Penguin Handbooks
Civil Liberty: The NCCL Guide to your Rights

D1325266

Civil Liberty:

The NCCL Guide to your Rights

Lawrence Grant
Patricia Hewitt
Christine Jackson
Howard Levenson

Drawings by Posy Simmonds

THIRD EDITION

PENGUIN BOOKS

Penguin Books Ltd, Harmondsworth,
Middlesex, England
Penguin Books, 625 Madison Avenue,
New York, New York 10022, U.S.A.
Penguin Books Australia Ltd, Ringwood,
Victoria, Australia
Penguin Books Canada Ltd, 2801 John Street,
Markham, Ontario, Canada L3R 1B4
Penguin Books (N.Z.) Ltd, 182–190 Wairau Road,
Auckland 10, New Zealand

First published as a Penguin Special 1972
Second edition 1973
Third edition published as a Penguin Handbook 1978

Made and printed in Great Britain by
Hazell Watson & Viney Ltd, Aylesbury, Bucks
Set in Monotype Ehrhardt

Contents

Acknowledgements

Contributors

The editors express their warmest gratitude to the following contributors to this book:

Geoffrey Bindman	Anthony Machen
William Birtles	Nic Madge
Anthony Burton	Tessa Moorhouse
Paul Cavadino	Clive Morrick
Lynda Clark	Bill Nash
Anna Coote	Greg Powell
Megan Doolittle	Brian Raymond
Jack Dromey	Brian Richardson
Sue Edwards	Nigel Rodley
Stuart Garcia	Rick Rogers
Alison Hannah	Mark Rowland
John Hendy	Catherine Scorer
Henry Hodge	Chris Studdart
Malcolm Hurwitt	Bill Thomas
Michael Jacoby	Peter Thornton
Helena Kennedy	David Watkinson
Martin Kettle	Janet Whelan

We should like to thank all those organizations which answered our queries during the compilation of this book, especially the Automobile Association which advised on the chapter on motorists – although we remain responsible for any mistakes that might remain.

We should also like to thank Alison Hannah, Catherine Scorer and Julia Keetch for their help in typing the manuscript and Lesley Fowler for assistance with editing.

A special thanks is due to Martin Kettle for organizing the contributions and ensuring that contributions reached the editors.

Introduction

This guide has three main objectives: to explain in simple terms the legal rights of people in the United Kingdom; to suggest ways of putting these rights into practice; and to highlight aspects of the law which adversely affect civil liberties.

There are few positive rights under the law. We have no written constitution and – unlike the United States and Canada – we have no Bill of Rights. Consequently rights in the UK are based on the negative concept that anything is lawful unless it is expressly forbidden by Act of Parliament or common law. We have had to devote much of the text to telling the reader what you may *not* lawfully do, leaving you to discover your rights by process of elimination.

We have tried to present as much straightforward and practical information as possible, avoiding legal complexities and theoretical discussion. Unfortunately the law is complex and there is always the risk that a simplified explanation will give an inaccurate impression of a particular aspect of law. We have sometimes resorted to imprecise terms such as 'generally', 'usually', 'normally' and 'reasonably', in order to avoid minor inaccuracies or the inclusion of endless detail. Where such words do occur, the reader is asked to bear in mind that there may be exceptions to the explanation given in the text.

We have tended to give greater emphasis in this book to subjects, such as public order, the powers of the police and immigration, where information is not readily available elsewhere. Conversely, a number of subject areas which might be expected in a book of this kind have either been omitted, or dealt with only briefly where there are other books dealing adequately with the subject.

The guide is aimed at people who need help in the many areas it covers. It is also designed to be of use to social workers, teachers, and others who act as advisers. We cannot hope to provide a complete answer to every problem, but where possible we have named specialist organizations who can give further help and advice. The NCCL is one of these and can help directly or indirectly on a wide range of matters. But we should warn readers that this guide deals with a number of subjects with which the NCCL has traditionally not been involved: the rights of tenants, motorists and consumers, in particular.

Many of the chapters indicate that there is a wide gap between principle and practice, which seriously inhibits the rights of individuals. It is a well-established principle, for instance, that a person has the right to be presumed innocent until proved guilty – yet the defects of the judicial system provide formidable obstacles for the accused. The Judges' Rules do not have the force of law and are not always obeyed. Many defendants face the courts unrepresented, because they cannot afford a solicitor, because they are not aware that legal aid may be available, or because the magistrate is reluctant to grant legal aid. Prisoners often have to wait so long for their appeals to be heard that they have nearly completed their sentence before they have had a chance to assert their innocence.

One of the most important aspects of NCCL's work is to encourage a greater awareness of the individual's rights under the law. There are those who believe that the administration will run more smoothly if people are kept in ignorance of what they are entitled to (one reviewer described the first edition of this guide as an 'urban guerrilla's manual'!). This is a philosophy we cannot accept. It is often ignorance of basic rights which results in people being locked up in prison although they may be entitled to bail, which prevents people claiming welfare benefits for which they qualify, which makes tenants flee from their homes immediately they receive a notice to quit from their landlords, which prevents people obtaining legal advice because they believe it is too expensive. We hope that this book will make a contribution to an increased awareness of rights and will assist in combating the injustices which thousands of people experience in many aspects of their lives.

Rights are quite distinct from privileges or concessions. People should know their rights and understand the principles upon which they are based. Essentially a citizen's relationship with society involves cooperation. Power can be abused, but the proper functioning of public service does not in itself imply abuse. Police officers and other public servants have a right to public understanding as well as a duty to observe the rights of individuals.

In previous editions of the guide, we asked for comments, criticisms and suggestions for additional material. We are grateful for the constructive response of reviewers and those who wrote to us and we have tried to incorporate their suggestions in this edition. We extend the same invitation to readers of this edition, and would be grateful if correspondence about the guide could be sent direct to NCCL.

We also wish to express our gratitude to the many contributors acknowledged at the beginning of the book; without them this book would never have appeared. Grateful thanks are also due to Michael Dover, our editor at Penguins, for his patience and helpfulness.

It is impossible to produce a guide which is completely up to date. For example, as this book was being written, the Criminal Law Bill was being debated by Parliament, receiving the Royal Assent in July 1977. This Act affects the law relating to police powers, public order, the right to trial by jury and the penalties for a number of offences. We have tried to incorporate the provisions of this Act and to anticipate the effect of proposed legislation wherever possible, in particular by a note on the Criminal Law Act (p. 17). Except where we have stated otherwise, the law referred to in the Guide was in force on 1 August 1977.

August 1977

LAWRENCE GRANT
PATRICIA HEWITT
CHRISTINE JACKSON
HOWARD LEVENSON

A note on the Criminal Law Act 1977

As this book was being written, Parliament was debating the Criminal Law Bill which makes certain changes to the law covered by this book. The most significant proposals are listed here, but we have also tried wherever possible to incorporate references to the Act in the appropriate places in the text. The Act received the Royal Assent in July 1977 and will be brought into effect over a period of several months.

Conspiracy and Trespass

The offences of forcible entry, forcible detainer and conspiracy to trespass (see pp. 151 and 464) have all been abolished and will be replaced by five new offences. The new offences are all summary offences – that is, they will be heard in the magistrates' courts and there will be no right to trial by jury.

1. Using or threatening violence to a person or to property for the purpose of securing entry into premises against the wishes of someone present on the property at the time. It will be a defence to show that you are a **displaced residential occupier**, that is to say, that you were occupying the property immediately before being excluded from it. However, displaced residential occupiers can still be prosecuted for assault and other offences if they use excessive force in regaining occupation. The maximum penalty is six months' imprisonment and/or a fine of £1,000.
2. Remaining on property having entered as a trespasser, after being required to leave by a displaced residential occupier (or someone acting on their behalf) or a protected intending occupier. There are two categories of protected intending occupier:
   – someone who owns the property (freehold, or leasehold with at least 21 years still to run), requires it for his own occupa-

tion as a home, is excluded from it by a trespasser and has sworn a statement to that effect before a JP or commissioner for oaths; *or*

– someone who has been allocated the property as a home by a local authority or housing association and has an official certificate to say so.

The sworn statement or certificate must be shown to the trespasser on request at the time the intending occupier asks him to leave. The maximum penalty is six months' imprisonment and/or a fine of £1,000.

3. Being on any premises that you have entered as a trespasser and having with you any offensive weapon (see p. 153). The maximum penalty is three months' imprisonment and/or a fine of £1,000.

4. Entering or remaining as a trespasser on any diplomatic mission or consular premises. No prosecution for this offence can take place without the Attorney General's consent. The maximum penalty is six months' imprisonment and/or a fine of £1,000.

5. Resisting or intentionally obstructing an officer of the court executing a possession order, but only if you are a trespasser (e.g. a squatter without permission) not if you are a tenant remaining in possession at the end of a tenancy. The maximum penalty will be six months' imprisonment and/or a fine of £1,000.

For all of these offences a police constable may arrest without a warrant (see p. 37) anybody whom he reasonably suspects to be committing the offence, and in the cases of 1, 2 and 5 also anybody he reasonably suspects has committed the offence.

The police officer may also enter by force and search any premises in order to arrest a suspect.

Sentences

The Act makes the following changes:

1. The maximum penalty for conspiracy to commit an offence will be limited to the maximum for the offence itself. If the

offence does not carry a prison sentence, the maximum for conspiracy to commit it will be an unlimited fine. (For instance, while the maximum for obstructing the highway is a fine of £50, the maximum fine for conspiracy to obstruct the highway will be unlimited.)

2. The maximum fine for conviction of any offence in the Crown Court will be unlimited.

3. Where an offence can be tried in either the magistrates' court or the Crown Court, the maximum fine in the magistrates' court will be £1,000.

4. A number of specific sentences will be changed, the most important of which are as follows: (The new sentences should be compared with the existing sentences mentioned in this book. If a prison sentence is not included below, the maximum sentence of imprisonment for the offence is to remain unchanged.)

  – Endeavouring to break up a public meeting: six months' imprisonment and/or a fine of £1,000.
  – Allowing a person under 16 to be in a brothel: six months' imprisonment and/or a fine of £50.
  – Conduct conducive to a breach of the peace: six months' imprisonment and/or a fine of £1,000.
  – Assaulting a police constable in the execution of his duty: six months' imprisonment and/or a fine of £1,000.
  – Driving or attempting to drive while unfit through drink or drugs; driving or attempting to drive with excess alcohol in the bloodstream; failing to provide a specimen of blood or urine if driving or attempting to drive: all six months' imprisonment and/or a fine of £1,000.
  – Being in charge of a vehicle while unfit through drink or drugs; being in charge of a vehicle with excess alcohol in the bloodstream; failing to provide a specimen of blood or urine in cases where you were not driving or attempting to drive: all three months' imprisonment and/or a fine of £500.
  – The Public Order Act offences of wearing political uniforms, failing to comply with police directions, and possessing an offensive weapon at a public meeting will all carry a maximum fine of £500.

- Failure to secure the attendance of your child at school: maximum fine of £50 for any offence.
- Obstructing a police officer in the execution of his duty: one month's imprisonment and/or a fine of £200.
- Careless driving: maximum fine of £500.

Trial by jury

A number of existing offences on which a defendant can choose trial in the Crown Court at present will become triable only in the magistrates' court, particularly:

- a number of motoring and drinking and driving offences;
- offences of criminal damage (except arson) involving damage of not more than £200.

Your rights after arrest

If you have been arrested and are being held at the police station, the police must tell a person of your choice about your arrest and where you are being held. But the police can delay doing this if it is necessary 'in the interest of the investigation or prevention of crime or the apprehension of offenders'.

The Act does not say whether the police have to ask you if you want someone informed of your arrest. You should always take the initiative and tell the police the name and address of the person you want contacted.

If the police refuse to contact the person you ask them to, you should make a formal complaint (see p. 65). Refusing to obey this provision of the Act will probably be a police disciplinary offence.

The person contacted does not have the right to see you or be present while you are questioned. But the Judges' Rules will still apply (see p. 45).

1. The powers of the police

This chapter covers:

There are about 90,000 police officers in England and Wales. They are often over-worked and under-paid. Some – though by no means all – of the complaints against police officers result from an individual policeman losing his temper or over-reacting to a difficult situation.

The main job of the police is to prevent crime and enforce the criminal law. They are not to blame for bad laws which may bring them into unnecessary conflict with a particular section of the community. But the powers which the police are given to deal with crime are often very vaguely defined by law, and leave the police considerable discretion in deciding whether to search or arrest someone; how long to detain a suspect at the police station and what charges to bring; whether to oppose bail or accept sureties for bail. The courts will usually uphold the police interpretation of what they can lawfully do. For instance, despite the limitations on the length of time during which a suspect can be held at a police station, people have sometimes been held, without access to a lawyer, for days. When police powers are abused, protection for the citizen is, as this chapter illustrates, often inadequate.

This chapter describes the most important powers which the police have, and explains what your rights are.

Police inquiries and search

Being stopped in the street

This section covers police questioning in public places. The position on questioning at the police station is set out on p. 44. For information about when the police can enter your home to question you, see p. 26. In general, the police can ask you anything they like. With the few exceptions set out below, *you do not have to answer*. (See p. 44 for more information about your right to remain silent.)

GIVING YOUR NAME AND ADDRESS

In many cases a police officer can arrest you if you refuse to give your name and address, or if he thinks the name and address you have given are false.* The most important occasions when this can happen are:

1. In certain motoring situations (see p. 23).
2. If you are suspected of creating a disturbance at a public meeting (Public Meetings Act 1908) or an election meeting (Representati n of the People Act 1949).
3. If you are suspected of possessing a prohibited drug and the police officer believes you will abscond if he lets you go (Misuse of Drugs Act 1971).
4. If you are in possession of a firearm and fail to produce a firearms certificate (Firearms Act 1968).
5. If you are suspected of having an offensive weapon in a public place (Prevention of Crime Act 1953).
6. If you are suspected of committing an offence under the Children and Young Persons Act 1933 (e.g. murder, manslaughter, cruelty or neglect of a child).
7. If you are seen or found committing offences relating to protected birds, e.g. stealing eggs (Protection of Birds Acts 1954 and 1967).

*'He' and 'policeman' are used throughout this chapter to refer to both male and female police officers. The great majority of them are male.

8. If you fail to produce a railway ticket or pay the fare (Regulation of Railways Act 1889). (In other words, you cannot be arrested simply for travelling without a ticket, provided you give your name and address and the policeman believes you.)
9. If you are running a market stall, the police officer can ask to see your licence; if you do not produce it, you must give your name and address.

ON THE ROAD

The police have a number of powers which apply if you drive or own a car, motorbike or lorry, etc., or if you are riding a bike, or if you are a pedestrian.

1. A policeman in uniform can ask anyone driving a vehicle or riding a bike on a public road to stop. If you refuse, you will have committed a criminal offence (maximum fine £50).
2. Any policeman, uniformed or not, can ask you to produce your *driving licence* and give your *date of birth* if you are driving a motor vehicle on a road. It is an offence to refuse (maximum penalty £50 fine).
3. If the policeman has reasonable grounds to believe that you have been involved in an accident or committed a traffic offence, then he can ask for your driving licence and date of birth. This also applies to the person accompanying a learner-driver.
4. If the policeman has reasonable grounds to believe that a particular vehicle has been involved in an accident or a traffic offence, he can ask for the *name and address of the driver*, or the person he believes is the driver, and the *name and address of the owner*. He can also ask for the *insurance and test certificates* for the car. If you don't give this information, you are breaking the law (Road Traffic Act 1972).

PEDESTRIANS

A uniformed policeman directing traffic can ask for the name and address of any pedestrian who doesn't obey a 'stop' sign which he gives.

BREATH TESTS

If you are driving or trying to drive a car or other motor vehicle on a road or in any other public place, and a uniformed policeman has reasonable grounds to suspect that you are driving under the influence of alcohol, then he can stop you and ask you to take a breathalyser test. Failing to give a breath sample is a criminal offence (Road Traffic Act 1972). You will find more information about motorists and the police in Chapter 5.

Police searches in the street

This section covers police searches before you are arrested. Detailed information about being searched if you are arrested is given on p. 40. Information about searches of your home or other private premises is given on p. 28.

As a general rule, the police have no right to search you if you have not been arrested. But there are a number of exceptions. The police can stop you and ask to search you in all of the following cases:

1. If they are looking for prohibited drugs (Misuse of Drugs Act 1971).
2. If they are looking for firearms (Firearms Act 1968).
3. If they are looking for stolen goods in the Metropolitan Police area (most of Greater London except for the City and the Temples; Metropolitan Police Act 1839). There are similar local powers in Manchester, Liverpool, Newcastle and most other major towns.
4. If you are an airport employee and the police are looking for goods which were stolen or unlawfully obtained in the airport (Policing of Airports Act 1974).
5. If they want to find out if you have any papers or articles on you which could provide evidence that you are involved in anything relating to terrorism (Prevention of Terrorism Act 1976). More information about this law is given on p. 534.
6. If you are suspected of destroying eggs of protected birds (Protection of Birds Act 1967).

In all these cases, *the police must have reasonable grounds for suspecting that you have what they are looking for*. The police try to justify 'reasonable suspicion' for drugs searches because of a person's movements, dress and the time and place of the encounter. These are often not very satisfactory grounds, and a Home Office circular to chief constables suggests that long hair or hippie clothing should never in themselves be reasonable grounds to stop and search.

Where the police have the power to stop and search you, you can be charged with obstructing an officer in the execution of his duty if you refuse to be searched or try to resist.

REFUSING TO BE SEARCHED

The police have the power to stop and search you in the situations listed above. There is no *general* power to stop and search people, and therefore the police can only search you in most situations if you agree. The problem is that if you refuse to be searched when the policeman thinks that it would be reasonable for an innocent person to agree, then that may make him decide that he has 'reasonable' grounds for arresting you.

WHAT YOU SHOULD DO IF YOU ARE STOPPED

Unlawful searches do take place. Before you agree to be searched:

1. Ask if you are being arrested.
2. Ask what the police are looking for, and under what authority they intend to search you.
3. If they give no reasonable grounds for searching you, you need not agree to be searched.
4. You can use reasonable force to protect yourself against an unauthorized search. But it is usually better to make a complaint or bring an action later (see p. 64), rather than using force at the time.
5. Whenever possible, make sure that anyone who is with you stays to watch you being searched. They may be needed as witnesses.

6. If you agree to be searched, but want it done privately, ask to be searched at the police station. Try and take witnesses with you. Remember that you are going voluntarily, and can leave once you have been searched – unless you are then arrested.

7. If the officer is in plain clothes ask to see his warrant card. If he is in uniform, take a note of his number. As soon as possible, make a note of any conversation between you and the police officer. Sign and date it. It may be useful if you are later charged with an offence, or if you want to make a complaint (see p. 64).

Police powers to enter and search private premises

The extent of police powers to enter, search and take property from your home or other private premises is far from clear. The law is confused and contradictory. Police powers are rarely challenged in the courts or elsewhere. Although the police view of the extent of their legal powers may be wrong, it is seldom challenged in the courts.

This section explains the limits on police powers and also sets out usual police practice.

There are three stages involved:

– entering your home or private premises;
– searching your home or premises;
– taking away items found during the search.

Each of these things can take place with or without a warrant, depending on the circumstances. Each stage is dealt with in turn.

ENTERING PRIVATE PREMISES

The police have no general power to enter your home or any other private place without your consent. But they can often get a **search warrant** from a magistrate which allows them to enter even if you refuse. The section on p. 28 describes when this can happen. They can also sometimes get a search authority from a senior police officer; this is explained on p. 32.

There are also a number of occasions when the police can enter your home or premises, *even though you refuse and even though they do not have a search warrant*. These are:

– if the police reasonably suspect that someone on the premises has committed, is committing or about to commit an *arrestable offence*. Arrestable offences include theft, most crimes of violence, taking and driving away a motor vehicle, unlawful possession of drugs and some firearms offences (see p. 37 for details). In this case, the police can also *search* the premises;
– in order to arrest someone if the police have a warrant for that person's arrest (see p. 36 for more about arrest with a warrant);
– in order to prevent or stop a likely breach of the peace or stop an affray (see p. 147 for what these terms mean). The police can also enter to stop someone being seriously injured, but these powers are almost never used in private disputes, e.g. to protect battered wives or a tenant who is being unlawfully evicted. In these cases, the police have no right to *search* the premises, but only to enter.

The situations when the police can search your home without a warrant are described on p. 31.

If you refuse to let a police officer enter

If the police have a legal right of entry (i.e. with a search warrant or in one of the three special cases just described), then they should announce who they are and ask to be let in. If you unreasonably refuse to let them in, they can use force to enter.

Otherwise, the police have no right to enter your house, whether to make inquiries or to investigate a crime. They have no right to force an entry or to demand to be allowed to stay. A policeman has a right, like anyone else, to come to your front door and ask to be let in. *But he can only enter with your permission*, or permission from another occupier. He must leave when you or someone acting on your behalf asks him to go.

If a policeman enters unlawfully or refuses to go when you ask him, he is trespassing. (Although, of course, you have to give him reasonable time to leave.) You can then take action for damages in a civil court (see p. 73). Also, he is *not* acting in the course of his duty, so you cannot be prosecuted on these grounds for obstructing a police officer in the execution of his duty.

Using force to evict a police officer

It is extremely risky to try and use force to evict a police officer. Although you are legally allowed to use as much force as is necessary to evict a trespasser, you risk being accused of using excessive force. It is better to get his name and number, call witnesses if possible and consider bringing an action for damages (see p. 73) or making a complaint (see p. 65).

SEARCHING PRIVATE PREMISES

As explained earlier, the police may be able to get a warrant which will entitle them to enter your home or private premises, if necessary by force, and search it.

A search warrant is usually issued by a magistrate, or occasionally by a High Court judge. To get a warrant, the police officer has to state on oath that he has reasonable grounds for wanting to search the place. Although the magistrate is meant to examine the evidence in order to decide if the police are entitled to a warrant, sometimes warrants are issued in haste, without proper consideration of the evidence. But once a warrant has been issued, even if it has been given on the basis of wrong information, you cannot challenge its validity at the time the police carry out the search.

The police can get search warrants for a wide range of offences – including stolen goods, dangerous drugs, firearms, offences against the state, sexual offences and obscene publications. Some of the commonest search warrants are described in more detail on p. 30.

In some cases, the police can search without a warrant. This is dealt with on p. 31.

Police powers under a search warrant

Once they have a warrant, the police may:

– enter the place named in the warrant. Provided they announce who they are and ask to be allowed in, they can use force to enter if they are unreasonably refused entry;
– search any part of the place named in the warrant;
– seize and take away any articles mentioned or described in the warrant. In some cases, they can also take away things not referred to in the warrant (see p. 33).

Some search warrants also allow the police to search *people* found on the premises, and to arrest anyone named in the warrant or anyone found in possession of the wanted articles.

Most warrants expire after they have been used once, so the police cannot come back with the same warrant later if they do not immediately find what they are looking for. But some warrants can be used more than once and permit entry at any time. In any case, if the police do not find what they are looking for the first time, they can apply for another warrant.

What you should do if the police arrive with a search warrant

1. Always ask to see the warrant. You can ask to have it shown to you through the window. The warrant must be shown to you, but the police only have to produce it once, so *read it carefully*. It must state the reason for the search – e.g. suspicion that stolen goods are on the premises – and the Act under which the warrant has been issued. Note any limits on the time of entry and the items to be looked for.
2. Check the address of the premises to be searched in the warrant. You can refuse entry if the premises are not properly identified (e.g. the warrant names a block of flats without specifying the number of any flat). You can also refuse entry to adjoining premises, for example a flat over a shop if only the shop is named in the warrant. If the police force entry anyway and the search is unsuccessful, you may have grounds for legal action later.

3. Ask to see the warrant card of the police officer in charge. It will help you to check that the callers are genuine police officers, and help you to identify the police officer if you need to make a complaint about any illegality in the way the search is conducted.
4. If you are alone, try to contact a lawyer or other people to come and witness the search. If the police refuse to let you make a phone call, do your best to see what the police take. Ideally, someone should watch every area which is being searched.

Can the police search people as well?

A search warrant only covers search of a *place*, unless it specifically says that people found there can also be searched. You should insist on your right *not* to be searched unless the warrant authorizes the police to search you.

If you are arrested during the course of the search, then the police are entitled to search you (see p. 40).

Some frequently used powers of search

This section gives more details about the most common search warrants.

Theft

A warrant can be issued by a magistrate if there is reasonable cause to believe that you have stolen goods in your custody or on your premises. 'Stolen goods' includes goods obtained by blackmail, deception or fraud and the proceeds obtained from selling stolen goods. A policeman can use *force* to enter if necessary, and he can seize any goods he has reason to suspect are stolen, even if they are not specifically mentioned in the warrant (Theft Act 1968).

Drugs

The police can get a warrant to search for any controlled drug (as defined on p. 165) if there is reasonable suspicion that drugs, or papers relating to illegal drug transactions, are on the premises or in the possession of anyone on the premises. With a warrant, the police can search both premises *and* everyone on them, even if there are no reasonable grounds to suspect each individual. So if a public house or hotel is raided, the police can search everyone quite indiscriminately.

A drugs warrant is valid for one month. The police can come back as often as they like during that month, and they can enter by force if necessary (Misuse of Drugs Act 1971).

Explosives and damage to property

The police can obtain a warrant to enter premises, if necessary by force, and search for any explosives. They may seize any explosives which they suspect may be used to damage property by explosion (Explosives Act 1875 and Explosive Substances Act 1883).

The police may also obtain a warrant to search premises, if they believe that the owner has any items which the police have reason to believe have been used, or are intended for use, to destroy or damage property, or to endanger people's lives by destroying or damaging property. The police may seize any such articles (Criminal Damage Act 1971). The police have also sometimes searched for documents, especially diaries and notebooks, under the 1971 Act.

Prevention of Terrorism

A magistrate can issue a search warrant if there is reasonable suspicion of an offence under the Prevention of Terrorism Act 1976 or evidence which could lead to someone being excluded (i.e. deported) from Great Britain to Ireland. These two grounds are very wide and are explained on pp. 538–43. The police can enter by force if necessary. *Everyone* on the premises can be searched, and the police can seize anything which they have reasonable grounds to believe is evidence of an offence relating to a banned organization (i.e. the IRA) or an exclusion order. The police can also take anything which would justify the Home Secretary in banning an organization, or deciding to exclude someone.

Police powers to search without a warrant

The section on p. 27 describes when the police can *enter* your home or other private premises without a warrant. There are also three situations when the police can *search* private premises without a warrant. These are:

1. *If you give them permission* to come in and search. See p. 27 for what rights you have if the police refuse to leave when you ask them to.
2. *In order to make an arrest.* The police will either have an arrest warrant or they will be looking for someone who can be arrested without a warrant (see p. 37). Remember:
   - the police can search the premises to find the person who is to be arrested, but *not for any other purpose*;
   - if they cannot find the person they want, you have the right to ask them to leave. But the police may use the opportunity to conduct a general search of the place;
   - if the police do make an arrest, then they can search the person who has been arrested and take anything relevant in his or her possession. They can also take away other items on premises occupied by the arrested person, if they believe these items are material evidence of an offence he or she has committed. They may also try to justify taking away anything which they believe to be evidence of a crime committed by someone associated with the arrested person.
3. *If a search authority is issued by a senior police officer* (superintendent or above), this permits the police to search premises and take articles away. This can happen in a number of situations, set out below.

Stolen goods
A senior police officer can issue a search authority if:

- someone occupying the premises has been convicted in the past five years for handling stolen goods or any other offence of dishonesty punishable by imprisonment; *or*
- someone who has been convicted of handling stolen goods within the last five years has occupied the premises within the last twelve months (Theft Act 1968).

This means the police can easily get permission to search any house if someone with the right kind of criminal record has lived there within the last twelve months. The police do not need any reasonable suspicion that any stolen goods are actually on the premises.

Explosives

A senior police officer can issue a search authority if he believes that there are explosives on your property which are about to cause immediate damage or injure people (Explosives Act 1875; Explosive Substances Act 1883).

Official Secrets

In an emergency, a senior police officer can issue a search authority if he believes that an offence under the Official Secrets Act 1911 has been or is about to be committed (the Act is described on p. 325).

Prevention of Terrorism

Again in an emergency, a senior police officer can issue a search authority to look for evidence relating to terrorism where 'immediate action is necessary in the interests of the state' (Prevention of Terrorism Act 1976).

Police powers to remove items found in a search

The extent of police powers to take away items found during a search depends on whether or not the search was made with a *warrant*.

If the police have a search warrant

they can take away:

– anything which is evidence of the offence for which the search warrant was issued (e.g. a warrant for stolen goods means that the police may take away anything they reasonably believe to be stolen);
– anything which is evidence that the *occupier* of the place named in the warrant has been involved in some other offence. This power depends, however, on an unsatisfactory decision in the Court of Appeal, which needs to be clarified. At any rate, the police should *not* take items simply because they believe that someone other than the occupier is involved in an offence other than the one for which the warrant was issued.

The effect of these rules is that the police can now justify going on a fishing expedition for evidence of other offences. For instance, after one of the conspiracy trials in 1971, a judge upheld the seizure of documents belonging to a defence committee as possible evidence of contempt of court and conspiracy to pervert the course of justice, even though the police had entered the premises with a warrant to search for explosives.

In a subsequent trial the police can use evidence which they have seized *unlawfully*, provided the judge is prepared to allow it.

If the police take away property from your premises, and you are later charged with an offence, the property will normally be kept until the trial, when the court will decide what to do with it. In some cases (e.g. obscenity trials), the courts have the power to order that the property should be confiscated or destroyed if you are *convicted*. If you are *acquitted*, you are entitled to have your property back but, to avoid problems, you should ask the judge to order the police to return it to you. You may have to provide proof that you do in fact own the property.

People sometimes complain that the police take away material which can have no relevance to the crime being investigated. If the police officer in charge of your case will not return the articles, you or your solicitor should write formally to the chief constable for the area (Commissioner of Police in London), specifying the articles which were taken and asking for their immediate return.

There are much stricter rules when the property has been taken without a search warrant, as described in the next section.

If the police do not have a search warrant

and they take property away, it will usually be following an arrest (see p. 40) or because they are using their powers to stop and search you in the street (as described on p. 24). But the police also have limited powers to take away items from your premises, even though they have no search warrant and even though no one has been arrested. These powers were laid down by the Court of Appeal in 1971.

1. The police must have reasonable grounds for believing that:
   – the offence committed is so serious that it is of great importance to catch the offenders and bring them to justice;

and the article seized is either the fruit of the crime, or the instrument used to commit the crime, or is material evidence proving that the crime was committed; *and*

– the person in possession of the article has committed the crime or is an accessory to it or in some other way involved; or has unreasonably refused to hand it over.

2. The police must not keep the article for longer than is reasonably necessary to complete their investigations or to preserve it as evidence. If a document is involved, a photocopy should, if possible, be made and the original returned to you. As soon as the case is over or if the investigation is abandoned, the article must be given back.

3. The lawfulness of what the police do must be judged at the time and not justified in the light of anything that happens later. In other words, if the search was unlawful at the time, it cannot be justified by information discovered later. If the police action was unlawful, this may mean that evidence obtained during the search should be excluded in a subsequent court case.

If the police take anything away, you should insist that they give you a signed receipt for everything they take away. If they refuse, make a note as soon as possible of what you believe they took with them, and make a complaint to the chief officer of police (see p. 65).

A summary of your rights if the police search your home

If the police want to search your home or other private premises, you have the right to:

– know what the police are looking for;
– know what authority the police have for searching your premises or home;
– see and read carefully any search warrant which the police have, before the search begins;
– refuse to let the police search you or your premises unless they have the right to carry out the search;
– insist on contacting a solicitor or get other help. Someone

should watch all areas of the search, if possible, in order to check on what the police take away;

– withdraw your consent for the police to remain on the premises and ask them to leave at any time – unless, of course, they have a warrant or are making a lawful arrest;

– use 'reasonable' force to remove police who are unlawfully on your premises; but as explained on p. 28, this is a very risky course of action.

If you have any complaint about the behaviour of the police during the search, make it known to the senior officer present, and put it in writing as soon as possible afterwards (see p. 65).

Arrest

An arrest is a formal procedure which means that someone is detained – usually in order to be brought before a magistrate on a criminal charge.

When the police arrest you, they must make it clear that you are *compelled* to remain with them – a mere *request* to accompany a policeman to the station is not an arrest. Simply telling you that you are under arrest is not enough either, unless you submit, and the policeman arresting you will usually hold you firmly by the arm or shoulder.

The police can use reasonable force to make an arrest. It is hard to say what would amount to excessive force, but force can never be justified if you do not resist or try to escape. Handcuffing is only justified if it is reasonably necessary to stop you escaping or to prevent violence.

The police can make an arrest either with or without a warrant. Each of these is dealt with in turn below. It is also possible for a *private citizen* to make an arrest (see p. 42).

Arrest with a warrant

A warrant is a document signed by a magistrate which directs a policeman to arrest a named person who is suspected of an offence, and bring that person to the magistrates' court. In order to get a warrant, a policeman has to give the magistrate details of the case in a written and sworn statement. The magistrate then decides whether to grant the warrant. (Warrants are almost never issued to private individuals.)

The warrant must include the name of the person to be arrested, and a description of the offence in non-technical language. If the offence is created by Act of Parliament, there must be a reference to the appropriate section of the Act.

The warrant may include directions for bail. If it does, then the police must let you out on bail and tell you when to appear in court. The warrant may also require sureties for the bail and the police have the power to approve the people you offer as sureties. If they don't, you can apply to the court for bail. (More about bail on p. 8o.)

WHAT YOU SHOULD DO IF YOU ARE ARRESTED WITH A WARRANT

If you are arrested on a warrant, you should:

- ask to see the warrant. You are entitled to see it *before* the arrest if it relates to a civil debt – e.g. not paying maintenance or rates;
- if the policeman doesn't have the warrant on him or refuses to show it to you before arresting you, make sure you see it or have it read to you – whichever you prefer – as soon after your arrest as possible;
- make sure the warrant in fact refers to you;
- check whether it is 'backed for bail'. As explained above, some warrants will say if you are to be released on bail and, if so, on what conditions.

Arrest without a warrant

There are a wide range of offences for which a policeman can arrest you without a warrant. These include:

- *Arrestable offences.* A policeman can arrest you without a warrant if he has reasonable grounds for suspecting that you have committed, are committing or are about to commit an arrestable offence. An **arrestable offence** is usually one carrying a maximum penalty of five years' imprisonment or more; some offences, with lower penalties, are also arrestable offences. It is impossible to set out a complete list of these offences, but they include: theft, blackmail, obtaining property or other advantage by criminal deception, most offences of violence, unlawful possession of drugs, some offences connected with possessing firearms, and taking and driving away a motor vehicle.

– If the policeman believes you are a 'suspected person' loitering in a street or other public place with intent to commit an arrestable offence (Vagrancy Act 1824). Known as the 'sus charge' this gives the police a very wide power to arrest people in the streets even though there is no evidence that the person arrested has attempted to commit an offence.

– To prevent or stop a breach of the peace committed in the police officer's presence. (More information about breach of the peace is given on p. 149.)

– If the policeman reasonably suspects you of obstructing the highway (see p. 152).

– If you are reasonably suspected of possessing an offensive weapon in a public place. This has been interpreted in different circumstances as possessing anything from a penny to a gun. You can only be arrested without a warrant for this offence if you actually have the offensive weapon on you at the time (Prevention of Crime Act 1953).

– If you are reasonably suspected of possessing a loaded gun in a public place or a building which you are not allowed to enter. In addition, if you are suspected of possessing a firearm and have already served three years in prison (for any offence), you can be arrested without a warrant (Firearms Act 1968).

– If you are reasonably suspected of having an article used for theft (Theft Act 1968).

– Refusing or failing to take or pass a breathalyser test (Road Traffic Act 1972) (see p. 160).

– If you are a woman and are reasonably suspected of being a common prostitute loitering or soliciting in public (see p. 178).

You can also be arrested without a warrant under various other Acts of Parliament, in particular:

- Public Order Act 1936 (on reasonable suspicion of wearing an unlawful uniform, having an offensive weapon or behaving offensively);
- Road Traffic Act 1972 (on reasonable suspicion of driving or attempting to drive while under the influence of drink);
- Licensing Act 1902 (on reasonable suspicion of being drunk and incapable in a public place);
- Criminal Justice Act 1967 (on reasonable suspicion of being likely not to come to court after being released on bail).

The police must tell you why you are being arrested, although they do not need to give you the technical name of the offence. But they do not have to tell you if you are caught red-handed or if it is obvious that you know why. If you try to run away, it may be impossible for the police officer to explain why you are being arrested, but he should still tell you as soon as possible.

WHAT YOU SHOULD DO IF YOU ARE ARRESTED WITHOUT A WARRANT

If a policeman tells you that he is arresting you, you should:

- ask him what for. He has to tell you, except in the circumstances just described;
- remember carefully what he says and write it down as soon as possible (see p. 55);
- if he is in uniform, try to remember his number, and make a note of it as soon as possible;
- go quietly. If he is arresting you unlawfully, you can sue him later (see p. 73). Although you are, in theory, entitled to use reasonable force to free yourself (or to help free someone else who is being unlawfully arrested), you may find yourself convicted of an offence for using excessive force. Or you may find that the arrest was lawful.

'Helping the police with their inquiries'

It is very common for people to be questioned at a police station, under suspicion of being involved in an offence, without being arrested. They are said to be 'helping the police with their inquiries'. But unless the person agrees to be questioned, the practice is unlawful. The legal correspondent of the *Guardian* has said that 'the phrase "a man is helping the police with their inquiries" is a polite euphemism for "a man is being held illegally while the police decide whether or not they have enough evidence to justify a charge"' (*Guardian*, 5.7.76).

If a policeman asks you to go with him to the police station, but does not arrest you, you do *not* have to go. If you refuse, he may then decide to arrest you, but he must have legal grounds for the arrest.

If you do agree to go without being arrested, you should try and get a lawyer to go with you. People who have gone to a police station, thinking they were to be questioned as witnesses, have later found themselves being suspected of the offence. Since the police often refuse to allow people held at police stations to contact a lawyer, it is better, if possible, to speak to a lawyer before you get there.

What you should do if you think you were unlawfully arrested

If the police, or anyone else, lay their hands on you against your will and without a lawful reason, it is an *assault*. Assault is a criminal offence, as are unlawful detention and unlawful arrest. They are also civil wrongs, for which you can claim damages. Since the law in this area is very complex, you should get advice from a solicitor before taking any action (see p. 73).

Being searched when you are arrested

When they arrest you, the police can search you to obtain and keep evidence in connection with the crime of which you are suspected. They can also search for any weapon which you could use for violence or to help you escape; if they find something of this kind, they can take it away. The police usually keep all your belongings, not just the ones they are entitled to. The police are

only allowed to search you to the extent required by the nature of the offence for which you were arrested.

Usually you will be searched as soon as you are arrested. You will always be searched when you get to the police station. The police may also search the room where you were arrested, and probably other parts of the building if you own them or occupy them, however temporarily (e.g. a hotel bedroom) (see p. 32). But they have no right to search other parts of the building, nor can they search other people in the building or their belongings, unless they have a search warrant.

WHAT HAPPENS TO PROPERTY THE POLICE TAKE AWAY

After you have been searched, you should ask the police to return everything which you believe is irrelevant to the crime which they suspect you of. But they will usually refuse to return it immediately.

The police should at least package and seal in front of you anything taken away from you. You should take these precautions:

– make sure the property is all listed and properly described;
– check that the list is correct;

- indicate if any of the items taken from you belong to someone else;
- never sign for anything which you dispute was taken from you;
- refuse to sign the list if there is anything you are not happy about;
- if you sign the list, sign immediately beneath the last item so as to prevent any additions to it;
- ask for a receipt and keep it.

If you are released without being charged, or let out on bail, the police should return all your belongings except anything which is to be used as evidence. Check all the items against the receipt, in the presence of a police officer.

If you are sent to prison, all personal property, including cash, must go with you.

The police might keep property you think you are entitled to have back. You or your lawyer can write to the Chief Constable of the area, asking to have it returned. Or you can apply to a magistrate who can order the police to return the property if this is 'consistent with the interests of justice' and your 'safe custody'.

'Having a go': the citizen's power to arrest

As a private citizen, you have the right to arrest someone else if:

- you reasonably suspect that person is in the act of committing an arrestable offence (e.g. theft – see p. 37), or is guilty of an arrestable offence which has actually been committed; *or*
- you are trying to prevent or stop a breach of the peace committed in your presence (see p. 149).

A private citizen who arrests someone else must contact the police immediately and hand over the arrested person.

This power is most commonly used by store detectives, who are not policemen and have no powers beyond those of any other private citizen. Because theft is an arrestable offence, a store detective can arrest someone whom he reasonably suspects of shoplifting, but only if something has actually been stolen or an attempt to steal something has actually been made. If this happens to you, insist on telephoning a friend or solicitor, and remind the person who arrested you that he must either call the police in or let you go.

It is very dangerous to use the citizen's right of arrest. You can be sued for damages if you arrest someone you believe to be guilty of an offence when in fact no offence has been committed (a policeman is protected from being sued in these circumstances). It is difficult to know which offences are arrestable, what amounts to a lawful arrest, what exactly is a breach of the peace or what to do after arrest. Any mistake may result in your being sued for damages or prosecuted for false imprisonment or assault. Equally, if you are wrongfully arrested by a store detective, or any other private citizen, you may be able to take legal action.

There is an increasing tendency to encourage people to give more help to the police – and indeed if a breach of the peace occurs, it is a criminal offence to refuse unreasonably a request for help from a policeman. If you are injured while doing so, you should make a claim to the Criminal Injuries Compensation Board (see p. 108).

Police questioning

In many cases, you will want to help the police when they ask you questions. The police need public cooperation to do their job properly, and putting obstacles in their way just for the sake of being awkward isn't in anyone's interests. But there are situations when it is important to know your legal rights, and know when you are not legally obliged to cooperate, as explained in this section.

In general, you do not have to answer police questions, whether they are informal or part of an official inquiry, but:

– failing to answer certain questions about motoring is a criminal offence (see p. 23);

- failing to give your name and address may lead to your arrest in certain cases (see p. 22);
- refusing to answer questions, particularly where the police have the power to stop and search you in the street (see p. 24) may cause the police to become more suspicious and may lead to your arrest even though their suspicion is unfounded.

The right to silence

Your most important right is to remain silent. Obviously, there will be situations where you are convinced of your innocence and feel it is quicker and easier to clear the matter up by answering police questions. But even where you are innocent, the law can be complex and you may decide not to answer questions before getting legal advice. Rather than remaining completely silent, you may wish to say that you do not want to answer any questions until you have seen your solicitor. But it is often better not to give any further explanation.

There are very good reasons for not answering questions or giving a statement to the police, unless you have a lawyer with you:

- the atmosphere of a police station often makes it very difficult to give a coherent explanation and do justice to yourself;
- you may need more time to collect your thoughts than the police will give you;
- even the most strong-minded of people have been known to say untrue things about themselves, just to get the ordeal over with;
- once you have made a statement which doesn't reflect the true position, it is very difficult to stop the evidence being used in court. If it is used and you say something different in court, you will be seen to be inconsistent.

There have been a number of cases in which people have made what later turned out to be false confessions. In one case in Middlesex a young man made a written statement to the police confessing that he had stolen money from his employer, who owned a petrol station. However, the employer later found the money, which had in fact been banked.

The case of Colin Lattimore, widely reported in the media, concerned three young men (one of them mentally subnormal) who were taken to a police station for questioning and signed statements confessing to murder. It was later established that the death could only have taken place at a time for which all three had undisputed alibis. It was, however, three years before the truth was established. Following a fresh hearing in the Court of Appeal a public inquiry was set up into how the confession statements came to be signed.

Rules governing police questioning

When the police question you on suspicion of being involved in a crime, their conduct is governed by a set of rules called the *Judges' Rules and Administrative Directions*. But these are only guidelines. Even where the Rules are not obeyed, the magistrates or judge can allow your statement to be used as evidence if they believe it was made *voluntarily*. This gives the police little incentive to follow the Rules.

The main provisions of the Rules are set out in the following pages.

QUESTIONING

A police officer can question anyone, whether suspected of a criminal offence or not, if he thinks he can get useful information. He can do this without arresting you, provided that *you have not been charged with an offence or informed that you may be prosecuted for it.*

CAUTIONS

As soon as the officer has reasonable grounds for suspecting that you have committed the offence, he must *caution* you as follows: 'You are not obliged to say anything unless you wish to do so but what you say may be put in writing and given in evidence.' This may happen as soon as you are arrested or soon after. The writing down of what you say need not be done in your presence, and usually isn't.

Remember that anything you say voluntarily can be used in evidence – even if you have not signed a statement. Defence lawyers often complain that the caution comes rather late in questioning. So you should not assume that, just because you have not been cautioned, the police do not suspect you.

The police should caution you again when you are charged or told that you may be prosecuted for the offence. You should be asked if you wish to say anything, and told that you need say nothing, but that anything you do say will be taken down in writing and may be used as evidence. As a general rule, *you should not be questioned after being charged*, unless the aim is to prevent or minimize loss or harm to some other person; clear up any ambiguity in answers or a statement you have already made; or if the questions are about a different offence. If the police do ask such questions, they must caution you for a third time.

Anything you say to the police should only be used as evidence in court if the judge believes that you said it voluntarily. Even if the statement is taken in a way contrary to the Judges' Rules, the judge can still decide that it was made voluntarily.

If the police make any inducements or threats while questioning you, your statement or answers should not be treated as voluntary. If the police offer inducements (e.g. 'We can make it easier for you if you confess') or threaten you ('We won't give you bail until you make a statement'), ignore them if you can. You may spend longer in the police station, but it will be to your advantage later.

Never rely on a police suggestion that a confession will make things easier for you. It may not. People have been convicted on the basis of confessions later proved to be false (see p. 45 for an example of such a case). It is better not to say anything until you have seen a solicitor.

TAKING STATEMENTS

The Judges' Rules contain a number of directives to the police about the method of taking statements:

1. If you are questioned or decide to make a statement after being cautioned, the police should keep a record of the time and

place of questioning, who was present, and what refreshments were given. Alcohol must never be served.

2. Questions and answers should be recorded in full. The record must be signed by you or, if you refuse, by the officer questioning you. *Answers can be used as evidence whether or not you sign the record – there is no such thing as an 'off the record' statement.*

3. Any statement you make after being cautioned should be written on the proper forms. Police officers should only use their own notebooks when there are no forms available.

4. If you make a written statement, you must be allowed to do so without being prompted and in your own words. Or you can dictate it to a police officer, who will then ask you to sign it. If you refuse, the police officer must sign it himself. When the policeman writes down your statement, he should use your words, not translate it into 'official vocabulary'.

5. You must not be led to believe that any statement you make can only be used *against* you. For instance, an innocent person may make a statement, clearing him or herself of the charge, but implicating someone else.

WRITTEN STATEMENT OF THE CHARGES

Once you have been charged with a criminal offence, the charge must be entered in the police charge sheet or book. You must be given a copy of the entry. The precise offence must be shown, as in the example on p. 48. The details of the offence *should* be in non-technical language, so that you clearly understand it.

ENGLISH IS NOT YOUR FIRST LANGUAGE

If English is not your first language, you are allowed to make a statement in your own language. If you have any difficulty understanding the police officer's questions, insist on having an interpreter. You may also want to contact your embassy (see p. 50).

Name & address JOHN CITIZEN, 20 SOME STREET, ANYTOWN

Sex MALE   Date & Place 10. 7. 48   Height 5'6"
            of Birth @ SOMEWHERE

Occupation COOK   Nationality UK

You are charged with the following offence (s):--

Charge one   That you did on 1 April 1977, at Anytown,
              steal one 'Monsieur Grand' atomizer spray,
              value, £5.80p, property of Chemists Ltd.

              Contrary to sections 1 & 7 of the Theft Act 1968

    Reply:--   'No'

Charge two   That you did, on 1 April 1977, at Anytown, by
              a certain deception, namely purporting to be
              the owner of a 'Monsieur Grand' atomizer, with
              intent to obtain a cash refund of £5.80p for the
              same, attempt dishonestly to obtain certain
              property namely £5.80p belonging to Chemists Ltd,
              with the intention of permanently depriving the
              said Chemists Ltd of the said property, against
              the peace.

              Contrary to common law

    Reply:--   'COS I WANTED THE MONEY'

IF YOU ARE AGED UNDER 17

The Directions say that as far as possible, people aged under 17 should only be interviewed in the presence of a parent or someone who is not a police officer and is the same sex as the child. This applies whether the young person is suspected of an offence, or is simply being questioned as a witness. A child should *not* be arrested or questioned at school if this can possibly be avoided. If it is essential, it should only be done with the consent of the headteacher and in the presence of the headteacher or someone he or she nominates. (See p. 365-9 for more information on children's rights.)

COMFORT AND REFRESHMENT

The police should make reasonable arrangements for your comfort and refreshment. Whenever possible, both you and the interrogator should be seated.

TELLING YOU YOUR RIGHTS

You should be told about your rights, and the facilities for getting help which are described in the next section. Notices should be displayed in conspicuous places in police stations, and drawn to your attention.

Getting help and legal advice

At every stage of a police investigation, you should be able to contact a solicitor and consult him or her in private – even if you are being held in custody. If you are at the police station, you should be allowed to contact a solicitor or friends for the purpose of your defence. But the Judges' Rules offer a let-out to the police, who can stop you contacting a lawyer if it causes 'unreasonable delay or hindrance to the investigation or the administration of justice'.

The police often refuse to allow a suspect to see a friend or a solicitor, even when the suspect has been held for many hours.

C.L. – 3

Indeed, they will often refuse to allow anyone else to see you until you have been charged with an offence. The only thing which can be done about this is an action for *habeas corpus* (see p. 53). If you have been held unlawfully you can sue for damages later (as explained on p. 73).

The following points may help you if you are held at a police station:

1. You can ask the police to contact your family for you, and they should do so. They should automatically contact the parents or guardian of a child who has been arrested, although in practice this is not always done.
2. You can ask the police to send a telegram for you, at your own expense.
3. You should be given writing materials if you ask for them, and the police should post your letter for you. You should also take the opportunity to write a full note of everything that has happened (see p. 55 where the reasons for doing this are explained).
4. Telephone a solicitor or a friend, as soon as you are allowed to, and tell him or her:
   - the name and address of the magistrates' court where you will appear;
   - the time the court starts;
   - to take to court anyone who is prepared to stand surety (as explained on p. 80);
   - to contact a lawyer, if you have not done so, and get the lawyer along to court.
5. Be careful when speaking to friends or a lawyer on the telephone. Conversations, even with solicitors, have been deliberately listened to, and the courts have allowed evidence obtained in this way to be used at the trial.

CONTACTING YOUR EMBASSY

If you are a foreigner, you should always be allowed to contact your embassy, consulate or legation, if necessary by phone. Some countries – including Norway, Sweden, France and the USA – require the police to notify the embassy if they arrest a citizen of that country. The police must provide facilities for embassy staff to visit you.

How long can you be held at the police station?

The length of time for which you can be held at the police station depends on whether you went to the station voluntarily; were arrested without a warrant; were arrested with a warrant; or are being held under the Prevention of Terrorism Act. Each of these four situations is dealt with below.

IF YOU GO TO THE POLICE STATION VOLUNTARILY

You are free to leave at any time. If you are told that you cannot go, or you try to leave and are stopped, this means you are under arrest. The only way to find out the position is to ask to leave or start to walk out. If the police have no reasonable grounds on which to arrest you, you should consider suing for damages (see p. 73).

IF YOU ARE ARRESTED WITHOUT A WARRANT

You will be taken to the police station where the police will decide whether or not to charge you. If they decide not to charge you, you should be released immediately they make that decision.

You should be charged as soon as the police have enough evidence against you. You should not be detained while the police make further inquiries to decide whether or not there is a case against you. You should not agree to be taken from place to place, or to your own home, so that inquiries or searches can be made.

You should be brought before a magistrate within twenty-four hours of being *arrested* (forty-eight at weekends), or released on police bail, unless the offence appears to be serious. Even if it is, you must be brought before a magistrate 'as soon as practicable' and certainly within twenty-four hours (forty-eight at week-ends) of being *charged*. Police have different ideas about what a 'serious offence' means and tend to interpret it widely. It is not unusual for the police to hold people for long periods. This may not be surprising in really serious cases, but detention at police stations has sometimes continued for several days or, in a few cases, even more than a week.

If the police cannot complete their inquiries immediately – for instance, they may be awaiting analysis of a substance to see whether it is an illegal drug – you should be given bail and told to come back to the police station at a fixed time and date. You must come back to the station, unless the police write and say that you need not do so.

A child aged under 14 must be given bail, unless he or she is suspected of murder or manslaughter. Where someone aged between 14 and 17 is arrested, a senior police officer must inquire into the case and grant bail unless he believes:

- that the person should be detained in his or her own interest; *or*
- that the person has committed murder or manslaughter, or some other serious crime; *or*
- it would defeat the ends of justice if the person were released; *or*
- the person would fail to turn up at court if released. A child or young person can be released on condition that the parents attend court with the child.

If the police refuse to give you bail, you should ask for bail when you appear at the magistrates' court.

IF YOU ARE ARRESTED UNDER A WARRANT

The police must take you before a magistrate as soon as possible after your arrest. They can only let you out on bail if the warrant is 'backed' for bail (see p. 37). If the warrant does not direct the police to give you bail the magistrate can still grant bail. When you appear at the magistrates' court you should ask for bail.

IF YOU ARE ARRESTED UNDER THE PREVENTION OF TERRORISM ACT

You can be held by the police for up to forty-eight hours. The police can then apply to the Home Secretary for permission to hold you for a further five days. (The Home Secretary has never refused such a request.)

In theory, the Judges Rules' apply if you are held under this Act. But you should note the following points:

- you do *not* have to be charged with an offence, or taken to court;
- it is a criminal offence to refuse to give information to the police which might be useful to them in detecting terrorists;
- people held under the Act have usually been refused permission to make phone calls or receive visits from friends or lawyers, and in some cases the police have refused to tell relatives where a person is being held.

The Act is described in more detail on p. 534.

Habeas corpus

If you obtain a writ of *habeas corpus*, a judge of the High Court issues an order requiring the police or prison authorities to produce the person named in the writ, and give an explanation to the court as to why the person is being detained. (*Habeas corpus* is Latin, meaning, roughly, 'let the body be produced'.) If the police have a lawful reason for detaining the person, then the court will allow the detention to continue. But if the reason given is inadequate or unlawful, the court will order the prisoner to be released.

Habeas corpus is therefore a most important remedy if you believe that you are being held unlawfully by the police. It may also be used by someone who is being extradited to another country; being held in custody pending deportation (see p. 288); held against his will in a mental hospital, without a proper committal order (see p. 374); or if a magistrates' court imposes a sentence which is outside its powers (see p. 78). *Habeas corpus* can also be used against a private person (for instance, if a store detective arrests someone and does not call the police), if the police refuse to act.

Habeas corpus is most commonly used by people who are being held at a police station and believe that they have been unlawfully arrested or held for an unreasonable length of time. The police will often refuse to let someone in detention contact a lawyer, making it difficult to start *habeas corpus* proceedings. But someone else – for instance, your husband or wife – can instruct a solicitor to act on your behalf, without the lawyer needing to interview you at the police station. Usually, once the police know that an application for *habeas corpus* is threatened, they will start to act lawfully and either release you or bring you to the magistrates' court. If this happens, *habeas corpus* is no longer necessary, but you may be able to sue for false imprisonment (see p. 73).

In order to get *habeas corpus*, your lawyer applies *ex parte* (i.e. without informing the people holding you) to the Divisional Court of the Queen's Bench Division of the High Court, or to a High Court judge if the Queen's Bench is not sitting. The application can be made at any time of the day or night or at weekends, and the duty officer at the Law Courts will provide the name of the judge on duty. It is not, however, always easy to find a judge to hear a *habeas corpus* application.

The application should be backed up by an **affidavit** (a statement sworn by you) explaining the circumstances. If you are unable to swear an affidavit, because you are in custody, your solicitor can swear one instead.

A summary of advice if you are taken to a police station

If you are taken to a police station for questioning as a suspect, you should try to remember the following points:

– you do not have to answer police questions;
– if you have gone to the police station voluntarily and do not want to continue with the interview, find out if you are free to leave;

- don't let yourself be persuaded into making a statement by promises or threats;
- ask the police to release you on bail;
- try to telephone a solicitor or friend to let them know where you are and, if necessary, arrange sureties so that you can get bail;
- as soon as possible after the police have stopped questioning you, or after you are released, make a detailed note of everything you can remember. Write the date and time on the note, and sign it.

Making notes if you are questioned, searched or arrested

If you have been in court, you may have noticed that when police officers give evidence, they are allowed to refer to their notebooks to refresh their memory, provided that they can convince the magistrates that the notes were made at the time or shortly after the incident. These are called **contemporaneous notes**.

You have the same right, as a defendant or a witness, to use contemporaneous notes to help you remember what happened in your dealings with the police. The only reason why the police are usually the only people in court with notes is that they are trained to make notes, and most other people do not think of it.

If you are involved in an incident with the police, you may be at a serious disadvantage if you have to appear in court without a note of the incident made at the time. It will probably be months before your case is finally dealt with in court, and most people's memories fade quickly.

If you are questioned, searched or arrested by the police, you should:

- write out in detail, as soon as possible, what the police said and did (e.g. searched all the rooms in your house);
- record the name and number, if you know them, of the officers who spoke to you;
- write out what the police said, and your replies, quoting the exact words, as closely as you remember, and not just the gist of what they said;

– as far as possible, write out your notes in the order everything happened;
– put the time and date at the bottom, and sign it.

If there were any witnesses present, you should ask them to do the same.

Sometimes, particularly if you are kept at the police station, you will not be able to write your notes for some hours. Don't worry about this: the court may still allow you to use the notes. It is better to make notes some hours or even a day after the incident, than to have none at all.

If you have a solicitor, give him your notes as soon as possible. If you do not have a lawyer, take your notes to court with you. Remember that you will be asked in court how long after the event you wrote the notes, and you will have to satisfy the court that the notes were written shortly after the event. Courts usually accept a policeman's word that his notes were contemporaneous. There is no reason why they should not believe you too.

Identification

This section deals with the three methods which the police use most commonly to try to identify suspects: fingerprints, photographs, and identification parades.

Fingerprints

Fingerprints will sometimes help the police to investigate a crime, but more often they are a way of finding out from the central fingerprint registry whether you have been accused and convicted before. The police may try to make you believe that fingerprinting is a routine practice, but, as explained below, their powers to fingerprint you are in fact quite limited.

In general, the police have no power to take your fingerprints unless you consent. Once you have been *charged* with a criminal offence punishable with imprisonment and have been taken into custody, should you refuse to let the police take your prints, the police can apply to a magistrate for an order allowing them to take finger- and palmprints without your consent.

Consenting to be fingerprinted may make it possible to clear up an accusation against you more quickly. Alternatively, you can wait and see whether the police decide to apply to the magistrate, when you or your lawyer can object to the application if you think it is unreasonable. If the magistrate does make an order, your fingerprints will be taken either at the court or wherever the magistrate has decided you should be held in custody. (The magistrate can, however, order your fingerprints to be taken, even if you are to be released on bail.) If you still resist, the police can use 'reasonable force' to get the prints.

There are a few exceptions to this procedure.

– *If you are under 14*, the police have no power at all to take your prints unless your parents consent, and the magistrate has no power to make an order allowing them to do so.
  – *If you are aged 14 but under 17*, you can be fingerprinted in the same way as an adult. (Special restrictions under the Children and Young Persons Act 1969 have not been brought into force.)
– *If you are held under the Prevention of Terrorism Act*, the police can take any reasonably necessary measures to identify you – including taking palm- and fingerprints. They do not need a magistrate's order and, if you refuse, they can use 'reasonable force' to get the prints.

ARE FINGERPRINTS DESTROYED IF YOU ARE ACQUITTED?

Fingerprints and copies taken following a magistrate's order should always be destroyed if you are acquitted. Some people doubt whether this is always done. If you are not satisfied, write to the chief officer of your area asking for a written assurance that everything has been destroyed.

The police do not have to destroy fingerprints if you gave them voluntarily. You or your lawyer should write to the chief officer, asking that they be destroyed.

If your fingerprints were taken under the Prevention of Terrorism Act, they will be kept in the central fingerprint registry, even if you are not charged with any criminal offence. They will only be destroyed if the Act is repealed.

USING FINGERPRINTS AS EVIDENCE

Fingerprints are often used to help establish that the person accused of an offence is guilty. If the fingerprints were taken illegally (without your consent, and without a magistrate's order), they can still be used as evidence. You may, however, be able to sue the police for trespass (see p. 73).

AFTER YOU ARE CONVICTED

If you are convicted of an offence, the police will tell the judge if you have any previous convictions which can be taken into account in deciding your sentence. If you dispute what the police say about your previous convictions, the judge may ask for your fingerprints to be checked with the central fingerprint registry.

Photographing

In general, there is nothing to stop anyone taking a photograph of anyone else. The police have no *special* powers to photograph you while you are in custody. In 1974, an experiment took place in five London police stations in which people who had been charged with criminal offences were photographed. There is some doubt whether this is legal, but it has not yet been tested in a court.

You can refuse to be photographed – but if the police photograph you without your consent, there is nothing you can do except complain. If they use force in order to photograph you against your will, you should contact a solicitor to get advice about taking legal action.

If you are sent to prison before your trial, the police can apply to the magistrates' court for a warrant ordering you to be photographed.

IDENTIFYING YOU BY PHOTOGRAPH

When the police are trying to find out who may have committed a particular crime, they can show possible witnesses a number of photographs to see if they can pick out any which look like the suspect.

If the police do not know the identity of the suspect, they can allow the witness to go through all available police photographs. But they must not give the witness any information about the identity of the people in the photos.

If the police do know who the suspect is, his or her photograph should be shown to witnesses amongst a number of other photographs which are as close as possible to the suspect in appearance, age and race. The photos should be placed on a table in front of the witness, who should not be given any help by the police. The police officer in charge of the investigation should not be involved.

Where a witness has already identified a suspect in person, the police must not try to back up that evidence by showing the witness a photograph. Equally, once a witness has picked out an arrested suspect from a photo, the witness must not be shown the photo again before identifying the suspect in person (e.g. on an identification parade).

Identification parades

The aim of an identification parade is to make sure that the ability of witnesses to recognize a suspect has been fairly and adequately tested. But it is very easy for an innocent person to be picked out on identification parade. In a number of cases, the Court of Appeal has quashed convictions of people who have been wrongly convicted following identification at a parade. In the case of Patrick Meehan – given a free pardon after nearly seven years in prison – the key witness knew that Meehan was the police suspect before identifying him on the parade.

The way the police should conduct an ID parade is set out in a Home Office circular; the guidelines set out in this circular are described in this section. The circular is not binding on the police and is not always obeyed. Even when the police do not follow the circular, any identification made at the parade can still be admitted as evidence in court. (The circular may become binding in the future, following the recommendations of the Devlin Committee on identification.)

As a member of the public, you may be asked by the police to go on an ID parade, along with the person who is suspected. It is up to you to decide whether or not to do this: the police cannot force you to do so. The police often have difficulty in persuading people to go on the parade and this can lead to unfairness to the suspect. If you do agree to go on the parade you will probably get a lift home and may also get a cup of tea and £1!

CAN YOU INSIST ON GOING ON AN IDENTIFICATION PARADE?

Although you can ask to be put on parade, the police are not obliged to hold one. But you can refuse to go on parade if the police ask you to.

YOUR RIGHTS AT AN ID PARADE

The police should tell you your rights before the parade starts. They are:

- you cannot be compelled to take part;
- your identity will not be revealed to the witnesses;
- you can choose any position in the parade, and change it after each witness has left;
- you can object to any person on the parade with you, or to any of the arrangements made;
- you can have a solicitor or friend present.

Use your rights. In particular:

- do not go on an ID parade without first getting legal advice;
- insist on having your solicitor present. If you cannot get a solicitor there, get someone else like a doctor, priest or trade-union official, whose evidence will carry weight later;
- have some other clothing brought along to the parade. If necessary, change clothing with someone else on the parade to help ensure your anonymity;

- make sure you are allowed to wash and, if necessary, shave (someone who has been in the police cells overnight will stand out beside people who are reasonably well dressed);
- make sure everyone on the parade looks roughly alike – same sort of age, clothing, hairstyles (get everyone to comb their hair), shoes, spectacles (if only a few people are wearing them, they should take them off). Beware of striking differences: you should refuse to go on a parade if you are the only person there with red hair, or a beard, or of a different colour;
- ask everyone to take off all rings and other jewellery;
- you or your lawyers should ask for the names and addresses of the other people on the parade before it starts. Although this tells them who the police suspect, you may need these people as witnesses later.

THE PARADE ROOM

The police should choose a well-lit room with at least two doors (one for witnesses to come in, the other for them to leave by). Alternatively, three rooms should be used: one for witnesses waiting, one for the parade itself, and one for witnesses who have finished the parade. A policeman should be posted at each door of the parade room to ensure that there is no contact between witnesses or with them. Your solicitor or friend should check these arrangements carefully.

OTHER PEOPLE ON THE PARADE

The police must choose at least eight people, as similar as possible to you in size, build, age and life-style. If two suspects look roughly the same, they can be put on parade together with at least twelve other people. If there are more than two suspects, or if they do not look alike, the police must hold separate parades using different members of the public. No police officer should be a member of the parade.

The police should do their best to make sure that any deformity you might have cannot help identification. For instance, if the suspect only has one eye, everyone should wear eye pads.

The members of the parade should not be allowed to know who the suspect is.

THE WITNESSES

According to the Home Office circular, the witnesses must:

- not be allowed to see the suspect before the parade;
- not be taken before the parade one at a time;
- not be told anything about the suspect or his identity;
- not be given any help to identify the suspect (e.g. a photo or description);
- be told by the officer in charge, loud enough for everyone to hear, about the correct procedure for identification. Witnesses must be asked whether the person they have come to identify is on the parade, and told to say if they can make a positive identification. If they can, they must touch the person and say, 'This is the person' (but a child victim of a sexual assault can simply point to the person recognized);
- not be told that the person identified is or is not the suspect;
- be separated from witnesses who have not yet attended the parade;
- be allowed to ask someone on the parade to put on a hat, walk

around, speak, or say a particular phrase. Any member of the parade can in turn be asked to do the same thing.

CONDUCT OF THE PARADE

Whenever possible, the officer arranging the parade should have at least the rank of inspector. The officer in charge of investigating the case should take no part in organizing the parade. Once the parade has been lined up, everything should be done in your hearing, including telling each witness the procedure they are to adopt.

The police should keep a careful note of what happens, in particular:

- any complaint you make about the procedure;
- if a witness identifies someone, but is unable to do so positively;
- if a witness asks someone on the parade to do or say something.

KEEPING A NOTE OF WHAT HAPPENS

If your lawyer or a friend is at the parade, they should make a detailed note of what took place on the parade. If you are alone, do this yourself. In particular, list any problems that occurred or objections you made, and note if any of the procedures set out above were not followed. Note down how many witnesses there were, and how many of them identified you, how many identified someone else, and how many could not identify anybody. Write this down immediately after the parade is finished, add the date and time, and sign it. Then give it to your solicitor as soon as possible.

ID PARADES IN PRISON

If a prisoner is willing to take part in a parade, it should be held in the nearest convenient police station. A parade should only be held in prison if there are special security reasons and must be conducted in the same way as a parade at a police station. The prison governer is responsible for getting people onto the parade, and a prison officer must be present throughout, in charge of the discipline of the prisoners taking part.

Complaints against the police

In 1975, 19,609 complaints were made against the police, using the official system described in this section. All the complaints were investigated, but only 1,369 people had their complaints upheld. Many of the complaints (6,637) were against the London Metropolitan Police; 301 people had their complaints upheld.

It is often difficult to decide whether or not to make a complaint against the police. Serious complaints are largely concerned with allegations that the police did not follow the Judges' Rules on police questioning (see p. 45), or that the police have assaulted, harassed or wrongfully arrested someone, or that a policeman has demanded or accepted a bribe.

You should never be discouraged from bringing a complaint if you have a genuine grievance, but trivial complaints (e.g. about an isolated instance of rudeness) are a waste of everybody's time and will not be taken very seriously by the police. It is very important, when making a complaint, not to exaggerate, to be sure of all the facts and, if possible, to have at least one reliable witness.

There are a number of different ways of pursuing a complaint against the police. These are:

– *Official complaints to the police.* Under this procedure, your complaint is investigated by another police officer, usually from a different force; the case may go to the Director of Public Prosecutions if a possible criminal offence is involved; the results of the investigation will be sent to the independent Police Complaints Board, to be set up during 1977. This procedure should not be used for making a complaint against a police officer in his or her private capacity (e.g. if you have a complaint against a neighbour, who happens to be a policeman); civil proceedings would be more appropriate.
– *Complaints in court.* When you are brought in front of the

magistrates' court, you can use the opportunity to register a complaint about police behaviour during your arrest or questioning.

- *Complaints to MPs and the press.* By complaining to your MP or the press, you may be able to publicize your case and pursue it beyond the official machinery.
- *Civil proceedings.* It is possible to bring a legal action for damages against a police officer who has assaulted you or unlawfully arrested you. If you win, you will be financially compensated for the harm done to you.
- *Criminal proceedings.* It is possible to bring a private prosecution against a police officer who has committed a criminal offence, such as assault. If you win, you will not usually be compensated, but the court will decide what punishment the convicted officer should suffer.
- *Independent inquiry.* The Home Secretary has the power to set up an independent inquiry into a serious incident concerning the police, or any other aspect of the way a police force works. Such inquiries are very rarely held.

Each of these methods is described in more detail below. What NCCL can do to help is described on p. 75; and information about special police forces, such as the transport police, is given on p. 75.

Official complaints to the police

The police complaints procedure was changed by the Police Act 1976, which will come into effect during 1977, and under which the Police Complaints Board has been set up. The board is to be independent of the police and will have up to nine members (none of whom can be a serving or retired policeman) appointed by the Prime Minister. Although there is now an independent element in the procedure, it will take some time to see if complainants believe that the new system is fairer than the old. The address of the Board is: Waterloo Bridge House, London SE1 (01-275 3072).

A NOTE OF WARNING

Under the new police complaints system, the chief officer has to give the accused police officer a copy of the complaint at the end of the case. The Government has promised an amendment to the Police Federation Regulations, so that the federation (to which all policemen up to the rank of chief inspector belong) can finance actions for libel or slander against a member of the public who has maliciously made a false complaint against a police officer. You should consider this possibility when deciding whether or not to make your complaint, but do not let it put you off if you have a genuine complaint.

SHOULD YOU COMPLAIN IF YOU HAVE BEEN CHARGED
WITH A CRIMINAL OFFENCE?

It is difficult to decide whether to complain against the police if you have already been charged with a criminal offence arising out of the same incident. (For instance, if you have been charged with assaulting a police officer, you may also want to make a complaint that the police officer assaulted you.) You should always take legal advice before making a complaint, since the complaint could harm your case. Usually the complaint will not be investigated until after the case has been completed, but it is sometimes better to give notice as soon as possible that you intend to complain when the case is over. In practice, you have little chance of succeeding with your complaint if you are found guilty.

HOW TO MAKE YOUR COMPLAINT

Leaflets explaining how to make a complaint should be provided at every police station, and a copy given to everyone who makes a complaint or who asks for the leaflet from the police. But police stations do not always have these leaflets available, and may be reluctant to hand them out to everyone who asks for a copy.

You should make your complaint to the chief officer of police in the area. Outside London, he is known as the **Chief Con-**

stable; in the Metropolitan and City of London areas, he is called the **Commissioner of Police**. You can call at any police station and make your complaint in person, but it is better to do it in writing direct to the chief officer (name and address from the local police station or town hall).

You should also be able to make your complaint by letter to the Police Complaints Board, and they will forward it to the chief officer. (Address on p. 65.)

Always keep a copy of the letter setting out your complaint.

WHO WILL INVESTIGATE YOUR COMPLAINT?

The chief officer of the police force has to register your complaint and have it investigated by a senior police officer. Although the investigating officer does not have to be from a different force, it is usual for the chief officer to call in an officer from another area. The Home Secretary has the power to direct the chief officer to bring in an investigating officer from a different force.

A complaint against a member of the Metropolitan Police may be made to the police station or to A10 Department at New Scotland Yard, which was set up to deal with serious complaints. However, most complaints will be dealt with by an officer from a different division from the policeman you are complaining about. Serious complaints will be dealt with by A10 itself.

The investigating officer will contact you and ask to interview you. You should ask for the interview to take place in the presence of a witness at your home or somewhere else, such as a solicitor's office, rather than at the police station. You are obviously less likely to feel intimidated if you do not have to go to a police station.

When you make a statement to the investigating officer, make sure that the final written version sets out accurately what you said and explains your complaint properly. Check that the most important points are properly emphasized. If you are not satisfied with the statement, ask for it to be changed *before* you sign it.

Ask for a copy of your statement. It is unlikely that you will get a copy unless you ask for it, and some people have found it difficult to get copies later.

If there are any witnesses who saw the incident, give their names and addresses to the investigating officer, so that they can also be interviewed. Tell them to make sure they get copies of their statements. As explained on p. 74, this is most important if you later decide to bring a civil action against the policeman.

When the investigating officer has finished his inquiries, by interviewing you, your witnesses, and the police officers involved, he will draw up a report for the chief officer. If the report shows that the police officer may have committed a criminal offence, it will go to the Director of Public Prosecutions (DPP), who will either decide to prosecute the policeman, or will return the report to the chief officer. If the report does not go to the DPP, or if the DPP takes no action, the chief officer has to decide whether or not to bring disciplinary charges against the policeman. Each of these stages is described in detail below.

If the DPP decides to prosecute the police officer, the case will be dealt with in the criminal courts in the usual way (see p. 77). The Police Complaints Board will get an interim report on the case when the chief officer sends the investigator's report to the DPP; it will get a final report after the DPP decides to prosecute.

If the DPP decides not to prosecute, the report of the case will be sent back to the chief officer. The Police Complaints Board will get an interim report on the case when the chief officer sends the report to the DPP, and a further report when the DPP decides not to prosecute. The board can then ask the chief officer to provide additional information, if it thinks the investigator's report is incomplete, and ask that this information be sent to the DPP for further consideration.

If the prosecution is unsuccessful, the report goes back to the chief officer.

If the complaint does not involve criminal proceedings, (either because the report does not go to the DPP, or the DPP decides not to prosecute), the chief officer will decide whether or not to bring a disciplinary charge against the policeman. Where the DPP has decided not to prosecute or the policeman has been prosecuted and acquitted, any disciplinary charges must be different from the criminal charge which might have been brought. There are three possible results: the chief officer may decide not to bring disciplinary charges; he may bring disciplinary charges and the police officer *admits* the charge; or he may bring disciplinary charges, which the police officer denies. The procedure is different in each of these three cases.

1. If the chief officer does not bring disciplinary charges, he will send a copy of your complaint to the Police Complaints Board, together with the investigating officer's report and a memorandum setting out his opinion of the case and why he has not brought disciplinary charges. The board can ask the chief officer for more information about the case. If it disagrees with the decision not to bring charges, it can recommend what disciplinary charges should be brought. If the chief officer is unwilling to bring charges, the board can, in the last resort, order him to bring charges. This is unlikely to happen very often.

2. If the police officer admits the charges made against him, the chief officer will decide what punishment is appropriate (see 'disciplinary hearings', p. 70). The board will only get a report on the case after the disciplinary proceedings are completed and has no power to take any action. But once the disciplinary charges have been made, they cannot be withdrawn except with the board's consent.

3. If the police officer denies the charges made against him, the board will receive a copy of your complaint and the investigating officer's report, together with a memorandum from the chief officer giving: his opinion of the case; what disciplinary charges have been brought; and whether there are any special circumstances affecting the case which mean that a disciplinary tribunal should hear the charges. The board can ask the chief officer for more information about the case and, in exceptional circumstances, can decide that the disciplinary charges should be heard by a tribunal (see 'Disciplinary hearings', below).

There are two special circumstances where the board will not become involved in your complaint at all. These are:

- if you have withdrawn your complaint, or said that you do not want any further steps taken; *or*
- if your complaint is against a senior officer above the rank of superintendent, in which case disciplinary charges are drawn up by a solicitor and heard by a person nominated by the Lord Chancellor. Complaints against a chief constable are dealt with by the local police authority, and those against the Commissioner of the Metropolitan Police by the Home Secretary.

DISCIPLINARY HEARINGS

If the chief officer decides to bring disciplinary charges, or the board directs him to do so, the charges will usually be dealt with at a private disciplinary hearing.

In exceptional circumstances, however, the board can decide that the charges should be heard by a special tribunal. It is not yet clear what 'exceptional circumstances' will mean in practice, but a case of special public interest should merit a tribunal hearing. The tribunal will consist of a chairman (usually the chief officer of the force which the policeman belongs to) and two members of the board. The tribunal can reach a unanimous decision, or two members can decide by a majority. Punishment will be decided by the chief officer of the force involved, after consultation with the other members of the tribunal.

Most cases will be heard by the chief officer of the policeman's force, without any members of the Police Complaints Board being involved. If the chief officer is a witness in the case or has some other special interest, the case will be heard by the chief officer of a different force. Punishment is always decided by the chief officer of the policeman's own force.

You should be present at the disciplinary hearing, although you can be excluded when confidential matters are discussed. You can be accompanied by a friend, but you cannot bring a lawyer or other professional representative. You should be called as the first witness and told what the charges are arising from your complaint, and whether the policeman admits or denies the charges.

The policeman will also be represented by a friend. Like you, he has no right to a legal representative. (Many police officers feel they should have the right to proper legal representation. NCCL has pressed for both the complainant and the police officer to have the right to legal representation.)

At the hearing, you can question the policeman, but the chief officer can stop you asking questions which he thinks are irrelevant. Under the regulations, questions about previous disputes between you and the police officer can be ruled out as irrelevant, although you may think that previous troubles with the same officer are extremely relevant to your case.

WHAT HAPPENS IF THE POLICEMAN IS FOUND GUILTY?

If the policeman is found guilty of a disciplinary offence, the chief officer of his force decides the punishment. (If a different officer heard the charges, he will be consulted about punishment. If a tribunal heard the charges, its members will be consulted.)

The police officer can be punished in a number of ways, from a reprimand or caution, to a reduction in rate of pay or rank, a requirement to resign, or dismissal.

The police officer has a right of appeal to the Home Secretary. If he is a member of the Metropolitan Police, he must appeal to the Commissioner of Police first.

You will be told whether or not the disciplinary charges have been upheld, but you are not allowed to know what punishment is given.

In summary, your complaint will result in one of the following decisions:

- *Your complaint is unsubstantiated.* You will be told this in a brief letter. The investigating officer's report is confidential and you will be given no reason for the decision.
- *Your complaint is substantiated, but trivial.* In this case, you will be given an apology. This happens all too rarely. If there were more apologies, there might be less suspicion about the method of investigating complaints against the police.
- *There are reasonable grounds for a complaint under the Police Discipline Code.* Your complaint will usually be heard by the

normal disciplinary machinery, but in 'exceptional circumstances' the Police Complaints Board may decide that it should be heard by a disciplinary tribunal.

- *A criminal offence may have been committed.* The papers on the case will go to the Director of Public Prosecutions who decides whether or not to prosecute. If he does not prosecute or the prosecution is unsuccessful, the papers go back to the chief officer who decides whether or not to bring disciplinary proceedings. Disciplinary charges cannot be identical to the possible criminal charge.

Complaints in court

Magistrates in criminal courts seldom seem to take complaints against the police very seriously. They either refuse to listen altogether, or tend to say that they do not believe that the complaints are true. Nevertheless, if you feel it is necessary to make a complaint in court, you should do so. If enough defendants made similar complaints in court, even the most unsympathetic magistrate should begin to take notice.

If you have been charged with a criminal offence, you should get your lawyer's advice before making a complaint through the official machinery described in the last section; see p. 66.

Complaints to MPs and the press

In some serious cases, it may be worth complaining to your MP or publicizing your complaint through your local paper or the national press. The police are naturally sensitive to public opinion. But they are also prompt to take legal action against defamation, and the Police Federation can finance libel suits.

Complaining to an MP may be the last resort. Unfortunately, it is unusual for either an MP or a sympathetic journalist to be able to bring about further investigations into a police complaint, but you may well feel it is worth getting publicity about your particular case and about the general shortcomings of the police complaints procedure.

Bringing a civil action

You may be able to sue the police in the civil courts for damages – instead of or in addition to making an official complaint. But you should get legal advice first. Once you have decided to bring civil proceedings, it might be better not to write an official letter of complaint since this might prejudice your case, as explained below.

The way the civil courts work and what you should do to start an action is described in detail in Chapter 11.

There is no point in bringing a civil action unless you have satisfactory supporting evidence. You will have to show the court that the police have committed a civil wrong (a **tort**). The most obvious grounds for a civil action are:

– *false imprisonment.* This covers wrongful arrest – i.e. being wrongfully detained or deprived of your freedom when the police have no lawful grounds for arresting or detaining you;
– *trespass to property.* An action for damages for trespass could be brought if the police forced their way into your house without a lawful reason and without your permission (see p. 26 for police powers of entry);
– *assault.* You could consider an action for damages if the police injure or frighten you.

To bring a civil action successfully, you will need witnesses to support your case, or other evidence, such as medical evidence.

The chief officer of a police force can be held responsible if one of his officers commits a civil wrong. So you do not have to identify the officer involved; you can sue the chief officer involved.

Because of the time and money involved in a civil case, people often prefer to make an official complaint first, knowing that they can bring a civil action if the complaint fails. It is often difficult to win a civil action if your official complaint has failed. The main reasons for this are:

– the police are well prepared to fight the case, since they have

all the statements you and your witnesses made during the
investigation;
- you have no knowledge of their case, since you cannot usually
see the police statements or the report of their investigation;
- you may not remember exactly what you told the investigating
officer unless you have kept copies of your statements and those
of your witnesses.

In addition, you will be told that disciplinary action will not be
taken against the accused officer until the case has been finished.

If you do want to bring a civil action against the police, you
may be able to get legal aid to help. If you are claiming less than
£100 in damages, you cannot usually get legal aid but in these
small cases, even if you lose, you will usually not have to pay the
other side's costs. There is more information about legal aid on
p. 496.

Bringing a criminal prosecution against the police

It is possible to bring a private prosecution in the criminal courts
if you believe that a police officer has committed a criminal
offence, but the Director of Public Prosecutions has decided not
to prosecute.

False imprisonment is a criminal offence, in addition to being
a civil wrong. So is assault. You could therefore apply for a
private summons for false imprisonment or assault in the magistrates' court, instead of issuing a summons for civil proceedings
in a county court.

The difference is that, in the civil courts, you are trying to get
compensation for what was done to you. The purpose of the
criminal proceedings is to punish the offender, and you cannot
always get compensation this way. If you do prosecute for assault
there is a rule that you may not be able to bring civil proceedings
later, whether or not you win your criminal case.

A private criminal case can be very expensive, and legal aid is
not available. You must get legal advice first, because, as with a
civil case, you will need strong evidence to bring a case.

Independent inquiry

The only kind of independent investigation provided by law is a
'local inquiry' which the Home Secretary can set up into 'any
matter concerned with the policing of any area in England and
Wales' (Police Act 1964, s. 32).

The inquiry can be held in public or private, and will be given
as much publicity as the Home Secretary decides in the public
interest. Local inquiries are very rarely held: only two have been
held since 1964. In June 1974, a student died as the result of
clashes between demonstrators and police in Red Lion Square,
and Lord Scarman was asked to hold a public inquiry at which
all the parties involved in the demonstration were legally represented. But the Home Secretary refused to order an inquiry into
another serious incident, the 1974 Windsor Free Festival, which
resulted in major clashes between members of the public and the
police.

How NCCL can help

NCCL has had years of experience of complaints against the
police. It does not have the resources to investigate many complaints itself, but will always give complainants as much advice
as possible.

NCCL pressed for many years for an independent system of
handling complaints against the police. The setting up of the
Police Complaints Board is an improvement on the earlier system, where complaints against the police were almost entirely
dealt with by the police themselves. But the new system has many
limitations.

NCCL is monitoring the results of the new procedure. If you
are making a complaint against the police, NCCL would like to
have details and, if possible, copies of all correspondence between
yourself and the police.

Other police forces

British Rail, the docks, the Atomic Energy Authority and similar
public bodies have the right to organize their own police force

to protect their property. Members of these forces have the same powers as members of the regular police forces, subject to certain limitations. In particular, they can only use their police powers within the area controlled by their employers or within a certain distance (usually a mile or less). The Atomic Energy police, who may be armed, will also be used to guard shipments of dangerous material.

You should make any complaint to the chief constable of the particular force. The address and other information can be obtained from any office of the docks, railways, etc. If you make a complaint in this way and are not satisfied with the result, you can take the matter up with the board which controls that police force, and then with the government minister concerned.

The Police Complaints Board can, if asked by the public authority involved, do the same job for complaints against these police forces as it does for complaints against the regular police. If the various authorities do not ask the board to become involved, then the Home Secretary can if he chooses impose this arrangement. (This only applies to forces in England and Wales.)

PRIVATE POLICE FORCES

The recent increase in private security organizations has given rise to some complaints, particularly when these organizations try to interfere with industrial spheres by using plain-clothes informers, and when they employ large numbers of uniformed men, including ex-policemen, on private security jobs.

Private police forces have no powers in addition to those of ordinary citizens. (See p. 42 for a description of the citizen's powers of arrest.) But the Home Office employs a private security firm to take care of potential immigrants at ports of entry, to ensure their safe custody and attendance at appeal tribunals.

If you have a complaint against a private firm, you should make it to the employer or, if it is serious and you have witnesses and other evidence to back up your case, you should report the matter to the police or consider a private prosecution or an action in the civil courts (see p. 73).

2. Your rights in the criminal courts

If you are charged with a criminal offence, you will have to appear in a criminal court. There are two ways in which you can be ordered to come to court: by a summons, or by being arrested.

The section on 'Arrest' in Chapter 1 (see p. 36) describes what happens if you are arrested. If you are summonsed, you will receive a document (called a summons), signed by a magistrate or his clerk, telling you what offence you are accused of, and what day you should appear in court. If you fail to turn up, the case will usually be changed to another date. If you still fail to come to court, a warrant will probably be issued for your arrest. A summons is a very useful way of getting people to court, without having to put them through the ordeal of being arrested. It is generally used for minor traffic offences and similar cases.

If you have been the victim of a crime, you should look at the sections on the Criminal Injuries Compensation Board (p. 108) and on compensation orders (p. 97).

The rest of this chapter deals with the following subjects:

The different criminal courts

The magistrates' court

Every criminal case starts in the magistrates' court and most of them never get any further.

Magistrates' courts usually consist of a panel of three part-time magistrates (Justices of the Peace), with a legally qualified clerk to advise them on the law. In London and some other big cities, the busier courts are staffed by full-time, legally qualified magistrates (called stipendiaries). A stipendiary magistrate deals with a case by himself, with legal advice from the clerk.

Many criminal offences *must* be dealt with in the magistrates' court, and neither the accused person (**defendant**) nor the prosecution can ask for trial by jury in the Crown Court. These include most petty offences such as drunkenness, minor traffic and driving offences, and offences under the Vagrancy Acts. Magistrates' courts also deal with maintenance, custody and separation claims, but these are *not* criminal matters and are described in Chapter 15.

Some cases can be dealt with either in the magistrates' court or in the Crown Court. In this case, the defendant can choose in which court the case will be heard. The magistrates can insist that a case should be heard by the Crown Court; they cannot stop the defendant choosing jury trial in the Crown Court.

The most serious charges – such as murder, manslaughter, robbery and rape – *must* be dealt with in the Crown Court, whether the defendant intends to plead guilty or not.

The division of cases between magistrates' and Crown Courts has been changed by the Criminal Law Act introduced in Parliament at the end of 1976 (see pp. 17–20).

WHAT PENALTY CAN THE MAGISTRATES' COURT IMPOSE?

The maximum penalty which a magistrates' court can impose depends on the particular offence. But it can rarely impose a fine of more than £1,000 or imprisonment for more than six months. It can never sentence someone to more than twelve months' imprisonment, even for a series of offences. But if the magistrates consider that their powers of sentencing are inadequate, they can send the defendant to the Crown Court to be sentenced. More information on sentencing is given on p. 93.

The Crown Court

The judges of the Crown Court hear cases at more than 100 centres throughout the country. The best known is the Central Criminal Court at the Old Bailey in London. If the defendant pleads 'not guilty' to a charge, the case will be heard by a jury of twelve people. If the defendant pleads guilty, the case will be dealt with by a Crown Court judge sitting alone or with two magistrates. A Crown Court can impose whatever is the maximum penalty for the particular offence concerned. Where someone is charged with an offence which can be dealt with either in the magistrates' court or in the Crown Court, the maximum penalty is usually higher in the Crown Court.

Courts of appeal

There are a number of courts which can hear an appeal by someone who has been convicted of an offence or someone who wants to challenge the sentence imposed by the court. Someone convicted in the magistrates' court may be able to appeal either to the Crown Court, or to the Queen's Bench Divisional Court of the High Court. Someone convicted in the Crown Court can appeal to the Criminal Division of the Court of Appeal. The final court of appeal is the House of Lords.

Appeals are dealt with in more detail on p. 98.

The magistrates' court

It is very important to get legal advice about your case, even if you intend to plead guilty.

If you are appearing by summons, and you need more time to prepare your case, write to the court asking them to change the date, or ask for an adjournment (often called a **remand**) at the hearing.

If you have been arrested, you will probably appear in court without a lawyer to represent you. Some courts have a duty solicitor who will advise you (see p. 492), but most do not.

It is generally unwise to go ahead with the case on your first appearance in court, even if you intend to plead guilty. You should get legal advice on whether you have a defence to the charge (since the law is so technical, you may in fact be innocent without realizing it). Even if you are guilty, you may need a solicitor to speak in mitigation on your behalf (see p. 88). The police may tell you, 'It's easier to get it over with.' It may be for them, but not necessarily for you.

So the first thing you should do, when taken to the magistrates' court is *ask for an adjournment* so that you can get legal advice. You should also ask for *bail* (described in the next section) and *legal aid* (see p. 500).

If the police are not ready to present their evidence against you, they will ask for an adjournment. You should still ask for bail and legal aid.

The lay-out of the court room varies from court to court. The magistrates always sit at the front, facing the rest of the court. Below them is the clerk of the court. The lawyers sit in seats facing the magistrates and the defendant may sit with the lawyers if the magistrate permits; otherwise the defendant will be in the dock, at the back or side of the court. The witness stand is to one side, near the clerk's desk, and there will also be seats for members of the probation service and other officials.

Bail

'Bail' means that you are allowed to go free, on condition that you come back to court on a specified date. If you are refused bail, you will be kept in custody in a remand centre or prison (or in local authority care if you are under 17) or, very rarely, in the police station. See p. 114 for the rights of prisoners on remand (i.e. waiting for their trial).

You can be asked to promise to pay a sum of money yourself if you are released on bail and then fail to turn up. (When the Bail Act comes fully into effect, this will be abolished except for people going abroad.) You can also be asked to provide other people who will act as sureties for you: in other words, they will undertake to pay a certain sum if you do not come to court for your trial.

When deciding whether or not to accept the people you offer as sureties, the magistrate should take into account:

– the person's resources (a householder is usually accepted, if he or she has sufficient assets);
– the person's character and any previous convictions;
– how close the person's contact is with you (e.g. if he or she is related, lives near you or works with you).

If the police object to your sureties, you can try and find other people, or you can ask the magistrate to accept them anyway.

IF YOU ARE ASKED TO ACT AS A SURETY

If you agree to stand bail for someone, you can be made to pay all or part of the agreed sum if the defendant does not appear in court at the right time. If you do not pay, you will almost certainly go to prison. It is a criminal offence for the person on bail to agree to pay the money for you.

If you think that the person you are acting as surety for will not turn up at court for the trial, you can protect yourself by telling the police and asking to be released from your obligation. You should do so in writing; hand the letter in to the police station if it is urgent. The person on bail will then be arrested, but can make a new application for bail.

IF YOU HAVE BEEN ACCUSED OF AN OFFENCE, FOR WHICH YOU CANNOT BE IMPRISONED

Even if you are found guilty, the court must release you on bail, unless:

– you have been released on bail on another occasion and failed to come to court; *or*
– the court considers that you should be kept in custody for your own protection.

IF YOU ARE ACCUSED OF AN OFFENCE WHICH IS PUNISHABLE BY IMPRISONMENT

The court must give you bail unless it believes that one or more of the following conditions applies:

– you would probably fail to turn up at court for your trial;
– you would probably commit an offence while on bail;
– you would probably interfere with witnesses or in any other way obstruct the course of justice;
– you should be kept in custody for your own protection.

In deciding whether or not to give you bail, the court can take into account the following factors:

– how serious is the offence that you have been charged with;
– your general character, background, associations and community ties (e.g. are you settled, with a permanent job and home; or are you on the move and perhaps less likely to turn up for trial);
– your previous record in turning up for trial after being given bail;
– the strength of the evidence against you;
– anything else the court thinks is relevant. (Bail Act 1976).

If the police object to your being given bail, you or your lawyer can question the police officer on any point where you think he is wrong or mistaken, or has misled the court. You can then explain to the magistrate why you think you should be given bail.

The court can impose certain conditions in giving you bail. For instance, you can be ordered to report to the local police station at regular intervals, to surrender your passport, or not to go to certain addresses.

IF THE MAGISTRATES REFUSE TO GIVE YOU BAIL

If the case cannot be heard in one sitting, and the court refuses to give you bail, you can be remanded in custody (i.e. detained) for up to eight days. The court must give you reasons for refusing you bail; this may help you make another application to the Crown Court or a judge in chambers (see below).

If you were not legally represented during your first appearance at the magistrates' court, you should apply for legal aid so that a lawyer can represent you the second time. Provided your income is not too high (see p. 502), you must be given legal aid for a second appearance, so that a lawyer can represent you. Make sure that you ask at the court office for a legal-aid form before you leave the magistrates' court the first time.

Instead of waiting to make a second application to the magistrates for bail, you may be able to apply to the Crown Court or to a judge in chambers for bail. Each of these procedures is dealt with in turn.

APPLYING TO THE CROWN COURT FOR BAIL

If your case is committed to the Crown Court for jury trial, you can apply to a Crown Court judge for bail, even if the magistrate has refused bail. (See p. 89 for details about committal proceedings.) If you have legal aid for your case, this will also cover an application for bail. You can apply more than once for bail. The circumstances when the Crown Court can refuse you bail, and the factors it takes into account, are the same as those set out on p. 82.

APPLYING TO A JUDGE IN CHAMBERS FOR BAIL

If the magistrate refuses you bail, you can apply to a 'judge in chambers' – that is, a High Court judge who hears the case in private. You can do this if your case is actually going to be heard in the magistrates' court, or if you have been committed for trial to the Crown Court, when you also have the right to apply for bail to the Crown Court, as explained in the previous paragraph.

There are two ways of applying to a judge in chambers: through the Official Solicitor, or privately through a lawyer. If you want to use the Official Solicitor, you can get a form at the prison. But the procedure is slow and inadequate. The Official Solicitor does not argue the case but presents information and documents to the judge. You are not allowed to attend. (The Official Solicitor is an official of the High Court with a number of different responsibilities. His address is **48-9 Chancery Lane, London WC2 01-405 7641**.)

You are more likely to get bail if you or your relatives can instruct a lawyer to make the application for you. Unfortunately, you will not be able to get legal aid for this so you or your family will have to pay the cost yourselves, which may be anything from £50 to £200.

APPLYING FOR BAIL AFTER BEING CONVICTED

If you are convicted of an offence in the magistrates' court, one of three things will happen:

– you will be sentenced immediately; *or*
– the magistrates will delay sentencing you until they get a medical or social work report; *or*
– the magistrates will decide that they want to impose a sentence which is outside their powers and commit you to the Crown Court for sentence.

If you are sentenced immediately, you may decide to appeal. How to appeal, and how to apply for bail while waiting for the appeal to be dealt with, are described on p. 100.

If the magistrates call for a medical or social work report, you should ask the magistrates to release you on bail. They can refuse bail if they believe that:

– you would probably fail to come back to court;
– you would probably commit an offence while on bail;
– you would interfere with witnesses or otherwise interfere with the course of justice;
– you should be remanded in custody for your own protection;
– it would be 'impracticable' to get the medical or social work report without remanding you in custody.

If you are released on bail, the case can be adjourned for up to

I have reason to believe that the defendant may commit an offence whilst on bail

four weeks. If you are remanded in custody, you will have to be brought back to court within three weeks, and you should then ask for bail again.

If the magistrates commit you to the Crown Court for sentencing, you should ask the magistrates for bail. If this is refused, you can apply for bail to the Crown Court or to a judge in chambers, as explained above.

IF YOU FAIL TO COME BACK TO COURT AFTER GETTING BAIL

It is a criminal offence to fail to return to court at the specified date after being released on bail, unless you can prove that you had good reasons for not turning up. Even if you had good reasons, it is a criminal offence not to turn up at court as soon as reasonably possible after the time and date fixed.

You can be sentenced by the magistrates to a fine of up to £400 or three months in prison or both, for failing to surrender to bail. If the magistrates decide that the offence is particularly serious (e.g. if you have repeatedly failed to come to court), they can either deal with the matter as contempt of court or ask the Crown Court to decide sentence. Either way, you can be sentenced to an unlimited fine or twelve months' imprisonment, or both.

Choosing trial by jury

One of the most difficult decisions you will have to make, if you are charged with an offence which can be tried either in the magistrates' court or in the Crown Court, is whether to opt for trial by jury in the Crown Court. You should get legal advice and discuss the matter with your family and friends. The following points may be useful:

- if you are dealt with by the magistrates the case will be heard more quickly;
- the Crown Court has heavier powers of punishment than the magistrates' court, if you are found guilty;
- magistrates have a tendency to become 'case hardened' while juries are often more open-minded;
- you will get copies of the prosecution statements before the trial in the Crown Court, but not in the magistrates' court.

If your case is going to be dealt with in the magistrates' court, the hearing is called a **summary trial**. If you or the prosecution have chosen to opt for jury trial, or if you are charged with an offence which can only be dealt with by the Crown Court, there will be a preliminary hearing at the magistrates' court called the **committal proceedings**.

Summary trial

IF YOU PLEAD NOT GUILTY

The order of proceedings will be as follows:

1. The prosecutor (a solicitor, barrister or police officer) will open the case by explaining to the court what the case is about. The prosecution will have to prove that you are guilty beyond all reasonable doubt. If there is any doubt, you are entitled to benefit from it.

2. The prosecution witnesses will give evidence:
   - each witness will be questioned ('examined') by the pro-secutor;
   - you or your lawyer will then be allowed to cross-examine the witness by asking questions about his or her evidence. You are not allowed to make speeches at this stage; you must ask questions;
   - the prosecutor can re-examine the witness about the answers given during cross-examination.

3. In some cases, you or your lawyer can then submit to the court that the prosecution has not produced enough evidence to deserve a reply from you, and that there is no case to answer.

4. If this submission fails or is not made, you or your lawyer call your evidence. You may do one of three things:
   - give evidence on oath and be cross-examined by the prosecution; *or*
   - make an unsworn statement in court, on which you cannot be cross-examined; *or*
   - say nothing at all.

   If you decide to say nothing, the court is not allowed to draw the inference that you are guilty. But usually you will want to give evidence or will have to in order to challenge the prosecution's case. You or your lawyer will then:
   - call your witnesses who give evidence and may be ex-amined, cross-examined and re-examined in the same way as the prosecution witnesses.

5. At the end of the evidence, you or your lawyer can make a closing speech. This should be used to point out to the magistrates the inconsistencies of the prosecution witnesses, and to remind them of your explanation in reply to the charge.

6. The prosecutor does not have a closing speech but can address the magistrates on any point of law (as distinct from the facts) involved in the case.

7. If the prosecution does this, the defence has a right of reply.

8. The magistrates will usually withdraw to consider their decision.

9. If you are found guilty, you or your lawyer has the right to address the court again in mitigation (see below).
10. The magistrates will then usually announce the sentence. They may delay the decision and call for a social-work or medical report. Or they may decide the sentence they want to impose is outside their powers, and you will have to be sentenced by the Crown Court. In either case, you should ask for bail (see p. 84).

IF YOU ARE ACQUITTED

Ask the magistrate for costs, if you have had to pay lawyers' fees, travelling expenses or any other costs. In some cases, someone who is acquitted will have any costs paid out of prosecution funds. But the magistrate can refuse you costs, for any reason (e.g. if they think that you brought the prosecution on yourself). If this happens, there is no right of appeal, but you should inform NCCL and complain to your MP.

IF YOU PLEAD GUILTY

The magistrates will only have to consider any points you or your lawyer make in mitigation (see below), and what sentence to impose. If you are pleading guilty to a summons, you may be able to plead guilty by letter. (You do not have to use the form which the court will send you.) But it is better to go to court, since the magistrates may be more lenient if you appear in person, and you may be able to explain things more clearly by attending than by writing. If you have been arrested, then of course you have no choice about being taken to court.

Mitigation

If you plead guilty, or the magistrates decide that you are guilty, you or your lawyer has the right to try to persuade the court to deal leniently with you.

If you are defending yourself, tell the magistrates about the following points:

- your previous good character, if you have not been found guilty of any offence before;
- if you pleaded guilty, the circumstances which led you to commit the offence;
- your work record if this is favourable, or any definite job prospect you have;
- any family you have to support;
- your income, expenditure and savings.

You can call witnesses (e.g. from work, or a relative) to support any points which you make in mitigation.

If you are pleading guilty by letter, you can also write down for the magistrates any points you want to make in mitigation. It is best, if possible, to type and number each point, since magistrates often find it difficult to read people's handwriting.

Committal proceedings

If you or the prosecutor choose jury trial, or you are charged with an offence which can only be dealt with by the Crown Court, you will still have to appear before the magistrates. They have to decide whether there is enough evidence to **commit** (i.e. send) you for trial to the Crown Court.

In most cases, there is enough evidence. If you are represented by a lawyer, the prosecution will send him or her copies of the statements made by their witnesses in advance. Your lawyer will tell the court that there is sufficient evidence to commit you for trial; the magistrates will accept this and the proceedings will be over in a few minutes.

If you are not represented, the prosecution witnesses must be called to give evidence, and their statements will be recorded by the clerk of the court. If the magistrates decide to commit you for trial, you will receive copies of these statements (called **depositions**) to help you prepare your defence.

Sometimes, even if you are legally represented, it is worth calling the prosecution witnesses in order to:

- get the case thrown out by the magistrates;
- test certain statements made by the prosecution.

The danger of doing this is that the witnesses may improve by the time they give evidence in the Crown Court, since you have given them the opportunity of a dry run.

The defence never in practice gives evidence at committal proceedings although it has the right to. The magistrates only have to decide if the prosecution evidence establishes a case for you to answer. They do *not* decide if you are guilty or not.

The Crown Court

Before the trial, the prosecution must set out the charges in a formal document called an **indictment**. Further charges can be added, provided that they are connected with the original ones and depend on the same evidence. Additional charges and evidence may be put in at any time, as long as the defence is not taken by surprise. Defendants often regard this as unfair practice, but the only remedy is to try to persuade the court to exclude the new charges and evidence, or grant an adjournment.

Unlike the American set-up where the defendant sits with the lawyers, the defendant in a British court nearly always sits in a dock, cut off from the rest of the court. The defendant can only communicate with his or her lawyers by passing notes or attracting their attention. The judge sits at the front of the court room; the jury sit on one side; the lawyers sit in front, facing the judge (with the defence lawyers on the same side as the jury and the prosecution lawyers on the other side); the witness box is on the side of the court, between the lawyers and the judge and opposite the jury; and the public sits in the public gallery, to the side and above the rest of the court.

The basic procedure is as follows:

– charges are read out;
– you plead 'guilty' or 'not guilty';
– if you plead 'not guilty', the jury is sworn in;
– the prosecution counsel makes an opening speech and calls his witnesses; each witness is questioned by the prosecutor, and can be cross-examined by the defence and re-examined by the prosecutor;

- the defence counsel puts forward the case for the defence and calls witnesses; each of them can also be cross-examined and re-examined;
- each side makes a final speech;
- the judge sums up;
- the jury withdraws and then gives its verdict, which must be unanimous (or by a majority of ten to two or eleven to one, provided that the judge has given permission for a majority verdict);
- the judge decides his sentence immediately, or postpones sentence until a medical or social work report has been obtained.

As in a magistrates' court case, you have the right to choose whether to say nothing, to make a statement on oath and be cross-examined, or to make an unsworn statement. (This is explained on p. 87.)

There are many variations on the procedure set out above, which are too detailed to explain in full. One of the most important is **plea bargaining** which often happens in contested cases involving several charges. The prosecution agrees to withdraw the most serious charges if the defendant pleads guilty to one or more of the less serious. The practice is open to abuse and has been criticized by the Court of Appeal. The choice should always lie with the defendant: no matter how strongly the lawyer feels that a deal would be in your interests, the lawyer should never bring pressure to bear if you want to fight on and assert your innocence.

If you are found guilty, you are entitled to proper advice from your solicitor and counsel about the possible grounds for appeal. You should not let yourself be fobbed off with a few hurried words in the cells after the verdict has been given. (See p. 98 for more on appeals.)

Jury service

You may be summoned for jury service if:

- you are on the electoral register; *and*
- you are aged between 18 and 65; *and*

– you have been resident in the UK, Channel Isles or Isle of Man for five years since the age of 13.

Certain groups of people are **ineligible** for jury service:

– members of the judiciary (including retired judges);
– lawyers, barristers' and solicitors' clerks, legal executives, etc.;
– prison officers, governors and members of a board of visitors;
– probation officers;
– police officers and members of a police authority;
– clergy;
– the mentally ill, if resident in a hospital or other institution; receiving regular treatment; under a guardianship order; or determined to be incapable of managing their own property.

Apart from the judiciary, who are ineligible even if retired, people in the remaining categories are ineligible for jury service for ten years after leaving the job or profession mentioned.
The following people are **disqualified** from jury service:

– people who have served a prison sentence of three months or more, or a period of borstal training, within the last ten years;
– people who have at any time been sentenced to life imprisonment, imprisonment for five years or more, or detention at Her Majesty's pleasure.

You may be **excused** jury service if you:

– are a peer, MP, or officer of either House of Parliament; member of the armed forces, practising doctor, dentist, nurse, midwife, vet or pharmaceutical chemist;
– have served on a jury (except a coroners' jury) within the last two years;
– convince the court officer that there is a good reason why you should be excused e.g. illness (you may appeal to the court if the officer refuses to excuse you).

It is an offence not to attend for jury service if you have been summoned and not excused, or to be unfit when you attend for jury service because of drink or drugs. The maximum penalty is £100. But you must have been sent the summons for jury service at least fourteen days in advance; and you will not be convicted if you can show the court that you had 'reasonable cause' for not attending.

Jurors will be paid an allowance for travelling, subsistence and loss of earnings or social security benefit, etc. (Juries Act 1974).

Sentences

If you are found guilty or plead guilty, the court has a range of sentences from which it can choose. What these sentences mean is described in this section. On p. 84, you will find details of how to apply for bail if the court does not sentence you immediately; on p. 98, you will find information about how to make an appeal – either against your conviction, or against the sentence imposed, or both.

ABSOLUTE DISCHARGE

This means that you are found guilty but no restrictions are placed on you. Although a conviction, it is usually an indication by the court that the charge should not have been brought or the circumstances are such that any form of punishment would be unjust:

A reporter was sentenced to nine months' imprisonment for possession of cannabis. On appeal he was given an absolute discharge because it was established that he had the cannabis only for the purpose of writing an article about the ease with which drugs could be obtained.

CONDITIONAL DISCHARGE

This is a similar method of convicting you without punishing you. It is used where any other form of punishment would be unfair but where the court wishes to have some method of keeping a check on you. The discharge can be made conditional for up to three years. If you are found guilty of any other offence within that period you can then be sentenced for the original offence. The court must explain this to you when giving the conditional discharge.

BINDING OVER

(The term 'binding over' is used elsewhere to mean the procedure by which you are required to pay a sum of money if you
fail to keep the peace and be of good behaviour. This can be
done even where there has been no conviction – see p. 148.)

Binding over as a form of sentencing has a different meaning. You may be bound over 'to come up for judgment',
usually subject to some specific condition. It is similar to a conditional discharge although there is no limit to the period for
which it can apply and conditions may be attached to a binding-
over order which may not be to a conditional discharge (e.g.
residence in a hostel). This can only be done by the Crown Court.

FINE

A fine may be imposed for almost all offences in addition to, or
instead of, any other sentence (except discharge and probation).
The maximum fine for most offences is fixed by Act of Parliament; otherwise, the court can impose an unlimited fine.

The main principle governing the use of fines is that the
offence must be one for which a sentence of imprisonment would
be wrong. Your ability to pay may reduce the amount of the fine
but should not affect the type of punishment (i.e. it would be
wrong for the court to imprison someone because he or she
cannot afford a fine). The court may make an order fixing a
period of imprisonment up to twelve months to be served in
default of payment. But you cannot be sent to prison for not
paying a fine unless one of the following four conditions is satisfied:

– you appear to be able to pay immediately;
– you are unlikely to remain in the country and to obtain the
  money by any other method;
– you are already in prison or detained for some other offence.
– you are already serving a term of imprisonment or detention.

It is considered incorrect to impose a fine which the convicted person cannot afford. Fines given in magistrates' courts are limited to £400. (The Criminal Law Bill proposes to raise the limit, see pp. 17–20.) You can ask for time to pay or to pay by instalments.

PROBATION

A probation order may be made for a convicted person aged 17 or over, but you must give your consent to this. An order may be made if the court is 'of the opinion that having regard to the circumstances, including the nature of the offence and the character of the offender, it is expedient to do so'. The order is made instead of any other sentence and when on probation you must be under the supervision of a probation officer for a period of between one and three years. The probation order may require you to comply with certain restrictions (e.g. residence in a probation home or hostel); usually these conditions may not include submitting to psychiatric treatment. Before making the order, the court must explain to you in ordinary language the nature and terms of the order, and must tell you that if you fail to obey the order or if you commit another offence, you can be brought back and sentenced for the original offence.

The probation order may be discharged on the application of the probation officer or the probationer. The order is usually discharged by the court which is supervising the order. The court may, instead of discharging the order, substitute a conditional discharge for the same period as the original order.

A probation order is not only for young offenders but can be used for anyone where it is the most appropriate form of punishment and where some degree of supervision is required.

IMPRISONMENT

Most offences have a maximum period for which a person can be imprisoned, although certain common-law offences (e.g. riot) have no maximum. It is not possible to discuss here the merits and demerits of prison sentences.

In a magistrates' court the maximum term of imprisonment that can be awarded is usually six months, but the court can also impose a period of imprisonment in default of payment of any fine. If you are tried for more than one offence and the sentences are made to run consecutively, the total term of imprisonment should not exceed six months, or, in the case of offences which could have been tried in the Crown Court, twelve months.

No one under the age of 17 may be imprisoned. A convicted person between 17 and 21 should be imprisoned only if there is no other appropriate punishment. The reasons for the choice of imprisonment must be recorded. The same is true of people aged 21 and over who have not previously been imprisoned.

SUSPENDED SENTENCE

When a court passes a prison sentence for two years or less, it can order that the sentence shall not take effect *unless*, during a specified period between one and two years, you commit a further offence punishable with imprisonment: if that happens, the court orders the original sentence to take effect. A suspended sentence can be combined with a supervision order (similar to a probation order, but where you do not consent).

On passing a suspended sentence the court must explain to you in ordinary language that if you are convicted of a further offence during the period of the suspended sentence, you will be brought back to the court that gave you the suspended sentence and may be ordered to serve all or part of it. Not every conviction will result in the suspended sentence being brought into operation. If you are aged 21 or over, and get a prison sentence between 6 months and 2 years, the court can suspend *part* of it ($\frac{1}{4}$ to $\frac{3}{4}$). This power had not, however, been brought into effect by August 1977.

DEFERRED SENTENCE

Any court may defer (i.e. put off) passing sentence for up to six months from the date of conviction to enable the court to take into account a defendant's behaviour after conviction (e.g. reparation, keeping out of trouble, good employment record).

COMMUNITY SERVICE ORDER

In some parts of the country, a court, instead of sentencing you to imprisonment, may order you to do unpaid community work under supervision, provided you consent, for between 40 and 240 hours. A breach of the order may incur a fine of £50 and the court can also proceed to sentence for the original offence (e.g. by imprisonment).

COMPENSATION ORDER

A person who is convicted may in addition to any other sentence be ordered by the court to pay compensation for any personal injury, loss or damage resulting from the offence. The amount ordered depends on the ability of the offender to pay, but a magistrates' court cannot impose a compensation order of more than £1,000.

CRIMINAL BANKRUPTCY

Where a person is convicted of an offence in the Crown Court and loss or damage (other than that attributable to personal injury) exceeds £15,000, the court may in addition to any other sentence declare the offender to be a criminal bankrupt. There is no appeal against this order, although there is against the conviction on which it was based.

Young people

Young people between 17 and 21 are not, except in very rare circumstances, sentenced to a term of imprisonment (see p. 96). They can be fined, put on probation, or discharged, but special forms of punishment can also be given such as detention and borstal training (see below), supervision or care orders (see pp. 361–4).

DETENTION CENTRE

Detention may be ordered in the case of an offender aged between 14 and 21 where the court would otherwise have power to pass a sentence of imprisonment. Where the maximum term of imprisonment for the offence is more than three months, the sentence of detention must be between three and six months. In all other cases it must be for three months.

BORSTAL TRAINING

Sentence of borstal training may be passed where a person aged between 15 and 21 is convicted of an offence punishable with imprisonment 'where the court is of the opinion having regard to the circumstances of the offence and after taking into account the offender's character and previous conduct, it is expedient that he should be detained for training for not less than six months'. Before passing a sentence of borstal training the court must consider any report prepared by the prison department but there is no obligation to obtain such a report. You may be detained for any period between six months and two years unless the Home Secretary directs your release earlier. You must remain under supervision for two years from the date of your release. If during that period you fail to comply with any conditions on which you were released, you may be recalled to borstal.

Appealing against conviction and sentence

A convicted person can appeal against conviction and sentence. As a rule you cannot appeal against conviction if you pleaded guilty, unless you did so by mistake, or were bullied into pleading guilty, or pleaded guilty after the court decided a point of law against you. You can appeal against sentence even if you pleaded guilty, unless the sentence was one that you had to agree to, such as a probation order or a community service order. You can also appeal against an order that you pay costs. (But if you are found not guilty and still have to pay costs, you cannot appeal against that.)

If you had legal aid at the Crown Court then this should also cover your lawyers advising you on the question of appeal and helping you set the appeal going. If they do not advise you on this then you should ask help from the **Registrar of Criminal Appeals, Royal Courts of Justice, Strand, London, WC2.** If you are in prison there is a special form that you can complete and which will be passed on to your solicitor, asking for advice on the question of appeal.

The appeals procedure depends on which court heard your case. If you were convicted in the magistrates' court and sent to the Crown Court to be sentenced, you need not do anything about appealing until the Crown Court has sentenced you. If you were convicted in any court and the sentence was postponed, again you need not do anything about appealing until you have been sentenced.

Appealing from the magistrates' court

If you want to appeal because you think that the magistrates made a mistake in law, you will usually appeal to the Divisional Court of the Queen's Bench Division of the High Court (see p. 79). Within fourteen days of the court dealing with you, you must write to the clerk to the justices, referring in your letter to the names of the justices who heard the case, the details of the date and place, etc., saying why you think they were mistaken in law and asking the justices to 'state a case for the opinion of the High Court'. The justices might ask you to guarantee a certain amount of costs (e.g. £100) before they do so, or might refuse to do so, in which case there are special rules for appealing to the High Court. Since this type of appeal can be complicated and expensive it is usually essential to obtain legal advice first. If you had legal aid at the hearing your lawyers will help. If not, you can get advice under the green-form scheme (see p. 494) or you can apply for legal aid, but you have to do so under the civil legal aid scheme (see p. 496). Since the time limits are very tight you should apply for emergency legal aid (see p. 499). If you have been given a custodial sentence you should ask the magistrates to release you on bail until the appeal is heard. If they refuse you can apply for bail to a judge in chambers (see p. 83). You can delay paying any fine until the appeal is heard.

If you wish to appeal on the facts or against sentence, or on a mixture of facts and law, you will usually appeal to the Crown Court. If the appeal is against sentence all the arguments on both sides will be heard again. The court can increase the sentence but only up to what the magistrates could have passed. Usually the most a sentence can be increased to is six months' imprisonment and/or a fine of £1,000 on each count. However, the court can order you to pay costs if you lose, which might be very expensive.

If the appeal is against conviction the whole matter will be re-heard with all the witnesses giving evidence and being cross-examined afresh and the court making up its own mind.

You can apply for legal aid for any appeal to the Crown Court. You can ask the magistrates' court to grant legal aid for the appeal and you can also ask the Crown Court itself. You should obtain the legal aid forms from the court (see p. 501).

If you are appealing to the Crown Court and you have been given a custodial sentence, you should apply to the magistrates for bail until the appeal has been heard. If they refuse you can apply to the Crown Court itself. Your solicitor (or a prison officer if you are in prison) will help you to arrange this.

You appeal to the Crown Court by completing and sending in appeal forms which you can obtain from the magistrates' court or from the Crown Court. You must also send a copy of the form to the prosecutor (e.g. the prosecuting solicitor or the police officer). The forms are sent to the magistrates' court and must be sent within twenty-one days of you being sentenced, although in very exceptional cases the Crown Court can give you permission to appeal after this time limit has expired.

Appealing from the Crown Court

In any matter except a trial, you can appeal from the Crown Court to the High Court on a point of law (e.g. if the Crown Court dismisses your appeal against a magistrates' court decision).

In all other cases (including conviction or sentence after a trial on indictment) the appeal will be to the Court of Appeal (Criminal Division).

You must apply for leave to appeal on a notice of appeal and give the Court of Appeal the grounds of your appeal. You should ask your lawyers for help with this. If you are waiting for detailed advice you can say that the grounds are 'provisional grounds' and that you are waiting for further legal advice. The forms for appealing can be obtained from the Crown Court or from the Registrar of Criminal Appeals (see p. 99 for his address) or from the prison authorities if you are a prisoner, and should be sent to the registrar.

There are separate forms to be completed if you wish to apply for bail, for permission to be present at the appeal, or to call fresh evidence. The notice and grounds of appeal must be sent in within twenty-eight days of your being sentenced. The other forms can be sent in later, but it is better to send them in as early as possible. You will not be given bail except in the rarest of cases unless you have been given a very short sentence which might be over before the appeal is dealt with.

The form of notice of appeal includes an application for legal aid for the appeal, but you will not be given legal aid unless you are also given leave to appeal (see below), or your application for leave to appeal is referred to the full court.

Most applications for leave to appeal are dealt with by one judge who decides whether leave is to be given or refers the matter to a court of three judges (the **full court**). Appeals which raise questions of law only should be referred directly to the full court.

If the judge refuses any of your applications you have fourteen days in which to ask for it to be heard by the full court, but you will not usually be given legal aid at this stage.

If leave to appeal is granted, you will be given legal aid, usually consisting of a barrister only, unless the appeal raises complicated details of background or fact. The barrister will be chosen by the registrar and will usually be one that you had at the trial, although you can ask for a different one.

Appeals take a long time to be heard because the court has to obtain a transcript of the trial. The court hears argument on all sides but does not usually take any new evidence, relying on the evidence given in the Crown Court. The court cannot increase the sentence but it can order that some of the time you have spent waiting for the appeal to come on should not count towards your sentence.

You can appeal to the Court of Appeal (Criminal Division) against sentence, and also against conviction on a point of law or fact (that is, alleging that the Crown Court has misapplied the law or has made an error in its findings of fact).

Appeal to the House of Lords

You can only appeal to the House of Lords if you are given permission to do so by either the Court of Appeal or the House of Lords itself and if you are appealing on a point of law which the court certifies to be a point of 'general public importance'. The procedure is very complicated and expensive and legal advice is essential before appealing to the House of Lords. The House of Lords hears only a handful of criminal appeals each year.

Using an adviser instead of a lawyer

You may prefer to defend yourself instead of using a lawyer, or you may not be able to get legal aid. In either case, you are entitled to have a friend with you, to sit beside you and give advice, take notes and give moral support. The friend can be a lawyer, but is not allowed to speak on your behalf. The friend is often known as a **McKenzie adviser**, following a court decision in the case of McKenzie which confirmed this right.

As soon as possible after the case begins (probably just after you have been asked to plead guilty or not guilty), you should say: 'I would like to request to have a friend sit beside me in court to assist me in representing myself. I make this application under the Court of Appeal ruling in McKenzie against McKenzie in 1970.'

If the magistrate objects or hesitates, you should make a formal application along these lines:

I want to make a formal motion to have a friend to assist me in representing myself. Every party to a case has the right to have a friend, qualified or not, to help and advise in the conduct of the case. The main authority for this is the recent Court of Appeal decision in McKenzie against McKenzie, 1970: Volume 3 *Weekly Law Reports*, p. 472.

If possible, have a copy of the law reports with you to show the magistrates.

In the case of McKenzie, a defended divorce action involving difficult and complex questions, the husband appeared with a young Australian barrister sent by the husband's former solicitors. The judge told the lawyer that, since solicitors were no longer employed to instruct him, he could not assist. The lawyer then left the court. McKenzie appealed against the decision dismissing his divorce petition. The Court of Appeal unanimously held:

– every party to a case has the right to have a friend present in court beside him to assist by prompting, taking notes and quietly giving advice; and
– that the judge's intervention had deprived McKenzie of that right. As a result, McKenzie had been prejudiced in presenting the case and a new trial would be needed.

If the magistrates refuse your application, you should ask the court for an adjournment to seek legal advice. The High Court has the power to compel magistrates to accept the presence of a McKenzie adviser, and you can get civil legal aid (see p. 494) to apply to the High Court. Or you could use a skilled McKenzie to help you apply to the High Court yourself!

The McKenzie ruling applies to all courts, not only magistrates' courts. You can choose to have a McKenzie adviser instead of legal aid: the court cannot force you to accept legal aid.

Rehabilitation of offenders

In the past anyone who was found guilty of a criminal offence, especially if they were imprisoned, would have had to carry that conviction round with them for the rest of their lives. Even if that person had 'gone straight' since the conviction, they would probably have met discrimination from employers, landlords, creditors and others, because so many people assume that anyone who has at any time tangled with the law is at best unreliable and dishonest, and at worst a confirmed criminal.

New legislation came into force in 1975 which attempts to improve this situation. The Rehabilitation of Offenders Act 1974 establishes that a person who has a previous conviction and has kept out of trouble for a certain period of time should usually be treated in law as a person who has no criminal record. This means that if you have served a sentence of less than six months and left prison over seven years ago (the **rehabilitation period**), your conviction is regarded as **spent** and you become a **rehabilitated person**. If, for example, you apply for a job, you may leave out reference to your imprisonment in your application or interview, or if you come before an industrial tribunal your past record may not be mentioned.

THE REHABILITATION PERIOD

The rehabilitation period depends on the sentence passed and runs from the date of conviction. Conviction means being found guilty of a criminal offence in any court in the world. It includes a finding under the Children and Young Persons Act, s. 1 that an offence has been committed; a decision that a ground has been accepted or established for referral of a child's case to a children's hearing (in Scotland); a decision to place someone on probation or give an absolute or conditional discharge; and conviction of certain offences in service disciplinary proceedings.

The following table sets out the various rehabilitation periods according to sentence.

TABLE 1

Sentence	Rehabilitation period	
Imprisonment or corrective training for between 6 and 30 months (2½ years)	10 years	All of these periods are reduced by half if the offender was under 17 at the date of conviction.
Imprisonment for 6 months or less	7 years	
Cashiering, discharge with ignominy or dismissal with disgrace from Her Majesty's service	10 years	
Dismissal from Her Majesty's service	7 years	
Detention in respect of conviction in service disciplinary proceedings	5 years	
Fine	5 years	
Borstal training	7 years	
Detention for between 6 and 30 months (2½ years) under the Children and Young Persons Act 1933, s. 53 (or in Scotland the equivalent provision)	5 years	
Detention for 6 months or less under the above provision	3 years	
Detention in a detention centre	3 years	
Committal to a remand home, approved school, etc., attendance centre order	1 year after date on which order ceases to have any effect	
Hospital order under mental health legislation	5 years, or 2 years after order ceases to have any effect, whichever is the longer period	

TABLE 1—*continued*

Sentence	Rehabilitation period
Fit-person order, approved-school order in Scotland, care or supervision order under Children and Young Persons Act 1969	1 year, or period ending with the date on which the order ceases to have any effect, whichever is the longer
Absolute discharge	6 months
Conditional discharge, binding-over or probation order	1 year or the period of the duration of the order, whichever is the longer
Disqualification or disability	The period during which it is in force

The following sentences can never be spent:

– a sentence of imprisonment or corrective training of more than 30 months (2½ years);
– a life sentence;
– detention during Her Majesty's pleasure;
– preventive detention. (This sentence was abolished in 1967.)

If you are convicted of an indictable (more serious) offence during the rehabilitation period and receive a sentence which is not excluded from the Act, the earlier rehabilitation period is extended until the new one expires. If you are convicted of a summary (more minor) offence during the rehabilitation period, it will carry its own rehabilitation period and will have no effect on the earlier one.

The effect of rehabilitation

Subject to certain exceptions, a rehabilitated person is to be treated for all purposes in law as a person who has not committed or been charged with or prosecuted for or convicted of or sentenced for the offence(s) for which the conviction has been spent.

EVIDENCE IN LEGAL PROCEEDINGS

If you are a rehabilitated person, your conviction cannot be used in evidence in a civil court, tribunal, arbitration or disciplinary or similar hearing. You cannot be required to answer any questions which would involve disclosing information about your conviction. You should not be asked questions about spent convictions and you need not answer them if they are asked unless you agree to do so. This does not apply in:

- criminal proceedings;
- service disciplinary proceedings;
- proceedings relating to adoption, guardianship, wardship, marriage, custody care or control of any minor, or care proceedings under the Children and Young Persons Act 1969, s.1 or a children's hearing (Social Work (Scotland) Act 1968);
- proceedings where the rehabilitated person is a party or a witness and consents to the determination of the issue or the admission of that evidence;
- where the court or tribunal is satisfied that justice cannot be done except by hearing the evidence involved.

EMPLOYMENT AND SERVICES

If you are a rehabilitated person you do not have to answer questions relating to spent convictions or the surrounding circumstances, and you can answer questions as though the conviction never took place on application forms for a job, or to join a union, or to take out an insurance policy, etc. Also, you cannot lose your job because you have a spent conviction or because you have failed to disclose it.

This does not apply:

- if you apply for admission or work as a medical practitioner, lawyer, chartered or certified accountant, dentist, vet, nurse, midwife, optician, chemist, for a post in the courts or police services or prison services, in certain types of social work, work with children under 18, in the health services, in certain types of insurance and unit trust work or as a firearms dealer;

- in proceedings relating to professional disciplinary action of some of the above professions, or before the Gaming Board;
- or if you are subject to national security vetting.

REVEALING A SPENT CONVICTION

There are three ways of dealing with someone who illegally reveals that you have a spent conviction.

You can:

1. Sue the person involved for defamation (libel if it is written, slander if it is said – see pp. 320–25) *even if what has been said is true*, provided it relates to a spent conviction and you can show that the person has acted with malice in disclosing it. This can also be done if anyone mentions details about your spent conviction which a court has ruled inadmissible (unless it is mentioned in a law report or similar document). It is not possible to get legal aid to bring proceedings for defamation.

2. Make a formal complaint to the police who may, with the consent of the Director of Public Prosecutions, bring criminal proceedings against someone who knowingly discloses information from official records kept by any court, police force, government department, or local or other public authority, which relates to your spent conviction. This offence can only be committed by someone who has access to the information in the course of official duties but it is not an offence if it is committed in the course of those duties. The maximum fine for this offence is £200.

3. Make a formal complaint to the police who may bring criminal proceedings against someone who obtains information relating to your spent conviction from any official record by means of fraud, dishonesty or bribe. The maximum fine for this offence is £400 and/or six months' imprisonment. If the police take no action you may take out a private summons (see p. 74).

Criminal Injuries Compensation Board

The Criminal Injuries Compensation Board (CICB) was set up in 1964 to provide compensation for victims of violent crime.

The scheme is financed by government, and administered by an independent board, with thirteen legally qualified members appointed by the Home Secretary and the Secretary of State for Scotland.

In the year 1975–6 the CICB received 16,690 applications and paid out a total of £6,437,967.

You can apply to the CICB if:

- you received a personal injury in Great Britain or on any British ship, aeroplane or hovercraft, on or after 1 August 1964; *and*
- your injury was directly caused by one of the following:
  - a crime of violence (including arson and poisoning); *or*
  - the arrest or attempted arrest of a suspected offender (even though the suspect was not involved in a violent crime); *or*
  - the prevention of an offence (whether a violent offence or not); *or*
  - helping a police officer do either of the last two things.

If you were injured in Northern Ireland, you cannot apply to the CICB since there is a different scheme (see p. 554).

You can only claim compensation for *personal* injury, and not for damage to goods or property. (If your goods or property are damaged, you will either get a court compensation order if the offender is convicted, as described on p. 97, or you will have to bring legal action in the civil courts, as set out on p. 243).

If you are the dependant of someone who died because of injuries received in any of these circumstances, you can also claim compensation from the CICB (although you will have to use a special form).

If you wish to claim compensation, you should get the application form from the Secretary, **Criminal Injuries Compensation Board, 10-12 Russell Square, London WC1 (01-636 2812)**.

MAKING THE APPLICATION

You can complete the application form yourself (it is not very complicated). You may also be able to get a lawyer to help you under the green-form scheme (see p. 494). You will have to include on the form details of the injury and how it happened. You will also be asked to authorize the CICB to make inquiries from the police, doctors who have treated you, your employers (for details of your earnings) and government departments (for details of your social security payments).

HOW THE CICB DEALS WITH YOUR APPLICATION

The CICB will only pay compensation if it is satisfied that:

– your injury is severe enough to deserve a payment of at least £50 (given inflation, a sprained ankle or severe bruising would probably be compensated for by £50 damages in the civil courts); *and*
– the person who caused your injury was prosecuted in the criminal courts, or that the incident was reported to the police without delay (although this requirement may be waived); *and*
– you have given the CICB every reasonable help, especially in making medical reports available.

The CICB will *not* pay compensation in the following circumstances:

– you were living together with the person who injured you, as members of the same family or as man and wife (whether or not you were actually married);
– the injuries were caused by a traffic accident, unless there was a deliberate attempt to run you down. In most cases, motorists are insured against injuring someone (see p. 158) and the driver's insurance company will pay you compensation. If the driver was not insured, you should apply to the Motor Insurers' Bureau (see p. 159);
– the CICB decides that, because of your conduct and character, it would not be appropriate to pay you compensation. This may exclude for instance, someone who joined a violent gang and was then injured in an internal gang fight. If you are assaulted in prison by another prisoner or a prison officer, you can still claim compensation but you will have to show that the

assault was criminal and not just the use of reasonable force; the amount of compensation may be reduced if you were partly to blame (e.g. by provoking the assault, or striking the first blow).

There are special rules in cases of rape and other sexual assault. The CICB will consider applications for compensation for pain, suffering and shock in such cases, and also for loss of wages due to pregnancy resulting from rape, and childbirth expenses for someone not eligible for a maternity grant (but *not* the costs of maintaining a child born as the result of a rape). But in cases of sexual assault or assault arising from a sexual relationship (e.g. a prostitute injured by a client), the CICB will look at the case carefully to see if the victim provoked the assault or was in any other way partly responsible.

As a general rule, the CICB will award the same amount of compensation as the civil courts would have awarded if you had brought a successful legal action – including loss of wages, expenses, and compensation for pain and suffering. The CICB *must* deduct the value of any social security benefits you are entitled to (e.g. sickness benefit) and may deduct a sum for any pension received as a result of the injury.

Your application will initially be decided by one member of the CICB looking at the papers. This may take several months. If you are dissatisfied with his decision, you can appeal to three other members who will hold a hearing where you can submit evidence, and call and cross-examine witnesses. The CICB will not pay any of your legal expenses, but can pay witnesses' expenses. You cannot get legal aid to cover the cost of having a lawyer at the hearing, although you may be able to get legal advice about the case under the green-form scheme (see p. 494). Alternatively, you can be represented by your trade union, a friend, your employer or a social worker.

If you have been awarded a sum of compensation by one member of the CICB, you should think carefully before appealing to the full board, since they have the power to reduce the sum awarded to you or even to pay you nothing at all.

Compensation which you obtain from another source (e.g. the

courts or an insurance company) will be deducted from the compensation you are awarded by the CICB. If you receive any other compensation after the board has awarded you money, you will have to pay it to the board, up to the total of what the board awarded you.

More information

See Chapter 25 on Legal Services, especially pp. 500–503.

3. Prisoners

This chapter covers:

Prisoners have few rights, but guidelines to their privileges are laid down in the Prison Rules 1964. A prison governor or other prison authority can withdraw privileges for a variety of reasons and failure to keep to the Rules will not lead to legal action against the prison authorities unless accompanied by some other breach of law such as assault.

The Home Secretary has ultimate responsibility for prisons. Prisoners or their families can petition him on certain issues such as an application to re-open a case after the appeals procedure has been exhausted, for permission to conduct business from prison, or an application to attend court proceedings.

Each prison has a board of visitors which is a small group of people including magistrates whose job is to overlook the running of the prison on behalf of the public, deal with disciplinary offences and review complaints and problems raised by prisoners. In practice the board of visitors is very much guided by the prison governor.

Reception into prison

On reception into prison the prisoner will be searched and may be photographed. Any property which the prisoner is not allowed to keep will be taken into the governor's custody. An inventory (list) of the prisoner's property will be made and the prisoner must be given an opportunity to see that it is correct before signing it. All cash must be paid into an account under the governor's control.

Prisoners must be given a written account of certain prison rules including information about earnings, privileges and the method of making complaints and a prison official must make sure that the prisoner has read and understood this information within twenty-four hours of reception.

Unconvicted prisoners

Prisoners who are remanded in custody to await trial are allowed certain rights which convicted prisoners do not have:

- they may wear their own clothes and arrange for clothes to be sent in by family or friends;
- they should not be forced to have their hair cut or beard shaved except for reasons of hygiene;
- they do not have to work though they may apply to work in the same way as convicted prisoners if they choose;
- they may send and receive as many letters as they like though the letters will be censored;
- they may receive as many visits as they like though in practice this is usually limited to one a day;
- they may receive food but apart from fruit, chocolate and similar 'extras' the food must be a complete meal which is then substituted for a prison meal (in some prisons half a bottle of wine may also be sent in);
- they may buy or be given books, papers and writing materials which are not considered 'objectionable' by the prison authorities;
- they may have a visit from a doctor or dentist who is not attached to the prison if they are willing to pay any expense incurred;
- they may see their legal adviser during normal working hours and as often as necessary – these meetings will be in the sight but not the hearing of a prison officer.

Convicted prisoners

Categorization

When they first go into prison, prisoners are placed in one of four categories according to the extent to which they are regarded as a security risk. This is done by:

- the governor at the local prison who classifies first offenders serving four years or less and those with previous convictions serving under five years;
- the regional director at a regional allocation centre who makes the final decision about those serving other sentences;
- the prison department of the Home Office who make decisions about placing prisoners in Category A (the highest security risk).

There is no appeal against the categorization decision but the position is regularly reviewed and changes can be made. If it is felt that there are grounds for reclassification representations should be made to the Home Office by the prisoner's relatives, solicitor, MP or NCCL.

The four security categories are:

CATEGORY A: Prisoners whose escape would be highly dangerous to the public or the security of the state.

CATEGORY B: Prisoners who do not need the highest conditions of security but for whom escape must be made very difficult.

CATEGORY C: Prisoners who cannot be trusted in open conditions but who do not have the ability or the resources to make a determined escape attempt.

CATEGORY D: Prisoners who can reasonably be trusted to serve their sentences in open conditions.

Allocation

Allocation to a particular prison is made after assessment of the offence and sentence, category, individual history, training needs and the domestic situation of the prisoner. No appeal is allowed against this decision but the prisoner or the prisoner's family can write to the prison department of the Home Office asking for a transfer if the decision seems inappropriate. Prisoners have no right to be sent to a prison near their home.

Visits

Prisoners are entitled to one visit every four weeks although the governor may allow more visits depending on facilities and staffing in different prisons. Extra visits are allowed by the governor or board of visitors if it is considered necessary for the welfare of the prisoner's family or for other special reasons such as to assist a prisoner with an appeal.

Visitors must first get a **visiting order** which is usually sent by post and covers up to three visitors or visits. Visitors to Category A prisoners must complete an inquiry form with a photograph and this will have to be verified by the local police.

Prisoners who have served more than two years after being transferred from a local prison and who still have at least six months left of the sentence are eligible for **accumulated visits** if it is difficult for family or friends to travel long distances to visit. Prisoners can accumulate up to a maximum of twelve visits.

A prisoner's wife, husband or next of kin who is receiving social security can claim an allowance for the cost of the fare from the DHSS. Some probation offices are prepared to help out if the visitor is not claiming social security but is having difficulty finding the fare.

Visitors may give prisoners cigarettes to smoke during visits but this is a privilege which may be withdrawn and visitors are liable to a fine or imprisonment if they give the prisoner anything else. Visitors must not take notes of the conversation nor use the information gained from a visit for publication.

If the authorities feel that a prisoner has or might abuse a visit they can impose certain restrictions:

- by refusing visits from certain people;
- by granting only 'closed' visits where the prisoner meets the visitor in a small room with a prison officer present; *or*

– by granting only 'screened' visits where there is a glass partition between the prisoner and the visitor.

Prisoners may usually receive visits from relatives or friends only although the governor or the Home Office can use their discretion to allow other visitors.

Visits by voluntary prison visitors count as ordinary visits but prisoners can have extra visits from their ministers of religion.

MPs can get authority to visit a prisoner from the Secretary of State but otherwise must have a visiting order from the prisoner or a magistrate. If an MP visits a prisoner, the interview will be outside the hearing of a prison officer, unless the MP requests otherwise or there are special security considerations.

Interviews with the police: police officers may, with permission from the governor, interview a prisoner concerning future charges, inquiries for criminal investigations, appearance as a prosecution witness or participation in an ID parade. The prisoner is entitled to refuse to see the police officer or to answer his questions.

Letters

Prisoners may send and receive one letter a week but usually two or more letters out are allowed if the prisoner pays the extra postage. The rule is more strictly enforced for Category A prisoners.

The prison authorities may read all letters to and from prisoners except correspondence between prisoners and their legal advisers about appeals. The governor may stop any letters considered to be 'objectionable' or too long and letters may be censored. 'Objectionable' can be widely interpreted to include mention of other prisoners' offences, complaints about prison treatment or matters which may attract publicity.

The governor may refuse to allow a prisoner to write to people not known at the time of conviction. But the prisoner will usually be allowed to write to organizations such as NCCL, Justice or the National Association for the Care and Resettlement of Offenders about his case. Prisoners may write to their

MP after two months in prison but are not allowed to complain of treatment in prison unless the complaint has already been investigated within the prison. The governor may stop a letter to an MP if it is considered objectionable but the prisoner's family or friends can write on the prisoner's behalf.

Prisoners are not allowed to write business letters or conduct business from prison without the permission of the Home Office.

Gifts

All gifts will be inspected and the governor may confiscate any unauthorized article found in a prisoner's possession. Gifts of money will either be paid into the prisoner's account under the governor's control or returned to the sender. Other gifts may be delivered to the prisoner, or placed with the personal property to be given back on release or returned to the sender.

All goods and money received from unknown sources are paid into an account for the benefit of discharged prisoners even when the article or money is addressed to an individual prisoner.

Work

All convicted prisoners are required to work, usually in association with other prisoners, unless excused by the medical officer. It is a disciplinary offence for a prisoner to refuse to work or to be idle, careless or negligent at work.

The type of work varies from prison to prison and there is no overall training plan. Conditions also vary but the average working week is twenty-six hours and prison wages are from 35p to £2·19 maximum a week. Prisoners do not pay National Insurance contributions.

Prisoners employed in special hostels or pre-release schemes where they work outside, get the normal weekly wage and pay insurance and tax.

Prison workshops are exempt from the Factories Act and no claim for industrial injury can be made in the event of an accident. However, a prisoner injured at work may be able to bring a civil claim (see p. 258) against the Home Office for negligence.

Each prison has a labour allocation board and prisoners can apply for a change of job.

Education facilities

Local education authorities provide a programme of evening classes in all prisons but classroom space is often limited. Facilities for daytime study and remedial teaching vary. The governor is responsible for assessing the prisoner's needs and suitability for further study and can release individuals from work duty for study. Permission from the prison authorities can be obtained to enable a prisoner to follow a correspondence course. Education and recreation facilities are provided at the governor's discretion.

All prisons have at least one library and prisoners can take out between four and six books a week. Friends and relations may send in books for prisoners if the authorities consider them suitable. All books sent to prisoners must eventually be given to the prison library.

Food

Prisoners are entitled to three meals a day. The prison authorities will make provision for prisoners with religious objections to certain foods to be given a special diet. It is also possible to have a vegetarian diet. No alcohol is allowed.

Bread and water diet given as a punishment has now been abolished.

Access to lawyers

Prisoners are permitted visits from solicitors about any legal proceedings they are involved in. These visits are held in the sight but not hearing of a prison officer.

Prisoners can only consult a solicitor about their treatment or conditions of imprisonment after the complaint has been investigated by the prison authorities. A prison officer will be present when the prisoner first sees the solicitor but visits will be private once the prisoner has instructed the solicitor to act for him. Prisoners can seek legal advice about taking civil proceedings without first having to get permission from the prison authorities.

Prisoners wishing to seek legal advice are eligible for free legal advice under the green-form scheme which can usually be extended beyond the £25 limit for a prison visit (see p. 494).

Complaints procedure

Prisoners who wish to complain about their conditions or treatment in prison should first raise the matter with the prison governor and then with the board of visitors. If the prisoner feels the issue has not been satisfactorily dealt with it is possible to petition the Home Secretary for a decision. Prisoners can write to their MP to intervene on their behalf but the prison authorities will have to give permission for this.

Prisoners can try to raise a complaint with outside individuals or organizations such as NCCL but the censor can stop such letters, though permission will sometimes be granted when the internal procedure has been exhausted.

It is sometimes more effective for a friend or relative of the prisoner to write about the matter to the Home Secretary, the appropriate MP, or to approach a solicitor to arrange a visit.

When all remedies in this country have been exhausted a prisoner with a complaint about conditions or treatment whilst in prison can petition the European Commission for Human Rights (see p. 576).

Disciplinary charges

If the governor believes that a criminal offence has been committed in the prison, he may inform the police. If charges are brought by the police, the case will usually be heard in an outside court in the usual way. The governor may, however, choose to treat it as a disciplinary offence. Prisoners charged with a disciplinary offence (an offence against the Prison Rules) will be notified immediately and may be removed from association with other prisoners until the matter is settled. The governor will inquire into the case in the first instance and the prisoner will hear the charges and may present a defence. The prisoner has no right to cross-examine witnesses and cannot be represented. The governor can order loss of remission (see p. 124) for up to twenty-eight days.

If the governor thinks the offence too serious or the punishment he can give too small, the case will be referred to the board of visitors. If the case involves an 'especially grave offence' the board of visitors must include two members who are magistrates. Again the prisoner has no right of representation, cross-examination or legal aid. The board can recommend a punishment of up to 180 days' loss of remission (which is the equivalent of a nine-month sentence).

There is no formal machinery for appeal but the prisoner can use the same procedure as for complaints and ask the governor, board of visitors or Secretary of State to reduce the sentence.

If the prisoner's defence involves an allegation against an officer and the defence is rejected, it is possible that a further charge of 'making a false and malicious allegation against an officer' may be brought.

Solitary confinement

The governor may impose cellular confinement (solitary confinement) for a period not exceeding three days as a punishment for an offence against discipline. Where the offence is more serious or the governor feels such an award is insufficient, he may refer the charge to the board of visitors. The board has greater power to impose punishments, and for especially grave offences may impose cellular confinement for a period of up to fifty-six days. The prisoner must be seen daily by the medical officer and no prisoner who is medically unfit should be put in solitary confinement.

Prisoners can ask to be put on Rule 43, which means solitary confinement for their own protection, for instance if they feel they are in danger of being attacked by other prisoners. In this case prisoners should not suffer loss of other privileges such as the use of a radio.

Some prisons have greater facilities (for instance, permit some freedom of association) for Rule 43 prisoners. There are special units at Reading, Gloucester and Wakefield prisons for Rule 43 prisoners, which allow full association at work and in leisure time with other prisoners in a similar situation. Consequently, if a prisoner seems likely to remain on Rule 43 for a long period, the prisoner, friends or family can petition for a transfer to one of these prisons.

Women prisoners

There are far fewer women in prison than men, and women are generally sentenced for shorter periods. There is a strong belief that women in prison are in need of treatment rather than punishment and therefore more resources are allocated to psychiatric facilities in women's prisons.

Women prisoners do not have their hair cut and can wear their own clothes but all other prison rules apply equally to men and women.

Mothers are allowed to keep babies with them up to about nine months. When Holloway prison is rebuilt, it is planned that children will be able to stay with their mothers up to the age of 5.

Prisoners' families

Either spouse can start an action for divorce in the usual way (see p. 348) even if the husband or wife is in prison. Legal aid may be available (see p. 496).

A prisoner can get married with the permission of the prison authorities but this will only usually be given if the woman is pregnant.

Prisoners' families often face grave financial hardship but there are some courses of action which may help:

– the wife or husband of a prisoner may be entitled to supplementary benefits or family income supplement. The DHSS will give information about these;
– the DHSS office will sometimes help out with rates and rent or interest on mortgage repayments;
– explain the situation to the building society and ask them to allow reduced mortgage repayments for the period of imprisonment;
– wives are not normally responsible for debts incurred in their husband's name but are responsible for debts in joint names. Where bills for gas, electricity, etc. have been incurred before imprisonment, write offering to pay off a nominal amount each week from prison earnings;
– if the gas or electricity is cut off, the social services must provide cooking facilities if you have children;
– the social services also have funds to use at their discretion where children are deprived because of their parents' financial situation;
– if no funds are forthcoming the parent should contact the local probation office, social worker or MP.

Release

Remission

Prisoners sentenced to more than one month's imprisonment are entitled to remission of up to one third of their sentence for good conduct whilst in prison. The sentence cannot be reduced to less than thirty-one days. Prisoners released with remission have served their complete sentence and cannot be recalled.

Parole

Prisoners are eligible to apply for parole after serving one third of a sentence or after one year as a convicted prisoner whichever is the longer. Category A prisoners should petition for reclassification before applying for parole.

Each prison has a local review committee consisting of the governor, a probation officer, a member of the board of visitors and an independent member of the public. They will consider the case in the first instance and will usually review it every twelve months. The procedure is as follows:

- a member of the committee will interview the prisoner and report back;
- the prisoner can also make written representations to the committee if he or she wishes;
- the committee will consider reports from the governor, probation officer and medical officer;
- the prisoner should ask friends and possible employers to write supporting the application and giving details of where the prisoner could live and whether a job would be available.

The local review committee will then make a recommendation to the Home Office and the Home Secretary can either grant the parole or refer the matter to the Parole Board for further consideration. The Home Secretary can overrule a decision of the Parole Board to release a prisoner.

There is no appeal against a refusal to grant parole and no reasons are given for a rejection.

A prisoner will only be released on parole subject to certain conditions and may be recalled to prison if these conditions are breached or a criminal offence is committed.

The parole will end on the release date calculated after taking into account remission entitlement.

Release on licence

Prisoners who were under 21 at the time of sentence and prisoners serving extended sentences do not get remission on their sentence and so, if not released on licence, must serve the full term of imprisonment. However, if they are released on licence but recalled, they will be eligible for remission of one third of the sentence still to be served. An extended sentence is one above the maximum for a particular offence and may be imposed in certain circumstances on people with very bad records. Prisoners who are serving life imprisonment may also be released on licence but will not usually be recommended for release by the Parole Board until at least seven years have been served. Once released on licence a life prisoner remains subject to recall until death.

Pre-release

Prisoners may be granted home leave some weeks before release to visit family and make inquiries about a job. Welfare officers or probation officers may be able to help with employment, accommodation, and information about hostel schemes for ex-prisoners, though these are very limited.

Prisoners serving more than four years may be able to get a placement in a hostel or pre-release scheme where they can work outside the prison in the normal way.

Discharge facilities

On release prisoners' personal clothing is returned or, if this is inadequate, suitable clothing is provided. They are also given any money they had on reception into prison, their fare home and a discharge grant of £8·60 or £17 if they are homeless. Those serving under three months are not entitled to the discharge grant though the prison authorities may give a subsistence allowance to enable the prisoner to get to the local DHSS office.

More information

Home Office Prisons Department, 89 Eccleston Square, London SW1 (01-828 9848).

Howard League for Penal Reform, 125 Kennington Park Road, London SE11 (01-735 3773).

National Association for the Care and Resettlement of Offenders (NACRO), 125 Kennington Park Road, London SE11 (01-735 1151).

National Council for Civil Liberties (NCCL), 186 Kings Cross Road, London WC1 (01-278 4575).

Preservation of the Rights of Prisoners (PROP), 339A Finchley Road, London NW3 (01-435 1215).

Prisoners' Wives Service, Bishop Creighton House, 378 Lillie Road, London SW6 (01-385 0054).

Prisoners' Wives Union, 14 Richmond Avenue, London N1 (01-278 3981).

Radical Alternatives to Prison (RAP), Eastbourne House, Bullards Place, Bethnal Green, London E2 (01-981 0041).

4. Public order

Under the law any activity is permitted unless it is prohibited by the civil or criminal laws. What this means in practice, for example, is that anyone can organize or take part in a march or meeting but that march or meeting may be or may become illegal if certain laws are infringed.

The law of public order has developed in a piecemeal manner and there are many uncertainties for individuals or groups who wish to exercise their freedom of expression and action. The line between **public order** and **disorder** is difficult to define and often can only be described in terms of the powers used by the authorities, which usually means the police, to prevent what *they* define as disorder.

This chapter describes the main laws which *may* be used to prevent, control or prosecute people who organize or take part in any activity which involves the expression or physical demonstration of an opinion. Picketing and other activity which takes place in connection with an industrial dispute is dealt with on pp. 207–11.

This chapter is is divided into:

Processions and marches

Most processions or marches are lawful as they simply consist of people exercising their legal right to move along the highway. But there are a number of exceptions as follows:

1. The police have the right to regulate the route of processions and to redirect traffic and pedestrians where necessary. In addition, if a chief officer has grounds for suspecting that a procession is likely to cause 'serious public disorder' he may impose whatever rules or directions he considers necessary to preserve order. But a chief officer may not restrict the use of flags, banners or emblems unless this is necessary to prevent a breach of the peace. It is possible to be charged with 'Wilfully disobeying directions' given by the police. The maximum penalty is three months' imprisonment and/or a £50 fine.

2. In very special circumstances, the chief officer may apply to the local authority for a temporary ban on processions if he can satisfy them that he does not have sufficient power to enable him to prevent a 'serious public disorder'. The local authority may, with the consent of the Secretary of State, make an order prohibiting some or all processions in that area for up to three months. (In London, the Commissioners of Police for the Metropolis or of the City of London can make the order with the consent of the Secretary of State.) Failure to comply with such an order is an offence. The maximum penalty is three months' imprisonment and/or £50 fine.

3. The charge of obstruction of the highway may be used (see p. 152).

4. The charge of causing a public nuisance may be used (see p. 154).

Picketing private premises

(Picketing private premises in connection with industrial disputes is dealt with on p. 209–11.)

Until recently it was assumed that picketing of private premises was lawful so long as it was done merely to obtain or communicate information or peacefully to persuade. But a decision by the courts in 1975 suggests that picketing directed at individual premises may be restrained by an injunction and compensation awarded for any loss of business which occurs as a result of the picket.

The case concerned a campaign to protect tenants and tenanted property in Islington from being bought out by higher-income house-buyers with the assistance of estate agents. Small groups of demonstrators picketed a particular estate agent's premises for limited periods of time by standing on the pavement, carrying placards and handing out leaflets to passers-by. The estate agent alleged that the picketing amounted to a private nuisance, that is, that it was designed to interfere and did interfere with the use and enjoyment of his premises and that his trade had suffered as a result. He successfully obtained a temporary injunction to prevent the picketing even though it was orderly and peaceful and there was no obstruction of the highway.

As a result of this case it seems that picketing on a particular issue outside a number of different premises (walking up and down a street for example) is lawful if there is no obstruction of the highway or threat of a breach of the peace occuring, but that picketing directed at particular premises is not.

Public meetings

There is no unlimited right to hold meetings in public places such as streets, parks, squares, etc. The expression **public place** means any place where the general public has the right to 'pass and repass' or are permitted access, whether on payment or otherwise. All land (including the highway and other public places) belongs to somebody and the use of it for any purpose other than passing and repassing could lead to a civil action for trespass. Where criminal law is concerned, a meeting in a public place is not unlawful so long as no specific criminal offence is committed.

Meetings in public places may give rise to various offences: obstruction of the highway; conduct likely to cause a breach of the peace; threatening, abusive or insulting words or behaviour; or obstructing a police officer. These are dealt with on pp. 146–57.

There are also a number of local bye-laws, local Acts, and common law and statutory provisions which may be used to prevent or control the holdings of meetings in public.

Bye-laws and local Acts

Local authorities have wide powers to make bye-laws covering public meetings held in their area. These bye-laws may lay down special conditions for use of public parks and other public places. Police officers may be given powers under a bye-law to stop any activity causing persons to assemble and obstruct free passage of the highway.

Bye-laws can be challenged on the grounds that they are repugnant to the law of the land, that they discriminate unreasonably and unfairly, that their terms are uncertain, or that they invest a local authority with more power than is conferred on it by statute. The courts, however, normally uphold the validity of bye-laws when they are challenged.

If you intend to hold a meeting in a public place find out what the local bye-laws are from the officers of the local county or district authority. Make a copy of the bye-law and consult a solicitor or the NCCL to find out exactly what it means.

Local Acts often require that the organizers of a meeting or procession give advance notice to the local authority and the police station. This notice must be in writing and must state the time of the meeting and the route of the procession. It should be delivered at least thirty-six hours before the meeting is due to start. Penalties may be imposed on people who organize meetings without authorization.

Even if local Acts do not insist on this, it may be wiser to notify the police in advance about any public meeting anyway, especially if you are planning a large meeting with advance publicity which they are bound to find out about. If no objections are raised, you can safely assume that there will be no police interference unless the meeting causes some unexpected disturbance. The police may object to your holding a meeting or suggest certain conditions but they cannot do this unless they have express powers as described above. They can, of course, advise you. You are under no obligation to follow their advice but if you do not, you are more likely to meet with police interference.

Meetings near Parliament

Open-air political meetings and processions may not be held within one mile of the Houses of Parliament, north of the Thames, if:

- there are more than fifty participants; *and*
- Parliament is sitting on that day; *and*
- the purpose of the meeting is to consider or prepare 'any Petition, Complaint, Remonstrance, Declaration or other Address' to the Crown or to either House 'for alteration of matters in Church or State'.

In effect, there is a ban on any meeting dealing with a subject which is the concern of the Crown or Parliament and would, therefore, apply to almost any ordinary political meeting.

At the beginning of each parliamentary session, the Commissioner of Police makes an order banning *all* open-air meetings and processions within a certain distance of Westminster on any day when Parliament is sitting. The ban only applies to meetings and processions which actually obstruct the free passage of MPs to and from the House of Parliament, or which may cause disorder or annoyance in the neighbourhood.

The banned area is roughly within a mile's radius of Parliament. It is bounded by the south side of the Thames, from Waterloo Bridge to Vauxhall Bridge, along Vauxhall Bridge Road to Victoria Street, and from there to Grosvenor Gardens and Grosvenor Place to Hyde Park Corner, along Piccadilly, Coventry Street, and the north side of Leicester Square, through Cranbourne Street, Long Acre, Bow Street and Wellington Street, and over Waterloo Bridge.

The police have no right to ban meetings in this area on days when Parliament is not sitting.

Meetings in Trafalgar Square

Meetings in Trafalgar Square are governed by special regulations made by the Department of the Environment. The following actions are prohibited unless permission is first obtained from the Department:

– making or giving a public speech or address;
– placing or exhibiting any display or representation;
– using loudspeakers, etc.;
– causing any obstruction to free passage;
– using artificial light or a tripod or stand for photography;
– organizing, conducting or taking part in any assembly, parade or procession;
– selling or distributing anything;
– singing or playing a musical instrument.

The Department of the Environment should not exercise any discrimination in granting permission for one or more of these actions to take place and the only facts they should consider are:

– whether or not the meeting will interfere with the ordinary life of London by causing traffic congestion; *and*
– what advice is received from the police, who must be consulted in each case, on the maintenance of public order.

Despite this, there have been in the past a number of refusals which appear to amount to political discrimination. Also the Department of Environment have raised objections to less conventional forms of public meeting such as music or drama displays held in the Square. Also, all meetings concerned with Northern Ireland were banned as from March 1972, except that permission was given to the peace movement. If you are planning this kind of activity it is best to negotiate with the Department in advance and, if necessary, to seek advice and assistance from the NCCL.

Conduct of public meetings

It is an offence *to try to break up a lawful public meeting* by acting in a 'disorderly manner' or to incite others to do so. The maximum penalty for this offence is six months' imprisonment and/or £1,000 fine in a magistrates' court. For breaking up an election meeting the maximum penalty is £100 fine in a magistrates' court.

If a policeman reasonably suspects a person of *trying to disrupt a public meeting*, or of inciting others to do so, he may at the request of the chairperson of the meeting ask that person for their name and address and, if it is refused, arrest them. The police sometimes allow the person to leave the meeting instead. The police have claimed that under this power any names and addresses collected by them may be given to the chairperson. This has given rise to victimization by the organizers of the meeting. It has not yet been decided by the courts if a chairperson of a public meeting does have a right to these particulars.

The police often ask for the *names and addresses of the organizers of public meetings and speakers*. They have no right to this information unless they give a lawful reason (see p. 22), nor do they have the right to demand names and addresses of members of deputations visiting embassies. In most circumstances, of course, there would be little point in refusing to give the police this information.

Anyone has the right *to heckle* provided that it is kept within reasonable limits. If a heckler goes too far and acts in a disorderly way, he or she may be charged with trying to break up the meeting or with using words or behaviour likely to cause a breach of the peace (see p. 149).

At public meetings held on private premises a reasonable number of *stewards* may be employed to help keep order. They may be assigned certain duties and given badges. This is an exception to the general rule that it is illegal to train or equip stewards to take over the functions of the police or to make a show of force to promote a political object at a public meeting. In practice, this law is rarely enforced and, in any case, no prosecution can be brought without the consent of the Attorney General. Stewards have no right to ask people to leave if the meeting is held in a public place.

Meetings on private premises

The right to hold meetings

The right to hold a meeting on private premises (in or out of doors) depends on getting the permission of the owner or occupier, even where the land may appear derelict or unused. Failure to do this will make all those who attend trespassers. Under the civil law a trespasser who refuses a request by the owner or occupier to leave can be ejected with reasonable force. Under the criminal law the charge of conspiracy to trespass may no longer be used (see p. 17).

Refusals by owners to let halls

Owners of halls can refuse to let their halls to whomever they like, whenever they like, provided they do not discriminate on grounds of race or sex. But:

1. During general and local elections, candidates have the right, subject to certain conditions, to use rooms in publicly owned schools and certain other publicly owned meeting places.
2. Where the control over the use of halls has been established under trust deeds, the power of the trustees to refuse lettings may be limited. It is always worth looking into this possibility.

If owners of halls show unreasonable bias in refusing to let their property, local publicity and pressure can sometimes persuade them to change their policy.

It sometimes happens that owners agree to let a hall and then try to reverse the decision. Unless it is written into the contract that they reserve the right to do this, a civil action may be brought against them for an injunction and damages. You would need legal help for such a case and it may be very expensive.

The right to remove members of an audience

People who attend a meeting held on private premises or in a hall hired for the purpose do so technically at the invitation of the organizers. Therefore the organizers have the right to refuse admission to anyone without giving a reason, whether or not there is an admission charge. If someone forces their way in after being forbidden to enter, they are trespassing and the stewards may eject them provided they do not use unreasonable force.

If someone is already in a meeting held on private premises and the organizers wish to get rid of them there are three possible actions they can take. If the person they wish to get rid of:

- has not paid an entrance fee (or if there has been only a voluntary collection), the organizers have the right to ask them to leave, and if that request is refused, the stewards may use reasonable force to make them leave;
- has paid to go in, the organizers cannot normally make them leave without the risk of being sued for breach of contract, but they may reserve the right to eject any person who has been admitted by displaying a notice to this effect on the tickets or in the entrance hall;
- acts in a disorderly way during the meeting, the organizers can certainly ask them to leave and eject them if necessary, on the grounds that a breach of the peace may occur.

The rights of the police

The police have no right to attend meetings held on private premises unless they are invited by the organizers. However, it is part of the police's duty to prevent crime and if they reasonably believe that a breach of the peace is likely to be committed at a meeting to which the public has been invited, they have the right to enter without a warrant to prevent this happening.

There has been a disturbing tendency for plain-clothes police to turn up at political meetings without authorization and for prosecutions to be launched based on their evidence. Organizers and speakers should be aware of this possibility.

Propaganda

Posters

PARADES

The police have no special power to censor the wording on posters, but they have been known to interfere with poster parades for two reasons:

- that they are likely to cause a breach of the peace;
- that the wording on the posters is 'threatening, abusive or insulting' (Public Order Act 1936, section 5 and Race Relations Act 1976).

This kind of interference is justified only if the wording on the poster is extremely offensive, or if there are other exceptional circumstances.

On occasions, the police have used this provision in a way that is quite contrary to its purpose. The following case is an example – it seemed that the police considered that people practising racial discrimination were doing nothing wrong, whereas those trying to end it were potential criminals:

In 1967, eight members of the Oxford Committee for Racial Integration picketed a ladies' hairdresser which had refused to serve coloured customers. They carried placards saying 'This shop has a colour bar' and 'Other Oxford hairdressers serve everyone'. They were arrested and charged with displaying insulting signs contrary to section 7 of the Race Relations Act 1965. The magistrate dismissed the charge without hearing the defence evidence.

If the police put a ban on processions (see p. 128), poster parades are usually allowed, as long as the participants walk in single file in the gutter and are widely spaced out.

FLYPOSTING

Flyposting (i.e. sticking up posters in public places) is illegal – and that applies to any words, letter, signs, placards, notices, or anything else that might be considered as an advertisement, announcement or direction (Town and Country Planning Act 1971). The fine is a maximum of £100 on a first conviction, and £5 for every day after that until the offending poster is removed.

You cannot put up a poster anywhere without the consent of the local planning authority, which is usually the county council or, in London, the borough council. However, advertisements for local non-commercial events (those of a religious, political, educational, cultural, social, or recreational character, and parliamentary or local elections) can be displayed without the consent of the planning authority, provided the following conditions are observed:

– you have the consent of the site-owner;
– the poster does not block or obscure the view of a road;
– the poster is no bigger than six feet square (except election posters);
– election posters are taken down fourteen days after the poll;
– you comply with other minor conditions.

These conditions do not apply to advertisements displayed on vehicles, but it is illegal to use a vehicle purely for advertising purposes within six miles of Charing Cross (Metropolitan Streets Act 1867).

Local regulations also forbid flyposting. In the London area, for example, it is illegal to put up posters in any public place or to deface or write or paint on any building, wall, or fence (Metropolitan Police Act 1839; City of London Police Act 1839).

It is unlawful to display any advertisement or notice which might be understood as 'indicating an intention to do an act of unlawful discrimination' (Race Relations Act 1976 and Sex Discrimination Act 1975). You cannot be prosecuted by the police for this, only sued by the Commission for Racial Equality or the Equal Opportunities Commission.

Loudspeakers and bands

If you are planning to use a loudspeaker or a band, first check up on the local Acts and bye-laws, which often include special regulations to limit noise. You can get this information from your local authority.

To use loudspeakers for non-commercial purposes, you must usually give at least forty-eight hours' advance notice to the local police station. It is usually illegal to use loudspeakers in the streets for the purpose of advertising a trade or business. Loudspeakers, megaphones and all amplifiers are forbidden in any public place between 9 p.m. and 8 a.m. They are forbidden at all times if used to advertise an organized entertainment, trade, or business. Bands are usually allowed, provided they are not too loud or continuous, nor used at an unreasonable time so as to be a public nuisance (Noise Abatement Act 1960). But remember that something which is allowed by this Act may still be prohibited by a local Act or bye-law.

In the London area, it is unlawful to use any noisy instrument, including a loudspeaker, for the purpose of calling people together, announcing a show or entertainment, selling, distributing or collecting any article, or collecting money. However, this does not prevent you from using a loudspeaker at a meeting, provided that you are not calling people together or taking a collection. You can also announce a meeting, since this cannot be classed as a show or entertainment. Be careful how you phrase the announcement: if you say, 'Come to a meeting at the Town Hall tonight,' you may be accused of calling people together, but you can quite legally say, 'There will be a meeting at the Town Hall tonight' (Metropolitan Police Act 1839; City of London Police Act 1839).

Before you use a loudspeaker or band in a park or similar open space, make sure you know the local regulations. In Hyde Park, for instance, you cannot use loudspeakers without the prior consent of the Department of the Environment.

Selling and distributing literature in the street

NAME AND ADDRESS OF PRINTER

Any printed book or paper intended for publication or distribution (including duplicated sheets) must bear the name and address of the printer. If this is not done, both the printer and the distributor can be prosecuted. Printers must keep for six months a copy of everything they print, and must write on each article the name and address of the person who commissioned the work.

OTHER REGULATIONS

The publication and distribution of written material is also controlled by the libel laws (see p. 321) and the Race Relations Act (see p. 241).

Non-commercial organizations who are selling or distributing literature for propaganda are not usually covered by local regulations which control street trading and the distribution of advertising matter in the streets. Even when they are, they can often get a special exemption. 'Distribution' means distributing to the public at large, not to one individual, or to an association of which the publisher or distributor is a member.

You may not carry or distribute any print, board, placard, notice, or leaflet in any street within six miles of Charing Cross, unless you do so in a way which is approved by the Commissioner of Police (Metropolitan Streets Act 1867). Obviously, a lot depends on how the police exercise their discretion.

Literature may be sold at public meetings in Trafalgar Square, but only with written permission from the Department of the Environment. You must apply in advance. Permission applies to the period of the meeting but is not limited to one specific day.

It is unlawful to distribute leaflets on which the wording is 'threatening, abusive or insulting' with the intention of creating a breach of the peace or in circumstances where it is likely to create a breach (Public Order Act 1936). This section was given an unusual twist by the court's decision in the following case:

In 1968, Gwyneth Williams was prosecuted for distributing leaflets to American servicemen. The leaflet criticized the US Government for its involvement in Vietnam in restrained and unprovocative language. Yet the court held that it was 'insulting' because it invited its readers to consider deserting if they agreed with its arguments: it was 'insulting' to ask a soldier even to consider such a thing.

The main difficulty you are likely to meet when selling or distributing literature is that you may be accused of causing an obstruction. Try to keep to the kerb and be careful not to get in the way of cars or pedestrians. If a policeman thinks that you are causing a real obstruction, he should only ask you to move on. He has no right to confiscate your literature. If he asks you to move on, do so immediately, at a reasonable walking pace, keeping to the kerb to avoid obstruction. As long as you do this, the policeman has no right to follow you and tell you to go away. There is nothing to stop you selling or distributing your literature as you go.

After you have left the congested area you may, if it seems reasonable, stop again. The policeman may then, at his discretion, tell you to move on and it is advisable to do as he says. But if he seems to be following you around and ordering you to move on even in uncongested areas, take his number. You may wish to make a formal complaint later.

You may also find that the police interfere on the grounds that, owing to the content of the literature, your behaviour is likely to cause a breach of the peace. This charge may be justifiable, depending on the circumstances. If, for example, someone persists in distributing anti-immigrant leaflets in a predominantly immigrant area, he may justly be charged with this offence.

Collecting signatures in the street

There are no laws or regulations which forbid you to collect signatures in any street or public place, although you may be accused of causing an obstruction (see p. 152).

PETITIONS TO PARLIAMENT

If you want to organize a petition, to be presented to Parliament by an MP, you will have to use the following special wording:

To the Honourable the Commons of the United Kingdom of Great Britain and Northern Ireland in Parliament assembled: this humble petition of [a general description of the petitioners] sheweth that [statement of the complaint], wherefore your petitioners pray that [statement of what you want done], and your petitioners as in duty bound will ever pray, etc. . . .

A copy of the rules covering petitions to Parliament can be obtained from the **House of Commons, London SW1 (01-219 3000)**.

Raising money

Fund-raising

STREET COLLECTIONS

You may take a collection in the street with a police permit, but these are extremely hard to get, unless you are collecting for a big charity.

Find out from the local authority the regulations controlling collections. In the Metropolitan Police District (most of Greater London, excluding the City of London), no collections may be made without the consent of the Commissioner of Police. As a general rule, not more than one collection is allowed per week in one locality and the aim is to keep the number of street collections as low as possible. There is no system of appeal against the Commissioner's decision. The following conditions are also imposed:

1. Collectors should not be under 16.
2. They must remain in one place, at least thirty yards from one another.
3. They must carry written authorization, which must be shown to a policeman on demand.
4. No tables may be used if they are bigger than thirty inches by twenty inches.
5. Collectors must not be accompanied by animals.
6. Tins must be labelled.
7. Accounts of the collection must be submitted within one month.

You may make a collection at an open-air meeting without a police permit, provided that you operate within a reasonable distance of the meeting. A 'reasonable distance' has not been defined, but as long as you are walking around near the meeting, you have the right to collect from passers-by and from the audience. If the meeting is being held in a park or similar open space, collections may be prohibited by the bye-laws of the park.

HOUSE TO HOUSE COLLECTIONS

It is illegal to travel from house to house appealing to the public to give money or property to a charity, without a licence from the local police (House to House Collections Act 1939).

The Act applies even if the collector gives something in exchange for what he gets. It has also been known to apply in the case of a genuine sale of articles, when the salesman has made it known that part of the purchase price is to go to a charity. It does not apply to collections made by one member of an organization among other members of the same body.

Collectors must not be under 16, they must carry a collection box or receipt book, and wear a badge, and they must not recieve payment for their work.

A policeman may ask anyone whom he believes to be collecting for a charitable purpose to give his name, address, and signature.

The Act only applies to charitable collections, i.e. all benevolent and philanthropic concerns, such as relief of poverty and the advancement of religion and education at home and abroad; it would probably include fund-raising for a local club or for the relief of strikers. But an appeal for funds for a political party would not be subject to these regulations.

Borderline cases, of course, are determined by the views of the magistrate, but unlicensed door to door collectors have not normally been prosecuted unless they were not collecting for a 'charity' in the conventional sense of the word.

You can apply for a licence to the local chief officer of police. The procedure and conditions are rather complicated, but you can get information about this from your local police station. If the collection is confined to only one locality and is not likely to continue for long, you can sometimes get a certificate of exemption by a much simpler procedure; but it is left to the discretion of the chief of police as to whether or not to grant one.

If a charitable collection is made without a licence, both the organizer and the collector can be prosecuted and fined. The organizer is liable to a maximum fine of £100 and/or six months' imprisonment, but the collector can only be fined £5 for a first offence.

The House to House Collections Act 1939 also applies to the door to door sale of literature.

Gaming

The gaming laws are very complicated. This chapter deals only with non-commercial gaming for the purpose of charitable or political fund-raising, which is bound by a separate set of regulations.

'Gaming' is defined as games of pure chance (dice, roulette, bingo, etc.) and games of chance combined with skill (card games, chess, etc.).

GAMING ON UNLICENSED PREMISES

In private homes or semi-private institutions, any gaming may be carried on, provided that no one is charged a fee for taking part.

Elsewhere, games which involve playing or staking against a 'bank' and games in which chances are not equal are not allowed. Therefore in unlicensed clubs, for example, only games such as whist, cribbage, poker, and bingo may be played. There may be an inclusive charge of up to 50p. No levies may be made on the stake or on the winnings.

Games and amusements with prizes require a special permit. This may be obtained from the local licensing authority. Any kind of game may be played, provided that the following conditions are obeyed: the maximum charge for one attempt is 5p; no more than £2·50 may be taken in one game; £2·50 is the maximum amount of prize winnings at one time; the proceeds must not be devoted to private gain; the games or amusements must not be the sole or major attraction at the entertainment where they are carried on.

If slot machines are installed at non-commercial entertainments, the person who sells or supplies them must have a permit. There is no limit to the number of machines or prizes at one event. The proceeds must not be for private gain.

For any other gaming at entertainments held for a good cause, an all-in charge of 50p is allowed. The total value of prizes distributed at one event must not be more than £50. The proceeds must go towards the 'good cause'.

Other general regulations: no one under 18 may take part; the prohibition of public advertising of gaming does not apply to non-commercial entertainments or those held for a good cause (Gaming Act 1968 and Gaming (Amendment) Act 1973).

GAMING ON LICENSED PREMISES

If gaming is carried on in licensed premises, most of the above regulations (with the important exception of the final paragraph) do not apply. A person applying for a licence must first obtain a certificate from the Gaming Board and then apply to the local licensing authority.

Inspectors appointed under the Gaming Act 1968 have the power to enter licensed premises without a warrant to inspect equipment and books.

Lotteries

As a result of the Lotteries Act 1975, it is now lawful for non-commercial organizations and local authorities to organize lotteries, provided they comply with certain regulations.

A charity, an organization concerned with athletic sports, games or cultural activities (e.g. a club) or some other organization which is neither commercial nor organized for purposes of private gain, must apply to the local authority to be registered in order to run a lottery. The fee for registration is £10, with a further £5 payable on 1 January each year. If the local authority refuses registration (on the grounds either that someone connected with the proposed lottery has been convicted of an offence relating to lotteries, or an offence of dishonesty or fraud, or that the society does not meet the conditions required), the society may appeal to the Crown Court.

The following conditions must be met by any society organizing a lottery:

- the organizers must make a return to the local authority as to how much money was raised; the amount spent on expenses and prizes; the purposes for which the profit was used; and the date of the lottery;
- the person organizing the lottery must be a member of the society, authorized in writing by the committee;
- proceeds must be devoted to the purposes of the society;
- no more than fifty-two lotteries can be run in one year (although two or more lotteries run on a single day may count as one); seven days must elapse between lotteries, unless the lottery is linked to a particular sporting or athletic event;
- every ticket must cost the same and must be printed with the price, the name and address of the organizers and the date of the lottery;
- no ticket may cost more than 25p;
- the maximum value of the tickets to be sold must be £5,000 or less (if it is to be higher, the lottery must be registered with the Gaming Board before tickets are sold);
- the amount devoted to expenses must be no more than 25 per cent of the proceeds (15 per cent if the lottery's value is over £5,000, unless the Gaming Board authorizes a higher percentage for expenses);
- no more than half the proceeds of the lottery can be used for prizes; no prize shall be more than £1,000 if the total value of the lottery is £5,000 or less (higher sums are allowed if the lottery is registered with the Gaming Board, depending on the frequency of the lottery);
- no tickets may be sold in licensed betting offices, amusement and prize bingo arcades, licensed bingo or gaming clubs or in the street (except from a kiosk), or from a vending machine;

– no ticket may be sold to anyone under the age of 16;
– lotteries may be advertised on radio or television.

It is an offence to disobey any of the regulations governing society lotteries; the maximum penalty is a fine of £400 in the magistrates' court or two years' imprisonment and/or an unlimited fine in the Crown Court (Lotteries Act 1975 and Regulations 1977).

Similar conditions apply to local authority lotteries.

LOTTERIES WHICH ARE PART OF AN ENTERTAINMENT

Lotteries may be held at bazaars, fetes, dances and sports events, etc., provided that:

– the lottery must not be the major attraction of the event;
– proceeds, after deduction of expenses, may not be devoted to private gain;
– expenses are limited; no more than £50 may be spent on prizes;
– money prizes are not allowed;
– both the sale of tickets and the announcement of the winners must take place during the entertainment.

PRIVATE LOTTERIES

Private lotteries are those organized exclusively for people who work or live in the same premises or belong to the same society (other than a gambling society). Only the cost of stationery and of printing tickets may be deducted as expenses. The rest of the proceeds must be spent on prizes or on the purposes of the society. Each ticket must cost the same and be printed with the price of the ticket and name and address of the organizers; tickets must be sold at their face value; and the lottery must not be advertised.

Public order and related offences

Many of the offences listed here are commonly charged following incidents arising from meetings and processions. A summary of these offences is set out in Appendix B, pp. 592–600.

Affray

It is an affray if there is fighting or a display of force without actual violence. It need not be in a public place but must occur in such a manner that reasonable people might be frightened or intimidated.

Aiding and abetting

It is an offence to help bring about any offence by helping the person who is committing it or by 'counselling or procuring' its commission.

Assault

There are four kinds of assault charges.

1. In law, a **common assault** is any act which intentionally or recklessly causes another person to expect or fear immediate violence. It is the *intended* use of unlawful force to another person without that person's consent. An assault can be committed without touching a person, for example, by aiming a

blow or throwing something at somebody which misses. You can defend yourself against a charge of assault if you acted in self-defence in that you honestly and reasonably thought it was necessary to threaten force in order to defend yourself, or someone else, or, in some circumstances, property.

The maximum penalty is two months' imprisonment or a £200 fine in a magistrates' court.

2. **Assault occasioning actual bodily harm** means that there is some bodily injury, like a graze or a black eye. The maximum penalty is six months' imprisonment and/or a £1,000 fine in a magistrates' court, or five years' imprisonment and/or an unlimited fine in the Crown Court.

3. There are other more serious assault offences which include **wounding** or **causing or inflicting grievous bodily harm** to any person with or without intent to do some grievous bodily harm. Grievous means serious.

4. It is an offence **to assault a police officer** (or anyone assisting a policeman) in the execution of his duty. This charge would not stick if the officer was exceeding his authority, but a policeman's duty has been widely interpreted by the courts and includes all actions which appear to him to be necessary for keeping the peace, preventing crime, or protecting property from criminal injury. It is no defence to claim that you did not know that the person you assaulted was a policeman or that you did not know he was acting in the execution of his duty.

The maximum penalty for assaulting a police officer in the execution of his duty is six months' imprisonment and/or a fine of £1,000. The maximum penalty is the same for a first and any subsequent offence. Magistrates often impose a prison sentence for a first offence.

Binding over

If you are arrested for conduct likely to cause a breach of the peace (see p. 149) or any of the other public order offences mentioned in this section, you may be 'bound over'. This means that the court will ask you to enter into a **recognizance**, with or without sureties, to keep the peace or to be of good behaviour for a specified period of time. A recognizance is an amount of money you promise to pay to the court if you do not fulfil the request made by the court. Sureties are amounts of money which other people promise to pay the court if you do not fulfil the request made by the court. So if you fail to keep the peace for the specified period of time, you and the people who have promised sureties will have to pay the money. If you fail to pay the money, you can be imprisoned for up to six months by a magistrates' court or twelve months by a Crown Court.

The purpose of binding over is to prevent offences being committed. It should not be used as a punishment. You should be allowed to address the court before an order is made. In some cases defendants are acquitted of offences and then bound over to keep the peace. If you believe that a magistrate has bound you over unreasonably, you can appeal to the Crown Court, or the Divisional Court on a point of law (see p. 79).

The courts have the power to bind over anyone giving evidence or involved in the case, but must first of all hear what they have to say.

You can also be summonsed 'to show cause' why you should not be bound over to keep the peace. The police sometimes use this procedure instead of charging people with a criminal offence.

Breach of the peace

If you act in a way likely to cause a breach of the peace you can:

- be brought before a magistrates' court to show cause why you should not be bound over to keep the peace (see above) even though you are not charged with a criminal offence; *or*
- be charged with the criminal offence of using threatening, abusive or insulting words or behaviour.

You should not be arrested just because your behaviour might lead to disorderly conduct, abusive language, or excessive noise. *You should only be arrested on this charge if it is suspected that your behaviour might lead to a genuine use or threat of force:* that is, the possibility of a breach of the peace occurring must be real.

In practice, however, the police may regard a disturbance amongst a large group of people as sufficient grounds for believing that a breach of the peace will occur.

You will commit this offence if you distribute or display any writing, sign or visible representation which is threatening, abusive or insulting, with intent to provoke a breach of the peace or which might cause a breach of the peace to occur. Threats may be made by words or gestures and may be inferred from the way you behave. If a speaker addresses an audience in a way which may provoke a breach of the peace, he or she may be guilty of the offence. Words which are rude or offensive are not necessarily insulting.

The maximum penalty for this offence is six months' imprisonment and/or £1,000 fine in a magistrates' court.

Conspiracy

You are guilty of conspiracy as defined by the Criminal Law Act 1977 if you agree with someone else to follow a course of conduct which will necessarily amount to or involve the commission of a criminal offence if the agreement is carried out in accordance with your intentions. For example, if you agree with someone else to go into a bank with a gun and ask the cashier for money which does not belong to you. If this is carried out it will involve the offence of robbery, if it is not carried out for any reason (e.g. you have planned the robbery for a Bank Holiday) then you are not guilty of robbery but you are guilty of *conspiracy to rob*. There is also an offence of conspiracy to defraud which is not defined by the 1977 Act.

Until the 1977 Act was passed (see p. 17) you could also be prosecuted for conspiracy if you agreed to commit a civil wrong (e.g. trespass) even though that civil wrong did not itself constitute a criminal offence. It is now only possible to prosecute you for conspiracy to commit a criminal offence *except* that you can still be prosecuted for conspiracy to corrupt public morals or conspiracy to outrage public decency. These charges are used as a means of censorship (see p. 314).

The offence of conspiracy occurs when the agreement is made.

The agreement can be orally, in writing, or even by some action ('a nod or a wink,' said the judge in one case). You do not actually have to do anything to carry out the agreement in order to be guilty of conspiracy.

The offence is often used as a 'blanket charge' in political trials: a means of catching and charging a number of people without having any evidence of any other crime being committed. The laws of evidence are relaxed in a conspiracy trial, so the court can hear all sorts of potentially prejudicial evidence about your life-style and beliefs that would not be allowed in a normal criminal trial.

You will not be guilty of the offence of conspiracy if the agreement was with your husband or wife, with a child under the age of criminal responsibility (10 at the time of writing) or with an intended victim of the offence; nor will you be guilty if you are yourself the intended victim.

Conspiracy charges are always heard in the Crown Court (see p. 79) even if the offence you were conspiring to commit could only be heard in the magistrates' court (e.g. obstructing the highway) although in such cases you cannot be prosecuted without the consent of the Director of Public Prosecutions.

The penalty for conspiracy is linked to the penalty for the offence you have conspired to commit. If the latter carries a prison sentence, then conspiracy will carry the same maximum sentence. If the offence itself carries a fine of any amount the maximum penalty for conspiracy will be an unlimited fine.

Criminal damage

It is an offence to destroy or damage another's property intentionally or recklessly and without lawful authority.

The maximum penalty is ten years' imprisonment and/or an unlimited fine.

Incitement

To incite another person to commit a crime is itself an offence whether or not the crime is committed or the other person is influenced by the incitement.

There are a number of specific Acts of Parliament which concern incitement. The Incitement to Disaffection Act 1934 and the Incitement to Mutiny Act 1797 are dealt with on pp. 400–401. Section 53 of the Police Act 1964 prohibits causing or attempting to cause disaffection amongst members of any police force. For incitement to racial hatred see p. 241.

Obstruction of the highway

There is a right to pass along and stop on the public highway if your behaviour is reasonable. For instance, it is not illegal to walk along with a small group of people, to window-shop, or to stop and talk to a friend. The charge of obstructing the highway may be used if your behaviour is regarded as **unreasonable**, which means that it is likely to prevent other members of the public from freely crossing or passing along the street.

This can arise if you take part in a march, procession or public meeting, or distribute or sell literature in a public place. On the whole, a moving procession is less likely to amount to an unreasonable use of the highway than a stationary meeting. If you use a site which has been used frequently for public meetings and has become a traditional meeting place you can *normally* assume that there is no danger of causing an obstruction in that place.

If you are taking part in an activity in a public place and the police order you to disperse, you should point out that you are exercising your right to use the highway. If the police persist you must decide if you are making reasonable use of the highway and are prepared to risk arrest. In determining what is reasonable many factors may be taken into account by the police and the court, like the time of day, the amount of traffic, the width of the road, and the number of people present.

The prosecution must prove that the obstruction was wilful, that is that your actions were intentional or reckless. If the prosecution can prove actual obstruction, they will have little difficulty in proving that it was wilful. But they do not have to prove that an actual obstruction took place, and it is no defence to claim that there was a way round the obstruction you caused.

It is up to the magistrates to decide what is unreasonable and it is often worth pleading not guilty and arguing the matter out in court, but few prosecutions are defended successfully. The maximum penalty that can be imposed by the magistrates is £50 under the Highways Act 1959, or £20 or fourteen days' imprisonment under the Town Police Clauses Act 1847.

Obstructing the police

It is an offence to resist or wilfully obstruct a police officer (or anyone assisting him) in the execution of his duty. Obstruction includes any deliberate act which makes it more difficult for the police to carry out their duty (e.g. refusing to obey police instructions, physically blocking their way, or warning a friend who is committing an offence that the police are approaching).

Refusing to give information or to assist will not usually amount to obstruction. Generally there is no legal duty to answer questions (see pp. 43–5) but giving false information may be an offence.

The maximum penalty is one month's imprisonment and/or a £200 fine in a magistrates' court.

Offensive weapons

It is an offence to have with you in any public place or at a public meeting, without lawful authority or reasonable excuse, any offensive weapon for use in causing injury, *or* which you intend to use for causing injury. An offensive weapon means any article:

- which is made as an offensive weapon (e.g. a knuckle duster or cosh);
- which has been adapted to become an offensive weapon (e.g. a bottle which has been purposely broken); *or*
- which you intend to use as an offensive weapon (e.g. a kitchen knife or spanner).

A police officer has 'lawful authority' to carry a truncheon, but a security guard (e.g. a steward at a dance hall) does not have such authority.

It may be a 'reasonable excuse' to claim that you carried the offensive weapon for self-protection if you can show that there was an immediate fear of attack and the weapon was for self-defence.

The maximum penalty is three months' imprisonment and/or a £200 fine in a magistrates' court, or two years' imprisonment and/or a fine in the Crown Court.

Public nuisance

It is an offence to do an act or fail to carry out a legal duty if the effect of the act or the failure is to endanger 'the life, health, property, morals, or comfort of the public, or to obstruct the public in the exercise or enjoyment of its rights'.

This offence and the offence of incitement to commit a public nuisance have been used frequently to curb processions, meetings and sit-ins. The nuisance, whether it takes the form of obstruction of free passage along the highway, noise, smell, or any other form of inconvenience (e.g. a hoax bomb call) must potentially affect a sufficient number of people for them to be called 'the public', not just a collection of particular individuals.

The maximum penalty is an unlimited fine and/or imprisonment.

Quasi-military organizations

It is an offence to participate in a body trained to usurp the functions of the police or army, or to participate in a group using or
showing force in promoting a political object.

No prosecutions can be brought without the consent of the
Attorney General. There has only been one conviction since
1936.

The maximum penalty is six months' imprisonment and/or a
£100 fine in a magistrates' court, or two years' imprisonment
and/or a £500 fine in the Crown Court.

Riot

A riot occurs in law where:

– there are at least three people present; *and*
– they have a common purpose; *and*
– they carry out that common purpose; *and*
– they are prepared to help one another, by force if necessary,
  against anyone who opposes them; *and*
– force or violence so as to 'alarm at least one person of reasonable
  firmness' occurs.

This means that if the common purpose of an unlawful
assembly is carried out with force it becomes a riot. A case in
1970 underlined that it is possible for a person who takes part
in a demonstration, not knowing in advance whether or not the
crowd will act 'for some common purpose' or whether the disturbance will be 'tumultuous', to be prosecuted for riot.

The maximum penalty is life imprisonment and/or an
unlimited fine.

Rout

There have been no prosecutions for rout in recent times. It falls
somewhere between unlawful assembly (see p. 157) and riot (see
above). The offence can only be committed if an actual move is
made towards the execution of a common purpose but it is less

serious than a riot in that the common purpose is not actually carried out.

The maximum penalty is life imprisonment and/or an unlimited fine.

Sedition

A wide range of actions might be interpreted as seditious. Generally the charge can only be used if there is some incitement to public disorder. One definition of sedition states:

It embraces all those practices, whether by word, deed or writing, which fall short of high treason but tend to have for their object to excite discontent or dissatisfaction; to excite ill-will between different classes of Sovereign subjects; to create public disturbance or to lead to civil war; to bring into hatred or contempt the Sovereign or the Government, the laws or constitution of the realm, and generally all endeavours to promote public disorder.

A plot to overthrow the government by force would amount to a seditious conspiracy.

Sedition and seditious conspiracy are very serious offences and the maximum penalties are life imprisonment and/or an unlimited fine. There have only been a few prosecutions in the last sixty years and most of them were unsuccessful.

Uniforms

Apart from the provisions of the Prevention of Terrorism (Temporary Provisions) Act 1976 (see pp. 534–5), it is also an offence under the Public Order Act 1936 to wear in public uniforms signifying association with any political organization or with the promotion of any political object. This offence has been used recently to convict people wearing black berets at a Provisional Sinn Fein anti-internment rally.

The maximum penalty is three months' imprisonment and/or a £500 fine in a magistrates' court.

(i) O.K.

(ii) Not O.K.

Unlawful assembly

It is an offence if three or more persons assemble intending to commit a crime by open force *or* intending to carry out any common purpose lawful or unlawful in such a manner as to endanger public peace or to make 'firm and courageous' people fear a breach of the peace.

This offence has been used in recent years to prosecute demonstrators, pickets and football fans.

The maximum penalty for unlawful assembly is life imprisonment and/or an unlimited fine.

5. Motorists

Legal requirements

The driver

You must hold the appropriate valid driving licence before you can drive a motor car, three-wheeled vehicle, motor cycle or other vehicle. To qualify for a licence you must pass a test and be able to read a number plate at twenty-five yards (with spectacles, if necessary). Epileptics can get a licence under certain conditions.

The vehicle

You must not use, nor allow another person to use a motor vehicle on the road unless it is covered for third-party insurance, including injury to passengers. Your policy must be with an authorized insurer who is a member of the Motor Insurers' Bureau. The maximum penalty for not having insurance is a fine of £200 with an obligatory endorsement and possible disqualification.

If your vehicle is more than three years old it is subject to an annual Ministry of Transport (M o T) test. If a vehicle fails a test, the owner can appeal to the Department of the Environment.

There are also a number of legal requirements concerning the roadworthiness of vehicles, details of which can be found in the Highway Code.

Accidents

If you are involved in an accident which causes injury to another person, damage to another vehicle or its trailer, damage to roadside property or injury to certain animals you must immediately stop. Failure to stop is an offence carrying a maximum fine of £100 and endorsement and you can also be disqualified from driving.

You must give your name and address and the registration number of your car to anyone with a legitimate interest such as the injured person or the owner of the damaged car or property. If you do not give your name and address when requested you must report to the police within twenty-four hours or you will have committed an offence. If you do not own the vehicle you were driving you must also give the name and address of the owner. If someone was injured and you did not have your insurance certificate with you at the time, you must produce it at the police station specified when the accident was reported to the police, within five days.

Compensation

The Motor Insurers' Bureau, Aldermary House, Queen Street, London EC4 (01-248 4477) can compensate you for death or personal injury caused by an uninsured or 'hit and run' driver provided you follow their strict timetable and procedure. They do not allow claims for damage to vehicles. If compensation is not provided automatically by an insurance policy you can take civil action in a county court or the High Court (see p. 243).

Driving offences

In most cases of dangerous driving, speeding, and disobeying certain traffic signs you will be informed within fourteen days whether you are to be prosecuted – either verbally at the time of the incident, by a summons or by a notice of intended prosecution. A summary prosecution cannot be brought more than six months after the facts come to the knowledge of the prosecutor or more than three years after the event.

In practice legal aid is rarely granted for minor traffic offences but it may be available in criminal cases if it is desirable in the 'interests of justice'. The RAC and AA provide free legal advice to their members and sometimes free legal representation. Some motor-insurance policies also provide for legal representation. Advice can also be obtained under the green-form scheme (see p. 494).

Causing death by reckless or dangerous driving

Manslaughter charges are rare and the most serious offence usually charged is causing death by reckless or dangerous driving. Conviction carries a maximum penalty of five years' imprisonment as well as disqualification and endorsement.

Dangerous driving

A charge of dangerous driving will only be brought if there is some fault on your part. Maximum penalty is four months' imprisonment or a fine of £1,000 if tried at a magistrates' court, or two years and/or an unlimited fine if tried at the Crown Court, as well as obligatory endorsement. Disqualification is obligatory if the offence is committed within three years of a previous conviction for this offence or for causing death by dangerous or reckless driving or for careless driving. In other cases the court can use its discretion regarding disqualification.

Careless driving

This is tried in a magistrates' court and carries a maximum penalty of £500, obligatory endorsement and discretion to disqualify.

The difference between dangerous driving and careless driving is not defined in law and you should always seek legal advice before you decide how to plead.

Drink and drugs

It is an offence to drive or to try to drive with more than 80 milligrams of alcohol in 100 millilitres of urine (i.e. 'excess alcohol').

A uniformed police officer can administer a breathalyser test if there is reasonable cause to suspect you have alcohol in your blood, or you have committed a traffic offence, or after an accident. If you refuse to take the test you may be fined up to £50. If the breathalyser test is positive you will be taken to a police station for blood or urine tests. You can refuse a blood test but if you refuse a urine test you will be treated as having excess alcohol in your blood. You can ask for an extra sample of your blood or urine for you to have independently analysed.

The Crown Court can impose a maximum penalty of two years' imprisonment and/or an unlimited fine. A magistrates' court can impose a £400 fine or four months' imprisonment. You will almost certainly be disqualified from driving for at least one year. (But see p. 19.)

It is also an offence to be 'in charge' of a motor vehicle with excess alcohol in your blood, for instance if you were supervising a learner driver.

Even if the tests are not positive you can still be found guilty of a separate offence of being under the influence of drink (or drugs) if the police can prove that your ability to drive was impaired due to the effects of drink or drugs. The maximum penalty is a fine of £400 or four months' imprisonment in the magistrates' court and an unlimited fine or two years' imprisonment in the Crown Court. (But see p. 19.)

Following the Blennerhassett Committee report on drinking and driving, the law may be changed to give the police the power to stop and breathalyse any driver, whether or not they reasonably suspect the driver of being under the influence.

Speeding

It is an offence to exceed a speed limit even when no harm results. The opinion of a single police officer (except in Scotland) is sufficient evidence if supported by a mechanical device such as a radar unit. The maximum penalty is a fine of £100.

Traffic signs

It is an offence to disobey a traffic sign, road sign, or a policeman on point duty except in emergencies, or to fail to give a pedestrian right of way on a crossing or to fail to stop when ordered to do so by a uniformed police officer.

Parking

Traffic wardens are employed under the direction of the police and their powers are mainly confined to dealing with parking offences. No parking signs erected by private individuals have no effect in law. The penalty for dangerous parking can be a maximum fine of £100 and disqualification. If you park your car so as to cause an obstruction, the police can move the car and you will have to pay to get it back. For details of other parking restrictions see the Highway Code.

Other offences

It is also illegal to take part in a race on a public road; to carry passengers in a dangerous manner; to sound a horn when a vehicle is stationary between 11.30 p.m. and 7.00 a.m. in a built-up area.

Endorsements

Your licence will usually be endorsed if you are found guilty of any motoring offence (except minor parking offences). The most serious offences will result in disqualification. As a general rule you will be disqualified if your licence is endorsed three times within three years. If you receive more than one endorsement for offences arising out of the same incident (e.g. two endorsements for two faulty tyres found at the same time, or two endorsements for driving without due care and attention and failing to comply with a traffic signal when you have driven through a red light) they will be counted as one endorsement for disqualification purposes.

Endorsements for major offences (e.g. driving or attempting to drive while unfit through drink or drugs or with excess alcohol in the blood; failing to provide a specimen for a lab test, in most cases) remain for ten years. Endorsements for other offences remain on your licence for three years before they lose effect. Records of old endorsements remain on court and criminal records but you may be protected under the Rehabilitation of Offenders Act 1974 (see pp. 104–8).

Powers of the police

The police have a number of powers specially relating to the motorist:

– the police can arrest you without a warrant if they have reasonable grounds to suspect you have caused death by dangerous driving or have committed manslaughter by driving;

– a police constable in uniform can stop you whilst you are driving a motor vehicle or riding a bicycle. Failure to stop when required to do so is an offence carrying a maximum fine of £100;

– a police officer can request the name and address of anyone driving a motor vehicle on the road even when there is no suspected offence. For more information, see p. 23. If required you must also produce your licence, certificate of insurance, M o T certificate and in certain circumstances give your date of birth. The police can inspect your licence but are not allowed to check it to see if you have any endorsements. If you do not have the documents with you, you must produce them at a police station within five days. Failure to provide the required information is an offence carrying a £50 fine for each refusal;

– if you are suspected of dangerous, careless, inconsiderate or reckless driving and refuse to give your name and address or give a false name and address you are guilty of an offence carrying a maximum fine of £100;

– if you commit an offence of dangerous, careless, inconsiderate or reckless driving within the view of the police, you can be arrested without warrant;

– you can be arrested without warrant by a policeman in uniform if you are in charge of a motor vehicle or attempt to drive on a road while under the influence of drink or drugs;

- you can be arrested without warrant by a policeman in uniform if the police suspect you of driving whilst disqualified;
- the police can stop and search any vehicle they reasonably suspect contains dangerous drugs or is involved in any crime;
- a uniformed police officer can stop any motor vehicle to test its condition. The driver can postpone the test if it is inconvenient to have it done on the spot but it is an offence to obstruct such an examiner from carrying out a test.

6. Drugs

LSD, tea, sleeping pills, pot, tobacco, alcohol and tranquillizers are all drugs. People take them for comfort, stimulation or pleasure. Some of them are easily obtainable, some are illegal. Some are dangerous, some are harmless. There is no connection between the ease with which you can obtain and take drugs and the harm they may produce. Alcohol and tobacco are addictive and can be killers but their purchase and use is socially acceptable and largely uncontrolled. Millions of barbiturates are bought in chemists or prescribed by doctors to thousands of patients. More people are dependent on them than any other drug and in 1974, 1,700 people killed themselves by taking an overdose. On the other hand, cannabis, which is not addictive and does not kill people, is illegal, and those found using it or selling it are committing a crime for which the penalty is often imprisonment. No government has been prepared to take note of the recommendations of the Wootton report of 1969 that laws against cannabis are irrational and counter-productive.

This chapter is about the Misuse of Drugs Act 1971. Briefly, the provisions of the Act are that you can be fined or imprisoned if it can be proved that you have been in possession of, produced, supplied to another, offered to supply to another, been knowingly concerned in supplying to another, exported or imported a **controlled drug** (see below) without authorization. It is also an offence if you have incited anyone, or attempted to incite anyone to commit any of these offences, or if you have been an occupier or concerned in the management of premises and allowed them to be used for producing controlled drugs, supplying them, or smoking cannabis or opium, or for cultivating cannabis plants.

Types of drugs

The Misuse of Drugs Act classifies **controlled drugs** into three groups, according to the dangers they are supposed to hold. The principal drugs in each class are as follows:

- CLASS A includes heroin, morphine, cocaine, opium, methadone (and other narcotics), STP, LSD (and other hallucinogens), cannabinol and derivatives, and injectable amphetamines.
- CLASS B includes amphetamines, Drinamyl (purple hearts), cannabis resin and the fruiting and flowering tops of the cannabis plant (marijuana or grass), Benzedrine and Dexedrine.
- CLASS C includes various amphetamine-type substances and methaqualone (Mandrax).

Drug offences

Possession

Under section 5 of the Act it is an offence to be in possession of a controlled drug except where the drug is legally obtained on prescription. You can be prosecuted for having traces of cannabis – even the minutest amount whose presence would not be revealed except by chemical analysis. Under section 28 you can defend yourself on the grounds that you did not know or suspect, nor had reason to suspect that you were in possession. It is up to you to prove that you did not know rather than for the

prosecution to show that you did. You can also be prosecuted for 'internal possession' where controlled drugs are discovered by a urine or blood test. Opiates and amphetamines are easily detectable in this way.

It is not clear whether possession of cannabis *leaves* is illegal. If you are prosecuted for this, get legal advice from Release (see p. 170). Registered addicts can legally obtain methadone, heroin and other drugs in Class A on prescription from a doctor or at treatment centres and clinics licensed by the Home Office.

Production and supply

Producing or supplying drugs are much more serious offences under section 4 of the Act. This includes production of a controlled drug, supply of a controlled drug, offering a controlled drug to another and being knowingly concerned in any of the above. Also, under section 5 of the Act the additional offence of possession with intent to supply is created and this charge is often brought where substantial quantities of a drug are involved. Under section 28 you can claim 'lack of knowledge' in these cases (see above p. 166).

Importation and exportation

It is a serious offence to be involved in bringing controlled drugs into the country or being involved in their export. The Customs and Excise Act 1952 also covers these offences and customs officers have extensive powers of search (see p. 307).

Other offences

It is an offence:

1. To cultivate cannabis plants. This includes any attempt at growing, even if you are not successful.
2. Knowingly to allow premises to be used for the smoking of cannabis or opium, the preparation of opium, or the production and supply of controlled drugs.

3. To assist or induce the commission of an offence outside the UK punishable by 'a corresponding' law in that place.
4. Knowingly to give false information when purporting to comply with a demand for information.

In any of these cases the prosecution must prove that the defendant knew what was going on.

Police powers and arrest procedures

Police may stop and search on the street anyone whom they have 'reasonable grounds' to suspect of being in possession of a controlled drug. Similarly vehicles and vessels may be stopped and searched. Apart from a Home Office circular directing police that 'in themselves, modes of dress and length of hair do not constitute reasonable grounds' for a search, no guidelines have been issued as to the interpretation of what 'reasonable grounds' actually are. (See p. 24 for details of police powers of search and arrest.)

The police may arrest without a warrant anyone who has committed, or whom they reasonably suspect has committed, an offence under the Act if:

– they believe, with reasonable cause, that the person will abscond unless arrested; *or*
– the person's name and address are unknown to them and cannot be ascertained; *or*
– they are not satisfied that the name and address given is genuine.

Private premises may only be searched for drugs with a warrant obtained from a magistrates' court (but see pp. 27–31).

If you are suspected of possessing a controlled drug, the police will normally release you on bail for up to three weeks pending analysis of the drug under section 38 (2) of the Magistrates' Court Act. You will have to report back to the police station at a specified date. If the analysis is positive you will be formally charged. (See pp. 43–55 for details of your rights at the police station.)

If the forensic analysis shows that the drug is 'non-controlled' it is still possible to be prosecuted if you are charged with supplying, if it can be proved that you believed that what you supplied was a controlled drug.

Penalties

You may be tried summarily at a magistrates' court, or on indictment at the Crown Court before a judge and jury (see p. 86 for what this means).

The maximum penalties for *possession* are:

Class A   summary – six months and/or £1,000 fine
           indictment – seven years and/or unlimited fine
Class B   summary – three months and/or £500 fine
           indictment – five years and/or unlimited fine
Class C   summary – three months and/or £200 fine
           indictment – two years and/or unlimited fine.

The maximum penalties for *possession with intent to supply* are:

Classes   summary – six months and/or £1,000 fine
A & B   indictment – fourteen years and/or unlimited fine
Class C   summary – three months and/or £500 fine
           indictment – five years and/or unlimited fine.

The maximum penalties for *supply or production* are:

Classes   summary – six months and/or £1,000 fine
A & B   indictment – fourteen years and/or unlimited fine
Class C   summary – three months and/or £500 fine
           indictment – five years and/or unlimited fine.

The maximum penalties for *allowing premises to be used* are:

Classes   summary – six months and/or £1,000 fine
A & B   indictment – fourteen years and/or unlimited fine
Class C   summary – three months and/or £500 fine
           indictment – five years and/or unlimited fine.

The maximum penalties for *cultivation* are:

Classes summary – six months and/or £1,000 fine
A & B indictment – fourteen years and/or unlimited fine.

The maximum penalties for *importation or exportation* are:

Classes summary – six months and/or the greater of £1,000
A & B or three times the value of the goods
  indictment – fourteen years and/or unlimited fine
Class C summary – three months and/or the greater of £500
  or three times the value of the goods
  indictment – five years and/or unlimited fine.

Sentencing policy

There is great variation in sentencing policy towards drug offenders at magistrates' courts. The least serious offence – possession of cannabis – would usually be met with a small fine, though in some provincial areas the fine may be five times what it is in London. It would be most unusual for a first offender to be sent to prison for possession of cannabis, though this has happened. Importation and supplying of drugs are treated as serious offences and, even in cases involving relatively small quantities of drugs, the offenders have been sent to prison.

More information

For further information see:
Alternative London, Wildwood House.
S. Bradshaw, *Drug Misuse and the Law*, Macmillan.
J. S. Hotchen, *Drug Misuse and the Law: The Regulations*, Macmillan.

For advice and information contact:
Institute for the Study of Drug Dependence, Kingsbury House, 3 Blackburn Road, London NW6 (01-328 5541).

Release, 1 Elgin Avenue, London W9 (01-289 1123; 01-603 8654 – 24-hour emergency).

7. Sex

This chapter covers:

(For sex discrimination see under 'Discrimination' in the index.)

Age of consent

Age restrictions for females

As far as the law is concerned, a girl cannot consent to sexual intercourse with a man until she is 16. (See p. 175 for the law relating to lesbians.) Before 1885, the age of consent was 12; it was raised to stop adults procuring young girls for prostitution.

The law means that:

1. A man who has intercourse with a girl aged under 13 commits unlawful sexual intercourse which is punishable with life imprisonment and/or an unlimited fine. It is not usually a defence for the man to say he believed that the girl consented or that she was older.
2. A man who has intercourse with a girl aged over 13 but under 16 is committing an offence for which the maximum sentence is two years' imprisonment. If the man is aged under 24, it is a defence if he believed that the girl was over 16, provided that he has not been charged with the same offence before. If the

man has gone through a form of marriage with the girl, it is a defence for him to show that he had reason to believe she was his wife. A boy aged under 14 cannot be convicted of unlawful sexual intercourse.

3. While it is an offence to assault anyone, an indecent assault (see p. 182) by a man on a girl aged under 13 is more serious and carries a maximum penalty of five years' imprisonment and/or an unlimited fine.

4. It is an offence for anyone to allow a girl under 16 to use premises for sexual intercourse, or to encourage prostitution or illegal sexual intercourse; maximum penalty two years' imprisonment and/or unlimited fine. But it is not an offence for a doctor or clinic to give contraceptive supplies to a girl under 16 (see p. 173).

5. It is an offence to take an unmarried girl under 16 away from her parents without their consent, even if sexual intercourse does not take place; maximum penalty two years' imprisonment and/or unlimited fine.

6. It is an offence for a man to take an unmarried girl under the age of 18 away from her parents without their consent if he is taking her 'with intent to have unlawful sexual intercourse' (i.e. intercourse outside marriage). The only defence is for the man to show that he reasonably thought the girl was over 18. So if a 17-year-old girl leaves her parents to live with her boyfriend, he may be prosecuted, even though it is legal for them to have sex.

7. A girl aged under 16 cannot be prosecuted for having intercourse with a man; only the man can be prosecuted. But a girl who is under 17, and who is sleeping with her boyfriend or likely to do so, may find herself in the juvenile court if her parents, the police or the social-service department think she is in 'moral danger'. **Moral danger** in this case means being under 16 and likely to have sex, or being under 17 and away from home and likely to be having sex. In this case, the court can make a supervision order or a care order (see pp. 361–4).

A girl is less likely to get into this kind of trouble if she lives in 'conventional' surroundings, even if she is sleeping with a boyfriend. She is more likely to be brought to court if she lives in a mixed flat or commune or with a man, if she has left home or dropped out of school, or if she mixes with unconventional people. (Boys are not taken to court for being in 'moral danger', unless they are thought to be in danger of homosexual contact.)

Age restrictions for males

Boys of any age can have sex with a woman without fear of prosecution provided that she is over 16 and consents. But it is unlawful for a man to take part in homosexual acts until he is 21 (see p. 175 for details of the law on homosexual behaviour).

The law presumes that a boy under the age of 14 cannot be guilty of unlawful sexual intercourse. A boy under 14 cannot be convicted of rape, but can be convicted of aiding and abetting rape or buggery, or of indecent assault.

A boy under the age of 10 is not responsible for any criminal action and therefore cannot be charged with a sexual offence.

Inability to consent

Someone who is mentally defective, whatever his or her age, is deemed unable to consent to sexual acts. Thus, a man who has intercourse with a mentally defective woman can be charged with rape. It is a defence if the man can show that he did not know that the woman was mentally defective.

Contraception

There are no legal restrictions on the rights of men and women to obtain contraceptives, although family doctors have a discretion to refuse to prescribe them. NHS family planning clinics will provide contraceptives to married and unmarried people.

It is not illegal for a girl aged under 16 to use contraceptives, although it is illegal for a man to have sex with her. It is not illegal for a doctor to give advice about contraception to a girl under 16. But it is usually illegal for a doctor to give a medical

examination or treatment to a girl under 16 without her parents'
consent (e.g. prescribing the pill or fitting a coil). But the doctor
can still treat her if he is acting 'in good faith' and has the consent of a second doctor. The Brook Advisory Centres specialize
in advising young girls on contraceptive matters.

Abortion

About 100,000 legal abortions are carried out on residents of
Britain every year, roughly half of which are on the NHS, the
rest in private clinics. You can get an abortion legally under the
following conditions:

1. Two doctors must sign a form saying that they genuinely
   believe:
   - that continuing the pregnancy would involve a risk to your
     life or the physical or mental health of you or any of your
     children, greater than the risk involved in ending the
     pregnancy; *or*
   - that there is a substantial risk that if the child were born it
     would suffer from a serious physical or mental handicap.
2. The abortion must be carried out in an NHS hospital or a
   clinic licensed by the Department of Health.
3. Abortion is also legal if it is carried out by one doctor who
   genuinely believes that it must be done immediately in order
   to save your life or prevent serious permanent injury to your
   physical or mental health (Abortion Act 1967).

For more information about medical rights, see Chapter 23.

Sterilization

Legally speaking, sterilization is just like any other operation:
it can be performed on anyone over the age of 16 who consents
to it or any child for whom consent is given (see pp. 471–3). In
practice, however, hospitals usually insist that, if a married
person is to be sterilized, the husband or wife must also consent. (Similarly, hospitals usually insist on the husband's signature for an abortion.) Although there is no law which demands

the spouse's consent, doctors fear that an aggrieved spouse might sue for 'loss of child-bearing capacity'. Someone who was sterilized without the spouse's consent would almost certainly be providing grounds for divorce.

Some doctors suggest to a woman who has decided to have an abortion that she should also be sterilized at the same time. But no doctor can insist that you should be sterilized and, if you are in any doubt at all or have not had time to think about it you should refuse to sign the form giving your consent to the sterilization.

Homosexuality

Women

There are no laws specially restricting lesbian behaviour, except within the armed forces, where women can be charged with committing 'disgraceful conduct of an indecent or unnatural kind'.

Technically, lesbians could be prosecuted for the following acts, but rarely are:

– insulting behaviour (see p. 180);
– indecent assault on another woman who did not consent or who is under 16;
– although there is no age of consent for lesbians, the Indecency with Children Act provides that a woman committing an act of gross indecency (see p. 177) with a girl under 14 would be breaking the law.

Men

It is lawful for consenting male adults over 21 to commit homosexual acts in private (Sexual Offences Act 1967). The rights of homosexual men are restricted in the following ways:

1. They cannot legally have sex before their twenty-first birth-day, although heterosexual intercourse with a woman is lawful when she reaches 16.

2. 'In private' does not include places such as public lavatories (even if no one can see) or where there are more than two people present, even if they all consent to be there. In other cases, the court will decide whether or not, depending on the circumstances, the act was 'in private' (e.g. a lonely wood or dark lane could be considered private).

3. Members of the armed forces are not protected by the Sexual Offences Act 1967. They can be court martialled for homosexual behaviour, and can be imprisoned for up to two years and given a dishonourable discharge (see p. 400).

4. Homosexual acts are illegal if committed by two UK merchant seamen aboard a ship where one or both of them is a crew member.

5. Men can be prosecuted for 'persistently soliciting or importuning in a public place for an immoral purpose' (Sexual Offences Act 1956). 'Importuning' can mean no more than smiling at another man; 'persistently' can mean trying repeatedly to pick people up or trying to pick up the same person more than once. This offence is not restricted to soliciting for the purposes of prostitution. In practice, the police generally only arrest people for this offence in public lavatories or places well known for pick-ups. (See Male prostitutes, p. 179.)

6. Policemen can use their discretion in order to carry out their duty of preserving the peace. Consequently, they can disrupt homosexuals' parties and close down their clubs more or less at will, if the people present are not behaving like heterosexuals.

AGENTS PROVOCATEURS

The police have been known to act as *agents provocateurs*, trying to lure homosexual men into committing an offence. This most commonly happens in a public lavatory. It is not a defence to say that you were tricked into committing an offence. If you are charged with indecent assault, you may be able to claim that the policeman invited you to touch him and was a willing partner, so that no assault could have taken place. But you could still be charged with importuning.

GROSS INDECENCY

'Gross indecency' is not fully defined by the law, but it can be any sexual act between homosexual men other than buggery (see p. 183). Actual physical contact need not take place, but the prosecution must show that a grossly indecent exhibition between men was taking place. The charge is most often used against men whom the police say were not acting in private, or where one or both was between 16 and 21.

A man aged 16 or over is presumed capable of consenting to an indecent assault, so both he and his partner can be convicted of gross indecency. The maximum penalty where one partner is 21 or over and the other under 21 is five years' imprisonment and/or an unlimited fine; where partners are either both 21 or over or both under 21, two years' imprisonment and/or an unlimited fine.

Indecent assault

If a homosexual act takes place and one partner does not consent, because he is under 16, or mentally defective, or simply does not give his consent, the other person can be charged with indecent assault. It is not an indecent assault to invite someone to touch you. (See p. 182 for the maximum penalty for indecent assault).

Transvestites

Although there is no law against wearing clothes traditionally worn by the opposite sex, the police sometimes charge male transvestites and transsexuals with insulting or indecent behaviour likely to cause a breach of the peace (see p. 149) or with importuning (see pp. 176 and 179).

Prostitution

It is legal for a woman over 16 to have sexual intercourse with a man for money. Call girls, whose appointments are arranged by phone, cannot be prosecuted. Nor is it in itself a crime for a man to solicit a woman in a public place (e.g. by kerb-crawling) but persistent kerb-crawling could be prosecuted as insulting words or behaviour likely to cause a breach of the peace. Nonetheless, there are a number of offences, related to prostitution, as follows:

1. It is illegal for any person to procure a woman to become a prostitute (maximum penalty two years' imprisonment and/or unlimited fine).
2. It is illegal for a man to live wholly or partly on the earnings of a prostitute. If the man has no regular employment and lives with a prostitute, even if she is his wife, it is up to him to prove to the court that he is not living off her 'immoral earnings'. The maximum penalty is six months' imprisonment and/or a £1,000 fine in the magistrates' court, seven years' imprisonment and/or an unlimited fine in the Crown Court.
3. A person can be prosecuted for allowing premises to be used for prostitution. If the owner of a place is to be prosecuted for keeping a brothel, the place must be used by more than one prostitute. The maximum penalty is three months' imprisonment and/or £100 for the first offence, six months' imprisonment and/or £250 for subsequent offences.
4. A man persistently soliciting women for prostitution in a public place could be charged with insulting words or behaviour likely to cause a breach of the peace.
5. A woman can be arrested without a warrant by a policeman who reasonably suspects her of being a common prostitute, and loitering or soliciting in a street or public place for the purposes of prostitution. A **common prostitute** is a woman who has been cautioned previously for soliciting. If the woman does not accept the policeman's accusation, the first time he cautions her, she can apply to the magistrates' court within fourteen days to have the record cleared. The police must prove that the woman was loitering or soliciting when she was cautioned. If the caution stays on the record, the woman is labelled a common prostitute and can be arrested if she is seen soliciting again. For a first offence, the fine will be small, but a woman who is brought to court repeatedly will probably be sent to prison. (Twelve per cent of the women in Holloway

Prison are there for charges connected with prostitution.) The maximum penalty for a first offence is a £10 fine; for a second offence a £25 fine; and for subsequent offences a £25 fine and/or three months' imprisonment. (Street Offences Act 1959.)

Male prostitutes

It is a criminal offence for a man to solicit another man to have sex with himself, or with a woman (**importuning**). The maximum penalty is a fine of £1,000 and/or six months' imprisonment in the magistrates' court, and unlimited fine and/or two years' imprisonment in the Crown Court.

Incest

A man can be prosecuted for having sexual intercourse with a woman he knows to be his mother, daughter, granddaughter, sister or half-sister. A woman aged 16 or over can be prosecuted for having intercourse with her father, son, grandson, brother or half-brother, even where the partner is under 14 and therefore in law incapable of intercourse. The partner can also be prosecuted, if he or she consents to the incest. The maximum penalty for incest is seven years' imprisonment (life if the girl is under 13) or two years' for attempted incest (seven years if the girl is under 13), and/or an unlimited fine.

Most offences occur between father and daughter. Only a few hundred cases come to the courts each year, although social work records suggest that incest is more common than supposed.

Indecent exposure

There are many laws, mainly bye-laws, dealing with displays of nudity and exposing the body. An indecent exposure seen by one person and capable of being seen by other people can be prosecuted as a common nuisance.

According to the Home Office Working Party's report on Indecency and Obscenity, 'the words "indecent" and "obscene" convey one idea, namely, offending against the recognized standards of propriety, indecent being at the lower end of the scale and obscene at the upper end of the scale'.

'Flashing' is dealt with usually under the Vagrancy Act 1824, which makes it an offence for a man 'wilfully, openly, lewdly and obscenely' to expose his person with the intention of insulting a woman. The delicate reference to 'person' means penis, and not any other part of the body.

Insulting behaviour

Insulting behaviour likely to cause a breach of the peace is something of a catch-all offence, used where public exhibitions which the police consider unacceptable cannot be prosecuted under any other offence. This can include kissing between homosexuals, 'streaking' or wearing topless dresses, simulating sexual intercourse or masturbation. Kerb-crawling (see p. 178) has also been prosecuted as insulting behaviour. (See p. 149 for more about breach of the peace.)

It is also an offence to commit any act which outrages public decency. The act would have to do more than offend or even shock reasonable people. Sexual acts in public or involving animals could be prosecuted as acts outraging public decency.

If the police find a man and woman having intercourse in a park or wood, they usually consider it sufficient to embarrass the couple, although the couple could be prosecuted for outraging public decency, or under park regulations or local bye-laws. A homosexual couple would not get off so lightly (see p. 176).

Rape and indecent assault

If a man has sexual intercourse with a woman who is not his wife, by force and without her consent, he is committing **rape**. Any penetration, however slight, amounts to rape. In legal terms a man cannot be raped; if one man forces another to have anal intercourse, it amounts to buggery or indecent assault (see below).

Rape can take place without actual violence if the woman is afraid, has been given drink or drugs, or is raped under false pretences, for instance if:

- she has sex with a man she mistakenly believes to be her husband;
- she has sex in the belief that she is undergoing medical operation.

For a man to be convicted of rape, he must either know that the woman did not consent, or not care whether she consented. It is a defence for the man to show that he honestly believed the woman consented, no matter how unreasonable the belief may seem.

The only circumstances where a man could be convicted of raping his wife are:

- where there is a judicial separation order or a separation order from a magistrates' court (see p. 345) which includes a 'non-cohabitation clause' (i.e. a clause ending the couple's legal duty to live with each other); *or*
- where there is a legal agreement to separate which contains a clause forbidding a husband from molesting his wife (i.e. a 'non-molestation clause'); *or*

– a *decree nisi* has been granted in divorce proceedings (see p. 348).

The police may be unwilling to prosecute a man for rape, if it is just the woman's story against his, and there are no witnesses and no obvious signs of struggle. The woman is more likely to be believed if she goes straight to the police after the rape, or is found by someone who can act as a witness. If possible, a woman who is raped should contact the Rape Crisis Centre 01-340 6145 (emergency) 01-340 6913 (office hours) or get a friend to go with her to the police station.

The Sexual Offences (Amendment) Act 1976 provides that both the man's and the woman's names will be kept out of the press during the trial, although the man's name may be published if he is convicted. Cross-examination of the woman about her previous sexual experience with other men will also be forbidden, unless the judge decides that there are exceptional reasons why it should be mentioned. The maximum penalty for rape is life imprisonment and/or an unlimited fine.

Indecent assault

Indecent assault is a legal term covering a range of sexual acts where one partner does not consent (or cannot consent because he or she is under age or mentally defective). Indecent assault can be between people of the same or the opposite sex and a woman can be charged with indecently assaulting a man. Technically, any sexual caress can be indecent assault – ranging from touching or fondling the other person's body, to forced oral sex or buggery. It is also an indecent assault if a man forces his wife to have intercourse against her will (even though the man cannot be convicted of rape). The maximum penalty for indecent assault on a *man* is six months' imprisonment and/or £1,000 fine in a magistrates' court; ten years' imprisonment and/or unlimited fine in the Crown Court. The maximum penalty for indecent assault on a *woman* is six months' imprisonment or £1,000 fine in the magistrates' court; two years' imprisonment (five years' if the girl is under 13) and/or an unlimited fine in the Crown Court.

Buggery

It is an offence for any person to commit buggery with another person or with an animal. But homosexual acts, including buggery, between consenting males aged over 21, in private, are lawful. As a matter of policy, the police do not prosecute a man and woman who consent to have anal intercourse in private. (It is hard to see how the police would know about it anyway!)

The maximum penalties for buggery are:

- if with a boy under 16 or any woman or an animal – life imprisonment and/or an unlimited fine;
- if with a man who does not consent – ten years' imprisonment and/or an unlimited fine;
- if you are over 21 and commit buggery with a man aged 16–21 who consents – five years' imprisonment and/or an unlimited fine;
- if both parties are aged 16–21 and both consent – two years' imprisonment and/or an unlimited fine.

More information

The following publications and associations may be helpful:
Anna Coote and Tess Gill, *Women's Rights: A Practical Guide*, Penguin, (revised edition 1977).

Anna Coote and Tess Gill, *The Rape Controversy*, NCCL (50p).

Know your rights: Homosexuals, NCCL Factsheet.

Albany Trust, 16–20 Strutton Ground, London SW1 (01-222 0701).

Brook Advisory Centre, 233 Tottenham Court Road, London W1 (01-580 2991).

Campaign for Homosexual Equality, PO Box 427, 33 King Street, Manchester M6 (061-228 1985). London office: 22 Great Windmill Street, London W1 (01-437 7363).

Family Planning Association, 27 Mortimer Street, London W1 (01-636 7866).

Friend, 274 Upper Street, London N1 (01-359 7371).

Gay Liberation Front, c/o South London Gay Centre, 78 Railton Road, London SE24 (01-274 7921).

Gay Switchboard, c/o 5 Caledonian Road, London N1 [mailing address only] (01-837 7324).

Grapevine, 296 Holloway Road, London N7 (01-607 0935).

Icebreakers, BM/Gay Lib, London WC1.

Paedophile Information Exchange, c/o Release, 1 Elgin Avenue, London W9 [no telephone].

Pregnancy Advisory Service, 40 Margaret Street, London W1 (01-629 9575).

Rape Crisis Centre, 01-340 6145 (24-hour emergency), 01-340 6913 (office hours).

Release, 1 Elgin Avenue, London W9 (01-289 1123; 01-603 8654 – 24-hour emergency).

Sappho, 20 Dorset Square, London NW1 (01-724 3636).

Scottish Minorities Group, 60 Broughton Street, Edinburgh 1 (031-556 3637).

8. The worker and the law

The law has traditionally been used to restrict the rights of workers. When strikes were illegal employers were able to impose almost any conditions of work on their employees that they chose. Over the last 150 years the labour movement has fought to establish minimum standards to govern the relationship of employees to employers. Some of these rights are contained in Acts of Parliament, some embodied in common law, that is, the past decisions of judges in courts. The law that has been created is vast and complex and it is only possible here to provide a brief guide to the main provisions.

This chapter covers:

If you have problems connected with your work, you should consult your trade-union official as trade unions provide the best protection for employed people. If you are not in a union, you may get help from a lawyer (see p. 489), but very few of them are trained in industrial law. Various other official and voluntary organizations exist which may advise workers about their rights and these are referred to in the relevant parts of the chapter.

Contracts of employment

The legal relationship between an employer and employee is based on a contract. A contract is defined as any agreement which the courts will enforce. It makes no difference whether a contract is in writing or was agreed verbally, although it may be harder to prove what was agreed if the contract was oral.

In common law, decisions by judges in thousands of cases over hundreds of years have established a number of **implied** terms of an employment contract, as well as the **express** terms which are actually agreed between the employer and employee. These implied terms can be enforced even if one or both of the parties is not aware of them. The implied terms establish that an employee's duties are:

– to obey all lawful and reasonable orders;
– not to commit misconduct;
– to give faithful and honest service; *and*
– to use reasonable skill and care in the work.

The employer's duties are:

– to take reasonable care for the employee's safety;
– to pay the agreed wages;
– not to require the employee to do unlawful acts; *and*
– to provide work for those employed on piece-rate.

If the employer breaks the contract (e.g., by not paying your wages) you can bring an action in a civil court for damages (see p. 243). Similarly, if you breach the contract, your employer may also bring an action. If it is a serious breach of contract, for example stealing from the till, the contract may be brought to an end and the employee may be sacked instantly.

Parliament has also legislated to determine the implied terms of contracts of employment and these statutes, in some cases, lay inescapable duties on employers regardless of the express terms of the contract. These laws are dealt with in the rest of this chapter.

Particulars

Contracts of employment vary enormously. Many of the terms which they contain are the result of collective agreements made between an employer (or a federation of employers) and a trade union (or trade unions negotiating together in a particular industry). For example, in local government, the terms and conditions of employment are set out in a book generally referred to as the 'purple book'. Most local government employees never see this book although they are entitled to, but it is referred to in the documents they are given when they start work.

Many people never receive a formal contract of employment signed by themselves and their employer. The terms and conditions of the job may be set out in a letter of appointment which details the wages, duties, hours, etc., but many people receive no piece of paper at all and become someone's employee by word of mouth or by having a shovel placed in their hands. If this happens, they are protected by the Contracts of Employment Act 1972 which has been amended by the Employment Protection Act 1975.

These Acts require an employer to give written particulars of the terms and conditions of work to persons who are employed full-time. **Full-time** means:

- working 16 hours a week or more for the same employer; *or*
- working 8 hours a week or more for five years for the same employer; *or*
- working 16 hours a week or more but for up to 26 weeks working between 8 and 16 hours.

Certain groups of employees are excluded from some parts of the Act, like registered dockworkers.
Particulars should include:

   name of employer and employee
   date employment began
   rate of pay
   interval between payments
   hours of work
   holidays and holiday pay
   sick pay
   pensions and pension schemes
   length of notice
   rights in relation to trade-union membership
   grievance procedure
   disciplinary procedure

any employment with a new employer which counts towards
continuous employment
the title of the employee's job

Although all these particulars should be made known to employees, the employer does not have to actually provide all these
things. For instance, with regard to sick pay, your particulars
might say, 'No wages will be paid in the event that the employee
is absent from work by reason of illness or injury.'

The particulars may be set out on notice boards at the place
where you work or they may be contained in a collective agreement between the trade union and employer. They do not have
to be signed by employees but they are a contract. If you cannot
find out what the particulars are for your job, or if the particulars you have been given are wrong, you can apply to the industrial tribunal who will decide what terms should be included
(see p. 203).

Terms and conditions of employment

Wages

The payment of wages is affected by a number of statutes.

1. The Employment Protection Act 1975 lays down that from
   the beginning of 1977 employers must provide itemized pay
   statements when paying wages. These must set out gross pay,
   net pay and must specify all deductions. If your employer
   does not do this, you can bring a case before an industrial
   tribunal (see p. 203).
2. The Truck Acts 1831–96 prohibit the payment of wages to
   manual workers in any form other than cash. Cheques can
   now be paid if you agree to this. The Acts also prohibit
   deductions from manual workers' wages except where certain
   conditions are observed. The calculation of deductions has to
   be made clear to employees. Deductions may be permitted for
   fuel, food, tools or accommodation supplied by the employer;
   if there is a union check-off agreement whereby union dues are
   deducted from wages; or if a court has made an attachment of

earnings order, for instance, on a man who has to pay maintenance to his wife. If you think that illegal deductions are being made from your wages you can bring an action for breach of contract in the county court (see p. 246). Employers making illegal deductions can also be prosecuted by the Wages Inspectorate (see below).

3. The Wages Council Act 1959 confirmed the establishment of a number of Wages Councils in certain low-paid industries. These set a minimum wage and fix certain other conditions such as holidays and hours of work. They operate mainly in the retail trade, catering and the clothing industry. The rates are enforced by the **Wages Inspectorate** who deal with employees' complaints. Contact the nearest office of the inspectorate, usually found at the regional offices of the Department of Employment, to see if you are receiving the right pay.

4. The Equal Pay Act 1970 came into force in 1976. It is intended to do two things.
   a. In certain situations, it gives individual women the right to the same rate of pay as men doing the same or similar work, or work rated the same under a job-evaluation scheme.
   b. It makes it illegal for wage agreements to discriminate against women by containing provisions which apply to men or women only.

The Act covers wages and salaries, overtime pay, shift-work allowances, night-work premiums, bonuses, luncheon vouchers and other fringe benefits, sick-pay schemes and health or medical insurance. It does not cover maternity leave or pension provisions or retirement age. The Act is extremely complicated and many employers have found ways round it in order to avoid paying women the same wages as men. If you think you are not receiving the same pay as someone of the opposite sex who is doing the same job as you, you can bring a case before an industrial tribunal (see p. 203). Seek advice from your trade union, from the **National Council for Civil Liberties, 186 Kings Cross Road, London WC1 (01-278 4575),** or from the **Equal Opportunities Commission, Overseas House, Quay Street, Manchester 3 (061-833 9244).**

Hours of work

Hours of work are usually established by agreement between employers and employees. But the law has established some maximum standards in certain industries and for certain kinds of employees. Where such standards have been set they are comprehensive and cover the maximum hours in each day to be worked, the length of periods of uninterrupted work, the length and frequency of breaks, the hours of the day in which work may be done, provision for time off in lieu and so on.

Hours of work for men who work in mines are controlled under the Coal Mines Regulation Act 1908, for those in night bakeries by the Baking Industry (Hours of Work) Act 1954, for those employed in automatic sheet-glass work under the Hours of Employment (Conventions) Act 1936, and lorry and other drivers under the Transport Act 1968.

Women's hours are regulated if they work in factories under the Factories Act 1961, in shops under the Shops Act 1950, and in mines and quarries under the Mines and Quarries Act 1954 (women are not allowed to work underground at all). There is no regulation of the hours of work of women who work in offices.

The hours of work of children and young persons (under 18) are regulated almost everywhere they might work by the Young Persons (Employment) Acts 1938 and 1964, and the Children and Young Persons Act 1963. In factories they are covered by the Factories Act 1961 and in shops by the Shops Act 1950.

Trade-union membership

Every trade union has its own rule-book, which sets out the terms of the contract between the union and its members. If a section of the union takes action against you in breach of the rule-book, you can complain through the union's own procedure, or you can take legal action to ensure that the rule-book is enforced.

It is also possible to take action through the courts if you believe you have been arbitrarily or unreasonably expelled from your union, or if the union failed to observe the rules of natural justice – telling you in advance of the allegations against you, in a disciplinary matter; and allowing you to state your case before a decision is made. You should take legal advice (see p. 489).

It is unlawful for a trade union to discriminate against a member or would-be member on grounds of sex, marriage or race. A complaint about discrimination can be made to an industrial tribunal (see p. 203); you can get advice from the **Equal Opportunities Commission, Overseas House, Quay Street, Manchester 3** or the **Commission for Racial Equality, 10/12 Allington Street, London SW1.**

Trade-union rights

The Trade Union and Labour Relations Act 1974 and the Employment Protection Act 1975 enable you to apply to an industrial tribunal for reinstatement, re-engagement (see below) or compensation if:

– you are dismissed for joining an independent trade union or taking part in trade-union activities – in the latter case there is a special quick procedure for reinstatement if application is made to the tribunal within seven days and supported by a letter from an officer of the union;
– you are victimized but not dismissed for joining an independent trade union or taking part in trade-union activities.

Trade unionists are permitted reasonable time off for union activities.

Closed shop

If a **union membership agreement** has been reached between the employer and one or more union in a company, then you can be required to join the union as a condition of being employed by that company. This applies even if you have previously worked for the firm, without being required to join a union. You can be dismissed for refusing to join the union, and the dismissal will be fair in law, unless:

- the closed-shop agreement was not properly enforced throughout the company (i.e. other employees continued to be employed without being required to join the union); *or*
- you genuinely object to joining a trade union on grounds of your religious belief (it should not matter whether your religion has written rules prohibiting union membership or not); (Trade Union and Labour Relations Act 1974 as amended).

If you are dismissed for refusing to join a union, you can make a complaint of unfair dismissal to an industrial tribunal (see p. 199 for more information on unfair dismissal, and p. 203 for more on industrial tribunals). But you are most unlikely to succeed unless one of the two conditions above applies.

Maternity rights

A provision of the Employment Protection Act came into force in April 1977 which guarantees a single or married woman six weeks' paid maternity leave if she has worked two years with the same employer. Provided she tells the employer before leaving, she will be entitled to have back her job up to twenty-nine weeks after the birth of her child. The maternity pay will be nine tenths of her full pay, less the flat-rate maternity allowance. At present if you have paid the full rate of National Insurance contribution, you can claim a maternity allowance and earnings-related supplement for eighteen weeks. It will almost always

amount to an unfair dismissal if your employer sacks you because you are pregnant. These provisions are enforced by the industrial tribunal (see p. 203).

Time off for public duties

Under the Employment Protection Act 1975, s. 59 employers should grant a reasonable amount of unpaid leave to employees who are magistrates, members of tribunals, councillors, members of health, water and education authorities, and other similar public offices. These provisions are enforced by the industrial tribunal (see p. 203).

Lay off, short-time and guarantee payments

Under the Redundancy Payment Act 1965 there is an extremely complicated procedure whereby an employee who is laid off (that is receives no wages at all) or is put on short time (that is receives less than half a week's pay) can claim redundancy payment. The lay off or short time must be for either four consecutive weeks or any six weeks in thirteen weeks.

Under the Employment Protection Act 1975 a provision came into force early in 1977 which entitles employees to receive guarantee payments in a situation where there is not enough work to do. The guarantee is a maximum of £6 per day for a maximum of five days in a period of three months.

These provisions can be enforced by the industrial tribunal (see p. 203).

Race discrimination

The Race Relations Act 1976 makes it illegal to treat a person less favourably than another on grounds of colour, race, ethnic or national origin. The Act covers recruitment, the terms and conditions offered, access to opportunities for promotion, training and other benefits, and dismissal, redundancy, etc. The **Commission for Racial Equality** (address p. 191), has the power to investigate discrimination and make orders preventing discrimination. If you think you have been discriminated against because of your racial origin, you can bring a case before an industrial tribunal. (See Chapter 10.)

Sex discrimination

The Sex Discrimination Act 1975 makes it unlawful for employers to discriminate on grounds of sex or marriage in recruitment, in the terms and conditions offered to employees, in relation to promotion, transfer or training and fringe benefits, and dismissal, redundancy and short time. There are a number of cases where the Act does not apply, in particular if the employer employs less than five people or if there is a 'genuine occupational qualification' which justifies discrimination, for instance in single-sex establishments or when actors or models are being hired.

If you think you have been discriminated against because of your sex or because you are married you can bring a case before an industrial tribunal (see p. 203). For help in bringing a case consult your trade union, the National Council for Civil Liberties or the Equal Opportunities Commission (addresses p. 191).

Suspension from work on medical grounds

Sections 29–33 of the Employment Protection Act 1975 give an employee who is suspended from work on medical grounds (that is, if a health and safety inspector has decided that a worker should, for instance, no longer work with a certain chemical process) a right to be paid whilst suspended. This provision is enforced by the industrial tribunal (see p. 203).

Health and welfare at work

Minimum standards of cleanliness and decoration of premises, overcrowding, ventilation, lighting, sanitation and so on are set by the Factories Act 1961 and the Offices, Shops and Railway Premises Act 1963. These provisions are enforced by the health and safety inspectors and local authority environmental-health officers.

Search of workers

In some circumstances, employers insist that their employees be searched on entering or leaving the works. This might be a precaution against theft, or to prevent anything dangerous being brought into the works. These searches may be carried out by 'security guards', or by private works police employed by the firm.

A contract of employment rarely makes provision expressly for employees to be searched. If you are searched without your consent – express or implied – you may have the right to sue for assault or, if you were detained on leaving, for false imprisonment. But the courts would usually find that your consent, however fictitious, had been given by implication. If you refused to give your consent, you would probably be told, 'If you don't like it, you don't have to work here.' But you would then be able to claim damages for unfair dismissal (see p. 199).

Safety at work

The law with regard to safety at work is in the process of being changed. The Health and Safety at Work Act 1974 is intended to replace all the old legislation. New regulations which come into force during the late 1970s will repeal old laws. As well as the old and new legislation, judges have established minimal standards for safety at work which can be enforced in a court of law (see p. 197).

The old legislation

Most contracts of employment say nothing about safety at work but many detailed and complex laws exist which impose obligations on employers to do or not to do certain things related to safety. If they fail to carry out their obligations they can, in most cases, be prosecuted by health and safety inspectors. The fines, however, are ludicrously small and are unlikely to deter employers who choose to ignore the legislation. But these legal obligations may be of use to trade unionists who can press for healthier and safer working conditions. And individual workers who are injured because of their employer's failure to carry out safety obligations may bring an action for damages (see p. 243).

The old legislation is very detailed and imposes rigorous safety standards in certain types of employment, for example the Factories Act 1961, Mines and Quarries Act 1954, Offices, Shops and Railway Premises Act 1963, and regulations concerning docks, asbestos and construction. The laws and regulations that do exist are precise and provide reasonable protection for those who work in these industries or on particular processes. But some six million working people are not covered by this legislation.

Health and Safety at Work Act 1974

It is unlikely that the codes of practice, regulations and guidance notes which will emerge from the Health and Safety at Work Act 1974 will be as comprehensive or as stringent as the old legislation. The Act is very general and employers are only obliged to do what is **'reasonably practicable'**. Since 'reasonable' could be interpreted in terms of possible interference with profit or inconvenience to the employer, it is important that trade unionists who are involved in the preparation of new regulations in their trades should ensure that this phrase is not used. For example, the National Union of Mineworkers insisted in 1953 during the passage of the Mines and Quarries Act that the phrase 'reasonably practicable' was replaced just by 'practicable' so that the only defence for an employer in a claim for damages by an injured worker was if it could be shown that it was 'not physically possible' to provide adequate safety precautions.

The Health and Safety at Work Act covers all workers. It is administered by the Health and Safety Executive who employ factory inspectors. Inspectors generally rely on persuasion to achieve their purposes but they have the power to prosecute employers who breach the old legislation whilst in force, or the new Act. They also have wide powers to enter premises, make inspections, look at documents, take samples and photographs. They can serve prohibition notices to prohibit the use of a machine or process where they think there is serious risk of injury; and serve improvement notices to require a machine or process to be improved in a specified way within a specified time. You can find the address of the local factory inspectorate under 'F' in the telephone directory.

The common law

Over centuries judges have established some minimal standards for safety at work which exist regardless of the old or new legislation. The common law imposes a duty on the employer to take reasonable care for the safety of employees in four ways by providing:

– a safe place of work;
– a safe system of work;
– adequate plant and equipment; *and*
– competent staff.

If you are injured at work or become ill as a result of inadequate safety precautions, you can sue your employer for damages. You will need legal help for this (see p. 496). You will have to show that your employer failed to take reasonable care. The judge will decide what 'reasonable' means.

In order to get some compensation, or damages as lawyers call it, for injury, ill health or death at work, you, or someone acting for you, will have to establish three things:

– that the employer had a duty of care;
– that the employer breached that duty; *and*
– that the injury occurred as a result of that breach of duty.

It often takes two or three years for this kind of action to complete its passage through the courts.

If you are partly responsible for the accident, you can still win a claim against your employer, but if you win the damages will be reduced to the extent that the judge thought you were to blame. This is called **contributory negligence.**

Industrial injuries benefit

National Insurance industrial injuries benefits provide some financial compensation for those injured at work. The compensation is small compared to court awards of damages but it can be obtained more easily and quickly.

The accident or disease must 'arise out of and in the course of the employment' in order for benefit to be awarded. There are three kinds of benefit.

1. Industrial injury benefit – a fixed weekly payment for a maximum of twenty-six weeks. To claim it you must be unfit for work.
2. Disablement benefit – a weekly pension or lump-sum payment depending on the degree of disablement. It is paid when injury benefit ends whether you return to work or not.
3. Industrial death benefit – a weekly sum paid to widows and dependents.

These benefits are paid by the state, not the employer. (See p. 412 for further information.)

Dismissal and redundancy

Your contract of employment may describe what will happen if the job comes to an end. Usually a period of notice is specified and there may be provisions relating to redundancy and so on. If a firm is going to close down the union will often negotiate arrangements and compensation. Such negotiation and any industrial action that may occur are matters of collective action rather than law and are not dealt with here.

Notice

The Employment Protection Act 1975 and the Contracts of Employment Act 1972 lay down minimum periods of notice for

most full-time employees who have worked for at least four weeks.
You are entitled to:

– one week's notice if you have worked for four weeks but less
than two years; *and*
– one additional week for each year's continuous service, up to a
maximum of twelve weeks for twelve years' service.

Your contract of employment may provide for longer periods
of notice than this which can be enforced in a court of law, *but
you cannot legally be given less notice than these minimum periods.*

An employer can give wages instead of notice and ask an
employee to leave immediately. Employees who are sacked for
'gross misconduct' or because of some other 'fundamental
breach' of their contract of employment are not entitled to any
notice at all.

If you have not received the proper notice to which you are
entitled you can sue for **wrongful dismissal** in the county
court for damages amounting to wages in lieu of the notice you
should have received. This is not the same as unfair dismissal
(see below). You could also get damages for wrongful dismissal
from an industrial tribunal if you are before the tribunal for some
other reason.

Reasons for dismissal

Section 70 of the Employment Protection Act 1975 requires
employers to provide within fourteen days written reasons for
dismissal if you have worked for the employer for at least six
months and have requested reasons. This provision can be enforced by application to an industrial tribunal (see p. 203) which
can declare what the reasons are and order the employer to pay
the employee two weeks' wages.

Unfair dismissal

Dismissal may take any of the following forms:

1. Sacking by the employer with or without notice.

2. Refusal by the employer to renew a fixed-term contract.
3. Resignation by the employee because the employer has behaved in such a way as to force the resignation. This is called **constructive dismissal**.

The Trade Union and Labour Relations Act 1974 entitles an employee who believes that he or she has been unfairly dismissed to apply to an industrial tribunal. You can only apply if you are under retiring age at the date of dismissal and have been working full-time for at least twenty-six weeks (see p. 187 for a definition of full-time). *The claim must be made within three months of the dismissal.* In some cases, tribunals can accept a late claim but they are very reluctant to do so.

Under the law it is up to the employer to show that the dismissal was fair, rather than for the employee to show that it was not. In other words, the emphasis of the hearing is on the employer's defence and not the employee's evidence. Normally, the employer's case will be put first and it is important that the employer or his or her representative is questioned about their evidence.

In order to prove that the dismissal was fair, the employer must show that the reason for the dismissal was due to one of the following:

– the conduct of the employee;
– the qualifications or capability of the employee;
– redundancy;
– 'some other substantial reason justifying dismissal'.

The employer must then show that 'he acted reasonably in treating [the reason] as a sufficient reason for dismissing the employee'. Some reasons are automatically unfair. For instance, the employer cannot dismiss anyone because of their trade-union activity, because they are pregnant, or because of their race or sex.

The industrial tribunal can, in certain circumstances, order that an employee be reinstated (which means going back to the same job with the same pay and conditions), or re-engaged (which means going back to a similar job). The tribunal also has the power to award compensation either as well as or instead of other remedies. In fixing the amount of the compensation the tribunal should take into account:

– loss of earnings from the date of dismissal until the estimated date on which a similarly paid job might be found;
– loss of expected wage increases;
– expenses in looking for a new job;
– loss of pension rights;
– loss of protection from unfair dismissal (usually estimated as a half-week's pay);
– losses because of the manner of the dismissal (for example because blacklisting may occur);
– loss of accumulated right to notice;
– a 'basic award' equivalent to redundancy pay (see p. 202) or two weeks' pay whichever is the greater.

From this is deducted any earnings after the date of dismissal. If the tribunal decides that you contributed in some way to the dismissal, the compensation will be reduced by the extent to which they find you to blame. Remember that you are expected to do everything reasonable to lessen the effect of the dismissal by signing on at an employment exchange and looking for other work. If you have not done this, the tribunal is likely to reduce the compensation.

Redundancy

A worker can be made redundant when an employer ceases to carry on business in a particular place (although employees may be required by contract to move with the employer), or when the employee's particular kind of work ceases because the requirements of the business have changed.

You are eligible for redundancy pay if:

– you have been working for the same employer for at least two years since your 18th birthday; *and*
– you are not working in certain jobs which are excluded from the Redundancy Payment Act 1965 (for instance, registered dockworkers or Crown employees); *and*
– you are under retirement age.

The amount of the redundancy payment is calculated by multiplying the number of years you have worked for the same employer by a certain number of weeks' earnings. Weekly earnings usually exclude overtime and are limited to a maximum of £80 per week. The maximum total payment you could receive is £2,400. Your employer must give you a written statement of how your redundancy pay has been calculated. You can get:

– half a week's pay for each year from your 18th birthday to your 22nd;
– one week's pay for each year between your 22nd and 41st birthday;
– one and a half week's pay for each year after your 41st birthday.

Redundancy payments are reduced by one twelfth for each month past the 64th birthday for men, or the 59th birthday for women.

Redundancy pay is paid by the employer who receives a rebate from the state. If the employer is bankrupt or in liquidation, the state pays the full amount.

You can lose your rights to redundancy pay if you accept alternative employment with the same employer, or unreasonably refuse 'suitable alternative employment' with the same employer. It is difficult to define what a tribunal will consider to be a suitable alternative. You must therefore be careful before refusing alternative employment with the same employer. If your employer offers you alternative employment, you can ask for this to be for a trial period but make sure this agreement is in writing. If the firm where you work is taken over, there are complex rules to determine whether you are entitled to redundancy payment from the old employer at the time of takeover or whether your continuity of employment carries over so that if your new employer makes you redundant, you can count the period of employment with the old employer.

If you know beforehand that you are going to be made redundant you are entitled to paid time off in order to look for a new job. But if you give notice to your employer before it is given to you, you could lose your entitlement to redundancy pay.

If you think you have been made redundant but your employer says you were dismissed for some other reason, or if your employer accepts that it is a redundancy but refuses to make the proper payment, you can apply to the industrial tribunal (see below). *You must do this within six months from the date of the dismissal.*

Industrial tribunals

Industrial tribunals hear cases concerning equal pay, redundancy, unfair dismissal, sex discrimination, racial discrimination, contracts of employment, industrial training and many other aspects of employment rights dealt with in this chapter. The tribunal hearings are open to the public.

If you wish to bring a case before an industrial tribunal you must get hold of form IT1 – called the **originating application** form – from an employment exchange, offices of the Department of Employment or from a citizens' advice bureau. The form must be completed and sent to the industrial tribunal. Describe the grounds for your case as briefly as possible. It is much better to save your detailed evidence until the hearing itself. A copy of this application will be sent to your employer who replies to your case on a form called a **notice of appearance**. You are entitled to see a copy of this if the case is to be contested.

Tribunal hearings are usually quicker and relatively informal in comparison with a court of law. The tribunal itself is made up of three people: a legally qualified chairperson, a representative of employers' organizations (usually a manager or boss) and a representative of the workpeople (usually an official or active member of a trade union).

The person bringing a case to the tribunal is called the **applicant**. The employer is called the **respondent**. Both sides are entitled to be represented.

Advice and representation

If you are a member of a trade union, consult your local full-time official, shop steward or branch officer who may advise you and help to arrange representation at the hearing. Some union officials represent their own members before tribunals; some will pay for lawyers to represent them. You can also seek advice from a solicitor under the green-form scheme (see p. 494). Under this scheme a solicitor can prepare a document setting out your case for the tribunal. But there is no legal aid available for representation at the hearing of an industrial tribunal so if a solicitor represents you, you will have to pay the fees. Make sure that the lawyer you approach knows something about industrial law: very few have any training or experience in this sphere. You can, of course, represent yourself or ask a friend to help you. In any case it is wise to have someone with you at the hearing to provide at least some moral support.

Procedure

Procedure varies depending on the type of case you bring. You must provide information about your job and the circumstances surrounding your application. You are entitled to call witnesses and produce any documents which you think are relevant. The tribunal and the employer's representative may question you. If you are presenting your own case the tribunal chairperson or other members of the tribunal may ask questions to draw out the full facts of the case. When the employers or representatives present their case, you may question them. Many employers contest cases vigorously and go to great lengths to win using barristers, company lawyers, personnel managers and the like to represent them or give evidence at the hearing. At the end each party summarizes their case.

The tribunal then makes their decision, usually in private. You are entitled to know the reasons for their decision.

If you want someone to attend to give evidence who refuses to do so, the tribunal can make an order compelling his or her attendance. Similarly, the tribunal can order the employer to bring relevant documents. Such orders must be applied for at least one day before the day of the hearing, but you should apply early wherever possible.

Appeals

If you lose your case at the industrial tribunal, you may be able to appeal to the Employment Appeal Tribunal. You will need a lawyer to help you and legal aid is available for such cases. If you lose at the Employment Appeal Tribunal you can appeal, but only if a mistake has been made in the law, to the Court of Appeal. This is a very formal court. Legal aid is available. If you lose you will usually have to pay the other side's costs (see p. 496).

Industrial cases in the courts

The courts deal with actions for damages in cases such as industrial accidents or unpaid wages. (See pp. 243–58 for information about your rights in civil courts.) The documents necessary for beginning an action in the civil courts can be obtained from court offices. Legal aid is available and it is usually necessary to be legally represented (see p. 489). Your union may assist in this.

Industrial action

There is no positive legal right to strike, to picket or to carry out other forms of industrial action. Nevertheless, the law provides some protection for people engaged in such action – providing they are acting 'in contemplation or furtherance of a **trade dispute**'. Trade dispute covers virtually every issue over which workers might wish to take industrial action, including sympathetic action on behalf of other workers. Trade dispute does *not* cover purely political industrial action.

Breach of contract

Any worker who refuses to carry on working in accordance with the contract of employment (see p. 186) is in **breach of the contract**. A strike, a work-to-rule, a go-slow, or an overtime ban where overtime is compulsory, are all breaches of contract.

Theoretically, employers could sue workers for breach of contract, although in practice they almost never do.

More importantly, an employer may dismiss workers involved in a strike or other industrial action. Provided the employer sacks *all* the workers involved, or refuses to re-engage all of them, the dismissal will be fair. The dismissal will be unfair in the following circumstances:

- the employer sacks only some of the workers involved, or sacks all of them but only re-engages some of them; *or*
- the industrial action is not the real reason for the dismissal, and the real reason (e.g. victimization for trade-union activity) is unfair. The employee who had been dismissed would have to show the industrial tribunal hearing the case that in fact industrial action had been used as an excuse to disguise the real reason for the dismissal. (See p. 199 for more information about unfair dismissal.)

ENCOURAGING PEOPLE TO BREAK THEIR CONTRACT

In general, it is lawful for trade-union officials, shop stewards or individual members to persuade other people to go on strike, black goods supplied to a firm where workers are on strike *or* threaten to go on strike or black goods. Such actions amount to inducing other people to break their contract (that is, their contract of employment, or their contract to supply goods); but provided the activity is carried on in furtherance of a trade dispute, the individuals involved cannot be sued for breach of contract.

Individual workers could, however, be sued if, in the course of persuading people not to work or to black goods, they libelled the employer, trespassed on the employer's property (see below for more on trespass) or physically prevented someone going to work. Libel, trespass and false imprisonment are all civil wrongs (torts); it is not a defence to a legal action concerning these or other civil wrongs to say that the activity was done to further a trade dispute.

Trespass – sit-ins, work-ins, etc.

Trespass means being on premises where you have no lawful authority to be. In most cases, it is a *civil* wrong (tort), not a criminal matter. (See p. 17 for information about criminal trespass.) Because it is a civil and not a criminal matter:

– workers who trespass on employers' premises (e.g. by sitting-in or working-in) cannot be prosecuted in the criminal courts simply because they are trespassers;
– in order to evict the trespassers, the employer will have to apply to the civil courts (the procedure is explained below);
– the police should not enter the premises to evict the workers, although they have the authority to enter if they fear that a breach of the peace will occur; see p. 27 for other circumstances where the police can enter private premises without a warrant. The police also have new powers (see p. 18).

EVICTION

In 1970, a new procedure was introduced in the courts to enable speedier evictions of squatters and other trespassers, such as students occupying college buildings, and workers occupying employers' premises. The procedure is contained in Order 113 (for the High Court) and Order 26 (for the county court).

Under the new procedure, it is not necessary for the employer to hand each individual a copy of the summons ordering him or her to leave the premises. Copies of the summons can simply be left at the main entrance. Nor is it necessary for the employer to know all the names of the occupiers; a summons can be obtained against some named people and 'other persons unknown'. Finally, a summons obtained against one group of people can be used to evict anyone who has moved in to occupy the premises named in the summons, even if the group of people originally named have left.

Once a summons has been obtained against workers occupying a factory or other premises, and the summons has been delivered to the workers or left in a prominent place on the premises, the workers can be evicted by court bailiffs if they do not obey the summons and leave.

CRIMINAL TRESPASS

Trespass is a criminal offence if the trespass involves breaking and entering; or an intention to rob, rape or inflict grievous bodily harm; or the trespass is on gas, electricity, water or rail authority premises.

In addition, however, it is proposed in the Criminal Law Bill, following a Law Commission report, to create five new criminal offences which would affect people occupying premises. These are set out on p. 17. Those which could affect industrial action are:

- using or threatening violence to a person or to property, for the purpose of securing entry into premises against the wishes of someone present on the property at the time (e.g. a security guard);
- being on any premises that you have entered as a trespasser and having with you any offensive weapon (see p. 153 for definition of offensive weapon);
- resisting or intentionally obstructing an officer of the court executing an eviction order.

A police constable will be able to arrest without a warrant anyone whom he reasonably suspects of committing these offences.

CONSPIRACY TO TRESPASS

Although trespass is in most cases only a civil wrong, in some circumstances (e.g. protestors sitting-in at an embassy), people used to be prosecuted for the *criminal* offence of conspiracy to trespass (see pp. 150–51). Conspiracy to trespass has now been abolished and replaced with five new offences (see p. 17).

Picketing

The 1906 Trade Disputes Act was intended to provide a right to picket peacefully in industrial disputes for the purpose only of peacefully obtaining or communicating information or peacefully persuading any person to work or abstain from working. Since then, a succession of court cases have whittled away the rights proclaimed by the 1906 Act, largely by upholding the powers of the police to restrict pickets' activities.

Depending on the circumstances, pickets could be charged with any of the following criminal offences, which are explained in detail in Chapter 4:

- obstruction of the highway (see p. 152);
- obstructing a police officer in the execution of his duty (see p. 153);
- using threatening, abusive or insulting words or behaviour with intent to provoke a breach of the peace (see p. 149);
- possessing an offensive weapon (see p. 153).

In addition, the Conspiracy and Protection of Property Act 1875 creates a number of criminal offences, as follows. It is an offence to:

- intimidate someone;
- persistently follow someone from place to place;
- hide somebody's tools or clothes;
- picket someone's house or the place where he works, or the approaches to such a place;
- follow someone around with other people, in a disorderly manner, in the streets;

if the intention is to prevent that person from doing something which he has a legal right to do (e.g. preventing him working) or to compel him to do something which he has a legal right not to do (e.g. compelling him not to work). The maximum penalty is a fine of £20 and/or three months' imprisonment. It is also possible to be charged with **conspiracy** to commit any of these offences; the maximum penalty for a conspiracy charge is an unlimited fine or an unlimited term of imprisonment. For example, in the

Shrewsbury case, Warren, convicted of conspiracy to intimidate, received a sentence of three years' imprisonment.

The Criminal Law Act proposes to restrict the maximum sentence for a conspiracy charge, to the maximum sentence which could be imposed for the substantive offence. (Thus, conspiracy to intimidate would carry the same maximum sentence – three months' imprisonment and/or £20 fine – as the offence of intimidation.)

In a series of cases, the courts have held that:

- police officers have a right to limit the number of pickets in a particular case, in order to prevent a breach of the peace or an obstruction;
- pickets have no right to march in a continuous circle round a factory entrance;
- pickets have no right to insist on stopping lorry drivers making deliveries, even though the pickets' aim is to communicate peacefully with the driver in an effort to persuade him to turn back;
- police may form a cordon between pickets and workers entering the factory, in order to prevent communication.

Before setting up a picket, it is wise to get advice from one or more experienced trade unionists and perhaps a sympatheitc lawyer as well. A few practical suggestions may be offered here:

- wherever possible, official pickets should be given badges, arm bands or other means of visible identification;
- pickets should be given precise instructions, written if necessary, so they are left in no doubt of what is expected of them;
- if slogans are to be used, care should be taken to see that everyone is familiar with the agreed wording and that the words used are unlikely to give rise to police action;
- all reasonable police instructions should be obeyed.
- if, in spite of precautions, a picket is arrested, it is essential to take the names and addresses of any possible witnesses immediately.

More information

You should consult your shop steward or trade-union official. If you are not sure which union to join, contact the TUC, Congress House, 23–8 Great Russell Street, London WC1 (01-636 4030).

Paul O'Higgins, *Workers' Rights*, Arrow (85p).

Maternity Rights for Working Women, NCCL (30p).

Rights for Women, NCCL (75p) – detailed guide to the laws on sex discrimination, equal pay, unfair dismissal and redundancy. Much of the law on employment has been brought together in the Employment Protection (Consolidation) Act 1977.

9. Consumer rights

The main sections of this chapter are:

Every time you pay for goods or services, you enter into a contract. Contracts for the sale of goods cover all purchases in shops, garages, supermarkets and include those made during sales – except auctions – virtually any point where goods change hands for money. Contracts for the supply of services cover, for example, the employment of a plumber, builder, solicitor; using a laundry, cleaners, car park, train, bus or plane; hiring a car or TV; arranging for goods to be repaired or serviced; buying a package holiday.

Sales of goods are protected by law – but so far there is no control by Parliament of service contracts.

TRADES DESCRIPTION ACTS 1968 AND 1972

These Acts impose criminal sanctions upon traders who:

- falsely indicate that goods are cheaper than they are prepared to sell them for;
- falsely describe goods – their size, quality, purpose, age, place of manufacture, etc.;
- give a false description about the service they provide (e.g. about accommodation or facilities at a holiday resort). But this only applies to descriptions which were false at the time they were made; it does not apply to descriptions of services to be supplied in the future. So only if it can be shown that the trader knew or ought to have known that what was said was false at the time, will you be able to make out a case.

Enforcement is by the local authority trading standards

department (known in some areas as the consumer protection or weights and measures department), and you should complain to them.

UNSOLICITED GOODS AND SERVICES ACTS 1971 AND 1975

If you receive goods which you have not ordered there are two things that you can do:

1. Write to the sender giving your name and address, saying that the goods are 'unsolicited' and that you do not want them. He or she then has thirty days in which to collect them at his or her expense. After that you may do as you please with them. *Or*
2. Keep the goods safe and wait for six months. If the goods have not been collected at the end of that time, they become yours to keep, throw away or sell.

It is a criminal offence for the sender to assert a right to payment for goods or services which you did not order; the maximum fine is £200. It is also an offence for the sender to threaten to take you to court or put you on a debtor's blacklist for not paying for something you did not order; the maximum fine is £400.

Until recently small business owners (and large ones too) used to receive bits of paper through the post claiming to be an 'invoice' for a directory entry. Many people paid the sum claimed believing they had to. Now all these so-called invoices are required to have large red overprints saying that they are not invoices and that there is no obligation to pay anything.

Sales of goods

Implied terms

Every sale of goods contract, however made, is controlled by the Sale of Goods Act 1893 as amended by the Supply of Goods (Implied Terms) Act 1973 and contains conditions known as implied terms.

There are four main implied terms laid down:

– that the seller has the right to sell – that means that no one else may claim the goods from you without your having a remedy against the seller;
– that the goods will meet the description applied to them.

These two conditions apply to all sales – private deals as well as deals by traders. So if you buy something through a small ad which turns out not to match its glowing description, you will have a claim against the private individual who sold it to you.

– that the goods will be of merchantable quality except for:
  – defects specifically drawn to your attention before you made the contract; *and*
  – if you *do* examine the goods, defects which you should have noticed then.

Merchantable quality means that the goods should not be broken and/or that they should work properly.

– that the goods will be fit for the purpose for which they were bought – in other words they should do what they are supposed to do.

These two conditions apply only to sales 'in the course of a business'. This primarily covers sales by a trader in his normal line of business, but if a greengrocer sells a secondhand office typewriter, that too is a sale in the course of a business.

If any of these implied terms are broken, the contract can be cancelled and you can claim back your money. They are fundamental to the contract.

Consumer sales

In a 'consumer sale' – when goods are bought by an individual for his own use – none of these implied conditions can be excluded. The seller cannot evade his legal responsibility. The notices you see in shops which say 'no money refunded' or 'no goods exchanged' – or similar terms in written contracts (all of which are called **exemption clauses**) – are of *no legal effect* at all where you are complaining about goods which have turned out to be defective. You can insist on your money back. Indeed, that is the only remedy which the law gives you – you cannot demand a replacement (although, of course, if the trader offers you one and that suits you, you can accept it).

Trivial defects

If the defect is trivial (e.g. a scratch or dent) or only needs a simple adjustment or the replacement of a small part – the trader has not broken a fundamental condition of the contract, which allows cancellation and a refund; but the contract is broken to a lesser extent. In this case you cannot claim back the price, but you are perfectly entitled to demand a reduction of the amount you paid, plus any out-of-pocket expenses you have incurred.

Delivery

When you buy goods, you have an obligation to take delivery of them and to pay for them; equally the seller has the right to hold on to them until he is paid. Note that delivery of goods to a carrier is equivalent in law to a delivery to *you*, although the law does say that the seller must make a reasonable sort of contract with the carrier. So failure to insure adequately goods sent by road, or to register packages of small but costly goods sent by post might well be treated by a court as an unreasonable act by the seller. This would mean that they still belonged to him and if they were lost or damaged, either you would not have to pay for them or would have a good claim for your money back.

Credit notes

Do not accept a credit note for defective goods. Your right is to have your money back. Accepting a credit note may mean that you cannot find anything in the shop that you want and result in you losing your money.

If you are simply returning the goods because you do not like them or because you have changed your mind, the trader has no obligation to accept them back. If he offers a credit note in this case, you should accept it.

If there is no time limit set on it, a credit note is valid for six years.

Guarantees

Many consumer goods come with a maker's guarantee. Always read a guarantee carefully. Some guarantees try to deny you the rights which the law gives you – like the right to claim against the trader – and which cannot be taken away (see p. 214). Others are only valid if you send the maker a card. Others even require you to send faulty goods back *at your expense and to pay* the makers labour charges for putting right faults caused by their carelessness.

You have no legal come-back against the maker of defective goods because your contract is with the trader, not with them. You should always go back to the trader before you try using the maker's guarantee: what went wrong may not have been the trader's fault – but it *is* his or her responsibility (see p. 214).

If the guarantee offers you, say, free replacement of faulty parts for one year, then it may be to your advantage.

Safety of some goods

A number of products have to meet stiff requirements on safety following regulations made under the Consumer Protection Acts 1961 and 1971. To sell in breach of the Acts is a criminal offence. Enforcement is by the local authority – so if you see anything being sold which you suspect infringes these regulations tell the trading standards (weights and measures or consumer protection) department of your local authority.

These are the items so far controlled:

oil heaters
stands for carry-cots
nightdresses
electric appliances
  (colour code for cable
  and flex; earthing)

cooking utensils
fireguards
pencils and graphic instruments
toys (for cellulose content)
glazed ceramic ware
electric blankets

Used goods on hire purchase

Generally if you buy secondhand goods from anyone – a trader or a private individual – you have no right to keep the goods if they turn out to be subject to an HP agreement. The true owner (the HP company) has every right to trace and re-take the goods. Your only remedy is a claim in the county court (see pp. 245–58) for the price and any out-of-pocket expenses against the person who sold them to you.

There is one important exception – motor vehicles. If you buy a used car in good faith and without notice of the existence of any HP agreement, the car becomes yours. The HP company has no claim against you either for money or for return of the goods. Some HP companies will try to bluff you into parting with a vehicle which was bought from someone who had it on HP. Do not be tricked into parting with your property. Simply tell them that you are now the owner by virtue of Part III of the Hire Purchase Act 1965.

Contracts for services

Terms of service contracts

At common law there are implied terms in service contracts. For instance, if you employ someone to do work for you he or she is expected to use the right sort of materials and a reasonable standard of skill; hired goods should be fit for their purpose, and equipment (e.g. in a launderette or car park) should work properly. But all implied terms – and many other terms relevant to the contract – *can be excluded* by the trader in a service contract.

If your service contract is made verbally, or in writing without any terms being imposed, you are protected by common law in much the same way as in the sale of goods.

If you have a written contract that sets out the terms and conditions on which the trader is prepared to do business with you, these terms may be in the contract itself, or in a notice in the shop, or on the ticket or receipt you are given. Provided the existence of the terms is sufficiently drawn to your attention before the contract is made, then signing the contract or taking the ticket means that *you are bound by the small print* (even if you did not see it, read it or understand it).

It is therefore possible for a trader to limit or avoid entirely his or her obligations for any breach of contract or negligence. In some cases, you have no remedy even for death or personal injury caused by their negligence – although this exemption is not allowed for carriage by British Rail, London Transport, in a 'public stage carriage' (a bus on a regular journey) or by air as a fare-paying passenger. Other carriers can and do exclude liability – so if, for instance, you hire a coach, find out what the insurance position is. You may need to take out a special insurance policy.

The moral is to READ AND RE-READ any contract before you sign it. If there are clauses you do not want, cross them out and tell the trader why you are doing so. If he or she will not agree to the deletions, then consider going elsewhere.

The Law Commission has recommended that there should be laws to give protection to the consumer on the same lines as for sales of goods. Some firms are already beginning to amend the worst of their trading terms. In any case, exemption clauses are being interpreted by the courts *against* the person who tries to rely on them.

WORK AND MATERIALS

If you make a service contract for 'work and materials' (e.g. for supplying and fitting new brakes to a car) and there is a term in the contract excluding liability for any defect in the materials, then you have no legal come-back if something goes wrong with them – even though, if you had bought the materials yourself, you would have been fully safeguarded under the Sale of Goods Act. The Law Commission recommends the ending of this inconsistency.

Repairs and services

A trader who repairs or does work to your belongings can keep them until he or she is paid. But if you do not collect them they can only be sold if:

– you have agreed beforehand that a sale can take place if you do not collect them within a limited time (shops often display a notice to this effect); *or*
– if the trader complies with the Disposal of Uncollected Goods Act 1952.

   To do this he or she must:

– display a notice that goods left may be dealt with under the Act;
– give you notice when the work is done;
– after twelve months give you a further written notice by registered post saying that the goods will be sold if you do not collect within fourteen days;
– sell by auction – unless he or she indicates to you the lowest price at which he would sell;
– retain any surplus (after deducting charges) for you to claim.

Food

All food which is sold for human consumption must be of the 'nature, quality and substance' which you ask for. If it is not, the trader – whether retailer or restaurateur – may commit a criminal offence. If you are sold bad food and become ill you have a criminal sanction – prosecution of the offender with a fine on conviction – and a civil remedy – an action in the county court for breach of contract. If you buy tinned or packaged food which is bad, you may also have a claim against the maker, but as your contract was with the trader, you may prefer to claim against him.

   Complaints about bad food should be made to the local authority's environmental health officer who enforces the Food and Drugs Act 1955.

   Of the many regulations about food, the more important cover:

– labelling;
– prepackaging;
– weight (the Common Market is insisting that we should indicate 'average' weight rather than a minimum weight);
– content (all dairy produce is closely regulated);
– weight of packages.

There are also rules about scales. Food which is not prepacked must have its weight made known to you either:

– by measuring or counting it in front of you – with the scales well in view; *or*
– by writing the weight on an invoice; *or*
– by providing you with scales.

Scales are part of the job of the local authority's trading standards officers.

Paying for goods and services

Down payments

There is an important difference between deposits and part-payments.

– A **deposit** is an indication of your desire to enter into a contract. Unless you agree beforehand that the money you are paying is in part-payment and can be repaid, you may not be able to claim it back if the contract falls through.
– A **part-payment** is part of the contract price and if the contract falls through you can claim part or all of it back.

In case of doubt or difficulty, you would do well to get legal advice, e.g. from a citizens' advice bureau or a local consumer advice centre.

Prices

An **estimate** is a guide to the price which the trader will charge. It is not a definite amount – it may vary, but the variation must be reasonable. If the final account is more than 10 or 15 per cent above the estimate you should immediately query this with the trader and refuse to pay unless you are satisfied. If you are not given a reasonable explanation, you may wish to let the trader sue you for the balance and defend on the ground that the amount claimed is excessive.

A **quotation**, once accepted, is a fixed and binding price for which the work will be done. In the absence of any exemption clause or terms in the contract permitting variation, the trader is stuck with the figure quoted; on your part, you must pay the price quoted, even is you think it is too much.

Credit

At present the civil law gives you protection only when you use certain types of credit facilities: e.g. hire purchase and credit sale. Within the next few years, however, as the Consumer Credit Act 1974 is put into effect (see p. 223), all forms of credit to individuals will be subject to control.

HIRE PURCHASE

Under HP the goods do not belong to you until you have paid the last instalment. They belong to the trader, or to a finance company to whom the trader sold them, and who in turn hired them to you. So:

– you cannot sell them or give them away without the owner's consent (but see p. 217);
– you must pay the instalments and take care of the goods;
– you will still have to pay even if the goods are lost or damaged.

Where the HP price (the cash price plus interest) is less than £2,000 you have the protection of the Hire Purchase Act 1965. These rights are:

– Once you have paid one third of the HP price, the owner cannot snatch back the goods if you do not keep up your payments; he *must* go to court for an order. If he acts illegally the goods will almost certainly become yours with no more to pay, or you will be able to recover all your money.

- You have a right to cancel the agreement by surrendering the goods. Usually you have to pay enough to make up one half of the HP price, although if you think that the owner has not lost that much, you can let him sue you and ask the court to decide. It *may* allow you to pay less than half.
- There are **implied conditions** in every HP agreement (whether for new or secondhand goods):
  - that the goods will be of merchantable quality (see p. 214);
  - that they will be fit for their purpose;
  - that they will meet their description;
  - that the seller has the right to part with them.

  The effect of these implied conditions is that serious defects enable you to cancel and recover all money paid. If there are trivial defects you can ask the HP company to put them right or pay for the repair and ask the HP company to pay. If they refuse you can deduct the cost from your instalments – but *write and tell them* what you are doing and why (and keep a copy of the letter), otherwise you will be treated as a defaulting debtor. The implied conditions cannot be excluded in the agreement.

- When you sign an HP agreement away from trade premises (e.g. in your living room) you must be sent a copy of the agreement within seven days. You then have a 'cooling-off' period of three days in which you may change your mind and cancel by notice to the HP company and by returning the goods. You are, of course, entitled to your money back.

Where the HP price is more than £2,000 you have at present no protection against snatch back nor a right to surrender. All will depend on the terms of the agreement, which you should read carefully BEFORE YOU SIGN.

CREDIT SALE

In this case the goods become yours as soon as you pay the first instalment. The Hire Purchase Act 1965 applies to agreements where between £30 and £2,000 is payable in five or more instalments. Because the goods belong to you, you can sell them and use the money towards payment of the instalments, if you need. If you stop paying, the seller cannot seize the goods, but he can go to the court and obtain an order for payment against you, and the court may order that they be handed back.

OTHER FORMS OF CREDIT

personal loans	credit cards
second mortgages	check trading
moneylending loans	mail order
pawnbrokers' loans	budget accounts

Apart from some control of moneylenders and pawnbrokers as traders, there has been virtually no control over the terms, rates of interest or rights of the lenders or borrowers in any of these forms of credit – as many people have found to their cost. For example, you may have bought goods using a personal loan. If the goods are defective, and the trader who sold them is unable or unwilling to put them right, you still have to pay the loan over, maybe, five years, with no redress against the lender.

When the Consumer Credit Act 1974 is fully in force, all kinds of credit will be covered by it.

CONSUMER CREDIT ACT 1974

This Act is designed to give better protection and more information to people who use credit to buy goods. It is being administered by a government agency, the Office of Fair Trading (OFT).

Most businesses who offer credit to consumers need to be licensed by the OFT. They will include moneylenders, pawnbrokers, debt collectors, debt counsellors, credit reference agencies, credit brokers and consumer credit businesses (i.e. any limited company giving credit and anyone giving credit of more than £30). When the licence system is in force, it will be a criminal offence for a trader to operate without an OFT licence, and agreements with unlicensed traders will be legally unenforceable.

These are the main changes under the Act (which is being brought into effect in stages):

– the sort of rights you have under the HP laws (see pp. 221–2) are to be extended to all credit and HP agreements up to £5,000 (except first mortgages on land and one or two other similar loans);
– the 'true rate' of interest is to be disclosed in all agreements and advertisements;
– 'canvassing off trade premises' (i.e. doorstep selling of credit) will be restricted;
– you will have the right to the name and address of any credit-reference agency asked about you (see p. 339);
– if you believe that you are being charged *too high* a rate of interest (even if your agreement was made under the old laws), you can complain to the county court (see p. 245) about an 'extortionate credit bargain' and ask to have it reviewed. This applies to any loan of any amount, whether from a relative or a commercial firm.

If you have any problems, you should contact your local citizens' advice bureau or consumer advice centre. Or you can write to the Office of Fair Trading (address on p. 229).

If you do not pay

Gas and electricity

The gas board can cut off supplies if a bill is not paid within twenty-eight days, but it must give written notice seven days beforehand.

The electricity board must give you twenty-one days' notice, and after a further seven days a final written notice must be sent, saying that if the bill is not paid, the supply will be cut off. Then an official will call and, if you do not allow him in, he has to get a warrant. (See p. 330 for the powers of gas and electricity boards' officials to enter your home.)

If you cannot pay the bill, you should contact the social services department of the local authority or the local DHSS office – although they will usually not help people in employment.

Hire purchase

If you do not keep up your instalments and

- you have paid less than one third of the HP price, the owner of the goods can come and take them away and end the agreement.
- you have paid more than one third of the HP price, the goods cannot be taken away unless:
  - you choose to end the HP agreement (paying the missed instalments up to date) and allow the goods to be taken away; *or*
  - the owner gets a court order for possession of the goods.

If you choose to end the agreement you will have to pay or have paid up to one half of the HP price.

Harassment of debtors

A useful sanction against people who accuse you of owing money is found in the Administration of Justice Act 1970, s. 40. This makes it a criminal offence to try to force payment of any debt (whether or not you owe it) by:

- harassing you in a way which by its manner or frequency or threat of publicity makes you or your family alarmed, distressed or humiliated; *or*
- falsely suggesting that, by not paying, you commit a crime; *or*
- falsely representing that he is officially authorized to claim payment; *or*
- issuing a document which pretends to be official. This covers the 'blue frightener' which some debt collectors use. (They look like a county court form.)

Though this section is useful in theory, the police are often reluctant to take any action. But very often a strong reference to the Act in a letter to the firm stops the harassment. If not, you can go to the magistrates' court and ask for a summons yourself (see p. 77).

What you can do if things go wrong

Go back to the trader

This is the first thing to do. Ask for the person in charge at the shop, showroom, station or company. Most difficulties are resolved at local level and can be solved quite quickly – even amicably. If this is not possible, then:

– for gas, electricity, coal, transport, Post Office, water: see pp. 518–22;
– for anything else:

Go to a citizens' advice bureau or consumer advice centre

They will be able to do two things initially: try to mediate with the trader and explain to you both what your legal position really is, and they can also help you to write a letter to the trader (you should keep a copy) setting out your case.

If this does not work . . .

What you do next depends on who you are dealing with

Many traders belong to a trade association. If the association is party to one of the Office of Fair Trading codes of practice (see below) the association has to help you.

There are trade or professional bodies for central heating, master builders, plumbers, shoe repairers, dry cleaners, coal merchants, painters and decorators, roofing contractors, furnishers, as well as many others. (For complaints against the professions, see p. 524; against doctors, p. 473; against lawyers, p. 503.)

Complaints about new houses may be investigated by the

National House Building Council, 58 Portland Place, London
W1.

Local authorities have statutory duties to supervise food,
hygiene, weights and measures, education, street lighting and
consumer protection in a wide sense. (For the complaints procedure, see p. 213.)

CODES OF PRACTICE

The Office of Fair Trading has helped in the introduction by
trade and manufacturing groups of codes of practice which set
out a system of dealing with complaints. The codes that have
had the blessing of the OFT now include:

– sales of new and secondhand cars;
– shoe repairs;
– sale of footwear;
– servicing of domestic electrical appliances;
– a used-car code for Scotland;
– vehicle body repairs;
– domestic laundry and dry cleaning;
– travel agents and tour operators.

Information about these codes is available from your local
advice centre, the trading standards department of your local
authority or from the OFT itself (address on p. 229).

A typical code contains a promise by the trade that they will
sell goods in reasonable condition; that they will be properly
serviced; that spare parts will be made available for a substantial
period; that complaints will be quickly and efficiently dealt with;
and that the trade association will try conciliation between the
customer and the trader concerned. They also contain arbitration schemes – but these are generally more expensive than
using the county court.

The codes only apply to traders who belong to the appropriate
association. If your trader doesn't belong, the association will not
be able to deal with your complaint.

If you cannot use the above methods, you can consider:

Making a claim in the county court

If the dispute is for not more than £200 you can make a 'small claim' in the county court. A citizens' advice bureau or consumer advice centre should be able to help you fill out the forms, or to put you in touch with a solicitor for larger claims (see p. 245).

It is quite easy to make a claim in the county court yourself. Recent changes enable small claims to be arbitrated without too much expense and without the use of lawyers. An excellent free booklet called *Small Claims in the County Court* is available from any county court. This sets out in detail the way to make your claim and explains the procedure and some of the pitfalls. (See also pp. 245–58).

In Manchester and Westminster there are also two independently funded schemes which exist solely to deal with small claims by private individuals, where the trader accepts this procedure (addresses on p. 229).

The trader is likely to be the person you sue, because of the contract between you. It is very rare to bring an action against the maker unless their negligence causes the goods to be dangerous.

Compensation

Quite apart from any civil claim you may have, when a trader breaks a criminal law, there is a useful power given to criminal courts to award compensation to the victim. This power is contained in the Powers of the Criminal Courts Act 1973, s. 35. Compensation is usually given where it is a clear-cut case and where there is no dispute about the amount you have lost. Common examples are cases under the Trades Descriptions, Consumer Protection, Food and Drugs, and Weights and Measures Acts, although the power covers all types of crime. You should tell the prosecutor or the court that you want to claim compensation.

More information

Citizens' advice bureaux.
Consumer advice centres.
Law centres (see p. 507).

Advertising Standards Authority, 15–17 Ridgemount Street, London WC1.

Consumers' Association, 14 Buckingham Street, London WC2 – publishers of *Which?*, *Motoring Which?*, *Money Which?*, *Handyman Which?*, *Holiday Which?* and many books of general help.

Office of Fair Trading, Field House, Breams Buildings, London EC4 (01-242 2858). Consumer credit licensing is based at Bromyard Avenue, Acton, London W3 (01-749 9151), and there is a *public register of licensed traders* at Chancery House, 53 Chancery Lane, London WC2.

Manchester Arbitration Scheme for Small Claims, 2 Ridgefield, Deansgate, Manchester 2.

Westminster Small Claims Court, 153 Ebury Street, London SW1.

10. Race discrimination

This chapter deals with:

The Race Relations Act 1976 replaces the previous Race Relations Acts of 1965 and 1968. The Act deals with race discrimination in employment and training; education; housing; the provision of goods, facilities and services; and advertising. It also sets up the Commission for Racial Equality, which replaces the Community Relations Commission and the Race Relations Board. The Act applies in England, Wales and Scotland, but not in Northern Ireland. Complaints by individuals who believe they have been discriminated against will no longer go to the Race Relations Board, but to the industrial tribunals (for employment matters) or the county court (in Scotland, sheriff courts).

Discrimination, under the Act, means treating someone less favourably on grounds of race, i.e. because of his or her colour, race, nationality or citizenship, ethnic or national origins. Discrimination can also mean **victimizing** someone for taking action under the Race Relations Act.

Discrimination can be of two kinds: direct and indirect. **Direct discrimination** means what it says: directly discriminating against you on racial grounds. Refusing to give you a job, sell you a house or rent a flat, or not allowing you to go into a pub, because of your race, are all examples of direct discrimination. **Segregating** people according to race is also discrimination.

Indirect discrimination means applying a condition or test which puts a particular racial group at a disadvantage, even though the test is apparently applied equally to everyone. The test won't necessarily be designed to disadvantage people of a particular race: its effect may be quite accidental. But it can still be unlawful if the effect is in fact to exclude a larger proportion of people of a particular race, and if the test is not 'justifiable'. The Act does not explain what 'justified' means: it just says that the test has to be 'justifiable irrespective of the colour, race, nationality or ethnic or national origins of the person to whom it is applied'.

The following is an example of indirect discrimination:

An employer tells an employment agency that the firm only wants candidates who speak good English, without foreign accents. Although the employer does not specify 'whites only', the effect of the requirement is to exclude many people from ethnic minority groups. The employer might try to argue that the requirement was 'justifiable' in terms of the job. This would be difficult to accept if the job did not involve contact with customers, or if the applicant's English, although accented, was quite comprehensible.

The following sections deal with the different areas where discrimination may be unlawful: employment and training; education; housing; goods, facilities and services (including clubs); and advertising. In each area, there are some exceptions, where racial discrimination is still permitted.

Employment and training

It is unlawful for an **employer** to discriminate against you on grounds of race in any of the following ways:

– refusing to hire you or consider you for a job;
– offering you a job on less favourable terms than other people;
– refusing to promote you or transfer you to another job;
– refusing to make provision for you to be trained;
– giving you less favourable fringe benefits;
– putting you on short-time work, dismissing you or making you redundant.

In order to bring a case to the industrial tribunal (see p. 203 for more information about making a complaint of race discrimination) you would need to show that you were being treated less favourably than someone of different racial or national origins would be treated.

The Act covers both permanent and temporary jobs, whatever the size of the firm. It covers apprentices and trainees as well as other employees; partners in a firm of six or more partners (such as a solicitors' firm); the police (who are not, technically, employees); sub-contracted workers (such as the 'lump' building workers or night cleaners) and employment agencies.

It will be unlawful for the Government to discriminate on race grounds in appointing people to serve on public bodies. It will also be unlawful for **trade unions and professional associations** to discriminate in any of the following ways:

– deciding who to admit to membership;
– refusing to let you join;
– only allowing you to join on less favourable terms;
– by giving you fewer benefits, facilities or services, or refusing to let you have any of these benefits (e.g. legal services, representation in a dispute);
– expelling you or subjecting you to any other disadvantage.

Similarly, it will be unlawful for any **licensing body** (e.g. the Law Society, which licenses solicitors; the Director General of Fair Trading, who licenses credit and hire businesses; the police, who license taxi-drivers) to discriminate on race grounds in deciding who can have a licence. Furthermore, whenever one of these bodies has to consider an applicant's 'good character' before giving a licence, they will be able to take into account any evidence about previous unlawful race discrimination. So, for instance, magistrates who are renewing a publican's licence should also take account of any evidence that he or his employees had previously refused to serve black people.

A complaint about race discrimination in the field of employment must be brought to an industrial tribunal (see p. 203) within three months.

Exceptions

Racial discrimination is still lawful in any of the following situations:

– employment in a private household;
– if an employer wants to employ someone who is not ordinarily resident in Great Britain, but who will be trained here before going to work abroad;
– employment of workers on ships who were recruited outside Great Britain;
– employment outside Great Britain;
– employment in dramatic performances, or for artist's or photographic modelling, where someone of a particular racial group is needed for reasons of 'authenticity';
– employment in restaurants, etc., with a particular setting where someone of a particular racial group is needed for reasons of authenticity (e.g. Chinese waiters in a Chinese restaurant);
– employment of someone to provide personal services to a particular racial group, where someone of the same racial group can do the job most effectively.

The last three exceptions are called **genuine occupational qualification** exceptions. In any of these cases, the employer must try to fill a vacancy from existing workers before discriminating on racial grounds.

Training

It is unlawful for any of the following training organizations to discriminate on race grounds:

– industrial training boards;
– Manpower Services Commission;
– Employment Services Agency;
– Training Services Agency;
– employers' organizations which provide training;
– any other organization designated by the Secretary of State.

These organizations will, however, be allowed to practise

positive discrimination where there have been no people of a particular racial group, or very few, doing a particular kind of work, either in the whole of Great Britain or in a region, in the previous twelve months. In this case they will be allowed to run training courses or provide facilities for that racial group only, or encourage people from that group to take up a particular kind of work.

Employers will also be allowed to run training courses for a particular racial group only, or encourage them to take up a particular kind of work, where there have been no people of that racial group, or very few, doing that kind of work in the firm during the previous twelve months.

Trade unions and professional organizations are also allowed to organize special training courses to encourage people from a particular racial group to hold posts within the organization (e.g. as shop stewards or officials), where there have been very few or no people from that group holding such posts in the previous twelve months.

Education

The Race Relations Act applies to schools or colleges maintained by a local education authority (LEA), independent ('public' or fee-paying) schools or colleges, special schools and universities. The Secretary of State can also designate other establishments to be covered by the law, such as polytechnics.

It is unlawful for any educational body (including the governors of a school or college and an LEA) to discriminate on race grounds in any of the following ways:

- the terms on which they admit students;
- refusing to admit you;
- providing more facilities or better facilities for particular racial groups;
- expelling you or in any other way putting you at a disadvantage;
- acting in any other way which involves race discrimination.

If you or your child has been discriminated against, you will have to make a complaint to the Secretary of State for Education (this does not apply to complaints against independent schools or universities). The Minister will have two months in which to do something about your complaint. If the Minister rejects your complaint, or the two months runs out, you can make a complaint to the county court. (See p. 245 for what this involves.) A county court action must be brought *within six months* (or eight months if the complaint has first gone to the Ministers).

The Act also puts a general duty on LEAs to ensure that educational facilities are provided without race discrimination. You have no way of enforcing this general duty, although of course you can draw the attention of local councillors and school governors to it. The only way it can be enforced is by the Secretary of State ordering the LEA to carry out its duties reasonably.

It is, however, lawful for LEAs and other bodies to provide special facilities to meet the particular needs of a racial group (e.g. for language classes).

Overseas students

There is only one exception to the education sections of the Act, and this concerns overseas students. It will be lawful for any organization or individual providing education or training to discriminate on racial grounds against people who are not ordinarily resident in Great Britain and who do not intend to remain in Great Britain after their period of education or training. This means, for instance, that it will be lawful for colleges or halls of residence to charge higher fees to overseas students.

Housing

Housing and premises, such as business premises, are covered by the Act. In general it is unlawful for someone to discriminate on race grounds, when selling, letting or managing property, in any of the following ways:

– in the terms on which you are offered the premises;
– by refusing to let you buy or rent the premises;

- by treating you differently from other people on a list of people wanting to buy or rent the premises;
- by refusing to agree to the transfer of a lease to you;
- by refusing you access to any benefits or facilities in premises you occupy;
- by evicting you or subjecting you to any other disadvantage.

The law covers private landlords and owner-occupiers, as well as local authorities.

Exceptions

There are three main exceptions. Firstly, owner-occupiers selling or letting their property are excluded, provided that they do not advertise or use an estate agent.

Secondly, small residential premises (e.g. small boarding houses or shared flats) are excluded. To qualify as 'small residential premises', the owner or occupier (or a near relative) has to live permanently in the house or flat; at least part of the house or flat, other than stairs or storage space, has to be shared with other people; and there must be only two households (other than the owner or occupier's household) or not more than six people (other than the owner or occupier's household) in the house or flat. A boarding house containing more than six lodgers, in addition to the landlord/lady's family, would not be allowed to discriminate, but a boarding house with fewer lodgers would be allowed to.

Thirdly, charities and voluntary organizations whose main purpose is to provide benefits for a particular racial group are allowed to provide housing for that group only. But these organizations will not be allowed to discriminate on grounds of colour, only on grounds of race, nationality or national or ethnic origin.

Goods, facilities and services

The Act covers any 'goods, facilities or services' which are offered to the public or a section of the public. This means, for instance, the services and facilities offered by hotels, boarding-houses, pubs and restaurants, banks, insurance companies, credit houses and HP firms, transport authorities and local authorities. Direct or indirect discrimination (as explained on p. 230) by any such organization will be unlawful.

If you have been discriminated against on race grounds by someone offering goods or services to the public, you can bring an action in the county court. You will find information about how to do this on p. 245. The Commission for Racial Equality (see p. 239) may also be able to help. *An action must be brought within six months.*

Any contract (e.g. to buy goods or supply services) which includes a term which discriminates on race grounds is void and can be amended by applying to the county court (see p. 249).

Exceptions

There are a number of situations where race discrimination remains lawful:

1. Any arrangement where someone takes a child, elderly person or someone needing special care and attention, into his or her home to be looked after (e.g. fostering children).
2. Goods, facilities or services provided outside Great Britain, or insurance arrangements to cover a situation outside Great Britain. (But the services of, for instance, a travel agent in this country, even though it arranges foreign travel, will still be covered.)
3. Charities and voluntary organizations whose main purpose is to provide benefits for a particular racial group (but these organizations will not be allowed to discriminate on grounds of *colour*, only on grounds of race, nationality or national or ethnic origin).
4. Special arrangements can be made for members of a particular racial group who have particular needs for education, training, welfare, etc. (e.g. language classes).
5. Discrimination on grounds of nationality, place of birth or length of residence is permitted in:

- selecting people to represent a particular place or country in a sport or game; *or*
- deciding who is eligible to compete in any sport or game, according to the rules of the competition.

Clubs

Under the previous race relations laws private clubs, such as political and working-men's clubs, were allowed to discriminate on race grounds. It is now unlawful for any club or society with twenty-five or more members to discriminate on race grounds in any of the following ways:

- refusing to allow you to join;
- offering you less favourable terms of membership;
- giving you fewer benefits, facilities or services or refusing to let you use or have any of these benefits (e.g. social facilities);
- expelling you from the club, or changing the terms of your membership;
- putting you at a disadvantage in any other way.

But a club or society whose main purpose is to provide benefits for people of a particular racial group, whatever its size, will continue to be allowed to discriminate on race grounds (although not on grounds of colour).

Advertisements

It is unlawful to insert or publish an advertisement which indicates that an employer, a company or anyone else intends to discriminate unlawfully. Only the Commission for Racial Equality (see below) will be able to take action against discriminatory advertisements, but if you see an advertisement which you believe breaks the law you should bring it to the Commission's attention.

Where there is an exception in the law which allows someone to discriminate on race grounds, then an advertisement which specifies race will usually be lawful. But an advertisement for employment in a private household must not be racially discriminatory.

Commission for Racial Equality

The Commission for Racial Equality (CRE) replaces the Race Relations Board and the Community Relations Commission. Under the previous laws, if you believed that you had been discriminated against, you had to take your complaint to the board, which would investigate it and, if necessary, try to conciliate between you and the person who had discriminated. Only the board could take a case to court.

Under the new law, individuals will be able to take their case direct to an industrial tribunal (in an employment case) or the county court (in a case concerning education, housing, goods or services). The CRE will be able to help individuals, especially if the case is complicated or is a 'test case', by writing letters to the company accused of discriminating or by providing legal representation. But the Commission's main job will be to attack general patterns of discrimination, even where no individual has made a complaint.

The Commission's chairperson is David Lane, and its address is on p. 242.

Investigations

The CRE can conduct 'formal investigations' into any subject it chooses – for instance, employment patterns in a region; the recruitment policies of a firm; housing-allocation policies in local authorities, and so on.

The CRE must give notice of its intention to hold a formal investigation, and publish terms of reference. If it is investigating a particular organization or person, and states in the terms of reference that it believes they are discriminating unlawfully, then it will be able to require them to give evidence or produce information. The power to get evidence and summon witnesses will also apply if it is holding the investigation at the request of the Secretary of State, or if the aim of the investigation is to see whether a non-discrimination notice (see below) is being obeyed. The penalty for disobeying an order requiring someone to produce information is £10 (although presumably the CRE can go on demanding the information until it is supplied); the maximum penalty for supplying false information is a fine of £400.

Either during or at the end of an investigation, the CRE can make recommendations for changes which would promote equality of opportunity. These recommendations will not be legally binding, but could be used to bring pressure on the organization or person, or as evidence in an individual case against them.

Non-discrimination notices

The CRE will be able to issue a non-discrimination notice if it decides, during a formal investigation, that an organization or individual has discriminated unlawfully.

The non-discrimination notice requires the organization or person named in it to stop discriminating unlawfully and, if necessary, to let the people concerned know what changes have been made in their procedures or arrangements in order to obey the non-discrimination notice. Before issuing the notice, the CRE must warn the organization or person concerned that it is thinking of doing so, and give it twenty-eight days to make representations. Once the notice is issued, the organization or person named can appeal to the industrial tribunal (in an employment case` or the county court. The appeal must be made within six weeks of when the CRE issued the notice.

If the appeal fails, or no appeal is made, the non-discrimination notice becomes final – in other words, it can be enforced. The CRE will keep a register of notices which have become final and anyone is entitled to inspect this register and take a copy of any notice in it.

Injunctions

A non-discrimination notice can only be enforced if the CRE goes to court and gets an injunction. It can do this at any time within five years of when the notice becomes final, if it thinks that the organization or person named in the notice will continue to discriminate unlawfully.

An injunction is an order by a county court or the High Court ordering someone to stop acting in a particular way. If the organization or person does not obey the injunction, they will be 'in contempt of court' and the CRE can apply to the court to have the people involved fined or imprisoned. (See p. 318 for more on contempt of court.)

The CRE may also apply to the county court for an injunction, without issuing a non-discrimination notice, in the following circumstances:

– someone has successfully brought a complaint against an individual or organization and the CRE considers that the individual or organization will go on discriminating unlawfully;
– if the CRE considers that someone has discriminated unlawfully and is likely to go on doing so; in this case, the CRE must itself apply to the industrial tribunal or county court to get a finding that the person concerned has in fact discriminated unlawfully;
– if the CRE considers that someone has published an unlawful advertisement (see p. 238); instructed an employee or agent to discriminate unlawfully; or put pressure on anybody else to discriminate unlawfully. Only the CRE can take action on these kinds of unlawful acts.

Incitement to racial hatred

It is a criminal offence to use threatening, abusive or insulting words in a public place in circumstances where racial hatred is likely to be stirred up. It is also an offence to publish or distribute threatening, abusive or insulting written material in circumstances where racial hatred is likely to be stirred up. It does not matter whether the person accused *intended* to incite people to racial hatred or not.

There is an exception for fair and accurate reporting of court proceedings, provided the report is published at the time, or of proceedings in Parliament.

A prosecution within England and Wales can only be brought with the consent of the Attorney General. The maximum penalty in the magistrates' court is six months' imprisonment and/or a fine of £1,000; in the Crown Court, two years' imprisonment and/or an unlimited fine.

More information

Commission for Racial Equality, 10/12 Allington Street, London SW1 (01-828 7022).

Community relations councils exist throughout the country. You can get the address of your nearest CRC from a citizens' advice bureau, the town hall or the telephone directory.

NCCL, 186 Kings Cross Road, London WC1 (01-278 4575) will advise people on their rights under the Race Relations Act; takes up cases involving race discrimination or alleged police harassment; and publishes factsheets on police powers in Urdu, Gujarati, Punjabi, Bengali and Hindi.

Runnymede Trust, 62 Chandos Place, London WC2 (01-836 3266) – an education charity which publishes information and pamphlets on immigration and race relations.

11. Your rights in the civil courts

This chapter deals with:

There is no clear-cut division between civil cases, which are dealt with in this chapter, and criminal cases, dealt with in Chapter 2. Generally speaking, a **civil case** involves a dispute between two individuals, or between an individual and a firm or a public body. Examples of civil cases are: matrimonial claims; an action by a landlord against a tenant for rent arrears or eviction; an action by a consumer against a company which sold faulty goods; a claim for damages for personal injuries, resulting from a road accident or an accident at work. While the police are involved in the vast majority of criminal cases, it is very rare for the police to be involved in a civil case.

The different civil courts

Although **magistrates' courts** are mainly concerned with criminal matters, they are also responsible for deciding some civil cases – especially maintenance claims and separation orders (see p. 345).

Most civil cases are dealt with by the **county courts**, which are responsible for claims for not more than £2,000 (and claims for more if both sides agree); claims involving the administration of estates, trusts and mortgages where the amount of the estate, etc. is not more than £5,000; landlord and tenant cases, and other actions concerning possession of land where the rateable value is not more than £1,000; and undefended divorce cases (only in some courts). There are county courts in all major towns.

The county court judge may in special cases sit with lay 'assessors' (e.g. in a case involving sex or race discrimination) who advise the judge on the facts of a case. There is also a court registrar who deals with rent summonses and claims, hire-purchase debts and so on, where the amount claimed is less than £200. The registrar can deal with a case involving more money, if both sides in the case agree. The registrar also deals with pre-liminary matters (see p. 250).

The **High Court** of Justice is based at the Royal Courts of Justice in the Strand, London. It also has a number of local offices called District Registries. There are three divisions of the High Court; Queen's Bench (which deals mainly with claims about breach of contract and personal injuries); Chancery (trusts, estates, wills, etc.); and the Family Division (which deals with ward-of-court proceedings, contested divorce and other matters involving the family). Most cases are heard by a High Court judge sitting alone. Where the High Court is hearing an appeal from the magistrates' court or a tribunal, there are usually three judges, who decide the case by a majority or unanimously. In this case, they are called the Divisional Court.

Magistrates' courts

Although magistrates' courts mainly deal with criminal cases, they also deal with some civil matters, particularly separation orders, custody applications and maintenance claims, and some actions for debt. The magistrates' court can normally only deal with complaints relating to something which happened within the area covered by the court. You will find the address of the local magistrates' court in the telephone directory under 'Courts'.

A civil case in the magistrates' court starts when someone makes a formal complaint to the court, asking the magistrate to issue a **summons** requiring the person complained about to appear before the court. The person making the complaint is called the **complaint**; the person complained about is called the **defendant**. If the magistrate agrees to issue a summons, a date will be set for the hearing. If the complainant appears in court, and the defendant does not (even though the summons was served on him or her), the court may decide to deal with the case in the absence of the defendant. Alternatively, the case may be adjourned, or a summons issued for the defendant's arrest. If the complainant loses the case, she or he may be ordered to pay the defendant's costs; if the defendant loses, she or he may be ordered to pay the complainant's costs.

The matrimonial and family matters that are dealt with by magistrates are described in detail in Chapter 15.

The magistrates' courts also deal with some cases of debt, e.g. non-payment of income tax. The court can make an order for payment, which may be by instalments to the clerk of the court. The order can be enforced by a distress warrant (which means that your goods can be seized) or by an order committing you to prison. These proceedings are very rare.

County courts

It is quite possible to bring a county court action without the help of a lawyer, although in a complicated case, especially where the sum involved is over £200, it may be sensible to get legal advice. Examples of when you could bring a county court action are:

– you have been hit by a car and want to claim damages from the driver;
– you have bought a faulty TV or washing machine and the firm will not give you satisfaction (see Chapter 9 for consumer rights and details of the small-claims procedure);
– you have been discriminated against on grounds of sex or race when trying to get a loan or a mortgage, buy goods or use some service or facility available to the public;
– your roof leaks and the landlord refuses to mend it.

The person starting a county court action (**suing**) is called the **plaintiff**; the person defending the action is called the **defen-**

dant. The rest of this section is mainly concerned with how to start an action. If you find yourself having to defend an action the procedure set out later (see p. 250) is equally applicable to you.

How to sue in the County court

Before you make your complaint, you have to decide who the defendant will be in your case. You also have to get full details of name and address, since the court has to make sure that the summons reaches the defendant. It is not the court's job to check the name and address.

If you are complaining against a *limited company*, the summons has to be delivered or sent to the registered office which may not be the address at which you have been dealing with the company. A limited company usually has the word 'Limited' or 'Ltd' after its name, on the writing paper or invoice, or in the telephone directory. If you cannot find the address, ask at the Companies Register, Companies House, 55–71 City Road, London EC1 (01-253 9393).

If the firm's name does not include 'Ltd', it is probably a one-man business or a partnership. In this case, you can use the address where the firm carries on business or where one of the partners lives. You should sue the firm without naming the partners individually: if you only sue one of the partners and win, but he is unable to pay, you won't then be able to sue the others, whereas if you sue the firm, you can be more certain of getting the compensation if you win. You may be able to get more information about a particular firm from the Registry of Business Names, Pembroke House, 40–56 City Road, London EC1.

PARTICULARS OF CLAIM

When you start an action you must give the court written details of what you are claiming. This is called the 'particulars of claim' and should set out quite briefly the facts of the situation which support your claim. You do not have to give the whole story, but simply enough to tell the defendant why you are making the claim and how much you want him to pay you.

The particulars should be headed with the name of the court, with a space for the plaint number which will be allocated when you issue the summons. Below this are the names of the plaintiff and the defendant. A specimen is on p. 248.

You then have to set out a brief statement of the facts of your claim and the sum of money or other remedy for which you are suing (see p. 256). It is usual to write in the third person and to set out your claim in numbered paragraphs. If you have trouble wording your claim, the court office will be able to help.

The particulars of claim don't have to be typewritten, provided that your writing is clear. You will need one copy for the court, and one copy for each defendant. You should make sure that you also keep a copy for your own use.

CHOOSING THE RIGHT COURT

England and Wales are divided into districts in each of which there is a county court. If you do not know which is the right court for your action you should inquire at the nearest county court office. County courts are usually listed in the telephone directory under 'Courts'.

THE REQUEST

To start your action, you must fill in a form called a 'request'. The court needs this in order to prepare the summons, which is the document that the defendant receives from the court telling him about your claim and what he has to do. A request form can be got from any county court office and the court staff will help you complete it.

COURT FEES

When you hand in your completed request form to the court, you will also have to pay the court fee, in cash. Court fees are based on the amount of damages you are claiming. The minimum fee is

IN THE ANYTOWN COUNTY COURT   Plaint Number:

                    BETWEEN

                        JANE SMITH   Plaintiff

                            and

            UNSATISFACTORY WASHING MACHINES LTD   Defendants

PARTICULARS OF CLAIM

1. On 31 March 1977 the Plaintiff visited the showrooms of the
    defendants at 3 High Street, Anytown and purchased a new
    washing machine, make Nogood Mark 1.
2. The full price of £.... was paid in cash.
3. The following week, when the washing machine was being used for
    the third time, the machine broke down, flooding the Plaintiff's
    kitchen.
4. On 11 April 1977 the Plaintiff wrote to the defendants requesting
    replacement of the machine. The defendants did not reply to this
    letter.
5. On 26 April 1977 the Plaintiff visited the showrooms of the defendants.
6. The defendants, through their servant or agent,[1] refused to supply a
    new replacement machine.
7. By reason of the matters aforesaid, the Plaintiff has suffered loss
    and damage.

AND THE PLAINTIFF CLAIMS

1. An injunction requiring the defendants to supply a new machine of
    the same make.
2. Damages listed to £.......[2]
3. Costs.

                                        Jane Smith
    1st May 1977   (signature)

    The Plaintiff's address for service is.......

---

[1] i.e. the manager or person who served you at the showroom.

[2] The court office will advise on how much you should claim. In this
case, damages should include a sum for the time and trouble involved in
cleaning the kitchen; the expense of using a launderette for the weeks between when the machine failed and the hearing; out of pocket expenses (e.g.
the cost of going back to the showroom, sending any letters to the company).

£5, which applies if you are claiming less than £50. Add to that 10p for each extra £1 you are claiming. The maximum fee is £15 which applies if you are claiming £150 or more. These fees vary from time to time but you can get advice from your local county court.

A court bailiff usually serves the summons on the defendant, and for this you will have to pay an extra £2.00 at the same time. You can serve the summons yourself, but it is better to let the court do it for you. That way, you are sure that the summons will be properly served.

DOCUMENTS TO BE LEFT WITH THE COURT

You have to leave with the court two copies of the particulars of claim. If there is more than one defendant, you need to leave an extra copy for each additional defendant. If you can't go to the court office in person, you can do this by post. You should send:

- the request form, properly filled in;
- the right number of copies of the particulars of claim;
- the fee (a crossed postal or money order, payable to the 'Paymaster General' – cheques are not accepted);
- a stamped envelope addressed to yourself. This is so that the court can send you the plaint note.

You should send all these items to the chief clerk at your nearest county court.

THE PLAINT NOTE

The court will now prepare the summons to be served on the defendant. You will be given a **plaint note**. This is a receipt for your fee and also contains a plaint number for your case. This number is very important because all court records are filed under plaint numbers and not under the names of the people involved. Always refer to the plaint number when writing or phoning the court about your case.

DEFENDED ACTIONS

It is very unlikely that the defendant will admit that you have a valid claim. If he or she wants to defend the action, he or she has to enter a defence within fourteen days after the summons is served. You will then be sent a copy of the defence.

The summons will fix a date, usually about six weeks ahead, when you and the defendant must attend court. This date will usually be a preliminary hearing, or a **pre-trial review**. The date will be shown on your plaint note, and you must attend yourself or send someone along to represent you.

If the action is for a debt or fixed amount, e.g. the price of goods sold, you will be entitled to 'enter judgment' by completing a form in the county court if the defence has not been sent within fourteen days. You will then have won your case. But a judgment can be set aside by the court if the defendant asks, and shows, there is a valid defence. If this type of case is contested, a pre-trail review will be fixed and the procedure below will follow.

THE PRE-TRIAL REVIEW

Unless you attend the pre-trial review, the action may be struck out (i.e. cancelled). If this happens you can apply to the court to restore the case to be heard another day. The registrar of the court (who acts instead of the judge in the pre-trial review) decides whether or not to restore the case. If he does, he may require you to pay any expense that the defendant has been put to as a result of your failure to turn up in court. If he refuses to restore it, your action is at an end and you will have to start all over again in order to make your complaint.

The pre-trial review usually takes place in private and is informal. It is really a discussion between the registrar and the parties as to how the action should be dealt with.

If the defendant does not attend, you may be able to have the case decided. You will probably have to give evidence, in which case the registrar will ask you to stand up and take the oath or affirm. You can then sit down and tell the registrar the facts of the case. You should remember to bring with you any letters, bills, receipts or other pieces of information which will help you to prove your case. If the registrar is satisfied that you have proved your case, he will give a decision and enter judgment.

When you and the defendant both attend the pre-trial review, the registrar will look at the papers and if he thinks that the particulars of claim don't give enough information, he may ask you to explain the matter more fully. He may then deal with the defendant's defence in the same way, or, if the defendant hasn't submitted one, he will find out whether he or she has a defence and if so, what it is. If you want more information from the defendant at this stage, you should say so.

You may find that you have left something out of your particulars of claim, or that as a result of further inquiries you want to alter them. You can do this before the pre-trial review, simply by sending copies of the amended particulars to the defendant and the court (and keeping a copy for yourself). If you want to alter them at the pre-trial review, you must ask the registrar for permission.

DIRECTIONS

After the pre-trial review, the registrar will give any directions which may be needed to prepare the action for trial and save unnecessary expense.

If the defendant wants to dispute your claim and has not filed a defence, the registrar will usually direct him or her to file it within a certain time (usually fourteen days). Very often, the defendant won't be allowed to defend the claim unless the defence is filed within this time limit. This is to stop a defendant who has failed to file a defence from turning up at the trial and asking to be heard; and it saves you the expense of bringing witnesses to court, who wouldn't be needed if the action is undefended. But the defendant can ask to have more time to file the defence, if he or she cannot do it within the time given; if you object, he or she can apply to the registrar who will decide whether or not extra time should be given.

FURTHER DETAILS OF YOUR CLAIM AND THE DEFENCE

You are entitled to know the facts on which your opponent is relying to defend the case. And he or she is entitled to know the facts on which you base your complaint. Without this information, neither of you would know what witnesses or documents to bring to court. It is possible that the registrar, without being asked, may direct either you or the defendant to supply extra details, but you should also consider whether there is anything more you need to know about the defence.

PRODUCTION OF DOCUMENTS

Although neither you nor the defendant can be required to say in advance what evidence you will call in support of your case, you can be ordered to produce all the documents you have which are relevant to the case. With some exceptions, each of you must, if ordered by the registrar or court, disclose to the other side all the documents that you are going to produce in court. This is called an **order for discovery**.

If necessary, the registrar will order the two of you to exchange lists of all your documents within a stated time and allow each of you to inspect the documents disclosed. Nowadays, many solicitors find it simpler to send each other photocopies of their client's documents, rather than go to the trouble of exchanging lists, especially where there are only a few documents involved. You are, of course, allowed to charge for the reasonable cost of supplying copies.

FURTHER HELP

Although the registrar cannot help you in preparing your case, it would not be wrong for him to indicate in general terms the sort of evidence you will need to prove your claim. He might suggest that you should try to find a witness who could support a particular aspect of your case, or that you should produce certain documents at the hearing. If you are in doubt, do not hesitate to put your problem to the registrar.

DATE OF THE HEARING

The registrar will fix a date for the trial. You should tell the registrar if there are any dates when, because of a holiday or work commitment, you or your witnesses cannot appear at court.

If, at a later date, you have to ask for the date to be changed, then you may have to pay any extra expense which this means for the defendant. If it is necessary to change the date, write to the defendant as soon as possible and see if he or she will agree. If so, you can write to the court enclosing his letter of agreement and ask for a new date. If he or she refuses, you will have to make an application to the court, in writing, for a new date.

PREPARING YOUR CASE

When your case is heard, the court will have to consider the evidence which is presented to it. It then has to decide whether or not you have proved your case. Sometimes the evidence will be so finely balanced that it will be almost impossible to say who is in the right. In such a case, the court is entitled to say that you have lost your case, because it is up to you to prove your claim. It is therefore vitally important that you give the court all the evidence that you can to support your complaint.

WITNESSES

In many cases, you and the defendant will be the most important, and perhaps the only, witnesses. Each of you will be giving your version of what happened, and your stories may conflict in many respects. If possible, you should bring along any other people who saw or heard what happened, or who can support your story. If you are relying on witnesses, it is essential that they come to court so that they can give their evidence on oath and can be questioned by the defendant and the court.

For various reasons, witnesses are sometimes reluctant to come to court. When you ask someone to act as a witness, find out whether he or she is prepared to come without being served with a witness summons. Ask them whether there are any dates when they could not attend court – this could affect the date of the hearing. If a witness is not prepared to come to court voluntarily, he or she can be compelled to do so: you should ask the court office for a request for a witness summons which the court staff will help you fill in. You will have to produce the plaint note, and pay a small fee for issue and service of the summons. You will also have to pay the court the money for the witness's expenses (travel to and from the court and loss of time at work); the court office will tell you how much this is.

You will have to be prepared to pay your witness's expenses. But if you win, the defendant will usually have to pay all or part of these expenses. The court will decide what is a reasonable sum for travelling and other expenses involved, and for the time lost attending court.

DOCUMENTS

Although spoken evidence from witnesses is most important, documents can sometimes make all the difference between success and failure. Letters written by you or the defendant, contracts and agreements, bills, invoices and receipts, bank statements and so on, could all be vital to your case. Remember to bring them with you when your case is heard.

THE HEARING

County courts normally open at 10 a.m. for a 10.30 start. Try to arrive at 10 a.m. so that you can find out which court room you will be in, and to give you time to discuss the case with your lawyer if you have one. Give your name to the usher so that he or she knows where you are when the case is called. The usher normally wears a black gown.

There may be other cases before yours, and you must expect to spend the day at court. It is a good idea to sit in court rather than wait outside, so that you can see how other cases are dealt with, and hear the sort of questions that are put to witnesses.

There is no reason why you should not bring along a friend

or relative to help you conduct the case yourself. (See p. 102 for more information about bringing a friend to court.)

THE COURT

The judge will sit at the front of the court room; he wears a wig and purple gown. The clerk of the court sits in front of him. If there are any barristers or solicitors appearing in court, then they sit at the front facing the judge. Barristers wear a wig and a black gown; solicitors wear a gown, but no wig.

GIVING EVIDENCE

When you come to give evidence in your case, you should come forward to the witness box where you will be asked to take the oath or affirm. Tell the judge about your claim from the beginning. If you have a lawyer representing you he will help you by asking questions. Try not to get excited and do not exaggerate. A person who stays calm and reasonable makes a better impression than one who is angry or incoherent. Remember to pause between sentences because the judge will be making a note – in longhand – of what you say. It is a good idea to watch his pencil; when he stops writing, you can go on speaking.

When telling your story, it may be difficult to avoid repeating what someone else told you. This is known as **hearsay** evidence, and generally speaking, it is *not allowed*. If you simply want to repeat what someone said to you in order to explain what happened next, the way to get round the problem is to say, 'As a result of what Mr X told me, I did so and so'. This is very difficult to remember, and when the time comes you will probably launch into details of what Mr X actually said. So do not be surprised if the judge stops you. The reason why what Mr X told you is not allowed, is that the truth of what he said cannot be tested unless Mr X is in court to be questioned. On the other hand, you are entitled to say what the defendant or his witness said because they can be asked about it when they give evidence.

CROSS-EXAMINATION

When you have finished telling your story, the judge will ask the defendant or his or her lawyer if he wishes to ask you any questions. In the same way, when the defendant or any of his or her witnesses gives evidence, you or your lawyer will be asked if you wish to question them.

There is nothing quite so dramatic as a devastating cross-examination, when the evidence given by a witness is utterly discredited. But cross-examination is a difficult art. Unless there are particular questions you want to ask, it may be wiser to remain silent.

Most judges dealing with cases where both you and the defendant are in court prefer to hear what each party has to say and then, if any explanations are necessary or there are points which need clarification, to question each of you in turn. At the same time, he will give each of you an opportunity to qualify or explain anything you have already said.

SPEECHES AND JUDGMENT

At the end of the evidence your lawyer and the defendant's lawyer may address the judge. If you don't have a lawyer the judge should ask you whether you have anything you want to say. If you want to, you can use this opportunity to sum up your complaint and stress the points which seem most important to you.

The judge will usually give his judgment straight away. If it is a difficult case or if he wishes to consider any point of law, he may reserve his judgment. You will then be sent notice of a further date to attend court when judgment will be given.

WHAT YOU CAN GET IF YOU WIN

If you win your case, the court can do one or more of the following:

– order your opponent to pay you **damages** (i.e. financial compensation), including damages for injury to feelings;
– order your opponent to do something to remedy the action you

complained about (e.g. carry out repairs). This is called an
injunction;
– make an order declaring what your rights are. This is called
a **declaration**.

COSTS

If you win your case, you should ask the court for your costs in
addition to any damages you have been awarded.

Your costs may include the following items:

– lawyers' fees (if any);
– court fees;
– witness expenses. In addition to the expenses for your witnesses, you can claim for your own expenses as a witness
(travelling costs and loss of time at work);
– out-of-pocket expenses. You may claim the expenses involved
in making searches in public registers, such as the Companies
Register. You may also claim fares, telephone calls or any other
expenditure that the court considers were reasonably necessary
for the preparation of your case. If you have had to spend a
night away from home to attend the hearing, or take a meal in a
restaurant during the trial, you can also claim these costs.

If you were not represented by a lawyer, you can be awarded a
sum to cover the work you did in preparing the case, as well as
out-of-pocket expenses as mentioned above (Litigants in Person
[Costs and Expenses] Act 1975).

PAYING THE OTHER SIDE'S COSTS

If you lose, you may have to pay your opponent's costs. The legal
fees which the defendant can claim from you depend on the
amount you were asking for. If you were asking for less than
£200, you cannot usually be ordered to pay anything. But if you
were asking for more than that, you could have to pay a large
sum. For instance, if you were claiming over £500, the case
could have cost your opponent over £100 in legal fees, which
you could be ordered to pay.

When deciding how much to claim in the first place, you should, if possible, get legal advice on your chances of winning and take into account the possibility of having to pay legal costs if you claim more than £200 and lose. If you claim a certain amount of damages and are awarded a figure on a *lower* scale, then you will not be able to get all your legal costs paid by your opponent. So it is important to ask for a realistic amount when making your claim.

APPEALS

If you lose your case, you may have grounds for appeal to the Court of Appeal. Before appealing, you should take legal advice. An unsuccessful appeal can be very expensive. The court office will tell you what you have to do in order to appeal against the court's decision, and the time within which this must be done (which is usually six weeks).

The High Court

The High Court deals with the more serious civil cases (especially personal injuries and libel). The procedure is similar to that in the county courts, but is much more formal. A case may take years to come to trial, although many are settled out of court. If it gets to court, the case will usually involve long legal arguments, points of procedure, and references to previous court judgments (**precedents**), often read out at length.

If you think that your case should be brought in the High Court (e.g. it involves a claim for more than £2,000) or if you are defending a High Court case, you should consult a solicitor and apply for legal aid (see p. 496). Legal aid is not available for either the plaintiff or the defendant in a defamation case (i.e. libel or slander), or in a case involving defamation.

Tribunals

A number of tribunals have been set up by the Government to settle disputes, usually between individuals and government officials without the formality, cost and complication of the ordinary courts. Most tribunals have a number of features in common, which are briefly described below. Individual tribunals are dealt with throughout the rest of this book, as follows:

Most tribunals are open to the public and the press, but the applicant may ask for a private hearing if the case involves disclosing highly personal information. Supplementary benefit appeal tribunals and mental health review tribunals are almost always held in private.

Tribunals are generally less formal than ordinary law courts, although the degree of informality depends on the attitude of the chairperson. The procedure to be followed in each case depends on the particular tribunal. Industrial tribunals in particular have become very formal. Tribunals deal with most cases in half a day or less, although a very complicated case may take much longer. It is very important for you to turn up to the tribunal hearing on your case, since you will have a better chance of winning than if you stay away.

Membership of tribunals

A tribunal usually consists of three people. The chairperson is usually a lawyer, while the other two members should have an expert knowledge of the subject dealt with by that particular tribunal.

Legal advice and representation

You can get help from a lawyer under the green-form scheme (see p. 494) in order to prepare a case for the tribunal. This can include drafting a written statement of your case which can be given to the tribunal members in advance. It is *not* possible to get legal aid for a lawyer to represent you at the tribunal hearing itself.

You should also be able to get advice on a tribunal case from the local citizens' advice bureau or, in an employment case, your trade union. There are a number of voluntary organizations which can provide advice and, in some cases, representation at tribunal hearings: these are given in the relevant sections of this book dealing with each tribunal. Finally, you may be able to get help from a local law centre (see p. 507 for addresses).

Costs

One of the advantages of tribunals is that, even if you lose, you cannot be ordered to pay your opponent's costs (except in very rare cases, where the tribunal decides that your application was 'frivolous or vexatious'). In most tribunals you can claim your travelling expenses and compensation for loss of earnings from the tribunal (ask the clerk for a claim form), but not your legal fees.

More information

Small Claims in the County Court: how to sue and defend actions without a lawyer (from the county court).

How to Sue in the County Court (Consumers' Association).

12. Citizenship, immigration and travel

This chapter deals with the following subjects:

This chapter explains in general terms the laws about citizenship and immigration. If you have a specific problem, you are strongly advised to consult one of the organizations listed on p. 310.

Immigration control is governed by the Immigration Act 1971 and the Immigration Rules made under the Act. The Act means that everyone entering or living in the UK is subject to immigration control unless they have a 'right of abode'. Those who do have a right of abode are called 'patrial' (see p. 265).

Non-patrials are subject to the controls and restrictions described in this chapter, although there are important exceptions set out on p. 266.

If you are refused entry, or not permitted to remain here, or only allowed to stay on certain conditions, you may have a right of appeal under the immigration appeals machinery (see pp. 296–300).

The Prevention of Terrorism (Temporary Provisions) Act 1976 gives the Government the power to exclude (i.e. deport) UK citizens from Great Britain or Northern Ireland, or to exclude foreign citizens from the United Kingdom completely (see pp. 538–42).

Who is subject to what immigration control?

Whether or not you (and your immediate family) can freely enter the UK and live here depends partly on what country you are a citizen of.

If you are a citizen of the UK and Colonies you will probably be a patrial (see p. 265) and so not be subject to immigration control. But some UK citizens are subject to immigration control – these people are called non-patrials (see p. 266).

Some Commonwealth citizens are patrials but most are not (see p. 265).

If you are a foreigner, see pp. 267–79 to find out what controls may apply to you.

Citizenship of the UK and Colonies

The laws relating to citizenship are extremely complex, and the Government has announced that it is reviewing them, with the intention of producing new legislation.

You can acquire citizenship of the UK and Colonies if:

– you are born in the UK or one of the colonies; *or*
– you are adopted by a UK citizen in the UK or one of the colonies; *or*
– you are the legitimate child of a man who is a UK citizen at the time of your birth; *or*
– you are a woman and register as a UK citizen on marriage to a UK citizen; *or*
– you are registered or naturalized as a UK citizen (see below).

If a woman who is a UK citizen has a child abroad (not in one of the colonies), the child will *not* be a UK citizen unless the father is a citizen and the parents are married. But there are two ways in which the child of a UK mother can acquire citizenship, despite being born abroad. These are:

1. If a child is born stateless and is always likely to be stateless, the child must be registered as a UK citizen provided the mother was a citizen at the time of the child's birth (British Nationality (No. 2) Act 1965).

2. Any child born abroad of a UK mother can be registered as a UK citizen, at the Home Secretary's discretion. This will normally only be done if the child's future is clearly within the UK (e.g. if the parents are separated, the mother has custody of the child and is living in this country). The father must consent to the application to have the child registered (British Nationality Act 1948).

Usually, however, a child born abroad will, if legitimate, take the father's citizenship.

COMMONWEALTH CITIZENS: BECOMING A UK CITIZEN BY REGISTRATION

If you are a Commonwealth citizen, you can apply to be registered as a citizen of the UK and Colonies if:

- you are 18 or over; *and*
- you have been here for over five years, and there have been no conditions attached to your stay for the five years before you apply for registration; *and*
- you satisfy the Home Secretary that you are of good character, have sufficient knowledge of the English language, and intend to live here after your registration.

In exceptional circumstances, the Home Secretary can accept you after a shorter period than five years.

If you apply for UK citizenship while in this country, you may lose your own citizenship. The UK allows you to have dual citizenship, but you will need to find out from your own High Commission whether your country also permits it.

FOREIGN NATIONALS: BECOMING A UK CITIZEN BY NATURALIZATION

If you are a foreign national, you can apply to be naturalized as a citizen of the UK and Colonies if:

- you are aged 18 or over; *and*

- you have been resident here for at least four out of the last seven years and also for the year before your application (i.e. five years in all); *and*
- there are no conditions attached to your stay at the date of application: *and*
- you satisfy the Home Secretary that you are sane, of good character, have sufficient knowledge of the English language and intend to live here after naturalization or be employed in Crown service.

You should contact your embassy to find out whether the laws of your own country allow you to have dual citizenship or whether you will lose your original nationality when you are naturalized.

Both registration and naturalization are discretionary. There is no appeal against a refusal to allow you to register or become a naturalized citizen. Your only remedy is to wait, and try again. Unless your circumstances change considerably, there is little point in making a new application for at least twelve months.

CITIZENSHIP BY MARRIAGE

A woman (whether Commonwealth citizen or foreign national) can register as a UK citizen as soon as she marries a UK citizen. But a man who marries a UK citizen has to fulfil the residence requirements set out above, before being entitled to register or be naturalized as a UK citizen (see above and p. 263). Until he becomes a citizen, he can still be deported (see p. 288). Discrimination on grounds of sex in the citizenship laws is not covered by the Sex Discrimination Act 1975.

CITIZENSHIP AND PATRIALITY

Being a citizen of the UK and Colonies does not automatically entitle you to come into this country. (See below for how you come a patrial.)

Patrials

You will qualify as a **patrial** (i.e. someone with a right of abode in the UK) if you come within one of the following categories: (An illegitimate child can qualify as a patrial through the mother, not the father.)

1. *You are a UK citizen* and:
   - you acquired your UK citizenship in the UK (by being born here, adopted here by a UK parent, or by registering or being naturalized here, see p. 263); *or*
   - one parent acquired UK citizenship in the UK; *or*
   - you settle and live in the UK for five years; *or*
   - you are a woman and marry a man who is a patrial. (You will continue to be a patrial even after divorce.)
2. *You are a Commonwealth citizen* and:
   - your mother was born in the UK (if your father was born in the UK, you will have inherited UK citizenship); *or*
   - you acquired your UK citizenship by registration here (or in a few cases abroad); *or*
   - you are a woman and marry a man who is a patrial. (You will continue to be a patrial even after divorce.)
3. *You are a foreign national* and:
   - you acquire UK citizenship by naturalization; *or*
   - you are a woman and register as a UK citizen on marriage to a man who is a patrial. (You will continue to be a patrial even after divorce.)

You can see that not all citizens of the UK and Colonies qualify for patrial status. East African Asians are one group who do not, as they are unlikely to have parents who were UK citizens. Yet certain Commonwealth citizens, most of them white (including many Australians and Canadians) do qualify.

It is up to you, not the Home Office, to prove that you are a patrial. You can obtain a certificate of patriality from the Home Office, or the British Embassy or the High Commission in your own country.

Non-patrials

If you do not come under any of the following groups, you will be subject to immigration control (see pp. 267–96.)

NON-PATRIALS WITH SPECIAL TREATMENT

You will qualify for special treatment if you are:

A citizen of a Common Market country

Because the Treaty of Rome permits free movement of labour between member countries, no condition will be imposed on you to restrict your employment or occupation here. You will be allowed in without a work permit to look for work, take up a job, set up business or work as a self-employed person. This applies whether you are a man or a woman. *But* it is more difficult to come as a student (see p. 271).

Normally you will be granted admission for six months. If you find work during this time, you will be issued with a resident's permit. The permit will normally be limited to the length of your employment if it is likely to be less than six months; otherwise it will be issued to you for five years. A resident's permit can be cancelled if you are found to be living off public funds and you are capable of work.

Once you have been in the country for three years, you can apply for settlement (see p. 279).

You are also entitled to bring into the UK with you your family: spouse, children under 21, other children who are still dependent on you, and the dependent parents of you or your spouse. Your family is entitled to the same extensions and resident's permits as you are.

Although you are still subject to the deportation laws and can be excluded for certain political and health reasons, these restrictions are not as extensive as for immigrants from other countries. In all cases, you have the right of appeal to the immigration appeals adjudicator (see p. 296) or to the courts. This applies even where other immigrants have no right of appeal. If your appeal is unsuccessful, you can appeal to the European Court of Justice in Luxembourg which administers Common Market law. You will need to get advice from a lawyer or one of the organizations listed on p. 310.

A Commonwealth citizen

If you were resident in the UK on 1 January 1973, you cannot be deported (see p. 292).

A citizen of the Republic of Ireland

You are free from most immigration controls, even though you are not patrial. However, if you were not resident in the UK on 1 January 1973, you can be deported in certain circumstances (see p. 292).

(There are also special provisions for seamen and crews on foreign ships and airplanes. Diplomats and certain consular officials are totally free from control.)

Entering the UK

As a non-patrial, you have no automatic right of entry to the UK. Even if you satisfy all the formal requirements, you can still only enter if you are given permission. This permission can be for an indefinite period, or it can be limited. If it is only given for a limited period, it can be made subject to **conditions** restricting your employment or occupation (see p. 270), and you can be required to register with the police (see p. 277).

You will not be allowed into this country without certain documents. You must produce a **passport** or equivalent document and, in some cases, an **entry clearance**. The Government encourages travellers to apply for entry clearance from the British Embassy or High Commission before they leave their own country. Although this is often not essential (see the next section for when it is), an entry clearance can make it easier to get into the country. But there is often a long delay in granting entry clearance. In many countries, entry certificate officers (who are appointed by the Foreign Office) conduct rigorous interviews, and appeals against a refusal to grant entry clearance can take up to two years.

Who must have an entry clearance?

Entry clearance is only essential for certain foreign nationals and dependants of people settled here. It is *not* essential for visitors, students and other people coming for a limited period. Nevertheless, if you are coming from a black Commonwealth country, you are usually safer if you apply for entry clearance before you leave, particularly if you are only coming for a short period. An immigration officer may suspect that you are coming to stay here permanently, and will ask you why you failed to apply for clearance and whether you did but were refused.

Refusal of entry into the UK

Immigration officers and medical inspectors have wide powers to question and examine people wanting to come into this country, and to refuse them entry. You can be refused entry in any of the following circumstances:

– you fail to produce travel documents;
– the immigration officer suspects that your entry certificate was obtained by fraud, or that there has been some change in your circumstances since you obtained it;
– you have a criminal record;
– you are already subject to a deportation order;
– the Home Secretary or an immigration officer decides that it is 'conducive to the public good' to keep you out of the country.

And if an immigration officer decides that you are not in good health, you can be examined by a medical inspector and may be refused entry.

If you get over these hurdles, you can still be refused entry if you fail to meet the requirements of the specific immigration rules which apply to you (e.g. visitor, student, wife or fiancé, etc.). The rules relating to the main categories of people entitled to come here are set out later, on pp. 271–6.

You should remember that an immigration officer has a general discretionary power and that the burden is on you to show that you are entitled to enter. But an immigration officer cannot refuse to let you in without first getting the authority of a chief immigration officer or an immigration inspector.

IF YOU ARE REFUSED ENTRY

An immigration officer can decide to admit you temporarily while the Home Office decides whether or not to admit you formally. You can appeal to the immigration appeals adjudicator against refusal of entry, or against any conditions which the immigration officer has imposed (see p. 296). But unless you have a current entry clearance or work permit, you must leave the country before appealing against the decision.

If you are told to leave or are in dispute with an immigration officer, ask to telephone a friend or relative, your High Commission or consulate, or the office of the United Kingdom

Immigrants Advisory Service (see p. 310), for additional help and advice.

REPUBLIC OF IRELAND

If you are allowed into the UK (including the Channel Islands and Isle of Man) you will be free to travel to the Republic. If you are refused entry to the United Kingdom, you will usually not be allowed to enter Ireland. Similarly, if you are not acceptable to the Irish immigration authorities, you will face difficulties in entering this country.

If you are admitted, how long can you stay?

You can only stay in the UK legally for the length of time given to you by the immigration officer, and stamped in your passport. If you stay longer without getting official approval, it is a criminal offence and you can also be deported (see p. 288). You can apply to the Home Office for an extension of your time-limit, or to have your conditions of stay changed.

You must apply for an extension before the period of your stay runs out. Otherwise, if your application is late, you will lose your right of appeal.

To apply for an extension, write to the **Home Office, Immigration and Nationality Division, Lunar House, Wellesley Road, Croydon**. You can visit the office there, but it is generally better to write, as misunderstandings have arisen between officials and immigrants at these interviews. You will have to qualify for an extension under one of the categories set out on pp. 271–6. If the Home Office refuses an extension, you will have a right of appeal, as set out on p. 296.

In general, remember:

– if you enter for a temporary stay (e.g. as a visitor or student), you must leave at the end of your stay, or at the end of any extended time period;
– if you are a visitor, you will not normally be allowed to work;
– students can only work in very limited circumstances (see p. 272);

– if you enter in a temporary capacity, you cannot change to full-time employment except in the most exceptional circumstances (see p. 275).

Visitors

You will generally be admitted if you can show that:

– you are a genuine visitor; *and*
– you intend to leave at the end of your visit; *and*
– you can support yourself and your family while you are here; *and*
– you can afford the return journey.

A time-limit will be imposed on the visit. Although immigration officers can admit you for up to twelve months, many people are admitted for a shorter period. Towards the end of your stay, you can apply for a renewal, but you will still have to satisfy the four conditions laid out above.

You cannot stay indefinitely as a visitor, and you will probably be prohibited from working.

Students

If you have obtained an entry clearance in your country of origin, you will normally have no difficulty coming in. In order to get entry clearance, you will have to meet the conditions set out in the next paragraph.

If you have not got clearance, you must satisfy the immigration officer that:

– you have been accepted for a course of study at a genuine educational institution; *and*
– the course will occupy the whole or a substantial part of your time (usually at least fifteen hours' day-time study per week); *and*
– you can meet the cost of the course; *and*
– you can maintain yourself.

Your dependants can also come here provided you can show proof that they will be maintained by you. You should have with you documents about your financial status (e.g. a bank statement or letter from your bank).

Immigration officers and the Home Office have wide powers to refuse to let you in if they are not satisfied that you meet the requirements. They have considerable discretion in the matter. For example, they can decide whether your qualifications are adequate for the course you intend to study and can refuse you admission if they are not satisfied. Assessment can be very subjective, so you should have a letter from a reputable educational institution or authority confirming that your qualifications are adequate for the course.

Students are often refused admission on the basis that they will not return home at the end of their studies. Try to produce evidence that you will return, and be very wary if the immigration officer asks if you would like to stay at the end of your course, if given the opportunity. Your answer may be taken as 'proof' that you do not really intend to leave.

You will be admitted for a maximum of twelve months only. You must then renew your application. You will have to show that you have been accepted to continue your studies, and can continue to support yourself and, where appropriate, your family.

You may be permitted to work in your spare time or vacations on condition that you get Department of Employment approval before you start work. Your wife is free to take up employment at any time, and her earnings may be taken into account in deciding whether you have sufficient funds to support yourself and your family.

As a concession, the Home Office will usually allow the husband of a woman student to enter with her and take up employment while she is here. The Home Office is particularly sympathetic where there are young children or the husband needs special attention from his wife because of some incapacity. The husband must leave when his wife's stay as a student ends (unless she successfully applies for permission to stay after the end of her course).

If you cannot satisfy all the requirements, the immigration officer has the power to admit you for a short period while the Home Office considers your case.

Businessmen

If you simply wish to transact business here, you are classified as a visitor, and should not be prevented from doing this during your visit.

If you wish to establish a business and remain here, you may be allowed to do so if you meet certain requirements.

If you propose to set up in business by joining an existing concern, you must produce evidence to show that:

– you are bringing money of your own into the business; *and*
– you will be able to bear your share of the liabilities of the business; *and*
– your share of the profits will be sufficient to support you and your dependants; *and*
– you will be actively concerned in the running of the business; *and*
– there is a genuine need for your services and investment.

You will have to produce audited accounts of previous years to show the exact financial state of the business. You will not be allowed to stay here if the partnership or directorship amounts to little more than 'disguised employment' or where it seems likely that you will have to supplement your business activities by seeking a job for which a work permit is needed.

If you propose to go into business on your own, you will have to show that:

– you are bringing enough money to establish the venture; *and*
– you can realistically be expected to support yourself and any dependants without taking a job for which a work permit is needed.

This last condition can produce arbitrary decisions by the Home Office who are often reluctant to accept that people can live on relatively small incomes.

Self-employed people

'Self-employed' appears to have a narrow meaning under the Immigration Rules. Some self-employed people will qualify as businessmen, but the Rules create a special category for people such as 'artists and writers'. To gain admission, you must show that you can support yourself and any dependants without recourse to public funds, and without taking a job for which a work permit would normally be needed.

If you have an entry clearance, you will usually be admitted for a period of about twelve months. If you do not have clearance, you may be allowed to enter for two months, and advised to put your case to the Home Office to be considered.

Entertainers and musicians (including members of pop groups) and members of sports teams are not counted as self-employed people and must obtain work permits before they are allowed to enter the UK.

People with independent means

If you are a person of independent means, and can show that you can support yourself and your dependants 'indefinitely', without working, then you may be admitted.

You will have to produce evidence of your income, e.g. bank statements or a letter of pension entitlement. You must show that this money is under your control and can be used in the UK. The money must be enough for the 'foreseeable future' – usually five years or more.

If you have an entry clearance, you will usually be admitted for an initial period of twelve months. If you cannot completely meet the requirements, you can be admitted for up to two months, and advised to put your case to the Home Office for consideration. People on extremely small incomes (e.g. retirement pensions) have been admitted to this country where it has been shown that they were used to living a frugal life!

Au pair girls

'Au pair' is an arrangement by which a *girl* of 17 and above may come to this country to learn English and live for a time as a member of a resident British family. Full-time domestic employment needs a work permit (see p. 275). In practice, many au pair girls are treated as domestic servants, paid very little and given little chance to learn English.

If you are admitted as an au pair girl, you have no claim to stay here in any other capacity. You cannot stay for more than twelve months without applying for a renewal, and you will not be allowed to take employment. You cannot be an au pair girl for more than two years in all.

Commonwealth girls can come to this country as au pair girls, but in the past permission has rarely been given.

There are no provisions in the immigration rules for au pair *boys*.

Coming here to work

There are severe restrictions on people coming here to take up employment. You must have a Department of Employment work permit unless you come into one of these limited exempt categories: patrial UK and Commonwealth citizens (as described on p. 265); young Commonwealth citizens on working holidays (see p. 276); those in 'permit free' employment, described below; and citizens of Common Market countries (see p. 266).

Permits can only be issued for a limited number of categories of employment. They include: professional and executive workers, skilled craftsmen, and workers in hospital and similar institutions. There are a number of other categories set out in a Department of Employment leaflet (number OW6, available from local employment offices).

Permits are not available for unskilled or semi-skilled jobs except for citizens of Malta and the dependent Territories, non-patrial UK passport holders, resident domestic workers, nursing auxiliaries and catering workers. These are admitted on a strict quota system.

Permits will only be granted to people aged between 18 and 54. They must be applied for by the employer, before you enter the country. A work permit is not an entry clearance, and although you do not have to have an entry clearance as well as a work permit, it is often advisable to get it anyway. *You will be*

*refused permission to work if you do not have the work permit on
arrival.*

If you have a work permit, you will normally be admitted for
up to twelve months on condition that you do not change jobs
without the Department of Employment's consent. Even then,
you will be expected to remain in the same type of employment
and permission will only be granted subject to the same conditions as the original permit. The new employer must apply to the
Department for the permit.

You can apply for an extension of your stay after the original
time-limit expires, provided you have a current work permit.

Unless you are admitted for seasonal employment, you will be
allowed to bring in your wife and children aged under 18. They
will be able to take jobs, without restriction (except the usual
restrictions on young people's employment, described on p.
434).

YOUNG COMMONWEALTH CITIZENS

Commonwealth citizens over the age of 16 (there is no official
upper age limit) may come to the UK for extended holidays of
up to five years before settling down in their own countries. You
will usually be admitted for twelve months, but you can apply
for extensions. You must leave at the end of your stay and you
will not be allowed to remain here permanently in employment.
The jobs you take are meant to be incidental to your holiday, but
the Home Office seems to take a broad view. Black Commonwealth citizens have difficulties qualifying under this category.

COMMONWEALTH CITIZENS WITH UK GRANDPARENTS

A Commonwealth citizen who can show that he or she has one
grandparent who was born in the UK will be allowed to come
here to work. An entry certificate is needed, but no work permit.
On admission, you will be allowed to settle here (see p. 279 for
what 'settlement' means).

Registering with the police

When you come into this country, you will have to register with the police if:

– you are a foreign national; *and*
– you are aged over sixteen; *and*
– you have been allowed to stay for over three months with a work permit, or over six months in a temporary capacity.

Your family will also have to register.

You should go to your local police station with your passport, and a photograph. Most of the information they need is in your passport, but they will also want to know your address here and your occupation. You will have to pay a small fee, and you will then get a certificate of registration.

If you change your address, status (e.g. by getting married), or occupation, or you get an extension of stay, you must notify the police within seven days. If you do not do so, you may be prosecuted and even removed from the country, although this is unlikely if you simply forgot to tell the police or had some other genuine reason.

Once you are allowed to stay here without any conditions attached to your stay, you will no longer have to register with the police. Until that happens, it is best to carry your Certificate of Registration with you at all times.

Civil and political rights of immigrants

IF YOU ARE A COMMONWEALTH CITIZEN

You can vote and be a candidate in both Parliamentary and local elections; you can become a magistrate; and you are liable for jury service. Citizens of non-Commonwealth countries cannot take part in these activities.

IF YOU ARE A CITIZEN OF A FOREIGN
(NON-COMMONWEALTH) COUNTRY

There are a number of further restrictions including limitations on joining the armed services. If you promote or attempt to promote industrial unrest in any industry where you have not been a genuine member for at least two years, you are liable on conviction in the magistrates' court to up to two years' imprisonment (Aliens Restriction (Amendment) Act 1919).

Apart from these restrictions, foreign nationals in general enjoy the same rights as UK citizens. In theory, therefore, you may engage in politics, but in practice, if your activities in this sphere become too marked, you may find that your application for an extension of stay meets with an unsatisfactorily explained refusal.

Refugee status and political asylum

The Immigration Rules state that where a person is stateless or a refugee, full account is to be taken of the relevant international agreements to which the United Kingdom is a party. Similarly, if you do not qualify for admission under the normal categories, you should not be sent away if this would mean returning to a country where you would face 'danger to life or liberty or persecution of such a kind that would render life insufferable because of race, religion, nationality or political opinion'. This applies whether you are seeking entry, applying for an extension of your stay, or are about to be deported.

The Home Secretary has to decide for himself, that it is probable that you would genuinely face serious danger. 'Persecution' can arise not only from the state authorities, but also from private individuals or groups if the law-enforcement agencies of the state are powerless to intervene.

If you feel you might be in such a position, you should contact the United Kingdom Immigrants Advisory Service (address on p. 310) which has a special officer to deal with problems of refugees and those seeking political asylum.

In many cases, political asylum may be difficult to obtain formally because the Government does not wish to upset publicly the government of another country, particularly one with which it has friendly relations. The Home Office has often been prepared to allow people to stay and work and eventually has lifted the conditions of their stay, without formally giving political asylum.

DESERTERS AND DRAFT-DODGERS

If you are a deserter from an army of a friendly country (including a NATO country), you cannot claim political asylum. You can be arrested and deported from this country without trial (Visiting Forces Act 1952).

The position of the draft-dodger is different. An immigration officer should not ask you if you are a draft-dodger if you are seeking to enter this country. In any event, you should not be refused permission to enter solely on this ground, and you should not be arrested or removed from the UK if this is the only offence you have committed in your own country.

Remaining permanently in the UK

If you are allowed to remain here permanently, you will be regarded as **settled** here. Settlement is a legal term which means that you are ordinarily resident here, without being subject under the immigration laws to any restrictions in the period for which you can stay.

How you can become 'settled'

You can acquire settlement in a number of ways.

1. *Whatever your nationality:*
   - if you were resident here when the Immigration Act came into effect on 1 January 1973, you are treated as having been given permission to stay here indefinitely; *or*
   - in practice, if you are granted political asylum or refugee status.

2. *Citizens of Commonwealth and other non-Common Market countries:*
   - if you were admitted to work you can apply for your time limit to be removed after you have finished four years in approved employment; *or*
   - if you are admitted as a businessman, self-employed person or person of independent means, you can also apply for the time limit to be removed after four years; *or*
   - if you are the husband of someone settled here or who is admitted for settlement at the same time; *or*
   - if you are the dependant of someone settled here – wife, child under eighteen, parent, grandparent or distressed relative; *or*
   - if you are a fiancée of someone settled here or who is admitted for settlement at the same time; *or*
   - if you are a Commonwealth citizen with a grandparent who was born in the UK.

3. *Citizens of Common Market countries*
   - if you have been here for four years in some form of employment and have a resident's permit; *or*
   - if you have been continually resident here for the last three years, or have been in employment here or another Common Market country for the last twelve months; and you have reached state retirement age or you qualify because you are disabled; *or*
   - you are a member of the family of a citizen of a Common Market country in one of these situations.

4. *UK passport holders who are not patrials:*
   - you and your dependants can only be admitted for settlement if you have a special voucher or entry certificate.

WHAT DOES 'SETTLEMENT' MEAN?

If you are accepted for settlement, you will not become a patrial (i.e. a person with a legal right of abode in this country), but:

- all restrictions on employment will be lifted;
- you should normally have no difficulty leaving or entering the

United Kingdom, provided that you do not stay away for more than two years. Even then you may be allowed back in, e.g. if you have lived here for most of your life;
– if you are a Commonwealth citizen and have been resident here for five years, without any conditions (e.g. time limits or employment restrictions), you can apply for registration as a UK citizen. If you are a foreign national you can apply for naturalization at an earlier date (see p. 264);
– you will automatically become a patrial if you are registered or naturalized as a citizen.

Until you do become a patrial, however, you can still be served with a deportation order (see p. 288).

When considering your application to become settled here, the Home Office has discretion in deciding whether to remove your conditions. The Immigration Rules set out the factors regarded as important, which include:

– whether you have observed the conditions under which you were admitted;
– whether in the light of your 'character, conduct or association', it is desirable to let you stay;
– whether you represent a danger to 'national security';
– whether you have been convicted of a criminal offence while in the United Kingdom.

Bringing in your family

If you are a citizen of a Common Market country, special rules apply about bringing in relatives (see p. 266).

If you are a non-patrial UK passport holder, coming in on a special voucher or entry clearance, you can bring with you your spouse and dependent children under 18.

The rules described in the following sections (pp. 282–7) only apply to Commonwealth citizens and citizens of foreign countries outside the Common Market. You are permitted to bring into this country for settlement your wife or husband and, in certain circumstances only, your children under 18, dependent parents, grandparents and other relatives. You must be able to show that you are able and willing to support your dependants without recourse to public funds. Your relatives must hold a current entry clearance showing that they are your dependants.

WIVES

Your wife will be allowed to join you and live here. If you are not married, but have been living in 'permanent association', your partner may also be admitted if it can be shown that there is a local custom or tradition which tends to establish the permanence of the situation. Admission under this rule will not, therefore, be given to partners who come from Western countries, who have chosen to live together without marrying.

The most serious difficulty facing wives applying for admission is proof of the marriage. This difficulty applies particularly to people coming from the Indian subcontinent where the absence of documentation and different traditions and customs can give rise to doubts about the relationship. The entry certificate officer will interview your wife and children over 12 in their own country, and will cross-examine them closely. If discrepancies arise between their statements and the information you have provided, the application is likely to be refused. The most likely discrepancies are those relating to the 'family tree': the names and dates of birth of the children; whether the husband was with his wife on the date of the conception; names, ages and places of residence of other relatives. Your wife may be questioned about minor details concerning possessions and about the marriage ceremony. You may be asked questions about tax relief claimed for your wife and children.

Wives and children may also face long delays before obtaining even a first interview with the entry certificate officer. In the Indian subcontinent, delays of up to two years are still common.

HUSBANDS

If you are a woman settled here, your husband should be admitted on proof of the marriage. You will not have to show that you can support him. But he will need an entry clearance. If the immigration authorities believe that it is a 'marriage of convenience' he will not be allowed in. Even if he is admitted, there may be conditions on his stay. After twelve months he can apply to have any conditions on his stay lifted.

FIANCÉES

If you are a man, your partner can come to settle here, if:

– you are settled here; *and*
– you can show the immigration officer that the marriage will take place shortly after entry.

Your fiancée does not need an entry certificate.

Normally, your partner will be admitted for three months and will not be allowed to take a job during that time. After the marriage, your wife should write to the Home Office enclosing the marriage certificate and your birth certificate or passport (to show you are settled here). Your partner will then be allowed to stay here permanently and allowed to work.

If the marriage is delayed your fiancée should apply to the Home Office for an extension of her time-limit. Explain why the delay has happened, and when the marriage will take place.

As soon as you are married, if you are a UK citizen, your wife can register as a UK citizen herself. If you are a patrial, she will automatically become a patrial too (see p. 265).

FIANCÉS

If you are a woman, your partner can come to settle here if:

– you are settled here; *and*
– you can show the immigration officer that the marriage will take place shortly after entry: *and*
– he has a current entry certificate (see p. 268).

But your fiancé will be refused an entry certificate if the immigration officer 'has reason to believe' that the marriage would be a marriage of convenience designed to get entry to this country, ard that you do not in fact intend to live together permanently. If your fiancé is refused entry on these grounds, he should appeal (see p. 296).

If your fiancé is admitted, he will normally be admitted for three months and will not be allowed to take a job during that time. After the marriage, your husband should write to the Home Office enclosing the marriage certificate and your birth certificate or passport (to show you are settled here). He should then be given a further extension of his stay for up to twelve months.

At the end of that period, he can apply to have the conditions on his stay removed. The immigration authorities will refuse his application if they have reason to believe that the marriage was simply designed to get the man admitted to this country, or that one of you no longer intends to live with the other. The application will also be refused if you are no longer living together. When making the application, therefore, you should state if you are still living together. You may be interviewed by the immigration authorities or the police, who are likely to ask questions about your private life in order to decide if the marriage is one of 'convenience' or not. If you consider that your privacy has been invaded or if your husband is refused permission to stay here you should contact NCCL or JCWI (addresses on p. 310) for advice and help.

Remember that your husband does not become a patrial on marriage. A man has to live here for five years before he can apply to become a UK citizen (see p. 263).

The law on fiancés and husbands discriminates on grounds of sex. Unfortunately, this is not covered by the Sex Discrimination Act 1975. In some cases, however, it will be possible to make a complaint to the European Commission on Human Rights (see Chapter 29): contact NCCL or JCWI (addresses on p. 310) for advice.

CHILDREN

Children aged under 18 can be allowed in for settlement if a number of conditions are met. These are:

1. Both parents are settled in the UK or are being admitted for settlement at the same time;
   or
   One parent – is settled here and the other is admitted for settlement at the same time as the child; *or*
          – is settled or admitted for settlement, and the other parent is dead; *or*
          – is settled here or admitted for settlement and has the sole responsibility for the child's upbringing.
   or
   The Home Secretary decides to admit the child to join one parent or another relative, because family or other reasons makes it undesirable to keep the child out (e.g. if the other parent is physically or mentally incapable of looking after the child) and suitable arrangements can be made for the child here. *And*
2. The adults whom the child is joining are able and willing to support and accommodate the child, without recourse to public funds. *And*
3. The child has an entry certificate authorizing him or her to come here.

Children aged over 18 must usually qualify for admission in their own right, not as your dependants. But an unmarried daughter of any age, and a son under 21 who is fully dependent, can be admitted provided that they formed part of the family unit overseas and the whole family are settled here or being admitted for settlement.

As with wives, children are sometimes refused entry because the immigration authorities do not accept that the child is really yours. The exact age of the child may be disputed to show that the father cannot have been with his wife when the child was conceived, or to show that the child is too old to qualify to come here. Problems are most frequent if you come from a country where public records are not kept in the same way as they are here.

A child may also be refused entry if he or she is coming to join one parent here. The parent has to show that he or she has had

sole responsibility for the child's upbringing. The Home Office will take into account factors such as:

- the length of time for which you have been separated from your child;
- the arrangements you made for the child before you came here;
- the existing arrangements;
- the proportion of costs of your child's maintenance which you have met (you should produce any documents you have to prove how much money you have sent for the child's upbringing);
- whether you have taken the important decisions about the child's upbringing;
- the relationship between you and the child.

But remember that the fact that somebody else has helped to bring up your child will not necessarily prevent you from proving that you have sole responsibility.

PARENTS AND GRANDPARENTS

You can only bring your parents here in very limited circumstances. If they come together, one must be aged 65 or over. A widowed father must also be aged 65 or over, but a widowed mother can be admitted whatever her age.

However, you must be able to show that:

- your parents are wholly or mainly dependent on you; *and*
- you have the means to support them and any other relatives who could come in as your dependants (see p. 281); *and*
- you have adequate accommodation for them; *and*
- they have a current entry certificate authorizing them to come here.

If one of your parents has remarried, she or he will not be admitted if she could look for support to the second spouse. Even if support is not available, entry will be refused unless you can show that you have sufficient means to support not only your parent and step-parent, but also any children of the second marriage who could be admitted as dependants.

You should always make sure that you can show the immigration officers proof of the accommodation you have for your parents. If is often helpful to get evidence from the local authority social services or environmental health departments. If you cannot provide satisfactory accommodation in your own home, genuine housing arrangements elsewhere should be accepted.

It is very rare for parents or grandparents to be admitted to this country as dependants. In 1975, only 279 people from Commonwealth countries were allowed to come here in this category.

DISTRESSED RELATIVES

The only other relatives you may bring here are those described as distressed relatives. The rules have been made very tight so that very few of your relatives will qualify. You will have to show that the relative:

– is aged 65 or over and is your brother, sister, aunt or uncle; *or*
– is aged under 65, but there are 'exceptional compassionate circumstances'; *and*
– is 'distressed', i.e. has a standard of living substantially below that of his or her own country; *and*
– is isolated, living alone with no relatives in his or her own country; *and*
– has a current entry certificate authorizing him or her to come here as your dependant.

So unless your relatives are almost destitute they have very little chance of joining you here.

Leaving the UK

For a temporary absence abroad

Only patrials (see p. 265) are guaranteed the right to enter *and re-enter* freely. If you are a non-patrial then . . .

If you come to this country for a temporary period (e.g. visitors, students), your passport will be stamped with the date when you must leave. If you do not get your stay extended, you commit a criminal offence by staying after that date. If you leave the country before that date and want to come back, you must qualify afresh. You will not be automatically re-admitted, even if there is time left on the original stamp.

If you are waiting here for your immigration appeal to be heard, it is safer not to go abroad until the appeal has been heard. Although the immigration authorities have allowed people to return for an appeal hearing, there is no guarantee that they will do so.

If you are settled here (see p. 279 for when this happens), you will be allowed to return if you have not been away for longer than two years. But you will have to show that you were settled here when you left, and that you did not receive assistance from public funds towards the cost of leaving. If you have been away for more than two years, you may still be allowed back if you have lived here most of your life or for a considerable period, and you have close family ties here. If you are admitted, your family will be allowed to come in with you.

You can be refused entry if you have a criminal record, are subject to a deportation order, or an exclusion order (see p. 538) or if it is decided that your exclusion is 'conducive to the public good'.

You do not need an entry clearance, but it is often safer to get one before setting out.

There is a special provision for Commonwealth citizens who were settled here on 1 January 1973 and at any time in the two years before they applied to return. If you are in this category, you and your family cannot be refused entry. Again, it is wise to obtain an entry clearance, although this is not essential.

Deportation

There are a number of circumstances in which you can be deported from the UK. These are:

1. *You have broken a condition of stay or overstayed your permitted time.* You will normally be considered for deportation if you

have 'persistently contravened or failed to comply with the conditions or have remained without authorization'. This is also a criminal offence and you can be prosecuted and recommended for deportation (see p. 290). If you are *not* prosecuted or recommended for deportation by a court, then you have a right of appeal against the decision to deport you to an immigration appeals adjudicator (see p. 296). But the chances of winning an appeal are small.

2. *The Home Secretary deems your deportation to be conducive to the public good.* The meaning of this phrase is vague and designed to give the Home Secretary wide powers, which may, for example, be used where someone has been convicted of a criminal offence but the court has not recommended deportation. A deportation order may also be made where 'strong and reasonable suspicion exists of criminal activities or associations, or moral turpitude, or both'.

You can appeal to the immigration appeal tribunal (see p. 297) unless the Home Secretary considers your deportation to be in the interests of national security or other political considerations. For these cases, there is a body of advisers, appointed by the Home Secretary. You can make oral and written representations to them although you cannot be legally represented. You will not be told the evidence against you. The advisers' recommendations are not binding on the Home Secretary.

3. *The authorities have decided to deport someone else in your family.* Only the immediate members of the family are liable to be deported: a man's wife and children under 18; a woman's children under 18. A wife will not usually be deported if:

– she has qualified for settlement in her own right (e.g. as a work-permit holder); *or*
– she has been living apart from her husband; *or*
– the marriage has been dissolved.

Even if the marriage has been dissolved, children aged under 18 can still be deported along with a parent. But they should not usually be deported if they have spent some years here or are nearing 18. Once aged 18, they cannot be deported.

The Immigration Rules set out factors which the Home Secretary must take into account in deciding whether to deport a wife or children of a deportee. They include: length of residence here; any ties the family may have apart from being the dependants of the deportee; the wife's ability to maintain herself and her children without recourse to public funds; any compassionate or other special circumstances; and any representations made on their behalf.

You can appeal to the immigration appeals tribunal (see p. 297) against a decision to make a family deportation. If a member of the family decides to appeal, remember that it is not possible to challenge the truth of any statement made with a view to getting permission to come here initially, unless you can show that the statement was not made by you or anyone acting on your behalf, *and* that when you entered the UK you did not know about the statement or, if you did, that you were then under 18.

4. *You have been convicted of an offence for which imprisonment could be imposed, and the court recommends deportation.* You can be recommended for deportation even if you have not

been sent to prison: the risk of deportation arises as soon as you are found guilty of an offence which could be punished by imprisonment.

You cannot be recommended for deportation on conviction if:

– you are under 17 when you are convicted; *or*
– you are a Commonwealth citizen and have been resident here for the previous five years.

The court must give you seven days' notice that you are liable for deportation, and they cannot make a recommendation for deportation until that notice has been given. You or your lawyer are entitled, after you have been convicted, to address the court about all the circumstances which should be considered and which might make the court decide not to recommend deportation.

The court cannot itself make a deportation order. It merely *recommends* a course of action to the Home Secretary. If the Home Secretary then decides to deport you, you have no right of appeal against his decision.

You can, however, appeal against the court's recommendation to deport you, through the normal criminal court procedure (see p. 79). You can appeal against the recommendation to deport you, even if you do not wish to challenge your conviction or the rest of the sentence.

The courts often recommend someone for deportation if they have broken their conditions of entry, but it is not automatic even in these circumstances. Magistrates who are reluctant to recommend someone for deportation are often wrongly led to believe by prosecution lawyers that they have no choice. But a recommendation should not be made unless it is appropriate as part of the sentence. In deciding whether to make a deportation order, the Home Secretary usually regards the existence of a recommendation from the court as a significant factor.

At the end of the court case, you will be detained in custody pending deportation unless the court orders that you are not to be detained, or the Home Secretary decides that you should not be detained. If you are detained, you cannot appeal against the detention or apply for bail. You can only make written representations to the Home Office, asking to be released.

WHO IS EXEMPT FROM DEPORTATION?

The only people who cannot be deported are patrials, and certain Commonwealth and Irish citizens. If you are not a patrial (i.e. someone with a right of abode in the UK), then you will only be exempt from deportation if:

– you are a citizen of a Commonwealth country or the Irish Republic and were a citizen of that country on 1 January 1973; *and*
– you were ordinarily resident in the UK on 1 January 1973; *and*
– you have been ordinarily resident in the UK for five years before the Home Secretary's decision to deport you (or, if you are recommended for deportation following a conviction, for five years before the conviction).

In practice, you will not be deported if the only country to which you can be sent is one to which you are unwilling to go for fear of persecution.

Remember that, *simply because you are settled in the UK, you are not exempt from deportation*. If you are married to a patrial, you can be deported unless you also become a patrial. Even if you are a citizen of a Common Market country, you are still not exempt. If you do not come within the special category listed above, the only way to become exempt from deportation is to become a patrial (as described on p. 265).

THE PROCEDURE FOR DEPORTATION

First, you will be served with a **notice of intention to deport**. This is not in itself a deportation order. You will usually have a right to appeal, which will be explained on the notice.

If you give notice of appeal, the Home Office will send you a statement setting out the reasons for the decision. Your appeal will be dealt with by the immigration appeals authority (see p.

297). As long as you have a right of appeal (i.e. for fourteen days after the notice of intention is served), or the appeal itself is waiting to be heard, the Home Secretary cannot sign the deportation order.

If your appeal fails, or the appeal period runs out and you do not make an appeal, the **deportation order** will be submitted to the Home Secretary for his signature. Until it is signed, the order is not effective, and you can legally remain here.

When you receive the notice of intention to deport, you will get another notice setting out the directions to secure your removal. You will usually be sent to the country of which you are a citizen. You can only be sent elsewhere if you can show that another country will take you, despite the deportation order, and the Home Office agrees. Although you can appeal against the directions of removal, it is pointless to do so unless you can produce documentary evidence that another country will accept you.

Providing that the proposed deportation does not arise out of a court conviction, you will not usually be detained in custody while waiting for your appeal to be heard. But the Home Secretary does have the power to have you detained pending an appeal. If this happens, you have a right to apply for bail to the immigration appeal adjudicator or tribunal (see p. 297), provided that you are also appealing against the notice of intention to deport you.

If you are recommended for deportation by the court following conviction, and the court does not sentence you to an immediate term of imprisonment, you will still be detained unless the court or the Home Secretary decide otherwise. It is therefore essential to ask the magistrate or judge to be released at the end of your case.

If you are convicted and sentenced to prison, the decision to deport you will not be made until towards the end of your sentence. You will not be allowed to leave the country until you have completed your sentence.

It can take some weeks for the Home Secretary to decide whether or not to deport you following a conviction. You may decide not to wait, but to leave the country immediately. The

Home Office will usually be quite cooperative, and arrangements can be made for you to leave even if you are in prison (provided that you are not serving a sentence, but only being detained while a decision is made).

But it is still important to make representations (see p. 300) asking the Home Secretary not to make the deportation order. This can be done more easily while you are still in the country, although in any event the Home Secretary should take into account your decision to leave. If you simply leave without the Home Office taking a decision whether or not to make the deportation order, you could have difficulty coming back.

FACTORS TAKEN INTO ACCOUNT IN MAKING A DEPORTATION ORDER

The Immigration Rules state that when a decision to deport is made, every relevant factor is taken into account. In most appeals against a deportation notice, the authorities will consider the following:

- age
- length of residence in the UK
- strength of connections with the UK
- personal history including character, conduct and employment records
- domestic circumstances
- compassionate circumstances
- any representations made on your behalf
- if you have been convicted of a criminal offence, the nature of that offence
- previous criminal convictions

THE EFFECT OF A DEPORTATION ORDER

A deportation order brings to an end any permission to stay in this country. If you return, the deportation order still exists and you will not be re-admitted; if you are admitted in error, you can be removed under the original order without a right of appeal.

HOW LONG DOES A DEPORTATION ORDER LAST?

A deportation order ceases to have effect if you become a patrial as described on p. 265). You can also apply to the Home Office, or the British Embassy or High Commission overseas, to have the deportation order **revoked** i.e. cancelled. If the authorities refuse to revoke your deportation order, you can appeal to the adjudicator (p. 297) unless the Home Secretary personally decides that your exclusion is 'conducive to the public good'. But you cannot appeal while you are still in the UK: you must leave the country and then make your appeal. You will not be allowed to attend the appeal hearing, but your representatives can do so.

In deciding whether to revoke the deportation order against you, the authorities will take into account the reasons for making the order originally, and the case made out in support of your application. The Immigration Rules state that 'the interest of the community (including the maintenance of effective immigration control) will be balanced against any compassionate circumstances'. If you have been convicted of a serious criminal offence, you can normally expect to be excluded from this country for a long period. In other cases, you would have to show changes in circumstances, new information not available when the original order was made, or simply the fact that a sufficient period of time has passed. No fixed time period is set out in the Rules. The Home Office works on the principle that at least two years must pass before revocation can be considered. But the immigration appeals tribunal has allowed at least one appeal where only fifteen months had passed.

If the deportation order is revoked, this does *not* entitle you to re-enter this country. It merely makes you eligible to qualify for admission under the Immigration Rules. You will have to apply for entry in the normal way under one of the categories set out on pp. 271–6.

CAN A MENTALLY ILL PERSON BE REMOVED FROM
THIS COUNTRY?

Any non-patrial person who is an in-patient receiving treatment
for mental illness can be removed from the UK on the Home
Secretary's order. But no Commonwealth citizen can be removed
unless it can be shown on medical advice that it would be in the
patient's own interests. The patient does not have to be removed
to his or her own country, provided that another country will
accept the patient. The cost of removing the patient and family
will be met by the Home Office.

Repatriation

The Home Secretary has the power to pay the expenses –
including the family's travelling costs – of those who wish to
leave the UK for a country where they intend to live permanently. *This is a voluntary scheme*. Politicians who talk about
forcible repatriation are advocating something which is not part
of the present law.

   The **International Social Service of Great Britain, Cranmer House, 39 Brixton Road, London SW9 (01-735 8941)**
administers the repatriation scheme. If you are considering
using it remember that you may have considerable difficulty if
you and your family ever decide to try to return here. Before
making a decision, it is worth consulting all members of your
family here and abroad.

Appeals and representations

Appeals against a decision by the immigration authorities

You have a right of appeal following a refusal by immigration
officials to allow you to enter or remain in the UK. In detail,
this means that you can appeal against:

– refusal to let you enter;
– refusal to give you an entry certificate;

- refusal to give you a certificate of patriality;
- the conditions on which you are admitted;
- the changes made to your conditions of entry, and any refusal to change them;
- most decisions to make a deportation order;
- most refusals to revoke a deportation order;
- directions for removal to a different country.

THE APPEALS SYSTEM

There is a two-tier system of appeal, with an adjudicator (appointed by the Home Secretary) and an immigration appeal tribunal (appointed by the Lord Chancellor). Appeals are normally heard by an adjudicator in the first instance and you may then be able to appeal in certain limited circumstances to the tribunal.

Adjudicators sit in most areas where there is a substantial immigrant community. The tribunal sits only in London.

If a decision is made against which you have a right of appeal, you will be served with a notice (by hand if you are at a port of entry, or by post to your last known address) informing you of your rights of appeal.

GETTING HELP WITH YOUR APPEAL

The appeal notice will tell you that you can go to the **United Kingdom Immigrants Advisory Service** (UKIAS) for advice. UKIAS is financed by the Home Office, although independent in its operations, and provides an advisory and representative service for appeals. The **Joint Council for the Welfare of Immigrants** (JCWI), an independently financed group, also provides help in many cases. NCCL can sometimes help in deportation cases (especially those involving a court case and deportations 'on grounds of public good') and cases of political refugees. (Addresses on p. 310.)

It is possible to employ a solicitor to help you with your appeal, although most solicitors have no experience of immigration appeal cases. Legal aid is not available to pay for representation at the appeal hearing, so you will have to pay for this yourself. But you can get advice from a solicitor under the green-form scheme (see p. 494).

APPEALING FROM OUTSIDE THE UK

In some important cases, you can only appeal once you have left the UK. In particular:

- if you are refused leave to enter, you can only appeal from outside the UK unless you have a current entry clearance or work permit;
- if you are appealing against a refusal to revoke a deportation order, you must appeal from outside the country.

In almost all other cases, you can appeal from inside this country. You should remember that if you are refused a certificate of patriality, you do not need to wait in your own country until the appeal is heard. You can come to Britain and appeal from here. But there are dangers in doing this unless you can bring enough evidence to prove your case, since otherwise you will lose your appeal and may be sent back.

HOW TO MAKE YOUR APPEAL

You will be told you have a right to appeal. You will be sent a letter telling you how long you have to make your appeal. *Check this date very carefully*. In most cases, where you are in this country, the time limit is fourteen days. If you are appealing against an immigration officer's refusal to let you enter the country, the time limit is twenty-eight days. If you are appealing against the entry certificate officer's refusal to give you an entry certificate, the time limit is three months. Although you will sometimes be allowed to appeal outside the time limit, this is rare.

Before the time limit ends, you must state your grounds for appeal to the Home Office. These should set out the general reasons why you wish to appeal. You should not set out all your evidence – save this for the hearing. As soon as possible after you give notice that you are appealing, the Home Office must prepare a written statement of the facts relating to the case, giving reasons for their decision, and send a copy to you and to the appeals adjudicator.

THE APPEAL HEARING

Most cases are heard by an appeals adjudicator. The proceedings are fairly formal, although not as formal as in a law court. If you are in the country, you should attend, and you will be expected to give evidence. Although you cannot be forced to give evidence, it is generally advisable to do so. The Home Office will have the opportunity at the beginning to expand on their written statement. You will be asked questions by your representative (if you have one), by the Home Office representative and by the adjudicator (or members of the tribunal, if the case is being heard by them). You can then call witnesses, who will also be questioned. The Home Office will rely on their explanatory statement and on cross-examining you and your witnesses, and do not usually call any witnesses themselves. You will therefore not be able to question anyone from the Home Office about your case.

Finally, you or your representative can make a statement to the adjudicator, stressing the reasons why your appeal should be upheld. The Home Office representative can also address the adjudicator. The adjudicator or tribunal may give you their decision immediately, but will always send written reasons to you or your representative for their decision.

MAKING A FURTHER APPEAL TO THE TRIBUNAL

Both you and the Home Office can sometimes appeal against the adjudicator's decision, if you are dissatisfied.

You must ask the adjudicator's permission to appeal to the tribunal immediately after the decision is given. Alternatively, you can apply to the tribunal for permission to appeal; this must be done within fourteen days if you are in the UK, or within forty-two days if you are outside the country. Permission to appeal to the tribunal must be given if it concerns a 'point of law' (that is, if you are arguing that the adjudicator made a wrong interpretation of the law) and in some other circumstances.

The tribunal consists of a chairperson, who is a qualified lawyer, and two other people. Normally the appeal will consist of legal argument about the adjudicator's decision. The tribunal cannot re-hear your case, although new evidence can be called if it existed but was not available when the original decision was made. The decision is usually given at the end of the hearing, with written reasons being sent later.

Making representations to the Home Office

If you have been recommended for deportation, you will have an opportunity to make representations to the Home Secretary asking him not to make a deportation order.

In other cases, where you have no right of appeal or the appeal has failed, nothing is lost by making representations to the Home Office. Even where an adjudicator has rejected your appeal, perhaps because there were no new circumstances in your case, the Home Secretary still has a discretionary power to allow you to remain in this country or to vary your conditions of stay.

The following points may be useful if you are approaching the Home Office.

1. Always try and find out the grounds on which the Home Office has decided your case, so that you can ensure that your representations include all possible relevant information.
2. Where possible, enlist the support of MPs, trade unionists and others who can make representations for you. Do not delay: speed is usually essential.
3. Remember that UKIAS and JCWI (addresses on p. 310) may be able to advise you and give help in drafting or making representations.
4. When setting out your representations in writing to the Home Office, make sure they are clearly laid out and that the important points are properly emphasized. Avoid repetition. Where-

ever possible, include documentary evidence to support your statements.

5. If you see a Home Office representative, make a short note of your interview immediately afterwards. This may help at a later date if there is a dispute about what has been said. Mistakes have been known to occur on both sides. If you are in any doubt about the effect of anything said to you at your interview, write to the Home Office for clarification, or contact the organization helping you or your MP for help.

Criminal offences under immigration law

The Immigration Act 1971 creates a number of criminal offences relating to immigration.

If you are a **non-patrial**, it is an offence to:

– enter the UK without leave;
– exceed your permitted stay;
– fail to comply with the conditions of your stay (e.g. by taking a job despite not being allowed to work without permission);
– fail to comply with certain instructions of immigration officers.

For all except the last offence, a police or immigration officer can arrest you without a warrant if they have reason to believe you have committed or attempted to commit an offence. The offences carry a maximum penalty of up to £200 fine and/or six months' imprisonment, and must be tried at a magistrates' court.

Assisting illegal immigrants

It is an offence for anyone to be knowingly concerned in making or carrying out arrangements for securing or facilitating the entry into the UK of anyone who you know or have reasonable cause to believe is an illegal immigrant. The offence is punishable by up to £1,000 fine and/or six months' imprisonment if tried in a magistrates' court, or by an unlimited fine and/or up to seven years' imprisonment in the Crown Court.

It is also an offence knowingly to harbour anyone who you

know or have reasonable cause to believe to be either an illegal immigrant or someone who has broken their conditions of stay. This offence must be tried at a magistrates' court, and is punishable by a fine of up to £400 or six months' imprisonment.

General offences

There are also a number of general offences in connection with the administration of the immigration laws. For example, it is an offence if you refuse or fail, without reasonable excuse, to submit to an interview under the Act or to produce any information or document in your possession when asked to do so by an immigration officer. It is also an offence to make false statements or forge entry certificates, certificates of patriality or work permits. Again, these offences can only be dealt with in the magistrates' court and the maximum penalty is £200 fine and/or six months' imprisonment.

The position of illegal immigrants

An illegal immigrant is someone who *enters without permission* under the immigration laws – i.e. someone who enters without presenting themselves to an immigration officer, or someone who enters in breach of a deportation order. Some people refer to 'illegal immigrants' when they talk about those who came here lawfully but have stayed here longer than permitted. But this is not what the law means.

Most illegal immigrants can be removed from the country without a right of appeal.

Special provisions were made for certain Commonwealth and Pakistan citizens when an amnesty was declared by the Home Secretary on 11 April 1974. The full text of the amnesty given by the Home Office to the press is as follows:

The Home Secretary told the House of Commons that he does not propose to exercise his powers under the Immigration Act 1971 to remove illegal entrants who came to Britain before 1 January 1973, and who were exempt from removal by the exercise of similar administrative powers under the old law.

This decision applies to Commonwealth citizens and citizens of Pakistan who entered the country illegally on or after 9 March 1968, and before 1 January 1973. It also applies to Commonwealth citizens and citizens of Pakistan who entered illegally before 9 March 1968 after having been earlier refused admission by an immigration officer.

The decision does not apply to those who were not affected by the retrospective provisions of the Immigration Act 1971. Accordingly it does not apply to foreign nationals, other than citizens of Pakistan, to seamen, to stowaways or to those who have overstayed or who entered in defiance of a deportation order. The decision does not apply to those who entered after 1 January 1973.

Quite separately from the Home Secretary's powers of removal some Commonwealth citizens and citizens of Pakistan covered by the Government's decision have remained liable to prosecution for illegal entry.

Commonwealth citizens and citizens of Pakistan who entered the country illegally before 1 January 1973 and who wish to have their position regularised should apply to the Home Office. They should apply to the Immigration and Nationality Department, Wellesley Road, Croydon, CR9 2BY, or to their nearest immigration office. They should enclose a passport if they have one and whatever evidence they may have of their period of stay in this country. There is no time limit for applying. Once a person has had his position regularised it will be open to his dependants to apply for entry certificates, in accordance with the immigration rules, to join him here.

Commonwealth citizens and citizens of Pakistan who have already been removed as illegal entrants, but who would have benefited from the Government's decision had they been here now, will be allowed to return here but it will be necessary for them to apply for an entry certificate.

Many people are frightened to apply for amnesty because of fears of implicating other people or not being accepted as an illegal immigrant. You should consult one of the organizations listed on p. 310; any information you give them will be treated in confidence.

Remember that if you leave the country before regularizing your position you will lose the benefit of the amnesty.

Travel

Travel inside the UK

There are no general restrictions on travel inside the UK. The following exceptions apply:

- members of foreign embassies may be restricted from travelling outside a certain radius from London;
- someone charged with a criminal offence may be released on bail, provided she or he does not visit certain places. Any such condition must not be too restrictive. For instance, an old age pensioner protesting outside Parliament against low pensions was charged with obstruction of the highway and given bail on condition that he did not enter the City of Westminster until after his trial. The High Court decided the condition was unreasonable and forbade him from going within 100 yards of the Houses of Parliament;
- under the Prevention of Terrorism Act, someone may be excluded from England, Scotland and Wales, and sent back to Northern Ireland or the Republic of Ireland; similarly, someone may be forbidden to enter Northern Ireland (see pp. 538–42).

Travel outside the UK

PASSPORTS

You should not try to leave this country without a passport. Although you may not be stopped by the immigration authorities here, airlines and shipping companies will insist on your producing a passport before allowing you to travel. Immigration authorities in other countries will usually not allow you to enter without a passport.

In many other countries, particularly in Europe, people are issued with national identity cards and can come into this country if they produce their card (see p. 266). Since we do not have ID cards, it is essential to get a passport.

Applying for a UK passport

Passports are issued by the Passport Office, which is part of the Foreign and Commonwealth Office. Any UK citizen (see p. 262) may apply for a passport. There are two kinds of passports:

– a full passport, valid for ten years (it cannot be renewed at the end of this time; you must get a new one);
– a passport valid for one year only. These are issued by main post offices, and are cheaper than the full passport, but the countries you can visit with this passport are limited.

To apply for a passport, you should get the application form from your post office or from the **Passport Office, Petty France, London SW1**. You will need:

– your completed application form;
– your birth certificate and any previous passport;
– two passport-sized photographs;
– the current fee (check this with the post office).

The application form and one of the photos will have to be signed by a 'responsible' member of the community who has known you for at least two years, e.g. a solicitor or doctor.

You are not entitled to a passport as of right, although normally you will have no difficulty getting one. Passports are the property of the government, and can be taken away from you for any reason. If this happens, you have no right to appeal against the decision. On rare occasions, people have been refused a passport because of their political sympathies. Problems can occur in the following circumstances:

– if you have been charged with a criminal offence, and the prosecution believe you will leave the country and not return;
– if you have travelled abroad and the Foreign Office has paid all or part of the costs of bringing you back, your passport will be confiscated until you have repaid the money.

Possession of a UK passport does not necessarily mean you can enter this country freely. You will also need to be a patrial (see p. 265).

Children under 18 need the consent of their parent or guardian before they can get their own passport. Children can be included on their parents' passports, provided they are UK citizens, until they reach the age of 16.

Foreign citizens may have problems if their embassy refuses to renew a passport. In some cases, the Foreign Office will provide a British Travel Document so that you can travel abroad.

PASSING THROUGH CUSTOMS

When you come back from abroad, you must pass through customs so that you, your baggage, and any vehicle you have can be examined by the customs officer. He may ask any relevant questions, require you to open your baggage, and search your car. When he has finished, it is up to you to repack and reload your belongings.

Some busier ports and airports have introduced a process of self-selection for passing through customs. If you have nothing to declare, you pass through the 'green channel' and go straight to your departure point. If you have something to declare or are uncertain, you pass through the 'red channel' to the customs bench. Occasional spot checks are made on people passing through the 'green channel'.

If you arrive in the United Kingdom by private transport, you should arrive only at a port or airport that has the approval of the Commissioners of Customs and Excise (although the rule is relaxed for private yachts), and you must report your arrival to the customs authorities.

Duty-free goods

If you have been abroad for more than twenty-four hours, you may bring back certain goods duty-free. Notices telling you what these are are displayed in customs halls, in departure areas if you are travelling by boat or aeroplane, in airport lounges and on cross-channel boats. A leaflet on *Passing through Customs* is available from travel agents and local Customs and Excise offices. These allowances only apply to the goods you bring back with you, not to anything sent through the post, or to unaccompanied luggage. There are no restrictions on what you can do with your duty-free allowances.

If you take anything valuable abroad which is foreign-made or not easily identifiable as British, but which you bought in the UK, it is advisable to take the receipt with you, as it is up to you to prove that you have paid the necessary duty or tax on it. (It is no use showing the camera, etc., to the customs officials on the way out.)

Imports

In addition to duty-free allowances, there is nothing to stop you bringing back as many goods as you like from abroad (apart from prohibited goods), provided that you can pay the duty. If you bring them as far as the British customs and then find that you cannot pay for them, the customs officer will keep the goods and give you a receipt. If you do not pay the duty within 3 months, the customs may, after giving you due notice, dispose of them.

If you are importing goods not as passengers' baggage, you must 'enter' them officially, or arrange for an agent to do so. The rates of duty and import prohibitions and restrictions are shown in the *Customs and Excise Tariff*, which can be found in the reference section of a public library or can be bought from any bookseller; it also tells you how to 'enter' goods.

POWERS OF CUSTOMS OFFICERS

Customs officers have wide powers of entry and search, but they are bound by the same Judges' Rules as the police (see p. 45).

If a customs officer is not in uniform and you have the slightest doubt as to his identity, ask him to produce his commission, which contains his name and indicates that he has been appointed an officer of Customs and Excise.

Search

A customs officer may enter any ship, vehicle or aircraft at any place or time and conduct a thorough search; he does not need a warrant. He may dismantle or break open any part of it and break any lock or container. (If considerable damage is caused and nothing is found it may be possible to claim compensation.)

If the officer finds any goods which appear to be smuggled, he may seize them, as well as the ship, vehicle, aircraft and any other equipment used for smuggling. He may order a ship or aircraft to go to a certain place for further inquiries; he may demand to see any papers or documents that might be connected with an importation, and make copies of them.

The officer may search anywhere for uncustomed goods if he has a warrant from a magistrate or a writ of assistance from a senior customs officer; you should always ask to see these documents and read them carefully. During the hours of darkness, the customs officer must be accompanied by a uniformed policeman.

Do not carry away the officer on your yacht, as it could cost you £100!

Search of person

If a customs officer has reasonable grounds to suspect that you have entered or are about to enter or leave the country, and that you are carrying an article on which the necessary duty has not been paid, or which is prohibited, he may search you. You may insist that he first obtains the authority of a magistrate or a senior customs officer, but you will probably be detained while this is being sought. A woman may only be searched by another woman.

Interception of literature

Customs officers have the duty of intercepting any obscene or pornographic literature which they find when they are examining cargo or passengers' belongings. They are not given any definition of obscenity, but there is a blacklist (not available to the public) which contains works thought to be obscene and which is claimed to correspond to the standards applied by British courts (see p. 315). In doubtful cases, the decision is referred to the Commissioners of Customs and Excise.

Exports

Customs officers also have powers to examine anything leaving the country, particularly currency, and anything that may contravene the Exchange Control Act 1947 or any export prohibitions.

Seizure

Illegally imported or exported goods, including obscene material, may be seized. This may be done with or without written notice, provided that the owner, his employee or agent, or the person whose action led to the seizure, is present. In other circumstances, a written notice of seizure must be delivered to the owner, if known.

The owner has one month from the date of seizure to claim that the goods should not be forfeited. The claim should be addressed to the Customs and Excise department named on the notice of seizure. The Commissioners of Customs and Excise must then take the case to court to prove that the goods were justifiably seized. If no claim is made within one month, the goods may be disposed of.

The owner can also appeal that an article be restored to him on compassionate or similar grounds. If the Commissioners are proved wrong in seizing goods they must restore them to the owner.

Arrest of offenders

If a person is caught smuggling, he may be detained, taken to a police station and charged; or proceedings may be started at a later date, by issuing a summons or a warrant. HM Customs and Excise conduct the case. If new evidence comes to light, the Commissioners of Customs and Excise have the power to remit fines or terminate prison sentences already imposed by magistrates and to restore goods that have been seized.

Organizations which can help with immigration problems

International Social Service of Great Britain, Cranmer House, 39 Brixton Road, London SW9 (01-735 8941) – prepares reports on family and children overseas for submission to Home Office and appeals bodies.

Joint Council for the Welfare of Immigrants (JCWI), 44 Theobalds Road, London WC2 (01-405 5527).

Kent Committee for the Welfare of Migrants, 39 Limes Road, Folkestone (0303 75920) and Lomgstraat 107, 8400 Ostend, Belgium – welfare organization serving channel ports.

NCCL, 186 King's Cross Road, London WC1 (01-278 4575) – only deals with political and court cases.

National Union of Students, 3 Endsleigh Street, London WC1 (01-387 1277).

MIND (National Association for Mental Health), 22 Harley St, London W1 (01-637 0741) – mental in-patients subject to removal from this country.

United Kingdom Council for Overseas Student Affairs (UKCOSA), 60 Westbourne Grove, London W2 (01-229 9268).

United Kingdom Immigrants Advisory Service (UKIAS), 7th floor, Brettenham House, Savoy Street, London WC2 (01-240 5176). (Central office – also has offices at ports of entry and cities where an appeals adjudicator sits.)

UK representative of United Nations High Commissioner for Refugees, 14 Stratford Place, London W1 (01-629 3862).

13. Censorship and secrecy

This chapter deals with:

These all concern restrictions on the publication of information or artistic works. The law may provide protection for the individual and the community (e.g. restrictions on publication of libellous material, or information relating to national security), but in other cases, it is used for more dubious purposes.

Obscenity, indecency and public morals

The right to publish, sell, exhibit and possess any book, picture, magazine, or other written or illustrated material depends initially on whether it is judged to be 'obscene'. The most important laws are the Obscene Publications Acts 1959 and 1964. Other laws in this field are discussed on pp. 314–16.

Obscene Publications Acts

The Obscene Publications Act 1959 makes it illegal to publish obscene matter, whether for gain or not. It is also illegal to possess any obscene article with the intention of making a *profit* out of it; this includes books, pictures, films and photographic negatives. Private collections of obscene material, not intended for further publication, are not illegal, although this does not, in practice, prevent the police from seizing such collections and refusing to return them.

WHAT IS 'OBSCENE'

No two people can be counted on to agree about the meaning of 'obscenity'. Not only have distinguished judges contradicted each other in their attempts to define it, but the word has changed its meaning considerably during this century. For instance, pubic hair, once thought to be obscene, is now freely depicted, and until 1970, it was an offence to display the words 'venereal disease' in public.

The definition provided by the 1959 Act is that an article is obscene if 'taken as a whole, it is such as to deprave and corrupt persons who are likely, having regard to all the relevant circumstances, to read, see or hear the matter contained in it'. 'Deprave and corrupt' clearly indicate a stronger reaction than 'shock and disgust' or 'outrage'. (Indeed, shock, disgust or outrage may indicate an effect opposite to that of corruption.) A more detailed definition was laid down by Lord Justice Salmon in 1968: to corrupt, is to induce or promote:

– erotic desires of a heterosexual nature
– homosexuality or other perversions
– drug-taking
– brutal violence

The definition is, of course, unreliable because no one has been able to prove that drug-taking, violence or perversions can be induced by books, pictures, films or magazines. Encouragement of drug-taking or brutal violence is dealt with by other legal controls. Thus, the Obscene Publications Acts appear to exist in order to punish the promotion of activities which in themselves may be both lawful and normal, and yet are equated with 'depravity'.

ENFORCEMENT OF THE LAW

There are two different procedures which may be used to enforce the Obscene Publications Acts. These are:

1. Someone accused of an offence relating to obscene publications may be tried, either in the magistrates' court (maximum penalties six months' imprisonment and/or a £100 fine), or in the Crown Court (maximum penalties three years' imprisonment and/or an unlimited fine). A defendant who wants to

fight the case always has the right to choose trial before a jury in the Crown Court.

2. The police may seize the allegedly obscene material, using a warrant from the magistrates' court (see p. 28), and apply to the magistrates for a **destruction order**. The occupier of the place where the material was found then has to show good reason, to the magistrates' court, why the material should not be forfeited or destroyed (Obscene Publications Act 1959, section 3). (This also applies to the use of a vehicle or stall if allegedly obscene material was found there.) The effects of this procedure are:

- the accused person has no right to apply for trial by jury;
- the defendant has to prove his or her innocence (i.e. that the material is not in fact obscene);
- the operation of destruction orders varies from area to area, making it impossible for booksellers in one part of the country to know whether the local police will follow the example of a different police force.

DEFENCES TO AN OBSCENITY CHARGE

Someone accused of an offence under the Obscene Publications Acts can defend the case on the grounds that publication is justified in the public good. This applies whether the case is heard in the magistrates' court or by a judge in the Crown Court. It is up to the jury or magistrates to decide, first of all, whether or not the material involved is obscene: no expert evidence may be called at this point. Even if the material is considered obscene, the jury must acquit the defendant if it is proved that publication is 'justified as being for the public good on the ground that it is in the interests of science, literature, art or learning or other objects of general concern'.

More recently, the 'public good' defence has been extended to cover unequivocal pictorial and other pornography on the basis that such material is beneficial to those with sexual problems, for whom viewing or reading pornography provides a harmless relief for frustrations which might otherwise have some sinister outlet. But in October 1976, the House of Lords ruled that the interests of the sexually deprived were not 'objects of general concern'.

The 'public good' defence may not be used in magistrates' courts proceedings where the police have applied for a destruction order.

Other laws relating to obscenity

CONSPIRACY TO CORRUPT PUBLIC MORALS

The publishers of 'obscene' or 'indecent' material may be charged with conspiracy to corrupt public morals. In 1960 a publisher of a guide to Soho prostitutes and their trade specialities was found guilty of this charge. Since then, the charge has been used against the owners of a shop selling bondage materials and equipment.

In 1972, the House of Lords upheld a conviction against the publishers of *IT* magazine, which had been prosecuted for publishing 'contact' advertisements for homosexual men, despite the fact that homosexual acts between consenting adults in private had been legalized some years previously. It was confirmed in this case that the offence of **conspiracy to outrage public decency** existed in order to control publications which were 'lewd, disgusting and offensive'. This offence has been used in private prosecutions of films (see p. 317). The 'public good' defence cannot be used.

In 1976, the Law Commission recommended the abolition of these conspiracy offences, as part of a reform of the conspiracy laws.

VAGRANCY ACTS

It is an offence to expose to view any obscene or indecent print, picture or other exhibition, in any street, public place, shop window or part of a building where the public can see it (Vagrancy Acts 1824 and 1838). The maximum penalty is a fine of £100 and/or three months' imprisonment.

Under the Vagrancy Acts, the prosecution only has to prove

Honestly Officer, we were just talking shop

that the display is 'indecent', a term which the law does not define but clearly indicating a lower level of offensiveness than 'obscene' and closer to 'shocking' or 'disgusting'. The test of whether the material is 'likely to deprave and corrupt' does not apply, and the defendant cannot use the 'public good' defence explained on p. 313.

It is also an offence to offer for sale, distribution or public exhibition any profane, indecent or obscene article, to sing profane or obscene songs, or use profane or obscene language, if this obstructs, annoys or endangers other people nearby. The maximum penalty is a fine of £2 or fourteen days in prison.

IMPORTS AND MAILING

It is illegal (Customs Consolidation Act 1876) to import indecent or obscene articles. Customs officers may seize books which have not yet been published and they are supplied with a Home Office blacklist to help them. Someone whose books are seized has one month to notify objections to the Commissioner of Customs and Excise (see p. 309). If no objections are made within that time, the books are automatically forfeited. If objections are made, the case goes to a magistrate. The 'public good' defence described on p. 313 cannot be used in such a case.

It is an offence to send through the post a packet containing obscene or indecent material, or material which has obscene, indecent, grossly offensive or libellous words or designs on the cover. It is also an offence for a person to order such a packet to be sent to him. The Post Office is entitled to detain and destroy such material. The penalty is a fine of up to £100 and/or up to a year's imprisonment (Post Office Act 1953).

It is also an offence to send unsolicited books, magazines or leaflets (or advertising material relating to them) describing or illustrating human sexual techniques. The Director of Public Prosecutions must give his consent before a prosecution is brought. The penalty is a fine of up to £400 (Unsolicited Goods and Services Act 1971).

CORRUPTION OF CHILDREN

It is an offence to produce, sell or hire any book, magazine or other work which is likely to fall into the hands of children and corrupt them: i.e. work which consists mainly of stories told in pictures and portraying crimes, violence, cruelty or incidents of a horrible or repulsive nature. The police must have the Attorney General's consent before prosecuting. The maximum penalty is a fine of £100 and/or four months' imprisonment. A defendant will be acquitted if he can show that he had not examined the work and had no reasonable cause to suspect that it fell into this category (Children and Young Persons (Harmful Publications) Act 1955). There have been no prosecutions under this Act.

The working party set up by the Arts Council in 1968 to investigate the operation of the law on obscene publications concluded that all legislation on this subject should be abolished, with the exception of the Children and Young Persons (Harmful Publications) Act and a section of the Post Office Act 1953 concerning unsolicited and offensive postal packets. They proposed a single law to protect people from being affronted by offensive displays or behaviour in public places. Nothing has been done to implement this recommendation.

Films

It is an offence under the Obscene Publications Acts (see p. 311) to publish, distribute, possess or exhibit an obscene film for gain. A prosecution can only be brought with the consent of the Director of Public Prosecutions. Someone accused of this offence can defend the case on the ground that publication of the film (or soundtrack) is 'justified as being for the public good in the interests of drama, opera, ballet or any other art, or of literature or learning'.

A magistrates' court can order the destruction of copies of an obscene film, provided the DPP consents (see p. 313).

The publisher, distributor or exhibitor of an obscene film can no longer be prosecuted for a common law offence of obscenity or indecency, nor for conspiracy to corrupt public morals or outrage public decency (Criminal Law Act 1977).

LOCAL AUTHORITY CENSORSHIP

Commercial film shows must take place on premises licensed by the local authority, who alone have the legal power to censor actual showings of films. Most local authorities used to delegate their powers to the British Board of Film Censors, which classifies films but has no statutory powers. After the Greater London Council and some other authorities began to use their powers more liberally and license films not passed by the Board of Film Censors, a private prosecution was successfully brought against a film licensed by the GLC on the grounds that it offended against public decency. As a result, local authorities must now refuse a licence to a film they consider *indecent* as well as censoring those films considered obscene.

NON-COMMERCIAL FILM SHOWS

Non-commercial shows include free showings, private showings, and public showings by non-profit-making organizations and film clubs. These showings do not require a local authority licence and are not subject to censorship. Premises must comply with certain safety regulations. Children's cinema clubs come under special control.

Theatres

Theatres must be licensed by the local authority. If a licence is refused, the applicant has the right to appeal to a magistrates' court. Local authorities may impose conditions in the interests of public safety, but may not impose any conditions or restrictions as to the content of plays or the way in which they are performed (Theatres Act 1968).

Those involved in presenting a play or other performance may, however, be prosecuted in the following circumstances:

1. Presenting or directing an obscene performance of a play is a criminal offence, unless it is justified as being for the public good, in the interests of the arts, literature or learning. Both the prosecution and the defence may call expert witnesses.
2. Staging a public performance which involves the use of threatening, abusive or insulting words, intended to incite racial hatred, is an offence if the overall effect of the play is likely to incite to racial hatred.
3. Using defamatory words (see p. 320 for the definition of 'defamatory') in the course of a play is an offence (Theatres Act 1968).

Prosecution for any of these offences must be with the consent of the Attorney General (Theatres Act 1968).

The police may, with a warrant from a magistrate, enter any premises if they have reasonable grounds to suspect that a play is being performed which involves an offence under the Act. A licensing authority or a policeman in uniform may enter licensed premises without a warrant.

A copy of the script of any new play which is publicly performed must be sent to the British Museum.

Contempt of court

Both the civil and the criminal courts have the power to punish someone for contempt of court. The purpose of this power is to make sure that the dignity of the court is maintained and that the administration of justice in the courts is not prejudiced or interfered with.

The following activities may amount to contempt of court:

1. Disobeying the orders or processes of the court. There are two circumstances in particular where contempt of court is involved:
   - refusal to obey an injunction (e.g. Robert Relf was imprisoned for contempt of court after refusing to obey an injunction ordering him to remove a racially discriminatory sign from outside his house);
   - publication of certain information from court proceedings (for example, it is forbidden to publish: details or pictures identifying children, unless the court specifically permits it; information about committal proceedings in criminal cases, unless the defendant asks and the court agrees to reporting restrictions being lifted; information other than names and an outline of the case in divorce proceedings. The courts have also claimed a much wider right to forbid the publication of witnesses' names, e.g. in blackmail cases. Under the Sexual Offences (Amendment) Act 1976 it is forbidden to publish the names of a complainant or defendant in a rape trial unless the court orders otherwise. The defendant may be named if he is convicted.
2. Abusing the judge during a court hearing, throwing eggs at him, or generally making a row. Anyone involved in such a case, including witnesses, or a member of the public who behaved in such a way, could be punished for 'contempt in the face of the court'.
3. Doing or saying anything which might affect judges' dignity or society's faith in their judgment.
4. Publishing a comment on a forthcoming case, which might prejudice the case by influencing the jury or even the judge. For instance, an injunction was granted to the Distillers' Company against the *Sunday Times* to prevent the publication of an article about the thalidomide tragedy before the families' claims for damages had been settled.

The law governing which court will deal with you if you are in contempt of court is complicated but the general rules are:

– if you are accused of contempt of the Court of Appeal you will be dealt with by that court;
– if you are accused of contempt of a magistrates' court, a tribunal or a court martial, you will be dealt with by three judges of the Queens' Bench Division of the High Court (see p. 79) sitting as what is called a 'Divisional Court';
– if you are accused of 'contempt in the face of the court' (see 2. above) or of breach of a court order, or of breach of the rules restricting publication (see 4. above) in any case in the High Court you will be dealt with by that court;
– if you are accused of 'contempt in the face of the court' in the Crown Court or of breach of an order of the court or undertaking given to the court, you will be dealt with by that court;
– if you are accused of any other contempt of court you will be dealt with by the Divisional Court.

If you do not have a solicitor or cannot afford to pay one the Official Solicitor (see p. 84) will help you. If you have legal aid (see p. 496) in civil proceedings that will also cover any proceedings in the case connected with contempt of court.

If you are convicted of contempt the maximum penalties are imprisonment for life and/or an unlimited fine, and the court can also ask you to undertake to be of good behaviour and to forfeit a sum of money if you are not. You can appeal to whatever court would usually hear appeals from the court which convicted you (see p. 79).

If you are imprisoned you may apply to the court for your release at any time on the grounds that you have 'purged' your contempt (e.g. by apologizing or complying with the court order).

Defamation (libel and slander)

Defamation means the publication of something untrue about a person which damages his or her reputation. (It can also mean the publication of a criminal conviction, in breach of the Rehabilitation of Offenders Act; see p. 104.)

There are two kinds of defamation: **slander**, which usually means the spoken word; and **libel**, which is more permanent than slander and includes writing, printing, drawings, photography, films, television and broadcasting.

Defamation can result in a civil action for damages against all those concerned, including the author, publisher, editor, printer and any distributor. In the case of libel, the person bringing the action does not have to prove that he or she has suffered any financial damage. But an action for slander can *only* be brought if financial loss can be proved (except where the slander concerns a person's profession or business, alleges a criminal offence – or suggests that a woman is 'unchaste'!).

Slander can never be a criminal offence. Libel can be a criminal offence, but possibly only where a breach of the peace is likely. A prosecution against a newspaper for criminal libel can only be brought with the consent of a High Court judge. Such prosecutions are extremely rare, but could be used to restrict freedom of the press. Blasphemous libel is also a criminal offence, but prosecutions are equally rare.

Bringing an action

Defamation cases are usually heard by a judge and jury, unlike most other civil cases which are dealt with by a judge alone. (See Chapter 11 for general information on civil cases.) Damages can be very high: in 1976 Lord Bernstein was awarded £36,000 against the *Observer* and the Court of Appeal decided that this was not excessive, considering 'the gravity of the libel and the high position of the plaintiff'.

Neither side in a defamation case can get legal aid, although costs are very high. An action for defamation must be brought in the High Court, although the court may order it to be transferred to the county court.

In order to prove defamation, the person bringing the action must show that the libel was **published**. 'Publication' means communicating the libel or slander to anyone other than the person defamed. Abusing you to your face when no one else is present is *not* defamatory. The extent of publication is relevant to damages: for instance, the jury will take into account the circulation of a newspaper when assessing the amount.

The person bringing the action must also show that the published material refers to him- or herself. The intention of the author or publisher is irrelevant: the question is whether the material could reasonably be understood as referring to him or her, even if the person is not actually named. Material defamatory of a group cannot be the subject of an action unless the group is so small that every individual in it could be identified. For instance, a member of an ethnic minority could not sue because defamatory remarks were made about that community. But defamatory remarks about a local community relations committee could well be actionable by any member of that committee.

Finally, the court will consider more than just the literal meaning of the words: an innuendo can amount to a libel.

DEFENCES

There are five major defences against an action for libel.

Justification

It is a defence to prove that the offending words were true, except under the Rehabilitation of Offenders Act (see p. 104). This is not easy, and it is entirely up to the defendant to provide substantiating details, dates and places in order to prove the truth of what was said. It is not enough to prove that the defendant accurately repeated the words of a third person. It is not a defence to show that the defendant genuinely believed that the offending material was true, if in fact it wasn't, although this may reduce the amount of damages which the court orders the defendant to pay.

Fair comment

It is a defence to prove that the offending words were 'fair comment', i.e. an honest opinion made without malice on a matter of public interest. This defence only applies when the material complained about constituted an opinion, not a statement of fact. The defence will fail unless the facts on which the comment is based are substantially true – i.e. the main facts must be true.

Criticisms which have been invited, either expressly or by implication, such as criticisms of books or films, can normally be defended as 'fair comment'. But fair comment is not usually regarded as a reasonable defence for an opinion about someone's moral character.

Privilege

There are certain situations where people are protected from being sued for libel or slander. This protection is known as 'privilege'. Absolute privilege gives complete immunity; qualified privilege gives protection only if the material is published without malice.

Absolute privilege covers:

- all statements made in the course of parliamentary proceedings and by MPs in the course of their duty;
- parliamentary papers or complete republications of them;
- judicial proceedings, including the acts and words of the judge, defendant, prosecutor and all others taking part;
- fair, accurate and contemporaneous newspaper reports of public judicial proceedings;
- reports of the Ombudsman and relevant communications to him by MPs.

Qualified privilege covers:

- fair and accurate reports of judicial proceedings in any publication, even if the report is not published at the time of the proceedings;
- extracts from parliamentary papers;
- fair and accurate reports of parliamentary proceedings;
- fair and accurate reports of public meetings (provided that the defendant, if requested, publishes a letter of explanation from someone claiming to be libelled);
- material dictated by an employer to a secretary (but publication

to someone other than the secretary and the person who claims to be libelled does not necessarily attract qualified privilege).

Qualified privilege may also cover other cases where there is a public interest in free communication, e.g. where an MP passes on constituents' complaints about a solicitors' firm to the Law Society, or where an employer gives a reference to a prospective employer.

Innocent defamation

If the defendant claims that the words were not intended to be defamatory, and he or she exercised all reasonable care to avoid making a mistake, the defendant may offer to make amends (usually a suitable correction and apology). The person defamed may refuse this and proceed to bring an action, but it is then a defence for the defendant to prove that the words were published innocently.

Apology

It is a defence to show that the libel was inserted without malice and without gross negligence, and to publish a full apology in

the newspaper where the original words appeared (or in another publication chosen by the person defamed, if the newspaper appears less than once a week). This defence is rarely used, because apologies are generally accepted before the matter goes to court.

Official Secrets

Much government information is kept secret and is protected by the use of the Official Secrets Acts 1911 and 1939. These Acts apply throughout the UK (i.e. in Scotland and Northern Ireland as well as in England and Wales).

Spying and prohibited places

Under section 1 of the 1911 Act it is an offence if a person 'for any purpose prejudicial to the safety or interests of the state:

– approaches, inspects, passes over, or is in the neighbourhood of or enters any prohibited place; *or*
– makes any sketch, plan, model, or note which is calculated to be or might be or is intended to be directly or indirectly useful to an enemy; *or*
– obtains, collects, records or publishes or communicates to any other person any secret official code word or pass word or any sketch, plan, model, article or note or other document or information which is calculated to be or might be or is intended to be directly or indirectly useful to an enemy.'

The maximum penalty for an offence under this section is fourteen years' imprisonment and/or an unlimited fine, on each offence, but on separate offences consecutive sentences can be imposed; thus the Soviet spy George Blake was sentenced to forty-two years' imprisonment.

This section is not limited to offences connected with spying, although that is what it is most commonly used for, and it has been used to convict members of the Committee of 100 who held a demonstration at Wethersfield Airfield, which was a prohibited place.

To be guilty of this offence you do not have to intend your actions to be prejudicial to the interests of the state, and you can be convicted even if *you* think that what you are doing is actually in the interests of the state.

The Government of the day determines what the policy and interests of the state are, and that must be accepted by the court. You will not be able to argue that the Government's policy is wrong.

Although the section refers to 'enemy', this means any potential enemy with whom there might be war. So if you take a drawing which might be useful to an enemy if war did break out, you will be guilty even though there is in fact no war.

A prohibited place is:

- any defence establishment or place being used temporarily for defence purposes, or where arms or defence documents are kept (even if the place does not belong to the Government and the arms, etc. are kept there under contract);
- any other place that the Government declares to be a prohibited place if it belongs to or is used on behalf of the Government or is a means of communication (e.g. a railway line) or for power supplies (e.g. gas works).

Defence establishments are therefore automatically prohibited places. The other examples are only prohibited if the Government declares them to be.

The Home Secretary can authorize a police officer of the rank of inspector or above to require a person to answer questions in relation to an offence under section 1. The penalties for refusing are the same as for committing an offence under section 2 (see below).

If is also an offence (carrying the same penalties) to 'obstruct, knowingly mislead or otherwise interfere with or impede' a police officer or any member of the forces engaged on guard, sentry patrol or similar duties in relation to a prohibited place.

Official information

Section 2 of the 1911 Act makes it an offence to:

- have in your possession or control:
  - any of the material covered above; *or*
  - any information of any kind obtained as or from any government official or civil servant or contractor; *and*
- communicate it to any person you are not authorized to communicate it to or use it for the benefit or any foreign power or in any other matter prejudicial to the safety or interests of the state or retain it without having right to do so.

The maximum penalty for this offence is: in a magistrates' court three months' imprisonment and/or £1,000 fine, and in the Crown Court two years' imprisonment and/or unlimited fine. Offences under section 2 are arrestable offences (see p. 37) although the maximum penalty is less than five years.

Section 2 is very wide indeed and it is possible that any civil servant who communicates information to the press or public without the authorization of the Government or the head of the department could be prosecuted under this section, while ministers and heads of department can never be prosecuted because they decide what is an authorized communication. There have been a number of prosecutions for disclosure of material that could not have done any real harm and governments have tended to use this section to protect themselves from political embarrassment. In some of these prosecutions juries have failed to convict. At the time of writing the Home Secretary has promised to introduce legislation in 1978 which will drastically amend the Acts. However, even if the scope of the criminal offences is restricted, civil servants will still be liable to dismissal from employment for unauthorized disclosure. Meanwhile this section is also used to prevent proper public knowledge of what goes on in such institutions as prisons and mental hospitals.

Since 1972 when the United Kingdom joined the Common Market the Acts have also covered people involved in Euratom who communicate or disclose classified information.

It is an offence under the Acts to harbour anybody you know

or ought to know has committed or might commit any offence under the Acts. The maximum penalty is: in a magistrates' court three months' imprisonment and/or £1,000 fine, and in the Crown Court two years' imprisonment and/or an unlimited fine.

No prosecution under the Acts can take place without the permission of the Attorney General.

More information

Tony Bunyan, *The Political Police in Britain*, Julian Friedmann, 1976.

Defence of Literature and the Arts Society, 18 Brewer Street, London W1 (01-734 3786/6800).

14. Individual privacy

This chapter covers:

There is no general legal right to privacy in the UK. If your privacy is invaded – by an official who enters your home without permission; a newspaper which publishes details of your private life; or a credit reference agency which refuses you credit on the basis of inaccurate information – there may be little you can do except complain. This chapter describes what remedies there are in the law.

The European Convention on Human Rights guarantees freedom from interference in private family life and correspondence. One successful case (concerning censorship of prisoners' letters) has been brought under the Convention; see p. 576 for more details.

Officials with the power to enter your home

There are tens of thousands of officials in the UK who have the power, in certain circumstances, to enter private premises. Many only have the power to enter business premises and are not dealt with here. This section describes the most important powers of entry, which may involve officials in entering your home.

The powers of the police to enter and search private premises are dealt with in Chapter I.

In general, if someone asks to come into your home, claiming to be an official, you should:

– ask to see the caller's identity card;

– ask the caller what authority he or she has to enter your home;
– if in doubt, refuse entry and contact the office from which the official claims to come in order to check his or her credentials.

If you have a complaint to make about the way an official behaves, you should complain to your local councillor, in the case of a local authority official; the gas or electricity board, in the case of a gas or electricity official; the collector in charge of VAT at the local office in the case of a VAT inspector; or the Commissioners for the Inland Revenue in the case of a tax inspector.

Fire brigade

A member of a local authority fire brigade who is on duty may enter any premises where a fire has broken out, or where there is reason to believe a fire has broken out. Other premises may also be entered if this is necessary for fire-fighting purposes. The fireman can force entry, if necessary. The permission of the owner or occupier does not have to be obtained. It is an offence to obstruct or interfere with any member of a fire brigade who is involved in fighting a fire; the maximum penalty is a fine of £20 (Fire Services Act 1947).

Foster homes

The Home Secretary can authorize someone (e.g. a social worker) to inspect any home where a child is being fostered. The inspector must produce an official document, proving that she or he has the right to enter. It is an offence to refuse to allow the inspector to enter; the maximum penalty is a fine of £5 or, for a second or subsequent offence, a fine of £20 (Children and Young Persons Act 1969).

Gas and electricity boards

An officer of the gas or electricity board may enter your home if:

– you agree to let the officer enter; *or*

- a magistrate has given the officer a warrant, authorizing the officer to enter; *or*
- there is an emergency and the officer has reason to believe that there is a danger to life or property.

A gas or electricity board official is entitled to ask to enter your home, or to apply to a magistrate for a warrant, in order to:

- inspect the meter or any other fittings;
- disconnect the supply in certain circumstances (see p. 224).

In order to obtain a warrant, the official must show that:

- you have been given at least twenty-four hours' notice; *and*
- he has asked to be admitted and you have refused; *or*
- the premises are unoccupied.

Entry must be at a 'reasonable' time, and the official must leave the house as secure against trespassers as it was when he or she arrived, and make good any damage caused.

It is a criminal offence to obstruct a gas or electricity board official who has a warrant or who asks to be admitted in an emergency; the maximum penalty is a fine of £5. It is *not* an offence to refuse to let the official enter if there is no emergency and the official does not have a warrant (Right of Entry [Gas and Electricity Boards] Act 1954).

Housing

An official authorized by the local authority may enter any house in the area at any 'reasonable' time in order to:

- make a valuation or survey, where a compulsory purchase order is being considered or has been issued;
- examine the premises and make a survey where a notice requiring repairs, a demolition order, a closing order or a clearance order has been served;
- measure the rooms, etc. to determine whether there has been overcrowding;
- ascertain whether there has been a contravention of any Housing Act regulations.

The official must have a written document of authority and must give at least twenty-four hours' notice. It is a criminal offence to obstruct the official, providing the official is authorized and has given notice; the maximum penalty is a fine of £20 (Housing Acts 1957 and 1969).

Mental health

A local authority mental welfare officer may, at any 'reasonable' time, enter and inspect any premises in the area where a mentally disordered patient is living, provided that the officer has reason to believe that the patient is not under proper care. It is a criminal offence to obstruct the officer; the maximum penalty is a fine of £100 and/or three months' imprisonment (Mental Health Act 1959).

Pests

An authorized local authority official can enter premises at any 'reasonable' time to carry out inspections, make sure that regulations are obeyed and take steps to destroy rats and mice. It is an offence to obstruct the official, provided that he or she has been authorized in writing to enter private premises; the maximum penalty is a fine of £5 for a first offence and £20 for a second or subsequent offence (Prevention of Damage by Pests Acts 1949).

Planning

An authorized local authority official may enter premises at any 'reasonable' time for various planning purposes, including:

– preparing or approving development plans;
– dealing with applications for planning permission;
– making a valuation in connection with compensation;
– making a survey in connection with a compulsory purchase order.

The official must give twenty-four hours' notice. It is an offence to obstruct the official, provided that proper notice has been given; the maximum penalty is a fine of £20 (Town and Country Planning Act 1971). The local authority must also pay compensation for any damage caused.

Public health

An authorized local authority official may enter premises at any 'reasonable' time in order to:

- find out if there has been any contravention of the Public Health Act 1936 (e.g. regulations concerning sanitation);
- take action on behalf of the local authority under the Public Health Act.

The official must give twenty-four hours' notice. It is an offence to obstruct the official, provided that proper notice has been given; the maximum penalty is a fine of £10 for the first offence and £20 for a second or subsequent offence (Public Health Act 1936 and Criminal Justice Act 1967).

Rating

A rating valuation officer, or any official authorized by the rating valuation officer, may enter any property in the area at any 'reasonable' time, in order to carry out a survey or make a valuation for the purposes of drawing up rating valuation lists. The official must give twenty-four hours' notice. It is an offence to obstruct the official, provided that proper notice has been given; the maximum penalty is a fine of £5 (General Rate Act 1967).

Social Security

A National Insurance inspector may enter business premises at any 'reasonable' time in order to interview employers, employees and self-employed people about their contributions record. It is an offence not to produce National Insurance certificates or other relevant documents. It is also an offence to refuse to answer the inspector's questions except that you are not obliged to give information which would incriminate you or your spouse (Social Security Act 1975). The maximum penalty for either offence is a fine of £50 and a fine of £10 for each day that the offence continues.

A supplementary benefits investigator (e.g. an official trying to find out if a woman is cohabiting) does *not* have a right to enter your home. If the official forces entry, or refuses to leave after you ask him to, he is committing a trespass and you may be able to take legal action (see p. 73).

Tax

A tax inspector can obtain a warrant from a High Court judge if he reasonably suspects that a tax offence has been committed. The warrant authorizes the inspector to enter and search private premises, and remove documents. Any application for a warrant must be made with the approval of a Commissioner for the Inland Revenue (Finance Act 1976).

VAT

A VAT official may enter any premises, at a 'reasonable' time, for any purposes connected with administering value added tax. The official may enter *without* a warrant, and may also inspect goods which are liable to tax. If the official has reasonable grounds for suspecting you of an offence related to VAT, he may apply to a magistrate for a warrant authorizing him to:

– enter, by force if necessary, at any reasonable time within fourteen days of the warrant being issued;
– seize any documents relating to the investigation;
– search any people on the premises (but a woman can only be searched by another woman).

Obstructing a VAT official could amount to an assault for which you could be prosecuted.

Water authorities

An authorized official of a water authority may enter any premises at a 'reasonable' hour in order to:

– inspect water meters;
– ascertain whether there has been any contravention of the law relating to water supplies;
– detect waste or misuse of water.

In the first two cases, twenty-four hours' notice must be given. In the third case, the official may enter beween 7 a.m. and one hour after sunset. It is an offence to obstruct an official; the maximum penalty is a fine of £5, with a further fine of £5 for every day the offence continues in either of the first two cases, or a maximum fine of £10 in the third case.

Intrusion or harassment by neighbours

There is very little you can do about neighbours who shout abuse, put things through the letter-box, watch you from their garden and so on. If you have a neighbour who is a peeping tom, you should complain to the police, since the person could be bound over to keep the peace by the magistrates' court (see p. 148 for more about binding over). If your neighbour harasses you severely, you may be able to bring a civil action for nuisance (see p. 243).

If a landlord harasses you by shouting abuse, banging on walls or doors, entering your room without permission, or going through your belongings, you may be able to take legal action. Where you have an exclusive right of occupation (in other words, you are a tenant, rather than a lodger or hotel guest), you will be able to sue the landlord in the county court for trespass. If you succeed, you will be able to get damages and an injunction preventing the landlord from repeating the behaviour (see p. 245 for more on county court actions).

You should also report a landlord who harasses you to the local authority, who have the power to prosecute in the criminal courts (Rent Act 1965; see p. 459 for more details).

Unsolicited mailing, etc.

People who come to your door to sell goods, ask you to give to charity, persuade you to support a particular religion or political party or ask questions for a market research or other survey, have no right to enter your home. You can refuse to talk to them, and they must leave when you ask them to.

If you are bothered by unwanted telephone calls, and know who the caller is, you can report the caller to the police. It is a criminal offence to telephone grossly offensive messages, or make indecent, obscene or menacing telephone calls, or calls which cause annoyance, inconvenience or needless anxiety (Post Office Act 1969). In the last resort, you can ask the Post Office, through the operator, to intercept your calls. Alternatively, you can change your number or go ex-directory.

If unwanted goods are delivered to your home or place of work, see p. 213 for what you should do.

It is also an offence to send obscene or indecent material through the post, or to send any unsolicited book, magazine, leaflet or advertising material describing or illustrating human sexual techniques. If you receive such material and object to it, you should complain to the police. (See pp. 315–16 for more on obscenity.)

Telephone-tapping

It is an offence for any official to disclose the contents of a telegram or of a telephone conversation (Post Office (Protection) Act 1884). Telephone-tapping by the security services must be authorized by the Home Secretary, although it is possible that tapping takes place without his consent. In the mid-1950s, there were over 200 authorized telephone taps per year, but official figures have not been given since then.

Unauthorized telephone-tapping, for instance by a private detective, is not an offence, unless it involves damage to telephone equipment, or wasting or diverting electricity (Theft Act 1968). A tap which draws power from the telephone lines is illegal, but a more sophisticated tap or bug does not necessarily involve any diversion of electricity. The maximum penalty for wasting or diverting electricity is a fine of £1,000 and/or six months' imprisonment in the magistrates' court or an unlimited fine and/or five years' imprisonment in the Crown Court.

It is illegal for someone who is an employee of the Post Office to tape-record a telephone conversation. Someone who is not a Post Office employee may tape-record a telephone conversation, but it is a breach of contract with the Post Office to attach any device to your telephone which has not been approved by the Post Office.

Personal information

Most people do not realize how much information is collected and stored about them – by Government departments; private agencies such as credit reference firms, market research departments of large companies; the health service; the police and so on. It is often difficult to find out whether or not a particular organization has a file on you, and usually impossible to get a copy of the file. This section explains what you can do to correct or control personal information about you.

Banks

Banks do not usually disclose their customers' affairs to someone else without authority. But it is usual for banks to give other banks confidential information about the credit-worthiness and reliability of their customers, even if the customer has not specifically authorized the bank to do this. The legal position is unclear. If you are worried about the possibility of your bank passing on confidential information, you should ask your bank what its practice is and ask it to get your specific permission before passing on information about you to anyone else.

Banks must make regular reports to the Inland Revenue about interest payments which are over £25 in a year. Otherwise, a bank should not disclose information about your account to a tax inspector without your authority.

The census

Every ten years, the Government conducts a national census to find out how many people live in the UK. The census also includes detailed questions about living conditions, size of household and so on. It is a criminal offence to refuse to complete a census form; the maximum penalty is a fine of £50.

Census information is collated by the Office of Population, Censuses and Surveys, which is responsible for making sure that the information is kept confidential. Census information should only be used for statistical purposes; nonetheless, after the 1971 census, the Department of Health and Social Security conducted a follow-up survey of ex-nurses, based on names and addresses obtained from the census. It is a criminal offence for any assessor employed by the census to collect the census returns to divulge information; the maximum penalty is an unlimited fine and/or two years' imprisonment.

Computerized data-banks

Personal information is increasingly being stored on computers – by national and local government, the police, banks, commercial firms and so on. In 1976, the Government established a Data Protection Committee to make proposals for legislation to protect personal privacy in relation to computers, and has promised to set up a Data Protection Authority to oversee computerized data-banks held by Government and by private firms.

Credit reference agencies

There are over 2,000 credit reference agencies in the UK. These agencies provide reports to commercial firms on the credit-worthiness of individuals. Many of them also act as debt-collectors. Between them, they have files on most adults in this country.

Some credit reference firms only collect information which is publicly available, especially lists of county court judgments against debtors, which anyone can inspect for a fee. Others maintain information about bad debtors passed from individual companies to a central office, so that other firms can check the record of someone asking for HP or a loan. Some agencies employ people to get more detailed information about people, by talking to neighbours or local tradesmen, for example.

It is a criminal offence to harass a debtor (see p. 225). Threatening to place you on a bad debtors' register might be harassment. If this happens to you, you should report the matter to the police.

The Consumer Credit Act 1974 gives you certain rights to see and correct any credit reference file about you. Under the Act, you have the right to:

– be given the name and address of the credit reference agency used by a firm whom you ask for HP or a loan;
– obtain a copy of any file held on you by any credit reference agency, provided that you pay a fee of 25p;
– give notice to the agency requiring it to remove inaccurate

information from your file, or correct it, if necessary by adding a statement from you of up to 200 words;
– report the matter to the Director General of Fair Trading, if the correction is not made within twenty-eight days.

The Director General of Fair Trading has a general duty to enforce the Consumer Credit Act, and in particular to license credit-reference agencies. If you have a complaint, you should write to the **Director General of Fair Trading, Bromyard Avenue, Acton, London W3.**

Some firms will refuse to lend money or enter into an HP agreement with you if a previous occupant of the same address has a history of bad debts. Provided that the information about the previous occupant is accurate, the Consumer Credit Act will not change this practice. If you are refused credit because your address has been blacklisted, you should complain to the Director General of Fair Trading. Although he will probably be unable to help on an individual case, he may eventually be persuaded of the need to recommend changes in the law.

Criminal records

Criminal records, which are kept by the police, are confidential. It is, however, quite possible for a private detective or some other person to build up a file of criminal records from a newspaper report. In some cases, it is a criminal offence to reveal details of a person's previous criminal record (see p. 104).

The police are *not* allowed to pass on details about someone's criminal record to an employer or anyone else. There are some exceptions to this rule. The police may supply information to professional bodies and prospective employers about the following groups of people: medical practitioners; lawyers; chartered or certified accountants; dentists; vets; nurses and midwives; opticians; chemists; employees in the courts, police or prison service; some social workers; workers with children under 18; some workers in insurance and unit trust companies; firearms dealers; civil service employees subject to positive vetting.

Employers' records and references

There is little you can do if a prospective employer asks you extremely detailed questions about your personal life. If you refuse to answer them, you may be refused employment and, in some cases, if you give false answers which are later discovered, you may be dismissed.

If your employer keeps personnel records on employees, which the employees are not allowed to see, you should ask your trade union to take up the issue. But you have no legal right to insist on seeing your personnel record.

If an employer or employment agency refuses to give you a reference, there is nothing you can do. Similarly, there is very little you can do if a previous employer gives you a reference which is misleading or inaccurate. You have no legal right to see the reference. If you do manage to obtain a copy of the reference, and consider that it is defamatory (see p. 320), you may want to get legal advice. In theory, it is possible to sue an employer who gives you a defamatory reference, but there are two problems: firstly, a reference is covered by 'qualified privilege', which means that you would have to prove that the employer was malicious in saying what he did about you; secondly, since there is no legal aid for libel actions, you would have to pay your own legal costs, and the other side's costs if you lost. NCCL is pressing for a reform of the law in this area.

The Department of Education and Science maintains a blacklist, List 99, of people who are not allowed to be employed in schools, colleges or within the youth service. Someone may be placed on the list following a criminal conviction, or after suspension as a teacher, if the Secretary of State decides that he or she is unfit for employment with children and young people. The person has a right to make representations, either in writing or at a hearing, before being placed on the list. The list, which is updated regularly, is circulated to principals of schools (including independent schools), colleges of further education and so on.

The media

If you consider that your privacy has been invaded by a newspaper or a radio or TV station, you may be able to bring an action for defamation (see p. 320). This is, however, an expensive matter, and you should take legal advice (see p. 496).

You may also wish to make a complaint against a newspaper to the Press Council (see p. 523). A complaint against a radio or TV station should be made to the BBC or IBA (see p. 522).

More information

Office of Fair Trading, Field House, Breams Buildings, London EC 4 (01-242 2858).

NCCL, 186 Kings Cross Road, London WC 1 (01-278 4575).

15. Marriage and cohabitation

There is only space in this chapter to give a brief outline of the law relating to marriage (and separation and divorce) and cohabitation. On p. 352, you will find a list of organizations and books which provide more detailed information.

Marriage

The man has a legal duty to maintain his wife; both parents have a legal duty to maintain their children. If the husband does not give his wife enough money for herself and the children, she can apply to the magistrates' court for maintenance (see p. 345). In exceptional cases, the man will be entitled to claim maintenance from his wife (see p. 346).

RESPONSIBILITY FOR CHILDREN

Both parents have equal rights and responsibilities for their legitimate child (Guardianship Act 1973). This means that decisions about the child's education or religion, consent to medical treatment for the child and so on, should be taken by both parents. If they disagree, they can apply to the court, which will decide the matter. Both parents should take legal advice separately or apply for legal aid (see p. 496).

OWNERSHIP OF PROPERTY

The following general rules apply to ownership of property during marriage:

- you each continue to own anything you yourself bought before the marriage or which you have bought with your own money since then, or which has been bought in your name;
- each of you owns half of the money in a joint account, or anything bought from it, provided you both contributed to it;

– the wife is entitled to half of anything bought, saved or won from housekeeping money from her husband.

If the home you live in (the 'matrimonial home') is in your **joint names**, neither of you can sell it without the other's consent or previous agreement. Even if the home is only in one partner's name, both of you have a legal right to stay there during the marriage. If your partner tries to evict you, you can apply for a court order. In very exceptional cases (e.g. if the husband is extremely violent or has committed incest), the wife can apply to the court for an order to evict the husband. In any dispute over property, both partners should take legal advice separately and apply for legal aid (see p. 496).

If your home is owned by one partner, that partner can sell it without the other partner's consent. But the other partner can prevent the sale by registering a right to occupy the home with the Land Registry or the Land Charges Registry (ask a solicitor how to do this).

CHANGING NAMES ON MARRIAGE

A woman is under no legal obligation to change her surname on marriage. If she decides to change her surname, she can, of course, continue to use the new name if she is widowed or divorced.

A legitimate child must take the father's surname unless the father consents to the child having a different name (see p. 354).

CITIZENSHIP

A foreign woman who marries a UK citizen can apply to be registered as a citizen immediately after the marriage. A foreign man has no such right, although, since 1974, the foreign husband of a woman entitled to settle in this country should be able to come and live here with her. (See Chapter 12 for more on citizenship and immigration).

NATIONAL INSURANCE CONTRIBUTIONS

Married women (although not married men) are allowed to opt out of paying full National Insurance contributions and rely instead on the partner's contributions. If the husband fails to pay contributions when he should, the woman may find herself entitled to only a reduced widow's pension in later years. It is a criminal offence not to pay contributions, except during illness or unemployment or if your income is very low. A woman who discovers that her husband is not paying contributions should try to persuade him to or, in the last resort, contact the Department of Health and Social Security who will chase him up (without revealing that she has contacted them).

IF ONE PARTNER IS VIOLENT

If your partner is violent towards you, you can apply to the county court for an **injunction** (a court order) ordering your partner to stop beating you. If the judge orders the police to enforce the injunction, your partner can be arrested by the police if he or she breaks the injunction. You can apply for the injunction without having to start divorce proceedings (Domestic Violence Act 1976). Emergency legal aid (p. 499) can be granted so that you can get legal advice for the application to the court. You should contact a solicitor, a law centre (see p. 507) or a citizens' advice bureau.

The National Women's Aid Federation, 51 Chalcot Road, London NW1 (01-586 5192) can put you in touch with a women's aid centre.

Separation order

A separation order does *not* end the marriage. It is an order from the magistrates' court which can direct the husband to pay a certain sum of money in maintenance for the wife and any children. It can also say which parent is to have custody of the children, and can include a 'non-cohabitation' clause ending the couple's legal duty to live together.

A man is only likely to get maintenance from his wife if he is unable to maintain himself (e.g. because he is physically incapacitated). The man can claim custody of the children, although the courts will usually only give the father custody of young children if there is some special reason why the mother is considered unfit to have custody. The most important factor in the decision is the interests of the child.

A separation order can be granted to the wife if the husband:

– fails to give his wife enough money to support herself and the children; *or*
– deserts his wife or forces his wife to leave him because of his behaviour; *or*
– is persistently cruel to his wife; *or*
– has committed adultery (provided that the wife has not lived with him for more than three months afterwards, or agreed to the adultery, or encouraged him by refusing to have sexual intercourse); *or*
– has been convicted in a criminal court of assault or indecency towards his wife or any of the children; *or*
– has forced his wife to practise prostitution; *or*
– has had sexual intercourse with his wife, knowing he has VD and not telling her; *or*
– is a habitual drunkard or a drug addict and is dangerous, cannot manage his affairs or is otherwise intolerable to live with.

Under a separation order, a wife cannot claim maintenance for herself if she has committed adultery.

The wife can apply for a separation order while the couple are still living together; this will help her if she wants to leave her husband but cannot until she knows that there will be money coming in. The order will not take effect until the couple separate.

A separation order should be applied for within six months of the incident on which the application is based. The partner applying for the order should contact a solicitor and apply for legal aid (see p. 496). Alternatively, you can go to the local magistrates' court (in the telephone directory under 'Courts') and make the application yourself.

You should go to the magistrates' court in the morning, before the court starts (most start at 10 a.m.). The court officer will help you with your application. The magistrate will hear the application in private and may ask questions. If the application is accepted, a date will be set for the case to be heard and your husband will be sent a summons telling him when to appear in court. You will be expected to be there too.

At the hearing, you and your husband will be able to produce evidence and call witnesses. Often the case is not finished at the first hearing, but another date is fixed some weeks ahead. When the case is finished, the court will decide whether to make a separation order, covering the following points:

1. **Non-cohabitation.** If the court includes a non-cohabitation clause, it means you are no longer legally obliged to live together. If the husband forces his wife to have sexual intercourse he can be prosecuted for rape. A non-cohabitation clause is usually only included if there is little hope of reconciliation or the wife needs protection.
2. **Custody** of the children. The court will order that one partner has custody of the children – i.e. lives with them and looks after them.
3. **Access** to the children. The parent who does not have custody is usually allowed to see the children at certain times, unless he or she is considered a danger to them.
4. **Maintenance.** The husband will be ordered to pay a certain amount each week to help support the wife and children. If the case is not settled at the first hearing and the wife needs money urgently, the court can make an interim order lasting for up to three months. A maintenance order ends if it was granted while the husband and wife were living apart and later start living together again. See p. 349 for what can happen if the husband stops paying maintenance.

Judicial separation

A judicial separation does not legally end the marriage, although it involves the same legal proceedings as a divorce. It is usually used by people who wish to separate but who have religious objections to divorce. You should consult a solicitor, since a judicial separation affects rights to inherit property, etc.

Divorce

You can usually only apply for a divorce after you have been married for three years. The courts will accept a shorter period in exceptional circumstances; you should get legal advice about this.

You can get a divorce if the marriage has broken down irretrievably because:

– you and your partner have lived apart for at least two years and both consent to the divorce (periods together which don't add up to six months or more since you first separated will not prevent you obtaining a divorce; but if you have lived together for more than six months since you first separated, you will need to start the two–year separation period again);
– you and your partner have lived apart for at least five years, even though one of you does not want the divorce;
– your partner has deserted you and stayed away for at least two years;
– your partner's behaviour is so unreasonable that you cannot be expected to live with him or her (e.g. persistent mental or physical cruelty);
– your partner has committed adultery and you find it intolerable to live with him or her.

If your partner wants a divorce and you do not, you should get legal advice. Even if you have lived apart for five years, the courts may refuse to grant the divorce if it would cause one partner grave hardship (Matrimonial Causes Act 1973).

It is now possible to get a divorce without going to a lawyer, provided that you both agree about any financial arrangements and about what should happen to the children. Even if you want a do-it-yourself divorce, you should get legal advice first, in case there are unexpected complications.

Every divorce starts with a petition to a divorce county court (see p. 244) or, in London, the Divorce Registry.

MAINTENANCE

Once either partner files a petition for divorce (or for judicial separation – see p. 347), the wife can apply for maintenance to the divorce court. An **interim order** can be made, until the divorce is finalized. After the divorce, you can ask the court to make the interim order permanent. Alternatively, if you and your ex-husband cannot agree about the amount you should get, your lawyer will apply to the court to fix a figure. You can apply for legal aid (see p. 496) to meet the costs of the application. The court will have to take into account the circumstances of each partner, how long you have been married and so on. As a rough guide, the wife may get one third of the total income and property of the couple, less what she earns herself. But if the wife is young, the marriage was brief and there are no children, the wife will get little or nothing. You should register the maintenance order in the magistrates' court to protect you if your ex-husband does not pay. (An interim order cannot be registered.) The husband is only likely to get maintenance from his wife if she is wealthy or if he is unable to maintain himself (e.g. because of a physical handicap).

WHAT TO DO IF MAINTENANCE IS NOT PAID

If the husband or ex-husband fails to pay maintenance, either under a separation order or following the divorce, the wife should apply to the magistrates' court for an **arrears of maintenance** summons. The court officer can explain how to do this. If this does not help and the man works for an employer, the woman can ask for an **attachment of earnings** order, which means that maintenance is deducted from the man's earnings. If the woman is claiming supplementary benefits, she should ask the local office to let her sign the maintenance order over to them, so that she receives full benefit and they collect the maintenance payments. The Supplementary Benefits Commission (see p. 414) can prosecute a man who fails to pay maintenance which a court has ordered him to pay.

CUSTODY OF THE CHILDREN

If both partners agree about what should happen to the children, it is unusual for the court to interfere. Otherwise, the court will decide who should have custody of the children. The other partner will usually be given access to the children at specified periods.

If the parent who does not have custody tries to take the children away from you or threatens to take them out of the country, you can have the children made wards of court (see p. 365). You should get legal advice urgently if there is any possibility of the children being removed.

Where the mother has custody of the children, she cannot change their surnames without the father's consent.

Cohabitation

The law has an ambivalent attitude towards cohabitation. On the one hand, if a man and woman cohabit, the woman will not be allowed to claim supplementary benefits for herself. On the other hand, the man will not be allowed to claim tax relief for

the woman. A man and woman living together without being married are often called 'common law' husband and wife, although this is not technically correct.

Neither partner has a legal duty to support the other while they live together or after they separate.

Both have a duty to support any children they have. The woman can take affiliation proceedings against the man, in order to claim maintenance (see p. 355). If the court orders the man to pay maintenance and he fails to do so, the procedure is as set out on p. 349.

CHILDREN

The father of an illegitimate child has few legal rights over his child. The mother has sole custody of the child – i.e. the right to make the decisions about how the child should be brought up. The child takes the mother's surname, unless she agrees to having the father's name put on the birth certificate.

The father can, however, apply to the magistrates' court to be given access to the child if the mother refuses to let him see the child. The court will usually agree to such an application, provided that he can prove that he really is the father (e.g. if the mother has accepted or claimed maintenance from him, or has admitted that he is the father in a letter or to some other person). A blood test can only prove that someone is *not* the father of the child: it cannot prove that he is the father.

The fact that a child is illegitimate does not alter its legal status. The parents can make the child legitimate by marrying. If the mother marries another man, she and the new husband can apply jointly to adopt the child or obtain a custodianship order (see pp. 357–61).

PROPERTY

The partner who owns or has a tenancy of the place where you both live can evict the other person. The only situation where a 'common law' wife has any rights to a home owned by the man is where the couple have lived together for a long time, have children, and the man intended the woman to live in the house. (There has never been a court case involving a 'common law' husband in similar circumstances.)

If the couple live somewhere which is jointly owned, then they are both entitled to live there. If they separate and cannot agree on what to do with the property, they can apply to a court to decide the matter. Both should get legal advice.

VIOLENCE

If one partner has suffered violence from the other partner, he or she can apply to the court for an injunction (see p. 345).

More information

Anna Coote and Tess Gill, *Women's Rights: A Practical Guide*, Penguin (revised edition 1977) – also gives details of how either partner can get an undefended divorce.

Getting a Divorce, Consumers' Association (£1·50) – a clear, detailed guide.

Battered Women, NCCL/Interaction, 186 Kings Cross Road, London WC1 – sets out how to get an injunction.

National Marriage Guidance Council, 3 Gower Street, London WC1 (01-935 2838).

One-Parent Families (formerly National Council for the Unmarried Mother and Her Child), 255 Kentish Town Road, London NW5 (01-267 1361).

Gingerbread, 9 Poland Street, London W1 (01-734 9014).

National Women's Aid Federation, 51 Chalcot Road, London NW1 (01-586 5192).

16. Children

This chapter deals with:

Custody is dealt with on pp. 350 and 351, guardianship on p. 343; sex on p. 171; education in Chapter 21 and consenting to medical treatment on pp. 471–3.

This chapter covers many aspects of the law designed to protect children, and to decide who has the obligation to look after them or the right to have custody of them.

There are various legal definitions of the word 'child'. For criminal and care proceedings the categories are:

>age under 14   – 'child'
>age 14 but under 17 – 'young person'
>age 17 but under 21 – 'young adult'

but these are not necessarily the same definitions that are used in other parts of the law.

If you are under 18 you may be restricted from certain activities, some of which are described in this chapter (see pp. 370–72).

A child becomes an adult on his or her 18th birthday. The most significant rights that are gained in practice are:

– the right to marry without parental consent; *and*
– the right to vote and be elected to public office; *and*
– the right to obtain a mortgage and own property.

However, while someone is still under 21 there are still restrictions on what he or she may do (e.g. the legality of any homosexual activity – see p. 175).

Registering and naming a child

A child's birth must be registered with the local registrar of births within 42 days (Births and Deaths Registration Act 1953). A birth certificate will be issued showing the names of the child, its sex and the date and place of birth. There are two versions of the certificate. The 'short' version is free of charge. The 'full' version has to be bought and contains further information including the full names of the child's mother and father, the mother's maiden name, the address and description or occupations of the parents.

Only the mother or the father (or else someone present at the birth – e.g. doctor or midwife) may register the birth of a legitimate child but anyone can obtain a copy of the certificate once it has been issued from the Chief Registrar, St Catherine's House, Strand, London WC2.

A legitimate child is usually given the father's surname. If the child is illegitimate the father's name will not be registered unless both he and the mother are present at the registration and he wants his name to be shown on the certificate or unless the mother can produce an affiliation order naming the father.

A mother cannot legally change the surname of a legitimate child without the father's consent even if they are divorced and she has custody of the child. A child of 16 or over must give consent if the parents wish to change his or her name. A child under 18 cannot alter the names given by the parents without the consent of the father if the child is legitimate, or the mother if the child is illegitimate.

Anyone aged 18 or over can change his or her name without parental consent, either by deed poll or informally. To change your name informally simply means that no legal documents are involved and that you start using the name of your choice. If you are under 18 and have left home there is nothing to stop you changing your name informally.

It is not possible to have your birth certificate changed to show your new name.

Illegitimacy

A child is illegitimate if the parents are unmarried at the date of birth but becomes legitimate if they marry after the birth.

If the parents of an illegitimate child die without making a will, the child has equal rights of inheritance with legitimate children and a right to claim from the estate as a dependent.

A father is under a duty to support his illegitimate child by making payments (i.e. **maintenance**) to the mother either voluntarily or as the result of court proceedings and an affiliation order.

A mother applies for an **affiliation order** by summons in the local magistrates' court. She can only apply for such an order:

– before the child's birth; *or*
– within three years of its birth; *or*
– at any time before the child reaches 13 if the father has made a voluntary payment within three years of the child's birth.

She must convince the court that the man is the father of the child. A blood test can prove that the man is *not* the father, but cannot prove that he is the father.

Although a child cannot make a claim, a person other than the child's mother might. For example, the Department of Health and Social Security may do so if they are supporting the child financially, or a custodian may do so, provided the custodian is not married to the child's mother and the application is made not more than three years after the custodianship order was made.

A mother of an illegitimate child has the rights and duties of a parent regardless of her age. A mother under 16 cannot in law be guilty of neglecting a child. If a local authority considers a child to be in need of supervision it may apply to the court for a care order. If the mother is under 18 it can also apply for a care order in respect of her.

A single mother may be encouraged to have her child adopted but if she decides to keep it she may claim:

– maintenance payments for the child from the father; *and*
– child benefit for the child; *and*
– supplementary benefit for herself and the child (see p. 414).

A mother of an illegitimate child can only lose her rights in respect of the child if she abandons or neglects it or treats it in such a way that the local authority can apply to take the child into care (see p. 361) or if the child is adopted (see p. 357).

The father of an illegitimate child has no automatic rights over a child but can apply to the court for an order for access to the child (which will usually be granted) and for custody (which will usually be refused).

Fostering

Foster parents look after a child but the natural parents continue to exercise all rights and duties over the child. However, if the child is being fostered as a result of a place-of-safety order or a care order, the natural parents lose their rights over the child and these are assumed by the local authority. Parents can appeal against a place-of-safety order or a care order (see pp. 361 and 364).

The local authority has a duty to ensure the well-being of all foster children in its area. Children are usually placed with foster parents by the social services department but there is some private fostering where arrangements are made direct between the natural parents and the foster parents.

In many cases children are fostered because the natural parent does not want the child adopted but is not in a position to look after it. This can sometimes be on a temporary basis, for instance where the child's mother is in hospital, but can sometimes continue throughout the child's non-adult life. The social services department usually hopes to return the child to its natural parents and full access is allowed.

Foster parents can apply to adopt a child who has been with them for twelve months but this is unlikely to be granted if the natural parents have maintained close contact with the child. Foster parents can also apply for a custodianship order (see p. 360).

If a child has lived with foster parents for five years, the child may only be removed with the permission of the court.

Foster parents are entitled to child benefit for the child, a boarding-out allowance unless they become custodians, and maintenance payments from the child's parents.

Children and the courts

Adoption

An **adoption order** is made by a court and transfers all parental rights and duties in respect of a child under 18 from the natural parents to the people applying for the adoption order, who are known as the 'adoptive parents'. The child becomes for all purposes the child of the adoptive parents and stops being the child of the natural parents. These purposes include upbringing, education, religion and inheritance rights.

An application for an adoption order may be made to a juvenile court (see p. 366), to a county court (see p. 243) or to the Family Division of the High Court (see p. 244). In practice most applications are made to a county court. The applications are dealt with in private (Adoption Act 1958).

Where one of the people making the application is a parent, step-parent, brother, sister, grandparent, uncle or aunt of the child, or where the child has been placed with the people applying by an adoption agency (see below) or by an order of the High Court, an adoption order cannot be made unless the child is at least nineteen weeks old and has lived with at least one of the applicants throughout the previous thirteen weeks.

In all other cases an adoption order cannot be made unless the child is at least twelve months old and has lived with at least one of the applicants throughout the previous twelve months.

An adoption order can only be made if:

– the child is 'free for adoption' (see below); *or*
– each parent of the child has agreed unconditionally and with full understanding of what is involved to the adoption order; *or*
– the court dispenses with the agreement of any parent on the grounds that he or she cannot be found or is incapable of giving agreement or is witholding agreement unreasonably or has persistently failed to discharge parental duties, or has abandoned, neglected or persistently or seriously ill-treated the child.

Any agreement by the mother to an adoption is not valid unless given at least six weeks after the child's birth.

An **adoption agency** is any adoption society approved under the Children Act 1975 by the Secretary of State for Social Services. In addition each local authority must establish an adoption service to provide for the needs of adults and children who might be involved in adoption and these services have the same rights as an adoption agency.

A child is **free for adoption** if a 'freeing order' has been made by the court on the application of an adoption agency. A freeing order cannot be made unless the parents agree or their agreement is dispensed with on the same grounds set out above for dispensing with an agreement to an adoption order. The difference between a freeing order and an adoption order is that a freeing order transfers the parental rights and duties to the adoption agency and not to any new adoptive parents. The agreement of the parents to a freeing order cannot be dispensed with unless the child is already placed with someone with a view to adoption or is likely to be placed. If there is a freeing order there is no need to obtain the parents' consent to a subsequent adoption order.

Before a freeing order is made the child's natural parents may make a declaration that they prefer not to be involved in future questions concerning the adoption of the child. If the parents make no such declaration the adoption agency must inform them within fifty-four weeks of the date of the freeing order, whether the child has been adopted or placed for adoption. If the child is still available for adoption the parents can apply for revocation of the freeing order and for their parental rights to be restored. During this period, the child may not be placed for adoption without the permission of the court.

Parents who wish to contest cases where their consent to adoption has been dispensed with or who wish to apply to revoke a freeing order, are eligible for legal aid (see p. 496).

If the child has been living with foster parents for five years and they have applied for an adoption order, the child cannot be taken away from them without the permission of the court.

The court appoints a **reporting officer** (usually a social worker) to inquire into the suitability of the proposed adopters. The reporting officer has the power to obtain details of the proposed adopters' criminal records (if any) from the police. The officer discusses the adoption with the proposed adopters to make sure they fully understand the implications of adoption. The officer also discusses the matter with the natural parent and explains that alternatives to adoption do exist.

First consideration has to be given to the welfare of the child. A person called a **guardian ad litem** is appointed to represent the child's interest at the hearing. (To avoid unnecessary expense the reporting officer usually acts as the guardian ad litem.)

The adoption agency must, so far as is practicable, consider the natural parents' wishes as to religious upbringing and they may keep the natural parents informed of other matters concerning the adoption. The agency also reports to the court on the suitability of the prospective adopters and any other matters of concern. The agency's responsibility continues until the adoption order has been granted.

Although the law does not say that only a married couple may adopt a child a single person is rarely allowed to adopt unless the child is a relative or a foster child. In the case of a married couple one of them at least must be domiciled in the UK and both must be at least 21.

Where the mother of an illegitimate child consents to adoption, the child's father should be given notice of the adoption and informed that he can apply for custody of the child.

Adopted children, once they reach 18 years, may apply to the Registrar General for the information necessary to enable them to trace their natural parents. However, they will first be informed that there is a counselling service which will discuss the desirability of tracing their natural parents with them.

Custody is covered on p. 350 and 351; Guardianship on p. 343.

Custodianship

This is a new term introduced by the Children Act 1975.

A **custodianship order** may be granted by a court to someone looking after a child under 18 who is not their own. The rights of the natural parents are suspended, unless the custodian is a step-parent, but the child retains a link with its natural parents. The order gives the custodian certain legal rights over the child. A child who has lived with a custodian for three years may not be taken away without the custodian's consent or the permission of the court.

The people who can apply to the court for a custodianship order are:

– a step-parent or relative (see p. 357 for list of relatives) of the child who has the consent of the person having legal custody (see p. 350) of the child and with whom the child has lived for the previous three months;
– any person with whom the child has lived for at least twelve months including the previous three months and who has the consent of the person having legal custody;

– any person with whom the child has lived for at least three years, including the previous three months, even if the person having legal custody does not consent to the order.

The granting of a custodianship order may make a number of changes in the financial provision for the child:

– The custodian can apply for child benefit for the child but will lose any boarding-out allowance payable as a foster parent.
– The natural parent may be ordered to pay maintenance for the child to the custodian, usually through the local authority or the DHSS.
– The custodian may apply for an affiliation order against the child's father within three years of the custodianship order. This does not apply if the custodian is a step-parent married to the child's natural mother.

Parents may apply to the court for access to the child whilst it is with the custodian. Legal aid (see p. 496) is available for parents who wish to apply for the custodianship order to be revoked in their favour.

Care proceedings

The law on this subject is complex: parents are advised to get legal advice.

A care order or supervision order may be made by:

– a juvenile court where a child under 17 has been convicted of a criminal offence (see p. 97); *or*
– a divorce court or other court dealing with matrimonial proceedings; *or*
– a juvenile court upon the application of a local authority or other authorized person such as the NSPCC.

A **care order** commits a child to the care of the local authority. This means the local authority takes over all parental rights and duties for the child and may remove it to a foster parent, a custodian, a community home or to wherever the authority directs. In some cases the child may be allowed to remain at home.

A **supervision order** means the child will continue to be looked after by its parents but a social worker will be allocated to the family to give help and assistance. If a criminal offence is involved the court may impose other restrictions on the child.

A judge hearing a divorce or an application for custody, or the magistrates hearing a complaint brought by one of the parents will first ask for a report on the child before making a supervision or care order.

LOCAL AUTHORITIES AND CARE ORDERS

Local authorities can apply for a care order in two ways:

1. The authority can pass a **resolution in council** to assume all rights and duties of the parent if:
   – they consider that a child has been abandoned; *or*
   – the child's parents are dead and no suitable guardians have been appointed; *or*
   – the parents or guardians are unfit to have care of a child; *or*
   – a child has been in the authority's care for at least three years; *or*
   – the child has been placed in voluntary care and the authority considers that important decisions have to be taken affecting the child's future.

If the whereabouts of the child's parents or guardians is known, they must immediately be informed of the resolution and their right to object. If the parents wish to oppose the resolution, a counter notice must be served within one month of receiving the notice. The resolution will then lapse unless the authority 'complains' to the juvenile court within fourteen days.

The authority must present its evidence to the court. Its witnesses may be cross-examined and the parents can call their own witnesses to support their opposition to the resolution. Legal aid (see p. 496) is available to the parents or guardians. The court must where possible give consideration to the child's wishes and may appoint a guardian ad litem, either a social worker or a lawyer, to represent the child's interests separately.

If the court find in favour of the authority, parents lose all rights over the child but they may appeal against this decision (see p. 364). Parents may apply to the juvenile court at any time to vary or discharge the care order as long as such an application has not been made in the previous six months.

2. The authority is under a duty to bring a child before the court if it considers the child is in need of **care or control** because:
   - the child is being ill treated or neglected; *or*
   - the child is exposed to moral danger; *or*
   - the child is beyond the control of parents or guardians; *or*
   - the child is not attending school or receiving suitable education.

The justices can deal with the matter in a variety of ways by:
- an order requiring the parents to agree to 'enter into a recognizance' (see p. 149) to exercise proper care and control of the child; *or*
- a supervision order placing the child under the supervision of the local authority or a probation officer; *or*
- a care order committing the child to the care of the local authority; *or*
- a hospital order; *or*
- a guardianship order.

Hospital orders and guardianship orders are made under the provisions of the Mental Health Act (see pp. 378–9).

At the hearing all concerned can present evidence and call witnesses who may be cross-examined. The child, as the subject of the application, is eligible for legal aid. In practice the parents' interests are often represented under the child's legal aid order. If the court consider there is a conflict of interest between the parents and the child, they will appoint a guardian ad litem, independent of the local authority, to represent the child or instruct a solicitor to do so. In this case the parents are eligible for separate legal aid.

If the court finds in favour of the local authority, the rights of the parents are suspended. The parents may make an application to vary or discharge the care order if an application has not been made within the previous three months. Parents can appeal against a decision and ask for a re-hearing in the Crown Court, or appeal to the Divisional Court on a point of law (see p. 79).

A care order continues until the order is revoked, or the child reaches 18 (or 19 if the child was 16 or over when the order was made).

An application for a care order cannot be made in respect of a person of 16 or over who is or has been married.

PLACE-OF-SAFETY ORDERS

In urgent cases a place-of-safety order may be made allowing a child to be removed from its parents or guardians until a full court hearing takes place. A social worker or other authorized person can apply to a magistrate for a place-of-safety order which remains in force for twenty-eight days. A police officer has power to impose a place-of-safety order on a child for up to eight days. The order will lapse after this period unless the local authority applies for a care order. A juvenile court will usually make an interim order pending the full hearing.

A place-of-safety order is difficult to oppose and because of the large number of cases before the courts, a child may be kept away from its parents for several weeks before the full hearing for the care order is heard. Even if the authority fails to prove its case and the child is returned to its parents, an aggrieved parent has no remedy against the authority provided it can show that it acted in good faith and believed the child to be in need of care and protection.

It is possible that the parents or guardians will not know that the authority intends applying for a place-of-safety order until after it is imposed and the child has been removed. If the parents consider the application for an order was not justified they can make the child a ward of court (see p. 365 below). The child will then be under the control of the court and not the local authority and parents can apply to the High Court for an order that the child be returned.

Wards of court

Anyone may apply to the Family Division of the High Court (see p. 244) to make any child under 18 a ward of court.

The procedure is usually only appropriate in the circumstances set out below. Usually disputes over children are between the parents and can be resolved by applying for a custody order (see p. 350). However, wardship can be used:

– where the person making the application is not a parent; *or*
– where one parent wants to stop the other parent removing the child from the country; *or*
– where the child between 16 and 18 wants to marry despite the lack of parental consent.

If a child is made a ward of the court, the court takes over all parental rights and may appoint a guardian and make any other order in respect of the child (e.g. an order giving consent to marriage). For example, in one case a child psychologist applied to make an 11-year-old girl a ward of the court to prevent her being sterilized on non-medical grounds, and the court agreed to the application (see also p. 472).

In most cases a child automatically becomes a ward of court for twenty-one days once the application is lodged at the court, but this will lapse unless the court orders otherwise at a hearing.

The court can appoint the Official Solicitor (see p. 84) to represent the interests of the child as guardian ad litem (see p. 359).

The wardship will last until the child is 18 unless the court revokes it earlier than that, and while it is in force the court can give directions concerning the upbringing of the child or any other matter.

Criminal proceedings

In England and Wales a child under 10 cannot be charged with a criminal offence. Any other child can be prosecuted for a criminal offence but:

– in most areas a child who is a first offender and who admits the

offence will be cautioned by the Police Juvenile Liaison Bureau instead of being brought to court, unless the offence is serious;
– it is rare for a child under 12 to be prosecuted;
– the government has power to implement restrictions on the prosecution of children but these have not yet been exercised.

Children under 17 are tried and sentenced in the juvenile court which has specially trained magistrates and should be in a separate building or part of a building from an adult court. If the child is charged jointly with a person over 16 they will both be dealt with in the magistrates' or Crown Court, but if the child is convicted he or she will be sent to the juvenile court for sentence. A child can appeal from the juvenile court to the High Court on a point of law, or to the Crown Court for a re-hearing (see p. 79).

ARREST AND BAIL

Children under 10 can be detained by the police for up to eight days under a place-of-safety order (see p. 364). Children over 10 can be arrested by the police and detained for inquiries but they must be released on bail unless a police officer of or above the rank of Inspector considers that:

– it is in the child's own interest to be detained; *or*
– there is reason to believe that the child has committed a serious crime and that release would defeat the ends of justice; *or*
– the child has committed a serious crime and would fail to appear to answer the charge.

QUESTIONING

A parent or guardian should be present when a child is interviewed by the police. In their absence someone who is not a police officer and is of the same sex as the child should be present (see p. 49).

A child should not be arrested or interviewed at school if this can possibly be avoided. If it is essential, the interview should only take place with the consent of the head teacher. Either the head teacher or someone nominated by him or her should be present.

If a policewoman is not available, a policeman may take statements from a female child witness, but a male officer should never interview a girl on a matter that concerns sex.

LEGAL AID

When a child wants legal aid in the juvenile court, either the child or one of the parents can fill out the application form but the parents will have to disclose their income and capital even if the form is filled out by the child. The court does have the power to disregard the income and capital of the parents when deciding whether to grant legal aid. If legal aid is granted, the solicitor is bound to accept instructions from the child, not from the parents. Obviously in the case of younger children the instructions will often come through the parents, but the solicitor's duty is to the child.

THE HEARING

A juvenile court hearing is conducted along similar lines to that in the magistrates' court (see p. 79) except that the hearing is in private and an attempt is made to simplify the language used. The court may insist that the child's parents be present and the child may be represented by his or her parents or by a lawyer. Criminal legal aid (see p. 500) is available for the juvenile court.

REMAND

The court might adjourn the case, or might adjourn passing sentence. This is called a 'remand'. The court might want to adjourn the case so that it can obtain reports on the child (e.g. from a social worker). If the child is not remanded on bail (see p. 80) he or she should be committed to the care of the local authority and will spend the period of remand (two or three weeks usually) in a community home.

However, if the court certifies that a child of any age who is charged with homicide, or a child aged 14–16 is 'of so unruly a character that he cannot be safely committed to the care of a local authority' the child can be placed in a remand centre (in which prison conditions apply) or in an adult prison if there is no vacancy in a remand centre.

There has been a great deal of public outcry at the number of children who are sent to remand centres or prison. At the time of writing the Government has promised to limit the powers of the courts to make what are called 'certificates of unruliness'.

SENTENCING

After conviction a child may be dealt with in the following ways:

- A child under 17 may not be imprisoned. But if the conviction is for an offence for which an adult could receive a sentence of fourteen year's imprisonment or more (e.g. homicide, robbery, burglary) the court can order the child to be detained for a number of years at such a place and on such conditions as the Home Secretary decides. This can include detention in a prison if the Home Secretary decides that is appropriate, for instance, if the child is certified as unruly. However, this should only be on a temporary basis and the child should not be placed with adult prisoners.
- Children aged 14–21 may be sentenced to serve a short period at a detention centre and young persons (aged 15–21) may be sentenced to borstal training.
- On conviction the child may be fined or given a conditional discharge but in addition the court may impose a supervision order or a care order.
- Under a supervision order a supervisor, usually a social worker, will be appointed to supervise and assist the child. The child usually remains with its parents. The court may also impose certain other provisions:
- as to where the child shall live for a period not exceeding ninety days; *and*
- for the child to attend a specified place such as a community home on a certain day or days (for instance every Saturday); *and*

- for the child to undertake certain activities such as community service work or to attend for group sessions with a child psychologist.
- If a care order is made, the local authority assume the rights and duties of the parents. The child will usually be sent to a community home, but may be allowed to return home under supervision.
- The child can apply to the juvenile court for a care or supervision order to be revoked, as can the local authority. Normally the child's application is made through the parents, who can apply for legal aid for the child.
- If they are not revoked, supervision and care orders last until the child reaches 18 (or 19 if he or she was 16 or over when the order was made).

Attending the courts

Generally, everyone has a right to be present in court if there is enough room and they do not disturb the proceedings. But a child (except for a babe in arms) cannot observe a criminal trial until the age of 14. There are no restrictions specifically relating to the presence of children at civil cases.

CHILDREN AS WITNESSES

A child who does not undertand the nature and consequences of the oath cannot give evidence in a civil case, but may do so in a criminal case if he or she is old enough to be understood and to understand the duty of speaking the truth.

CHILDREN AND CIVIL PROCEEDINGS

A child has the right to sue and be sued. However, children under 18 can only sue through a next friend. In practice, children cannot sue someone independently of their parents. In civil proceedings a child's 'next friend' must normally be the father but the mother may be accepted if a reasonable explanation is given to the court. If a child is sued by someone else, a 'next friend' is appointed by the court unless the parents volunteer. In some cases the court will appoint the Official Solicitor (see p. 84) to represent the interests of the child.

CHILDREN AND CONTRACTS

A child under 18 is free to enter into a contract but generally speaking such contracts are not enforceable by law. However, a child would normally be forced to abide by a contract if he or she received essential goods or services as a result of the agreement.

Religion

Children cannot prevent their parents from making them a member of any particular faith or from going through formal ceremonies such as baptism. Parents can insist that children living at home receive religious instructions and children have no legal right to prevent this.

A child's religion may be altered after birth without the child's consent. This sometimes happens as a result of a dispute between the parents. If a court thinks a child is old enough to hold an opinion the child's view may be taken into consideration but it may be overruled. Usually the court does not make comparative judgments between one faith and another but it tends to take the view that a child should have some form of religious instruction rather than none at all.

The law requires that all children in state schools receive religious instruction. Parents can withdraw their children from religious instruction at school but children cannot make this decision themselves (see p. 430).

Age restrictions

Drinking and smoking

With the exception of the landlord's child no one under 14 is allowed to go into a pub or any licensed premises. Young people are not allowed to drink or buy drinks for someone else in a pub until they are 18. However, people over 16 can have beer or wine with a meal.

There is no law preventing a child from smoking in private but it is an offence to sell tobacco to a child under 16 when it is for the child's own use. A child aged 10–16 can be charged with aiding and abetting the retailer who made the sale.

If a child under 16 is found smoking in a public place a uniformed police officer (or park-keeper) may seize all tobacco and cigarette papers. However, a pipe or tobacco pouch may not be seized.

Betting and gaming

You can go into a betting shop when you are 17 but you must not take part in any form of betting or gaming until you are 18. However, you may do so at any age in a private house in the presence of your parents or with their permission. A young person over 14 can play dominoes or cribbage in a pub.

Cinemas

Cinemas usually classify their films in a way which restricts the admission of children. The classifications are:

U   passed for general exhibition
A   parents are advised that they might prefer children under 14 not to see them.
AA   restricted to people 14 or over
X   restricted to people 18 or over.

These classifications are made by the British Board of Film Censors. They have no legal effect, but local authorities can and do adopt the same classifications thereby placing a legal obligation on the manager of the cinema (see p. 317). No criminal offence is committed by a child who goes to a cinema and sees a restricted film. The offence is committed by the exhibitor of the film who allows the child to enter.

Children who are too young to understand the nature of a film (probably children under 2 years) may enter most cinemas no matter what film is showing provided the cinema manager has no objection.

Driving

A person of 16 may hold a licence to drive certain tractors and to ride motor cycles or invalid carriages. At 17 you may drive any vehicle except certain heavy-duty vehicles.

Driving while under age is punishable in a magistrates' court by a maximum fine of £100. (There is usually a further charge of driving without insurance.) In addition the child may be disqualified from obtaining a driving licence for a certain period and may have a future licence endorsed. It may be useful to have a lawyer to plead mitigating circumstances so as to prevent the child from being disqualified.

Work

There are very complicated regulations covering what work a child may do. A child who is at school may be subject to restrictions on part-time work laid down by the local education authority (see p. 434).

A child who wants to work or an employer who wants to employ a child should seek advice from the Department of Employment and the local education authority.

Fireworks

It is an offence to sell fireworks to someone aged under 16.

More information

Childrens Rights Workshop, 73 Balfour Street, London SE17 (01-703 7217).

National Children's Bureau, 8 Wakely Street, London EC1 (01-278 9441).

National Society for the Prevention of Cruelty to Children, 1 Riding House Street, London W1 (01-580 8812).

17. Mental patients

This chapter covers:

Nearly half of all hospital patients are there because of some mental disorder. Anyone can apply voluntarily for treatment and may be admitted to mental hospital **informally**. Most patients are admitted to hospital in this way, and they are entitled to leave at any time (although as an informal patient you may be faced with the prospect of being compulsorily detained, by one of the means set out below, if you do try to leave). Some patients, however, are **compulsorily** detained. This chapter is mainly concerned with the position of compulsory patients and the rights of their relatives, as covered by the Mental Health Act 1959.

There are four categories of mental disorder which may result in your detention in hospital or under special care. These are *legal* and not medical categories:

– *Mental illness:* this means any mental disorder not included in the three categories below. It includes illnesses such as schizophrenia or paranoia, which may be of relatively short duration, or lasting brain damage resulting from an accident.
– *Severe subnormality:* when you suffer from arrested or incomplete mental development, which includes subnormal intelligence, and are therefore incapable of leading an independent life, or are in danger of being seriously exploited.
– *Subnormality:* a state of arrested or incomplete development which requires or responds to medical treatment or other special care or training, but which does not amount to severe subnormality.
– *Psychopathic disorder:* a persistent mental disorder, which may or may not include subnormal intelligence, which results in

abnormally aggressive or seriously irresponsible behaviour, and which requires or responds to medical treatment.

Before the 1959 Mental Health Act, it was quite common for people to be detained in mental institutions because of promiscuity or other 'immoral' behaviour. Such behaviour may not now be considered a form of mental disorder by itself, and someone behaving promiscuously should only be detained in hospital if he or she appears to suffer from an illness so severe that it warrants observation or treatment, and it would be in the interests of the person's own health or safety or the protection of others to detain him or her.

Applications for compulsory detention

You may be compulsorily detained in hospital as a mental patient on application by a **mental welfare officer** (i.e. a qualified social worker authorized by the local authority) or by a near relative. Except in an emergency (see below), the application must be supported by the recommendation of two doctors, one of whom should be the patient's own G P. The two doctors must not have family or business connections with you or with each other, and one of them must be approved by the local authority as having experience in dealing with mental disorder. If the application is successful, the applicant may authorize anybody to convey you to hospital, by force if necessary.

There are three kinds of application: observation, emergency, and treatment.

Admission for observation

An admission for observation may be made in cases where the medical officer needs time to decide whether you satisfy the conditions of mental illness and need for treatment as described above. You may not be detained for observation for more than twenty-eight days and after that the application cannot be repeated immediately (Mental Health Act 1959, Section 25).

Emergency admission

In an emergency, any relative or mental welfare officer can apply for admission with only one medical recommendation. Also, if you are already in hospital informally, you can be detained for seventy-two hours for observation on a recommendation by the doctor in charge of your treatment. You cannot be detained on this basis for more than seventy-two hours unless within that time a second doctor makes a recommendation, in which case the admission becomes an ordinary admission for observation.

Admission for treatment

An application may be made for treatment for a patient already admitted for observation, or for a person outside hospital. A mental welfare officer may not apply for admission for treatment until the nearest relative has been consulted, if that relative is easily available. The mental welfare officer has no power to make the application if the nearest relative objects. The nearest relative should make any objection known in writing to the local health authority or the mental welfare officer, although this is not laid down as being necessary. In an extreme case, the mental welfare officer may challenge the nearest relative in a court of law. An application for treatment cannot be made for a subnormal or psychopath over the age of 21.

A magistrate may issue a warrant authorizing a policeman to obtain entry, by force where necessary, to remove to a place of safety someone who is living alone and unable to care for themself or who is being neglected or ill-treated. A policeman who finds a person in a public place who appears to be in need of immediate care or control can take him or her away to a safe place. The policeman may not detain anyone compulsorily for more than seventy-two hours, and during that time an application should be made for admission for observation or treatment.

An admission for treatment is valid for one year. The **responsible medical officer** (i.e. the psychiatrist responsible for your case) may then renew it for another year and after that for periods of two years at a time. Subnormals and psychopaths must be released from hospital when they reach the age of 25 unless they are recorded as being dangerous.

Leave of absence from the mental hospital may be granted indefinitely or for a specific period. If you are continuously on leave for six months and if at the end of that time have not run away or been transferred to guardianship (see p. 378), you are automatically discharged.

If you are absent without leave you may be detained and forcibly returned to hospital. But a subnormal or psychopath over 21 may not be forced to return after an absence of six months and no other patient can be returned after twenty-eight days: in these cases you are automatically discharged.

The responsible medical officer or your nearest relative can discharge you at any time, but the medical officer can forbid discharge by the relative on the grounds that you are potentially dangerous to others.

The nearest relative

The **nearest relative** is the first of the following who is over 18 and resident in the UK: husband or wife, child, father, mother, brother or sister, grandparent, grandchild, uncle or aunt, nephew or niece. When there is more than one person in any category, for example two children, the eldest is taken first.

The major exceptions to this rule are:

- A husband, wife or parent under 18 years of age cannot exercise the rights of nearest relative.
- If a married couple are separated, the spouse will not be considered as nearest relative. Anyone who has been living as spouse with the patient for six months will be regarded as their spouse.
- If a child or adolescent patient has at any time been taken away from its parents under the Children and Young Persons Act, the local authority or guardian will act as nearest relative, unless the patient is married. The same applies when there is a legally appointed guardian, except when the guardian has been appointed under the Mental Health Act.

– An illegitimate child is considered as the child of the mother only.

Anyone who is a relative or spouse of the patient, or a mental-welfare officer, may apply to the county court for an order depriving the nearest relative of all his or her rights concerning the patient and appointing somebody else. This can be done on a number of grounds, the most important of which is that the nearest relative objects unreasonably to the patient being admitted to hospital, or misuses the power of discharge. In this case, the nearest relative, who is now called the **displaced relative**, may still appeal to a tribunal once a year on the patient's behalf (see p. 380).

If an order has been made displacing the nearest relative, and somebody else wishes to take over the responsibilities of nearest relative, he or she may apply to the court to have the order discharged. This might happen if, for instance, a relative reached the age of 18 or returned from abroad and therefore became eligible to act as nearest relative. On the other hand, the nearest relative may also renounce his or her rights in favour of anyone else over 18 and resident in the UK by giving notice to the hospital or guardian, and the local health authority. The right to act as the nearest relative may be resumed at any time by a similar procedure.

Appeals

No appeals may be made against admission for observation. In other cases, the patient or the nearest relative has the right to appeal to a mental health review tribunal (see p. 380).

A patient over 16 can appeal:

– at any time within six months of admission to hospital or of reaching the age of 16;
– within twenty-eight days when not released at the age of 25 (subnormals and psychopaths only);
– within twenty-eight days when reclassified from one of the four categories of mental disorder to another;

– at any time when the order for detention has been officially renewed.

A patient's nearest relative has the right to appeal:

– within twenty-eight days when the order for discharge is cancelled by the responsible medical authority;
– within twenty-eight days when a subnormal or psychopath is not released at the age of 25;
– within twenty-eight days if the patient is reclassified.

If a tribunal rejects an appeal, a further appeal cannot be heard for twelve months, except when appeals have to be made within twenty-eight days, and in a few other special cases.

Guardianship

If you are suffering from mental disorder and require treatment or care but are not likely to be a danger to yourself or to others, you can be put into the care of a guardian instead of being detained in hospital. The guardian may be a close relative or someone appointed by the local health authority. The procedure is subject to the same conditions as admission for treatment, with the following important exceptions:

– Subnormals and psychopaths must always be discharged at the age of 25.
– The nearest relative has an absolute right of discharge; it cannot be cancelled by the medical officer.

An application for guardianship should be made to the local health authority, which is responsible for making the necessary arrangements. Patients can be transferred from hospital to guardianship and vice versa. But a transfer from guardianship to hospital requires two medical recommendations. The patient can appeal to a tribunal at any time within six months of the transfer.

Detention of offenders

Detention by court order

If you are tried for any offence punishable by imprisonment, the judge or magistrate may make a **hospital order** on the recommendation of two doctors, if it is established that you committed the offence and suffer from mental disorder needing treatment (see p. 373). In that event, the court may not impose any sentence of imprisonment or fine nor make a probation order. Hospital orders are valid for one year unless discharged by the hospital. They may be extended for a further year by the hospital and then at two-year intervals.

This procedure is subject to the same conditions as an admission for treatment, with the following exceptions:

– The nearest relative need not be consulted.
– Subnormals and psychopaths can be subject to a hospital order above the age of 21 and will not automatically be released at the age of 25.
– The nearest relative has no right of discharge, but can appeal to a mental health review tribunal once every twelve months (see p. 380).

RESTRICTION ORDERS

When the Crown Court makes a hospital order, it may also make an **order restricting discharge**. If this happens, neither the patient nor the nearest relative may apply to a tribunal for discharge. The order does not have to be renewed at the normal times. Leave of absence can only be given with the consent of the Home Secretary, and patients absent without leave can be forced to return at any time. The Home Secretary becomes the only person who can release the patient.

The only right which remains to the patient is to ask the Home Secretary to refer the case to a tribunal for advice. The patient can do this whenever the hospital order comes up for renewal if there is no restriction order. The Home Secretary must accept this request but is not obliged to take the advice the tribunal gives.

A magistrates' court may not make a restriction order but may refer a case to a higher court for that purpose. When a restriction order ceases to have effect, the patient is treated as coming under a hospital order only.

Detention by direction of the Home Secretary

If you are serving a prison sentence you may, on the recommendation of two doctors, be transferred to mental hospital by direction of the Home Secretary. Such a **transfer direction** may also be made on anybody detained in a children's home, borstal, community home, or detention centre. It has the same effect as a hospital order made by a court.

When making a transfer direction the Home Secretary may also make a **restriction direction**, with or without time limit. This has the same effect as a restriction order made by a court, with one exception: it must lapse at the end of the prison sentence. After that, you can appeal to a tribunal for release from hospital.

Guardianship

A court can pass a guardianship order instead of a hospital order if an offender is suffering from mental disorder and requires treatment or care but is not likely to be a danger to him- or herself or to others (see p. 378). The Home Secretary can make a guardianship direction on children at community homes under the same conditions as a transfer direction.

Mental health review tribunals

Mental health review tribunals hear appeals by mental patients or their nearest relative for discharge from mental hospitals and institutions. Application forms can be obtained from the patient's hospital, from the tribunal, or from the local health authority if the patient is in the care of a guardian (see above). Patients detained under a hospital order made by a court which has imposed restrictions on their release can ask the Home Secretary to refer their case to a tribunal to obtain their advice on the patient's future.

The tribunal consists of three members, chosen from three panels representing lawyers, doctors and lay members with some knowledge of social welfare work. All three must be independent of the hospital and local health authority concerned in the case.

Procedure of the tribunal

The hearings are normally held in private at the patient's hospital. The patient may ask for a public hearing but this may be refused on the grounds that it would be harmful to the patient or for some other reason.

The applicant may ask for a 'formal hearing' which means that everyone concerned may be present and give evidence when asked and also ask questions if permitted by the tribunal, but the tribunal may refuse this. At a formal hearing the patient or the nearest relative, whichever has made the application, can call witnesses, but otherwise the tribunal conducts proceedings more or less as it likes. There is no right to a formal hearing in cases referred to the tribunal by the Home Secretary.

The tribunal has the power to take evidence on oath, to order witnesses to appear and to produce documentary evidence. It inquires into the conditions under which the patient will be living if discharged. The medical member examines the patient and inquires into all aspects of his or her health. The patient or the nearest relative, whichever has made the application, has the right to be heard.

Advice and representation

It is most important that a patient should receive advice and representation when appealing to the tribunal. This may be provided by the NCCL which operates a scheme to provide experienced representatives at mental health review tribunals, from MIND (see p. 590), from a welfare officer or from a solicitor, who can give advice under the green-form scheme (see

p. 494). Failing that, a relative can be of considerable help to the patient as moral support, by helping to provide the information the tribunal wants to know and by offering to make arrangements for the patient's care and accommodation if he or she is discharged. This last point is often an important factor in influencing the tribunal's decision.

Expenses may be paid to the nearest relative, representatives of the patient and of the nearest relative (unless they are lawyers), and any witnesses that the tribunal feels have been really useful in helping to decide the case. Expenses consist of rail fare, subsistence, and loss of earnings (if any), but some negotiation with the tribunal may be necessary.

The tribunal's decision

If an application is made to the tribunal and it considers that the patient:

– is not suffering from mental disorder; *or*
– does not need to be detained for health reasons; *or*
– is not a danger to him- or herself or others,

he or she *must* be discharged. This does not apply to cases referred by the Home Secretary.

The tribunal might not give a full explanation of its decision on the grounds that it may harm the patient, and the patient will not always be allowed to see medical reports.

There is a right of appeal from the decision of a mental health review tribunal but only on a point of law.

(The procedure of the tribunals is regulated by the Mental Health Review Tribunal Rules 1960.)

Your rights in mental hospital

Letters

A postal packet addressed to you may only be withheld if the medical authorities consider that the content may be harmful to you. If this happens, it must be returned to the sender. A postal packet sent *by* you may only be withheld if the addressee requests it, if the contents are unreasonable, offensive to the addressee or defamatory to other people (not including the hospital staff), or if your interests would be prejudiced.

No letters to the following people can be withheld under any circumstances: an MP, an officer of the Court of Protection, a manager of the hospital, the nearest relative or someone else acting in that capacity, a mental health review tribunal to which you can appeal, a solicitor nominated by you (unless that solicitor is unwilling to receive such letters).

Visitors

The medical superintendent can refuse to admit any visitor if he or she considers it would interfere with your treatment.

If you want to be examined by an independent psychiatrist this must be allowed, but you or your nearest relative must pay the bill.

Property

Your property cannot be interfered with unless you consent or unless someone is authorized to do so by the Court of Protection. The Court of Protection protects and manages the property of people who, through mental disorder, are incapable of managing their own affairs whether or not they are in hospital.

Maltreatment

It is a criminal offence to ill-treat or neglect a patient who is undergoing treatment for mental disorder. Unfortunately it is extremely hard for a patient to convince the appropriate authority that an offence has been committed, but hospital staff managers and visitors who are alert and careful can do much to protect patients.

Compulsory treatment

If you are an informal patient you can refuse to accept any treatment you dislike or disagree with.

The law is not clear if a patient who is compulsorily detained has the same right. In practice, hospital authorities assume they can treat these patients without their consent, but the courts have not yet decided the question.

Voting

In the past, no patient in a mental hospital or mental nursing home could be entered on the electoral register.

Informal patients, or patients who are resident in mental hospital but unable to leave simply because of lack of outside accommodation, are now entitled to be entered on the electoral register and to vote. (See p. 91 for information about jury service.)

Access to the courts

A patient or anyone else (e.g. a relative) cannot bring any civil or criminal proceedings against anyone in respect of anything purporting to be done in pursuance of the Mental Health Act 1959, unless the High Court is satisfied that the act was done in bad faith or without reasonable care, and gives permission to bring proceedings.

More information

Larry Gostin, *A Human Condition: The Mental Health Act 1959*, MIND.

CARE for the Mentally Handicapped, Burton Rough, Petworth, Sussex.

Ex-Services Mental Welfare Society, 37 Thurloe Street, London SW7 (01-584 8688/3351).

NCCL, 186 Kings Cross Road, London WC1 (01-278 4575).

Mental After Care Association, Eagle House, 110 Jermyn Street, London SW1 (01-839 5953).

MIND (National Association for Mental Health), 22 Harley Street, London W1 (01-637 0741).

18. Gypsies

This chapter differs from others in this book in that it is not addressed to those whose civil liberties may be threatened but to those who are called upon to give advice and support to Gypsies.

Who are Gypsies?

It is impossible to define Gypsies precisely. In the Caravan Sites Act 1968 they are described as 'persons of nomadic habit of life, whatever their race or origin'. They are not legally recognized as a racial group and so are not fully protected under the Race Relations Act (see p. 230). Settled people usually have romantic notions of 'real' Gypsies as fortune-telling, handicraft-selling Romanies in horse-drawn vehicles hidden away in woods and commons. The reality of present-day travellers (as some Gypsies prefer to be called) is more likely to be scrap-metal dealing in motorized transport encamped on the verge of a by-pass or on a demolished building site in town. Because of intermarriage and because former house dwellers have joined the travellers, they are not all of unmixed Romany descent. Gypsies define themselves as people who have at least one traveller parent.

They are nomadic in that they have little territory that they can claim as their own. They have to be adaptable in order to make a living. As casual agricultural work and the market for crafts have declined they have taken up the unpopular work of scrap reclamation. They are self-reliant because they are isolated from the settled community. They prefer to be self-employed and to seek assistance from one another in hardship or conflict with officialdom. Their children rarely receive regular schooling and few travellers claim their full rights in welfare and health benefits.

Where do they live?

The census of 1965 recorded 15,000 travellers scattered throughout the country, with the largest numbers on the fringes of the great conurbations in the south-east and west midlands. It is acknowledged that this is a low estimate and that a more realistic figure would be around 26,000. Some live in privately owned yards, some on officially provided sites, some on farms while undertaking seasonal work, but the majority have no permanent resting place and are illegally encamped on highways or are squatting on public or private land.

Their greatest problem is the lack of authorized stopping places. Wherever they camp they are likely to meet hostility from the settled population which finds expression in local government and police action against them. The difficult conditions they are forced to endure makes it hard for them to maintain hygiene, to earn a living, to get served in shops and pubs and for their children to be educated. The poverty, ill health and illiteracy that may result increases the hostility shown to them. Some health practitioners, some educationists and some local government officials do try to serve their needs, but the general picture is one of officially endorsed deprivation and social ostracism.

The legal position

The Highways Act 1959 specifically prohibits Gypsies from encamping on the highway. The Caravan Sites Act 1968 lays a duty on local authorities 'to provide adequate accommodation for Gypsies residing in or resorting to their area'. *But*, the Minister may exempt local authorities from this duty if suitable land is not available and metropolitan counties only have to provide accommodation for fifteen caravans at a time in each metropolitan district. London boroughs have an equally limited duty. The Secretary of State for the Environment has the power, under the 1968 Act to designate areas where he deems that adequate provision for Gypsies has been made. This power has been used on several occasions. The local authority can then prohibit and remove unauthorized encampments in the area

I see a tall, dark stranger who bodes ill

more swiftly and using the threat of heavier penalties than usual.

Even on the move, Gypsies have problems. As they now need to run lorries and as the cost of fuelling, maintaining, taxing and insuring commercial vehicles has increased, the often illiterate and poor travellers may run them illegally. The relentless checking of their vehicles by the police is another method of removing them from a district.

Legal advice for various situations

Below are listed some of the typical situations that arise, with a note of the advice a supporter might give.

Prosecutions for encampment

The traveller has been summonsed for stopping on the highway.

If the charge is under section 127 of the Highways Act ('did **encamp** upon the highway') the traveller is usually best advised to plead guilty and pay up to the maximum fine of £5, then stay put. The offence is 'encamping' and the charge cannot be brought again until a fresh 'encampment' is proved. If they are towed away by others and left on the highway, the Gypsies are not responsible and can defend an encamping charge brought against them.

If the charge is for **obstructing** the highway the fines are heavier and may be repeated daily. It may be worth attempting a defence by making the prosecution prove it is highway land and prove obstruction. If the offence is technical, the traveller should plead mitigation and refer to the lack of authorized sites. Some magistrates may be lenient. Again, if they are towed there, others should be blamed for the obstruction.

The traveller has been summonsed for stopping on public land (owned by borough, county or district council), or on a common.	The summons will be to go to the county court 'to show cause why order for possession should not be granted'. The judge will have to grant an order properly applied for but may be moved by moral arguments to delay the issue of it. It is worth making a spirited defence, reminding the court of the local authority's duties to provide adequate accommodation. Camping on a common is also likely to be a bye-law offence.
The traveller has been summonsed for stopping on private land.	This may be brought by a private owner seeking re-possession, often because the local authority has threatened the owner with planning infringement. Either try to persuade the private owner to get planning permission and a site licence or try moving the traveller to another bit of the same land and wait for the process to be repeated.

If the travellers are on the land of a farmer who is employing them, the farmer is exempt from planning and licensing requirements.

The travellers have camped on their own land and have been summonsed.	This is likely to arise from an enforcement notice to discontinue an unauthorized planning use. There are penalties for stationing a caravan without a caravan-site licence, which can only be obtained after planning consent. If planning permission is refused an appeal may be made to the Department of the Environment. If travellers are operating a farm or small holding, they should get Ministry of Agriculture backing for the viability of the enterprise. If this is granted, they can then apply for a site licence. The only difficulty then may be in meeting local authority standards of roads, sanitation, etc. If these are satisfied, the local authority must grant a licence.
The traveller has been prosecuted for camping in the district, but there is no authorized site; *or* the traveller has been prosecuted for camping after being refused space on an authorized site, possibly in a designated area.	This is the main campaigning issue for Gypsy supporters. The local authority has a duty under the Caravan Sites Act to provide adequate accommodation. If it fails to do so, a complaint should be made to a councillor and then, if necessary, to the local government ombudsman (see p. 516). The failure of the local authority does not give the traveller a defence to a prosecution, but may be used in mitigation. In other than London boroughs and metropolitan districts where accommodation is for '15 at a time', the duty to provide adequate accommodation is open-ended, except in areas where the Minister has made a designation order (see p. 387). Here the traveller is in a much

worse position: the penalties for unauthorized camping are severe, and the only defences recognized in the Act are 'illness, breakdown or other immediate emergency'. The Minister has the power to remove the designation order if he is dissatisfied with the accommodation provided in the area – but this has never been done.

The traveller cannot afford the rent on the authorized site.	Supplementary benefit is available to meet the rent, but any income has to be declared or the traveller will be prosecuted 'for obtaining money fraudulently'.
The traveller has been banned from authorized site(s).	There is no remedy for this, except to campaign for a sufficient variety of site types to suit all travellers.

Welfare services and education

The traveller has no money or work, and cannot get social security.	They can apply for supplementary benefit with the help of a literate friend who can insist that full allowances are granted. Using an 'accommodation' address of a sympathizer may be useful to ensure that regular payments are received. If the problem is because of non-payment of self-employed or unemployed National Insurance stamp, it may be possible to plead illiteracy and ignorance of the regulations.
The travellers have been refused a drink at a pub because they are Gypsies.	A complaint should be made to the brewery owning the pub and/or the Commission for Racial Equality. Although Gypsies are not covered by race relations legislation, the commission should use their influence and will generally succeed.

The traveller is ill and cannot get a doctor.	If urgent, the traveller can go straight to a casualty hospital. It is desirable to register the family with a local doctor when arriving in a district. If the doctor refuses to accept the Gypsy family, a complaint should be made to the area health authority (see p. 474).
The traveller has children who have been refused admission at a local school.	Visit the divisional office of the local education authority who must find them a place. If possible appropriate teaching should be provided on the site (see p. 424).
The traveller has been summonsed for not sending children to school.	This is a snag for a traveller who has registered children at school. It is only possible to complain that the appropriate education is not being offered and that work at home is part of Gypsy education.
The traveller has been summonsed for dropping litter.	If this is in the course of car-breaking work, it should be pointed out to the court that disposal of bulky rubbish is a local authority duty under the Civic Amenities Act 1967.
The travellers have been summonsed because their horses have strayed.	This is a troublesome matter deriving from the loss of traditional sites and the perseverance of the Gypsy tradition of horse keeping and dealing. The Caravan Sites Act empowers local authorities to provide facilities on camp sites for activities normally carried on by Gypsies. This does not oblige them to provide grazing land.
	If the local authority impounds and mistreats horses, legal action should be considered or a complaint made to the Ombudsman (see p. 516).

More information

Adams, *Gypsies and Other Travellers*, 1967 (from Government bookshops) – based on the 1965 census.

Puxon, *On the Road*, NCCL, 1968.

Zara, *Travelling People and the Law*, 1971 (from West Midlands Travellers School).

Advice Committee for the Education of Romany and Other Travellers (ACERT), 204 Church Road, London w7 (01-579 5708).

Adult Literacy Resource Agency, 33 Queen Anne St, London w1 (01-580 6862).

Department of the Environment, Gypsy Adviser, 17–19 Rochester Row, London sw1 (01-834 8181).

Gypsy Council and National Gypsy Education Council, 18 Poyntz Road, London sw11 (01-228 2884).

Minority Rights Group, 36 Craven St, London wc2 (01-930 6659).

Save the Children Fund, 157 Clapham Road, London sw9 (01-582 1414) – employs a Gypsy liaison worker.

19. The armed forces

Many Acts of Parliament regulate the position of servicemen,* and civilians in their dealings with servicemen. For the sake of simplicity only the provisions relating to the Army are quoted here although similar provisions generally apply to the Navy and Air Force.

The Army Act 1955 lists those who are subject to military law. They include all serving members of the regular Army, all persons employed expressly on condition that they are subject to military law and reservists who are actually serving or training.

The system of courts operated by the armed forces is quite different from that which applies to ordinary civilians (see p. 77). There are a series of specifically military offences and areas where military law differs from civilian law. In addition, all civilian offences, whether committed in the UK or outside, are offences under military law, though the most serious (e.g. treason, murder, manslaughter and rape) cannot be tried by military courts if they are committed inside the UK.

Military offences

There are a number of military offences and only the most important are dealt with here.

Desertion and absence without leave

The difference between desertion and absence without leave depends on the intention of the person concerned. To be convicted of desertion it must be proved that you intended to remain permanently absent from duty, that you intended to avoid service at any place overseas, or that you intended to avoid a particular

*'He' and 'serviceman' have been used throughout this chapter for any member of the armed forces, male or female.

service when faced with the enemy. Desertion is quite difficult to prove particularly if you surrender yourself, although the longer you have been away the more likely it is that it will be thought that you intended to desert.

The civilian police have the power to arrest any deserter or absentee, who must be brought before a magistrates' court as soon as practicable. At the court you can contest that you are a deserter or absentee and apply for legal aid to do this (see p. 500). However, if the court decides against you, it will order you to be delivered into military custody. Deserters and absentees from certain foreign armies may be returned to their own country's forces by a magistrates' court under the provisions of the Visiting Forces Act 1952. Again, you may apply for legal aid for the magistrates' court hearing.

Homosexuality

It is an offence under military law to be guilty of 'disgraceful conduct of a cruel, indecent and unnatural kind'. This may cover matters which are not offences under the civilian law, notably homosexual acts between women and homosexual acts between men even where the parties consent and are over 21.

It is up to the court to decide whether the conduct is 'disgraceful', and there are no hard and fast guidelines.

Scandalous behaviour

Similarly, if the court considers that an officer has behaved in 'a scandalous manner unbecoming the character of an officer', he can be found guilty under military law of actions which would not necessarily be an offence under civilian law. There are no guidelines for this charge, except that it may be 'either of a military or a social character'.

Other restrictions

The Queen's Regulations prohibit or restrict a variety of actions which would not be offences under civilian law. These include the following:

- Regular personnel may not take 'an active part' in the affairs of any political organization or party, though it is not an offence to be a member of a political party. Personnel may attend political meetings, in or out of uniform, provided that 'service duties' are not impeded. It is risky to get involved in political activities within service establishments.
- Regular personnel may not stand for election to Parliament or to local authorities.
- Gambling and moneylending are forbidden, as is borrowing money from subordinates.
- Without the permission of the commanding officer, no intoxicating liquor may be introduced into any part of a barracks or camp except clubs, messes, officers' quarters and married quarters.

Military courts

If you are charged with an offence, you are entitled to be given a copy of a booklet, *The Rights of a Soldier charged with an offence*. You should apply for legal aid if it is available and decide whether you need legal representation.

Legal aid

Legal aid is not available for disciplinary proceedings below the level of court martial. Civilian legal aid schemes do not apply to military proceedings, but you can apply for legal aid through service channels set out in detail in the Queen's Regulations. The commanding officer will forward the application and add to it, from his knowledge of the defence case, whether he considers that there are grounds for legal aid. There is no right of appeal against a refusal to grant legal aid.

The following are examples where legal aid may be granted:

- for the defence of a serviceman charged before a court martial; *or*
- for an application for leave to appeal to the Court Martial Appeal Court; *or*

– for the defence of a serviceman charged before a criminal court abroad in respect of an offence committed while off-duty.

There are various principles which must be followed in deciding whether the case justifies legal aid. For example, whether the defendant would have been granted legal aid had the case been brought in the civilian criminal courts in the UK. Each case is considered on its merits.

Legal representation

There is no right to legal representation on summary trial.

Before courts martial, or before the Court Martial Appeal Court, you may defend yourself, or you may be represented by a defending officer of your own choice, or by a civilian lawyer. If you state that you want a particular officer to defend you, the court should appoint that officer. If you are represented by a civilian lawyer, you may still have a defending officer to assist as well.

Before civilian courts, you are entitled to have legal representation.

Court procedure

SUMMARY TRIAL

Certain offences can be dealt with summarily by a commanding officer, without trial by a court martial. However, both the accused and the commanding officer have the right to secure court martial trial in a large number of offences. You should refer to the booklet, *The Rights of a Soldier Charged with an Offence*, for the exact procedures, which depend upon the nature of the charge and the rank of the accused.

COURT MARTIAL

At the court martial, there will normally be a panel of three or five officers, with a judge advocate in attendance, who is a qualified lawyer and who can direct the court on points of law in a summing-up at the end of the case.

An important difference exists between the sentencing of a court martial and a civilian court: if you are charged before a court martial with several offences, you will (if found guilty) receive one sentence for all the offences.

APPEALS BY PETITION

All findings and sentences of a court martial are subject to confirmation by a confirming officer who may, if he thinks there has been an error of law or a guilty verdict arrived at against the weight of the evidence, direct that the court reconsider the matter. He is also obliged to reconsider the sentence and may reduce, change or remit it. If a guilty finding is not confirmed, a retrial can be held if an order for it is issued within twenty-eight days.

You may petition the confirming officer against the finding or sentence at any time before you are told the decision of the confirming officer. The petition must be in a prescribed form, and your lawyer or defending officer will either draft it for you or help you to draft it. It is always worthwhile to petition against sentence as this often results in reductions.

Try to get the petition submitted before the confirmation is made, but even if you submit after the confirmation but before you have been notified, the confirming officer may reconsider his confirmation decision in the light of your petition.

If you are dissatisfied with the decision of the confirming officer, you may re-submit your petition against finding or sentence to the confirming officer and you may at any time petition a superior officer to the confirming officer, the Defence Council or the Queen. You should always try to get legal advice at this stage.

COURT MARTIAL APPEAL COURT

If your petition against a guilty verdict is unsuccessful, you may appeal to the Court Martial Appeal Court. You may not appeal against sentence unless you were a civilian both at the time of your conviction and when the offence was committed. The procedure is similar to the Court of Appeal Criminal Division (see p. 101) and your lawyer or defending officer will draft your grounds of appeal. The preparation of petitions and the preparation of applications for leave can be covered by legal aid.

Leaving the armed forces

Members of the armed forces do not have a 'contract of employment' and none of the usual provisions of employment law affect them. There are only a limited number of ways of terminating service.

Discharge by purchase

You can purchase a discharge by giving fourteen days notice if:

– you have been in the force for less than three months; *or*
– you joined up when you were under $17\frac{1}{2}$ years of age and have not completed six months' service; *or*
– you joined between the age of $17\frac{1}{2}$ and $18\frac{1}{4}$ years and apply for discharge before you reach the age of $18\frac{1}{4}$ years or before you have completed six months' service, whichever is the sooner.

Outside these categories you may purchase your discharge as a 'privilege' but not a 'right'. Normally there is a minimum period which must be served and various other criteria will be taken into account including length of service and availability of personnel with similar skills.

Compassionate grounds

You may receive a discharge if you have strong compassionate grounds such as an invalid parent whom no other member of the family can look after. A strict assessment will be made of such grounds.

Health grounds

Mental or physical illness may be grounds of discharge and you will be assessed by army medical officers.

Grounds of conscience

Any soldier or officer may be discharged if he can show objection to serving on genuine grounds of conscience either moral or religious. It is not clear how far this extends (e.g. whether you can object to just a particular war, service on behalf of a particular government, or whether your objection must be to all military service). This form of discharge cannot be obtained if you are awaiting a court martial. If your application is rejected by your commanding officer, you may request a hearing before a special advisory tribunal where you can be represented.

Other discharges

You may be discharged:

– on giving notice if you have a 'notice engagement'; *or*
– on termination of your engagement; *or*
– if your services are no longer required (a form of redundancy); *or*
– after conviction by a court martial (soldiers and officers who are requested to resign have the right to make representations against enforced resignation); *or*
– if you are an officer and make application to resign your commission.

Civilians and the armed forces

There are a number of laws (including the Incitement to Mutiny Act 1797) which restrict the freedom of civilians in their dealings with service personnel. The most important are:

Incitement to Disaffection Act 1934

Under this act it is an offence to 'endeavour to seduce any member of Her Majesty's Forces from his duty or allegiance'. In addition, it is an offence to possess any document which, if distributed, would constitute an 'endeavour to seduce'.

The exact definition of these words in any particular case is a matter for a jury to decide. Recent cases have indicated that the jury will be strongly influenced by the intention of the individual person. For instance, a pacifist will be more likely to be acquitted than a member or supporter of the IRA, even though they may possess or be distributing the same leaflet. Particularly if the leaflet refers to contentious political affairs (such as Northern Ireland), you should consult a lawyer about the wording of the leaflet before distributing it – you do not have to accept the lawyer's advice but it is important to understand the implications of particular phrases under the Incitement to Disaffection Act. In general, if a leaflet only gives information and does not seek to persuade a serviceman to a particular point of view, it will not be in breach of the law.

Under the Incitement to Disaffection Act the maximum penalties are: in the magistrates' court, four months' imprisonment and/or a fine of £1,000; in the Crown Court, two years' imprisonment and/or an unlimited fine.

An alien (a foreigner who is not a UK or Commonwealth citizen) can be imprisoned for up to ten years with an unlimited fine under the Aliens Restriction (Amendment) Act 1919.

Army Act 1955

Under the Army Act 1955 it is an offence in any way to assist a soldier who has already deserted or gone absent without leave. This means that doing anything, such as providing food, money or accommodation, which assists the soldier to remain absent is liable to be regarded as an offence.

This provision is of special importance to people counselling and advising soldiers who have gone absent without leave in order to come to a clear decision. Experience has shown that merely advising a soldier to return to duty before doing anything else may achieve nothing. It may be a defence to argue that any assistance given was merely for the purpose of allowing the soldier time to consider his position and was purely incidental to the main advice to return to duty and obtain a legal discharge. However, this is not certain. The maximum penalty for such an offence is: in the magistrates' court, three months' imprisonment and/or a fine of £1,000; in the Crown Court, two years' imprisonment and/or an unlimited fine.

It is also an offence to prevent any member of the army from carrying out his duty by supplying him with drugs or affecting his health in such a way as to make him unfit for service.

Obstruction of the army

There are a number of offences which are concerned with preventing the soldier or the army from carrying out their duty or work. The most important are:

- obstructing any member of the regular army in the execution of his duty (maximum penalty three months' imprisonment and/or a £50 fine (Army Act 1955);
- obstructing or interfering with the execution of manoeuvres (maximum penalty a £2 fine) (Manoeuvres Act 1958);
- removing flags or distinguishing marks, cutting or damaging telegraph wires being used for manoeuvres (maximum penalty a £5 fine) (Manoeuvres Act 1958).

Civilians and military courts

Under Part II of the Army Act (which deals with discipline, trial and punishment of military offenders), those civilians who are employees of the army, families and employees of service personnel are liable to the military courts described above. The major difference affecting civilians charged before military courts is that they can appeal against both conviction and sentence to the Court Martial Appeal Court.

There are a number of specific charges affecting civilians under this part of the Army Act, including:

- assaulting a sentry or person on watch or compelling a guard to let a person pass;
- obstructing a provost officer or refusing to assist him when called on to do so;
- contravening a standing order or routine order;
- resisting arrest by a duly appointed guard or provost officer or escaping from lawful custody by the same.

Helpful organizations

At Ease, c/o Release, 1 Elgin Avenue, London w9 (01-838 9794) – counselling service for those seeking legal ways of leaving the armed forces.

Central Board for Conscientious Objectors, c/o Endsleigh Street, London wc1 (01-352 7906).

NCCL, 186 Kings Cross Road, London wc1 (01-278 4575).

20. Welfare and social security benefits

This chapter briefly covers:

Grants for children at school are dealt with on p. 429.

The basic social security scheme in this country remains the National Insurance scheme but in practice many people dependent on National Insurance benefits require supplementary benefit in order to provide them with enough money to live. To most people 'social security' means supplementary benefit.

National Insurance contributions

Contributory benefits (see pp. 405–14) depend on contributions paid to the National Insurance Fund either by the contributor or, in some cases, by relatives. The theory is that people prefer to claim benefits only when they have contributed and that only then do they think that they are not asking for 'charity'. In effect, however, contributions are little more than a form of tax and you may be unable to obtain these benefits if you have not paid enough contributions in the right period.

There are four classes of contributions. Class 1 contributions are paid by both employer and employee at certain percentages of gross earnings up to £95 per week (8·75 per cent and 5·75 per cent respectively before April 1977). These count towards all benefits. A married woman can choose to pay reduced contributions at the rate of 2 per cent of gross earnings but those contributions do not help to make her eligible for benefits. See leaflet NI 40.

Class 2 contributions are paid by self-employed people and

towards all benefits except unemployment benefit. These are paid at a flat rate of £2·41 for men and £2·20 for women. Married women can opt out. See leaflets NI 11, 27A, 41.

Class 3 contributions are voluntary and may be paid by non-employed people. This does not include those who are sick or unemployed and signing on, as they get credited with Class 1 contributions. Class 3 contributions do not count for unemployment benefit, sickness benefit or maternity allowance and are paid at a flat rate of £2·10 weekly for men and women. See leaflet NI 42.

Class 4 contributions do not count for any benefit and are levied – some say unfairly – on the self-employed by the Inland Revenue at the rate of 8 per cent of all profits between £1,600 and £4,900 per year.

The DHSS leaflets mentioned at the end of each section contain information about contribution conditions for various benefits. We do not deal with the conditions here except to say that, as a general rule, entitlement to benefit depends on contributions paid at least a year before the claim.

The benefits themselves are awarded in the form of a basic benefit and 'additions' for dependants. Earnings-related supplement and other additions may also be payable.

Non-means-tested benefits

If you have contributed

UNEMPLOYMENT BENEFIT

This is paid after the first three 'waiting days' in any one 'period of interruption of employment'. It lasts for 312 days (not counting Sundays), in any one such period. Any two such periods separated by any more than thirteen weeks count as one period only. You must register as available for reasonable full-time work. The meaning of 'reasonable' depends on the circumstances and if benefit is refused because you place what are said to be unreasonable restrictions on the employment you are willing to do you should consider appealing to a local tribunal.

The main cause of disputes is the 'six-week rule' by which

you may lose benefit for up to six weeks if you lost your last job through misconduct, left 'voluntarily without just cause' or refused a reasonable offer of employment. Again you may appeal against the insurance officer's decision.

If you earn more than 75p a day you will lose benefit.

See leaflet NI 12.

SICKNESS BENEFIT

This is paid if you are 'incapable of work'. It is paid after three 'waiting days' for up to 168 days of any 'period of interruption of employment'. If you earn more than £7 per week you will lose benefit.

If the insurance officer does not think that your doctor was right to advise you to stay away from work, he or she may require you to be examined by a regional medical officer and benefit may be stopped. You may appeal against such a decision.

When collecting evidence for tribunal hearings it is important to remember that the condition for entitlement to benefit is that you must be 'incapable of work' – not just ill – so that doctors must be asked to give opinions on capacity for work. They often need to be reminded of this otherwise they tend to stick to a description of the symptoms and a diagnosis. You are not 'incapable of work' if you are capable of doing light work.

See leaflet NI 16.

INVALIDITY BENEFIT

Invalidity pension is paid for an indefinite period beginning when sickness benefit ceases to be payable. It is basically a higher rate of sickness benefit. It is increased by an invalidity allowance which depends on the claimant's age when he or she first becomes incapable of work.

See leaflet NI 16A.

MATERNITY ALLOWANCE

This is paid from the eleventh week before *expected* date of birth of the child for eighteen weeks or until the sixth week after the *actual* date of birth, whichever is longer. You should claim between the fourteenth and eleventh week before the expected date of birth. Maternity allowance depends on the *mother's* contribution and is only paid during periods when she is not working. Mothers under the age of 16 cannot claim maternity allowance or maternity grant.

See leaflet NI 17A.

MATERNITY GRANT

This is paid for each child born. Entitlement depends on the contributions of either the mother or her husband (if you are not married, you cannot claim benefit on the father's contributions.) The grant may be claimed before the birth if maternity allowance is payable then.

If you are expecting a baby or have a child under twelve months old you can have free dental treatment and prescriptions on the NHS. See leaflet NI 17A.

WIDOW'S ALLOWANCE

Like all widow's benefits this depends on the contributions of the claimant's late husband. It is paid for the first twenty-six weeks of widowhood. There is no limit to what you may earn and an earnings-related addition calculated like earnings-related supplement is paid for each week. Remarriage or cohabitation leads to disqualification.

See leaflet NI 13.

WIDOWED MOTHER'S ALLOWANCE

This is paid from the end of the widow's allowance period for as long as you are pregnant by your late husband or have a dependant child living with you or have a non-dependant child under the age of 19 living with you. There is no limit on earnings. Remarriage or cohabitation lead to disqualification.

WIDOW'S PENSION

This is paid provided you were over 40 when either your husband died or widowed mother's allowance ceased to be payable. If you were under 50 the pension is reduced by an amount equal to 7 per cent of the amount which would otherwise be paid for each year by which you were under 50 at the relevant time. There is no limit on earnings. Remarriage and cohabitation lead to disqualification.

CHILD'S SPECIAL ALLOWANCE

This is paid to a woman whose marriage ended in divorce and whose ex-husband is now dead. It is paid for any child for whom he was either actually paying or else legally bound to pay maintenance at the rate of at least 25p weekly. The child must be living with you or else you must be contributing at least £1·50 to his or her upkeep.

See leaflet NI 93.

DEATH GRANT

This is paid on the death of a contributor, the wife, husband or child of a contributor. It must be claimed within six months of the date of death and is not paid for people who were over pension age on 5 July 1948.

See leaflet NI 49.

RETIREMENT PENSION

To be entitled to a retirement pension you must be *both* over pension age (65 for men, 60 for women) *and* have retired. Anyone more than five years over pension age is automatically treated as retired. So is anyone whose earnings are less than £50 weekly. Otherwise you are only treated as retired if you have stopped work or you are or intend 'to be (an earner) only occasionally or to an inconsiderable extent or otherwise in circumstances not inconsistent with retirement'.

Category A retirement pension is payable to people entitled on their own contribution record. (Widows may include some of their late husband's contributions.) Category B retirement pension is paid to a married woman who is only entitled to a pension on her husband's contribution record and is paid only if *both* he and she are retired. If the man is retired but the woman is still under pension age, he may be able to claim an increase of his pension in respect of her as a dependant. The increase is equal to the amount of category B retirement pension. Category A retirement pension may also be paid to a widow. Category C and D retirement pensions are paid to those very old people who were over pensionable age on 5 July 1948.

A retirement pension is increased by 25p weekly if you are over 80. If you were receiving invalidity allowance within thirteen weeks of retiring, the pension will be increased by the amount of the invalidity allowance. A pension is reduced if you earn more than £35 weekly.

See leaflet NI 15.

EARNINGS-RELATED SUPPLEMENT

This is payable for the first six months during which you are entitled to unemployment benefit, sickness benefit, injury benefit, maternity benefit or widow's benefit. It is not paid for the first twelve days of any 'period of interruption of employment'.

The rate of supplement depends on earnings during the last tax year before the calendar year before you first claim. Leaflet NI 155A gives the figures.

ADDITIONS FOR DEPENDANTS

A claimant can have his benefit increased if he is living with his wife or children for whom he may claim child benefit, or is maintaining her or them at a weekly rate not less than the amount of increase. A claimant may be able to claim for a female who has the care of dependant children and certain dependant relatives. A woman may only claim for her husband if he is 'incapable of self support'.

No increase of unemployment benefit or sickness benefit, for adult dependants is payable if the dependants earn more than the amount of increase. In the case of invalidity pension or retirement pension the increase will be reduced if the dependant earns more than £35 weekly.

Even if you have not contributed

It is to be hoped that one day no benefit will depend on complicated contribution records. Many new benefits are noncontributory but they are paid at an absurdly low level and often leave people dependent on supplementary benefit.

ATTENDANCE ALLOWANCE

This is paid to those who are so severely disabled mentally or physically that they need frequent attention in connection with their bodily functions or need continual supervision to avoid danger to themselves or to others. It is paid at the lower rate if you need the attention or supervision during *either* night or day and at the higher rate if you need it during *both*.

First a doctor – often your GP – visits and reports to the Attendance Allowance Board at Blackpool. If it refuses to allow the claim you may ask for a review. Over half such reviews are successful. It is important to explain the practical effects of the disability rather than worrying about causes. A final appeal lies on a point of law to the National Insurance Commissioner (see p. 420). He has decided that people on kidney machines may claim and also that the danger to which people are exposed does not have to be constant as long as constant supervision is required in case of occasional danger. 'The object of supervision may be precautionary and anticipatory yet never result in intervention.'

See leaflet NI 205.

INVALID CARE ALLOWANCE

This is paid to those who are looking after a close relative who is receiving attendance allowance or equivalent from public funds and who have to stay away from work to do so. Married women looking after their husbands are not yet eligible.
    See leaflet NI 212.

NON-CONTRIBUTORY INVALIDITY PENSION

This is paid to those who have been incapable of work for at least 196 consecutive days. It is not paid to married women and is only of advantage to those who do not have sufficient contributions for sickness benefit and who therefore never become entitled to the ordinary invalidity pension.
    See leaflet NI 210.

MOBILITY ALLOWANCE

This is paid to those under pensionable age who are unable to walk or virtually so.
    The Pensioners' car allowance scheme is being withdrawn. The Department of Health and Social Security say that resources are being concentrated where they are most needed – the younger disabled person. However, pensioners who are giving up an invalid car will be able to get mobility allowance.
    See leaflet NI 211.

GUARDIAN'S ALLOWANCE

This is paid to a guardian where the child's parents are both dead or else one is dead and the other is either in prison or untraceable.
    See leaflet NI 14.

CHILD BENEFIT

This benefit, which has replaced family allowance, is paid to those who are responsible for a child under 16, or someone under

19 and in full-time secondary education. You are responsible for
a child if the child is either living with you or you are maintaining the child at a rate not less than the rate of child benefit. Only
one person may claim for any one child so there is an order of
priority. A person with whom the child is living takes precedence
over others. A wife takes precedence over a husband, and an
unmarried mother takes precedence over the father where the
couple is living together. In other circumstances a parent takes
precedence over another person. Two people with equal rights
must choose who is to claim, or a decision will be made for them.

See leaflets CH 1, CH 7.

Industrial injury benefits

These are payable if you suffer personal injury due to an industrial accident or else suffer disablement due to a prescribed
industrial disease.

An accident is something unexpected but if caused by the
misconduct of another person it may still be an accident provided
that you did not contribute by your conduct. The accident must
occur while you were doing something you were employed to do
and this includes travelling to work if the employer provides the
transport. You should report even very small accidents and get a
declaration that they are industrial accidents. This can be done
even if the accident does not appear to have affected you: it
safeguards your position should the effects of the accident
become apparent later.

Injury benefit is paid weekly if you are rendered incapable of
work because of the accident. It is only paid for periods within six
months of the accident. Earnings-related supplement is payable
and the benefit may be increased if you have dependants.

See leaflet NI 5.

INDUSTRIAL DISABLEMENT BENEFIT

This is paid for any period after injury benefit stops being payable
and during which you suffer disablement because of the injury.
Thus it can be paid even if you are working. The amount of

benefit depends on the extent of the disablement and this is assessed by the medical board who also decide whether the disability is due to the accident and for how long it will last. The extent of disablement is expressed as a percentage. For example, if you have lost one eye without complication, the other being normal, you will be assessed as 40 per cent disabled. You would therefore get 40 per cent of the disablement benefit paid to a person who was 100 per cent disabled (e.g. through loss of a hand and a foot) due to an accident. Those percentages are laid down by law but where there is a back complaint or mental illness, the board has to assess the percentage. You may appeal to a medical appeal tribunal against a decision of the medical board.

The way the benefit is paid depends on the percentage disablement. If you are 20 per cent or more disabled then you receive a weekly *disablement pension*. Otherwise you receive a lump-sum *disablement gratuity*.

If you are unable to return to your former job you will be entitled to *special hardship allowance* in addition to disablement benefit. Special hardship allowance is paid where your earnings are likely to be lower than those in the previous job would have been. Prospects of promotion are taken into account and the amount paid is the difference between likely future earnings and those that might have been obtained but for the accident, subject to a maximum. The amount of special hardship allowance is often much greater than the disablement benefit itself. If the accident has rendered you unable to work again *unemployability supplement* is paid instead of special hardship allowance. There are other increases of disablement benefit for those who due to an industrial accident require *constant attendance* or *hospital treatment* or who suffer *exceptionally severe disablement*.

See leaflet NI 6.

INDUSTRIAL DEATH BENEFIT

There are a number of death benefits payable if someone is killed in an industrial accident but the general rule is that relatives who were being supported by the dead person are entitled to a pension or in some cases a gratuity. The initial pension payable to a widow for the first twenty-six weeks is paid at a fixed rate with a supplement related to her late husband's earnings. It is then reduced to one of two rates. Widowers can only claim if they are permanently unable to support themselves and are paid at a flat rate. A woman who lived with the deceased before his death and looked after his children might be entitled to a small pension if he was contributing at least half of her maintenance.

See leaflet N I-10.

Means-tested benefits

Supplementary benefits

When the present social security system was developed it was planned that National Insurance benefits should be raised to a level sufficient to enable people to live on them without further support. The National Assistance Board was to provide income for those who were missed by the insurance scheme or whose insurance benefits were inadequate, but it was intended that its role would be reduced. In 1966 the National Assistance Board was replaced by the Supplementary Benefits Commission. The rate at which National Insurance benefits have increased has not been sufficient to enable many claimants to live without other financial support and $4\frac{1}{2}$ million people are dependent at least in part on supplementary benefit.

Supplementary benefits are not available to people in full-time paid work unless there is an urgent need.

WEEKLY BENEFIT

This is called a supplementary pension if you are over pension age; otherwise it is called a supplementary allowance. The amount of basic benefit is calculated by adding up the claimant's 'requirements' and subtracting any 'resources'.

The 'requirements' of a claimant are found by first adding up the rates allowed. Those either over pension age *or* who have been claiming benefit for more than two years without being required to register as available for work are entitled to the long-term rate. (An extra 25p is added if the claimant or a dependant is over 80.)

	Ordinary rate £	Long-term rate £
Married couple	23·55	28·35
Person living alone	14·50	17·90
Any other person aged: Not less than 18	11·60	14·35
16–17	8·90	
13–15	7·40	
11–12	6·10	
5–10	4·95	
under 5	4·10	

(NB: These are correct at November 1977 but are changed twice yearly.)

To this figure there must be added an amount for 'rent'. For a tenant this will usually be the actual amount of rent together with rates unless the rent is considered to be unreasonably high. For a householder with a mortgage the interest part of the mortgage, together with rates, will usually be paid. A non-householder receives a standard addition of £1·20 for 'rent' but this may be increased if the circumstances warrant it.

The 'resources' of a claimant include those of his or her dependants and consist of National Insurance benefits other than mobility allowance (and attendance allowance for practical purposes), child benefits, maintenance payments (only if actually received), and net earnings (less deductions and travel expenses). If you are required to register as available for work your first £2 of earnings is not counted as resources. Single parents can earn up to £6 and others up to £4 (£8 if husband and wife both work).

Benefit may be increased (or decreased in the case of people under pension age) in order to take into account exceptional circumstances. This is commonly done to help people who are in ill health or who live in poor housing, and so have difficulty heating their houses. Increases are also given to people who have to follow diets, have exceptional laundry expenses or HP commitments for essential household items. However, the law does not limit the payment of exceptional circumstances additions to those expenses only, so that any claimant with unusual and essential expenditure may ask for assistance. There is a right of appeal to a supplementary benefits appeal tribunal (see p. 421).

Claimants often have no idea how their benefit is calculated and the Supplementary Benefits Commission admits that mistakes are made in a very large number of cases. You can ask them to send you a notice of assessment (form A124) and this will explain the calculation. See also leaflet SB 1.

EXCEPTIONAL NEEDS PAYMENTS

Lump-sum payments may be claimed even if you are not receiving weekly benefit. However, you will have some difficulty justifying the request if your income is much above that of a supplementary benefit claimant. The payments will be made if it is considered 'reasonable' and if there is an 'exceptional need'. If the expense is something which you would not usually be expected to meet from your weekly benefit (e.g. removal expenses, or furniture) there is not too much difficulty. However, claimants are expected to be able to feed, clothe and heat themselves with the week's money so that you have to explain why you have not been able to do so when asking for a grant for clothing or to meet a fuel bill (e.g. because you didn't claim a grant for removal expenses when moving, or the children have suddenly grown out of everything at once). If hardship will result from a refusal to make the payment then that may by itself be a good enough reason for making it. There is a right of appeal against refusal of payment even if the person claiming is not claiming weekly benefit.

THE COHABITATION RULE

A couple not married but living together as man and wife are treated as a married couple. If the man is working full-time this means that they are not entitled to benefit at all. Living in the same household is an essential requirement but that alone is not enough to establish cohabitation. The relationship must be 'more than an occasional or very brief association'. Evidence of financial support is important. If the man is not supporting the woman (or vice versa) that fact should be stressed. A sexual relationship or a lack of one is not conclusive either way, it is, however, relevant, as is any public representation from the couple that they are married (e.g. the woman taking the man's surname). Whether the man treats any children as a father would is also important, but again not conclusive.

Family income supplement

This benefit is intended to help families with children where the breadwinner is in full-time work and therefore not eligible for supplementary benefit. It is paid to people who work at least thirty hours a week and whose income (before tax and insurance and including child benefits but not rent allowances or rebates) falls below the 'prescribed level'. This is at present (from July 1976) £39 per week for a family with one child and is increased by £4·50 for each extra child. The benefit paid is *half* the difference between the family's income and the 'prescribed level'.
    See leaflet FIS 1.

Exemptions from NHS charges

If you are getting supplementary benefit or family income supplement, you are exempt from most NHS charges for:

– appliances supplied by hospitals (including drugs supplied to outpatients);
– dental treatment;
– glasses;
– prescriptions.

You can also get free milk and vitamins if you have children or are expecting a baby.
    See leaflet M 11.

Rent and rate rebates

If you are a council tenant, or a private tenant, you may be able to pay less for your rent by applying to the local authority. Council tenants can receive a **rent rebate**, which means that the rent they pay is reduced; private tenants can receive a **rent allowance** to offset against their rent.

The amount you will receive depends on:

– your income;
– the size of your family;
– the amount of rent you pay (excluding rates and service charges).

The method of calculating rent rebates and allowances is complicated, so it is always worth applying in order to see if you qualify. You can get the claim form from your local council housing office. Even people on relatively high incomes can qualify: for instance, a couple or single parent with three children, an income of £60 weekly and paying a rent of £5, can get over £1. The maximum rebate you can get is £6·50 (£8·00 in Greater London).

You cannot receive *both* a rent rebate or allowance and supplementary benefits, since your supplementary benefit (see p. 415) should cover your rent. But you may be better off claiming rent and rate rebates instead of supplementary benefits; you should ask your local supplementary benefits office to work out for you which would be more advantageous to you.

RATE REBATES AND ALLOWANCES

It is not only owner-occupiers who pay rates. Tenants also pay rates, often as part of their rent. Both owner-occupiers and tenants can claim a rate rebate, which is calculated, like rent rebates, on the basis of your income, the size of your family, and the amount of rates you pay. The maximum rate rebate you can get is £2·50 (£3·00 in Greater London).

The method of calculating rent and rate rebates and allowances is set out in full in *Your Rights* (see p. 423).

Appeals

National Insurance

If you disagree with the insurance officer's decision about whether you are entitled to receive a National Insurance benefit, or how much you should get, you should appeal to the National Insurance tribunal. You can get an application form from the National Insurance officer, or else simply write a letter of appeal to the tribunal (address in the telephone directory).

The tribunal deals with appeals concerning the following benefits: unemployment benefit; sickness and invalidity benefit; invalidity allowance; some mobility allowance questions; non-contributory invalidity pension; maternity grant and allowance; widows' allowance, widowed mothers' allowance and widows' pension; guardians' allowance; retirement pension; child benefit; death grant; and industrial injury benefit, when the issue in dispute is whether there has been an accident.

ADVICE

If you belong to a trade union and you are claiming unemployment or sickness benefit or any other benefit connected with your employment, you should ask your branch secretary for advice and, if possible, to get someone to represent you at the tribunal hearing. You may also be able to get advice from a solicitor under the green-form scheme (see p. 494); a local claimants' union; or the Child Poverty Action Group (see p. 423).

THE TRIBUNAL HEARING

The tribunal consists of three people: a chairperson, who is usually a lawyer, and two others drawn from panels representing employers and employees. Members of these two panels are appointed by the Department of Health and Social Security, but they are not employed by the department. The atmosphere is very informal – the person appealing sits at the same table as the tribunal and does not have to take an oath or stand up when giving evidence.

The tribunal members will have read your letter of appeal, and the insurance officer's statement supporting his decision, so they will know the basic facts of the case. You present your case first. You or your representative can call witnesses and produce documentary evidence such as letters, doctors' certificates, pay-slips, time sheets, etc. The tribunal members will ask you questions, and so will the insurance officer. You can question witnesses and inspect documents produced by the insurance officer.

You will either be told the decision at the hearing or by post. The tribunal does not have to give reasons for its decisions unless you ask for them so you should ask for reasons, either at the end of the hearing or as soon as you get the decision. It is best to ask for a written decision with reasons in case you decide to appeal.

You can claim travelling expenses and compensation for loss of earnings; the clerk of the tribunal usually arranges this.

NATIONAL INSURANCE COMMISSIONER

If you disagree with the tribunal's decision, you can appeal against it to the National Insurance Commissioner. The appeal must be made within three months. You should get expert advice first, either from a solicitor or your trade union.

You can get the appeal form from the local National Insurance office. If you want the case to be heard at a proper hearing, so that you can attend, you should say so on the form. Otherwise, the case may be decided on the basis of the papers only.

National Insurance Commissioners are senior barristers, very like judges. The hearings are fairly formal, with the Commissioner sitting at a separate table, at the front. The Commissioners only hear cases in London, Edinburgh and Cardiff, so you may need to travel to the hearing. You can claim travelling expenses, subsistence and compensation for loss of earnings; the clerk usually deals with this.

The Commissioner will always give you a written decision, giving the reasons for the decision, some time after the hearing.

The only way to challenge the Commissioner's decision is by an application to the High Court, on the grounds that the Commissioner was wrong in law. You will need legal advice before doing this.

Supplementary benefits

If you are not satisfied with the local supplementary benefits office's decision about whether or not you are entitled to receive benefit, or how much you should get, you can appeal to the supplementary benefits appeal tribunal. You must make your appeal within twenty-one days of the decision (although the tribunal can allow you to appeal later). You can get an application form from the local supplementary benefits office, or you can simply write a letter saying 'I wish to appeal against the decision of ... [date] concerning ...' It is very important in this letter to set out every point about which you want to appeal.

ADVICE

You may be able to get help with making your appeal from the local claimants' union or the Child Poverty Action Group (see p. 423). They may also be able to arrange for someone to represent you at the tribunal. If you cannot get help from these sources, you should get a copy of the *Supplementary Benefits Handbook* (see p. 432) which sets out the policies of the Supplementary Benefits Commission.

THE TRIBUNAL HEARING

The tribunal consists of a chairperson, who is usually not a lawyer, and two other members, one from a panel representing workers and the other appointed by the Secretary of State for Social Services. The hearing is very informal and is always held in private, except that research workers may, if you agree, be allowed to attend.

It is very important that you should attend the hearing. You and your witnesses can claim travelling expenses and compensation for loss of earnings; the clerk of the tribunal is responsible for this.

You will rarely win your case simply by showing the tribunal that you do not have enough to live on. Although the statutes and regulations governing supplementary benefits are fairly simple, there are many discretionary decisions involved, which are usually taken in line with Supplementary Benefits Commission policy. Unless you have some knowledge of these policies, the officer from the supplementary benefits office will have more influence with the tribunal, as he is bound to have a thorough knowledge of the laws and practices of the system. You can produce witnesses and documents (e.g. doctor's letter, heating bills, evidence about clothing prices in your area) to back up your case, and you can speak on your own behalf if you want to. You may be questioned by the chairperson and sometimes other members of the tribunal. The supplementary benefits officer may also question you and your witnesses. You are entitled to question the officer and any witnesses he or she brings.

You will be told of the tribunal's decision by post. The tribunal must give you the reasons for its decision in writing, as soon as practicable after the hearing.

FURTHER APPEALS

If the tribunal has made a mistake on a point of law, you may be able to appeal to the High Court. You should get legal advice, for instance from the Child Poverty Action Group, about this.

Family income supplement

If you want to appeal against a refusal to give you family income supplement or against the amount you get, you should write to the local DHSS office within twenty-one days. Clearly head your letter '*Family income supplement appeal*'. The appeal will be heard by the supplementary benefits appeal tribunal (see above).

More information

DHSS publish about 100 leaflets – the ones you see in post offices. The leaflets contain up-to-date figures, and, in some cases, claim forms. If none of the ones on show seem relevant, ask for the right one at your local DHSS office or citizens' advice bureau or write to Information Division Leaflets Unit, Block 4, Government Buildings, Honeypot Lane, Stanmore, Middlesex.

Family Benefits and Pensions (leaflet FB 1) gives a summary of state and local authority benefits.

Supplementary Benefits Commission administration papers: in particular, *Supplementary Benefits Handbook* – from government bookshops or HMSO, PO Box 569, London SE 1 (01-928 1321).

R. Lister, *National Welfare Benefits Handbook* (sixth edition, 1976) CPAG (65p including post) – a guide to supplementary benefits, family income supplement and other welfare benefits. CPAG also publish both special guides for students and the unemployed (including strikers) and pamphlets on general social security issues.

C. Smith and D. C. Hoath, *Law and the Under Privileged*, Routledge & Kegan Paul, 1976 (£2·95) – good on National Insurance in particular.

Your Rights, Age Concern (30p including post).

Disability Rights, Disability Rights Alliance, 96 Portland Place, London W 1 (65p including post) – a guide for disabled people.

Your local DHSS office.

Your local citizens' advice bureau.

Age Concern, 60 Pitcairn Road, Mitcham, Surrey (01-640 5431).

Child Poverty Action Group (CPAG), 1 Macklin Street, London WC2 (01-242 3225).

Citizens' Rights Office, address as CPAG (01-405 5942).

21. Education

This chapter is divided into two sections:

Addresses of organizations who may be able to provide further information and advice are given on p. 442.

Schools

The right to education

Every child aged from 5 to 16 has the right to receive an efficient full-time education suitable to age, ability and aptitude. Parents have a legal duty to ensure that their child receives such an education.

Every local education authority (LEA) must provide enough primary and secondary schools for their area, but a child can be educated at an independent school or at home if the parent(s) can convince the LEA that the child is receiving a suitable education.

Attendance

The LEA is responsible for ensuring that parents carry out their legal obligations with regard to their child's education.

If a parent has not registered a child at a school, and the LEA decides that the child is not being satisfactorily educated, then the LEA can serve a **school attendance order**, naming a particular school, on the parents. If you object to the school named in the attendance order, you may ask the LEA to substitute another. You may also ask for the order to be revoked on the grounds that you have made arrangements for the child to be educated outside school. If the LEA refuses either to revoke the order or change the school named, you may refer the matter to the Secretary of State for Education. If the LEA considers that the alternative school you propose is unsuitable, they may refer the matter to the Secretary of State. If you are not happy with the Secretary of State's decision, you have a right to appeal to the courts and you should take legal advice.

If the LEA considers that the child is not being satisfactorily educated, and the parents do not obey a school attendance order, then the LEA can prosecute. The maximum penalty is a fine of £10 for a first offence, £20 for a second offence and imprisonment of one month and/or a fine of £20 for a third or subsequent offence. (But see p. 19.) It is also possible that a care order could be made on the child by a juvenile court (see p. 363).

If a child is registered at a school, the parents are responsible for ensuring the child's regular attendance. The head teacher of every school must keep a record of attendance and if any child of compulsory school age fails to attend regularly the parents may be guilty of an offence. Usually no action is taken if:

– the child was prevented from attending by sickness or some other unavoidable cause which affected the child, *not* the parents; *or*
– the child was absent on days exclusively set apart for religious observance by the religious body to which the child's parents belong; *or*
– the LEA failed in its legal duty to provide transport for the child to get to school (see p. 428); *or*
– the child was excluded from school for health reasons such as infectious disease or infestation; *or*
– the child had leave to be absent from school.

Some young children get over-tired from doing a full day at school. Legally, a child must attend school full-time from the age of 5, but many schools now recognize the problem of exhausted infants. If your child is over-tired you should talk to the school, which will probably arrange for a shorter school day for a while.

Choice of school

You do not have an absolute legal right to choose which school your child attends, although LEAs cannot legally refuse a child a place at a particular school without good reason. If more than one school offering the right type of education within the area has places available, LEAs should meet parents' wishes if possible about which school their child will attend. But the law is very vague on this point: 'The Minister and local authorities shall have regard to the general principle that, so far as is compatible with the provision of efficient instruction and training and the avoidance of unreasonable public expenditure, pupils are to be educated in accordance with their parents' wishes.'

Often, little real choice exists because school places are so limited. Some reasons have always been accepted as justifying parents' wishes for a particular school:

- the preferred school's religious instruction is more appropriate;
- the journey to school is safer and more convenient;
- the preferred school has special facilities (e.g. for a handicapped child or a child with a particular talent), or provides a midday meal when both parents work;
- the parents prefer a single-sex or co-educational school;
- the child has brothers or sisters at the preferred school;
- in Wales there is a special consideration as to whether the school holds its lessons in Welsh.

There are equally strong reasons why your application for a different school may be turned down:

- distance. As a rule, children should not be allowed to attend a primary school where the journey is over five or six miles or takes more than forty-five minutes, or a secondary school where the journey is over ten miles or one and a quarter hours;
- over-crowding. LEAs must keep to certain minimum standards of teaching space, and can set up catchment areas for schools which they consider overcrowded. This is called **zoning**, but you can appeal against the arrangement if you consider it unreasonable.

Some parents can exercise choice by moving house into the catchment area for the school they wish their child to attend.

Children from abroad

There may be difficulties in having a child admitted to a state school, if the family is only temporarily in this country. If the family has been admitted to the UK for one year or more, then the child should be accepted by a school in the usual way. If the family has been admitted for less than six months, then the child is unlikely to be accepted. If the family's period of stay is between six and twelve months, the school will use its discretion as to whether or not to accept the child. If you have any difficulties, you should contact the **Joint Council for the Welfare of Immigrants (JCWI), 44 Theobalds Road, London WC1 (01-405 5527).**

Private schools

A private or independent school has no obligations to its pupils beyond what is stated in the contract between the school and the parent. This may be incorporated in a formal document or simply in an exchange of letters. The terms are laid down in the prospectus and the school rules, and these are usually the only terms on which the school is prepared to accept a pupil. The parents have very little bargaining power. They do, however, have the right to appeal to the Secretary of State on the following grounds:

– the school has committed a serious injustice;
– unsuitable school premises;
– inadequate or unsuitable accommodation;
– insufficient or unsuitable instruction;
– the proprietor or any teacher is unfit for the post.

An independent school can apply to be recognized as efficient by the Department of Education and Science (DES) following a full-scale inspection by Her Majesty's Inspectors. Those schools which are recognized as efficient can be found in List 70 published by the DES.

The information in the rest of this chapter mainly applies to schools maintained by the state.

Special education

An LEA may decide a child is in need of special education if, for instance, the child is handicapped, deaf or educationally subnormal. No single test should determine the issue and the assessment should be made on the combined evidence of the educational psychologist's report, the teachers' opinions and the doctor's opinion. Parents have a right to be consulted and can appeal against the decision.

If there is a shortage of places at special schools in the area, an LEA must offer a child a boarding place. Alternatively, they may try to integrate the child into a local school, providing special resources where necessary, but they are not obliged to do this.

Sex and race discrimination

It is unlawful for any school, including a private school, to discriminate on grounds of race or sex (e.g. in the terms of admission, the provision of courses or facilities, or decisions to suspend or expel a pupil). Single-sex schools can continue to admit one sex only. It is also unlawful for an LEA to discriminate on grounds of race or sex (e.g. by providing a boys' school in the area with better facilities than the girls' school). If you have a complaint about race or sex discrimination, you should write first to the Secretary of State for Education, who has a maximum of two months in which to do something about your complaint. If the Secretary of State refuses to take action, or the two months run out, you can then make a complaint to the county court (see p. 245).

Transport

LEAs are legally obliged to provide free transport to get children to and from the nearest suitable school if:

– the child is aged under 8 and lives more than two miles away;
  or
– the child is 8 or over and lives more than three miles away.

LEAs can also provide free or subsidized transport at their discretion if the child does not attend the nearest school, or the child lives within the distance limit but has a particularly dangerous journey to school. Discretionary transport is likely to be cut back as a result of public spending cuts.

Uniform

There is no legal obligation for a child to wear school uniform, but if the head teacher requires it there is little you can do. A head teacher can forbid a child from coming to school without the prescribed uniform on the grounds that it is 'prejudicial to school discipline'. But the head should only give a general indication of what is 'suitable' for school wear and should not go into minute detail. Schools are not allowed to name a particular shop as the exclusive supplier of their uniform.

If you feel the head teacher's requirements are unreasonable, you can appeal to the school governors, the LEA and, if necessary, the Secretary of State.

Grants

LEAs can provide two kinds of grant aid to parents to help with their children's education: **statutory** grants, which they must provide by law, and **discretionary** grants, which they may decide to provide or not. As a result, the awarding of grants varies between LEAs. You can get information about grants in your area from your local education office, education welfare officer or the citizens' advice bureau.

You can apply for grants for the following items:

– boarding education, if boarding is the only way your child can get a suitable education;
– school uniform and other essential clothing;
– maintenance for children who stay on at school after 16;
– fees for school clubs, school outings and field trips;
– travel to and from school;
– provision for special talents;

– free milk (supplied to all children up to 7, and to children up to
  16 in special schools and to handicapped children aged 5–16
  who are not in schools);
– free school meals.

Course content

The Education Act 1944 gives the LEA legal control over the
curriculum in its schools, but in practice the head teacher has
overall control of the curriculum in his or her school. The LEA
can influence what is taught in each school by its provision of
resources and teaching staff. If parents and teacher disagree
about the subjects a child is to study, you may have grounds for
pursuing the complaint if you can show that the subjects proposed
by the school do not suit the age, ability and aptitude of your
child.

After the third year of secondary school, pupils are usually
given some choice of what to study. Parents and pupils should be
made aware of the choices available and should consult with
teachers about what subjects the pupil should study.

Schools are legally obliged to provide religious education.

Religion

State and private schools must begin every school day with
collective worship. The Education Act does not specify which
religion must be the form of worship, so there is nothing to prevent a school from holding a Hindu, Muslim or any other
religious ceremony if teachers, parents and pupils so wished.

Schools must also provide religious instruction according to
the 'agreed syllabus'. This syllabus is agreed by representatives
of the various churches in the area. An LEA can arrange for a
child to be taught a religion other than the one usually taught at
the child's school. This can be at the same or a different school,
as long as it does not interfere with the rest of the child's school
work.

Parents have a right to withdraw their child from religious
instruction and morning prayers. There must be a short break

between morning prayers and announcements, so that these children can be present for the announcements only. Teachers may also withdraw from giving religious instruction and attending morning worship if they wish. Pupils have no right, independent of the parents' wishes, to withdraw from religious instruction or worship.

Homework

Parents can forbid a school to set homework for their child. Since, however, the school decides what subjects a child does at school, which class your child goes into and what exams he or she takes, you may damage your child's progress at school if you do not allow homework. If you are worried about the amount or difficulty of your child's homework, talk to the school about it.

Contact with the school

Parents must get the head teacher's agreement before going into the school. You will usually be allowed to talk to the teachers, see the classrooms, look at your child's work and check on the type and quality of the school's facilities. But you have no legal right to do any of these things.

If you are concerned that your child is 'under-achieving' or being underestimated, discuss it with the school. If a dispute arises, you have a legal right to get an independent assessment of your child's ability, e.g. by an educational psychologist.

Every parent should receive regular information about how their child is getting on at school. You should also be consulted about your child's progress. Although there is no legal obligation for schools to issue school reports, most do so.

School records

School records are kept on most children in this country. They are different from school reports and cover not only the child's work, but also the child's personality, appearance, attitudes and family background. These records are usually secret and often based on anonymous sources of information. Records are usually transferred to the new school when the child changes schools. There is no legal right for a parent or child to see, comment on, challenge or contribute to the child's record. Only three LEAs claim to allow parents to see their child's record – Clwyd, Dorset and the ILEA (primary schools only). Parents should ask the head teacher and governors of the school to allow them to see their child's record.

Authority over the child

While a child is at school, the teachers exercise the normal rights and responsibilities of parents towards children; they are said to be '*in loco parentis*' (i.e. in place of the parent).

The LEA bears legal responsibility for any harm the child may suffer. For instance, if your child has an accident whilst in the school's care, you may be able to sue the LEA if you can prove that the accident was due to the school's negligence. The school must make sure that any child sent home early for any reason has a safe passage home.

A head teacher can also exercise some control over what a child does or wears beyond the school boundaries and after school hours by claiming that behaviour outside the school can be prejudicial to the maintenance of good discipline inside the school.

Punishment

All punishment must be 'reasonable', but, apart from that proviso, parents have little say in what a school can do to their child. If you consider your child has been punished unreasonably, you should take the matter up with the head teacher.

The school must ensure that **detentions** are given for a good reason, are supervised by an adult and that extra traffic hazards to children kept in late are taken into account. You can forbid the school to keep your child in after school hours, but the school will usually impose an alternative punishment.

Each LEA makes its own rules about corporal punishment.

Schools are supposed to keep a book which records corporal punishments, to be submitted to the school inspector. In practice, these books seldom record all corporal punishments. The following points may be helpful:

- No parent can insist on a teacher using corporal punishment on a child.
- A parent who keeps the child away from school, rather than letting the child be caned, risks being prosecuted for not sending the child to school (see p. 425). Parents in this position should ask the LEA to intervene and, if necessary, arrange a transfer to another school.
- If a teacher contravenes the punishment rules of your LEA, or gives a punishment which is not in line with the practice of the school, you should report the matter to the head teacher or the LEA.
- If your child receives a punishment which causes bodily harm, the teacher should be prosecuted for criminal assault. The LEA cannot be held responsible for a teacher's criminal act, if it can prove that the teacher acted contrary to express instructions.

Suspension and expulsion

Each LEA makes its own rules about suspension and expulsion contained in the articles of government for each school (see p. 436). You should check with the local office to establish the position in your area.

No child under 16 can be expelled from a state school. A pupil aged 16 or over can only be expelled from a state school by decision of the school governors and/or the LEA. Private schools have the right to expel a pupil of any age.

A child who seriously misbehaves, is regarded as a potential danger to other children, fails to work or is absent for a prolonged period can be suspended by the head teacher. The LEA is still obliged to provide facilities so that a suspended pupil of compulsory school age can be educated: either by a return to school after a brief 'cooling-off' period, or a transfer to another school, truancy centre or refuge.

LEAs must inform parents of their rights if their child is suspended. If you consider your child's suspension or expulsion unreasonable, you can appeal to the school governors, the LEA and if necessary the Secretary of State.

Medical inspections

The area health authority must arrange for children at school to be given a medical and dental inspection at appropriate intervals through their school life. This usually means when the children start school, when they transfer to secondary school and around the age of 12. Parents must be told of any such inspection and can be present if they wish. It is no longer an offence for parents to refuse to allow their child to have an inspection – whatever the reason – except in the case of assessment for special education.

Lost property

If your child loses anything at school, you cannot make any legal claim on the school unless you can prove that the school was grossly negligent or fraudulent. An LEA may give a discretionary sum as compensation, without admitting liability, but this is rare.

A teacher does not have to look after your child's property. But if the teacher does, or if he or she confiscates anything, then he or she must take reasonable care of the item, since the teacher is liable for its loss or any damage done if reasonable care is not taken. But this is very difficult to prove, and it is best not to allow your child to take anything valuable to school. If a teacher confiscates something, he or she *must* return it.

Employment of schoolchildren

No child is allowed to work until the age of 13, with two exceptions:

- his or her parents may allow the child to do light agricultural or horticultural work if local bye-laws permit this;

– a child may with a special licence take part in films or stage shows, but until he or she reaches 16 cannot take part in a public performance if 'life or limb' is endangered.

At the age of 13, a child may do light work if local bye-laws permit, but for no longer than two hours on school days and Saturdays. On school days, a child may work for one hour beginning not earlier than 7 a.m. and finishing before school begins. The school medical officer's consent must be obtained first. On Sundays, a child may only work for one hour, before 7 p.m.

You should check with your local LEA to find out the exact position under local bye-laws. The Employment of Children Act 1973 is designed to replace all local bye-laws with a standard set of regulations, but this had not been brought into effect by January 1977.

The LEA can ask for information about a child's employment from the parents or employer. It can stop anyone under 16 from working outside school hours if they consider the work is prejudicial to the child's health or education. It is an offence to refuse to provide the information requested by the LEA or to disobey the LEA's instructions.

If the child is 16 or over, the LEA cannot restrict or prohibit his or her employment. But it can impose conditions on the child's continued attendance at school. Head teachers can make it a matter of school discipline that pupils must not have part-time jobs, and they may even apply other sanctions such as refusing to supply references for college entrance or prospective full-time employers.

Complaints

Parents have few legal rights where their children's education is concerned, but a complaint to the head can often have the right effect. If you feel the complaint is serious, you can take the matter to the school governors or managers; then to the local education office (address in the telephone directory); and then to the Chief Education Officer for the local authority. Ultimately, you can go to the Secretary of State for Education and Science, who has powers to intervene if LEAs, school governors or head teachers are failing to fulfil their duties or are using their powers unreasonably.

If you feel the LEA or school has been guilty of maladministration, you can appeal to the Ombudsman (see p. 516).

If you consider that the LEA, the school or the teachers have done something involving sex or racial discrimination, you should complain to the Secretary of State and then, if necessary, bring a county court action (see p. 245).

School governors and managers

Every primary school must have a board of managers and every secondary school a board of governors. Managers have to abide by 'rules of management' and governors by 'articles of government'. Each LEA draws up rules and articles for primary and secondary schools in its area, although the articles for secondary schools have to be approved by the Secretary of State. These rules and articles set out the functions of the LEA, the governors and the head teacher, i.e. who is responsible for what. They always give the governors 'oversight of the conduct and curriculum of the school', including responsibility for such things as finance, suspensions, the use of school premises, appointing and dismissing the head and other teachers. The LEA has responsibility to determine how many governors there shall be and who should be represented, when and how they are to meet, and so on; this will be set out in the 'instrument of government'. Articles and instruments of government vary from one LEA to another, but copies should be available from your local education office.

Further and higher education

Further and higher education includes apprenticeships and day-release courses, colleges of further education, the Workers' Educational Association, adult education colleges, polytechnics and universities (including extra-mural departments), the Open University and professional training. Most colleges or courses require you to have certain qualifications before they will accept you. But even if you meet these requirements, you have no legal right to be admitted to the course. See p. 443 for addresses of organizations which can provide information about further education.

Sex and race discrimination

It is unlawful for any institution which provides education or training to discriminate on grounds of sex (except single-sex colleges) or race. A detailed description of the law on race discrimination is given in Chapter 10; the law on sex discrimination will be found in *Rights for Women* (NCCL, 75p) or the Penguin *Women's Rights: A Practical Guide*.

If you believe that you have been discriminated against, you should contact the **Equal Opportunities Commission,** Overseas House, Quay Street, Manchester M3, the **Commission for Racial Equality,** 10/12 Allington Street, London SW1 or the NCCL, 186 Kings Cross Road, London WC1.

You can make a complaint against an employer or a statutory training body (e.g. an industrial training board) which has discriminated on grounds of race or sex to the industrial tribunal; any complaint must be made within three months (see p. 203). You can make a complaint against any other organization which has discriminated on grounds of race or sex to the county court; any complaint must be made within six months (see p. 245).

Apprenticeships and day release

Employers are *not* legally obliged to release young workers for training or allow part-time students time off to take exams during working hours. Many employers do have day-release or apprenticeship schemes, often depending on an agreement with the union. There are **industrial training boards** throughout the country, which are responsible for organizing training in different industries. You can get the address of the appropriate board from the *Education Committees Year Book* (from the local library).

Employers must give shop stewards a reasonable amount of time off for training (Employment Protection Act 1975).

If your employer has apparently discriminated against you on grounds of race or sex, in refusing you opportunities for training, you should consult your trade union or one of the organizations listed above.

Local authority courses

You can be refused a place on a non-vocational, part-time or evening course, even though the only entrance requirement is your willingness to pay a fee. Local authorities run such courses entirely at their discretion and can cancel them once they have been arranged if they are under-subscribed.

Grants

The local authority of the area where you live must give you a grant to follow a:

- first degree course;
- course recognized by the Department of Education and Science as equivalent to a degree course;
- Higher National Diploma course;
- course leading to a Diploma in Higher Education;
- initial teacher-training course.

These grants are called **mandatory** grants; the courses for which they are given are called **designated** courses.

The authority can refuse you a grant if:

- you have not been resident in the UK for the three years immediately preceding 1 September of the year in which your course starts, unless you can satisfy the authority that your spouse or parent was for the time being employed outside the UK; *or*
- the local authority decides that you have by your conduct shown yourself to be unfit to receive an award; *or*
- you have already attended all or part of a designated course; *or*

– you are under 25 and have already attended a full-time course of further education of more than two years or have successfully completed its part-time equivalent, or you have attended a comparable course outside the UK (this does not apply to O- and A-level courses); *or*

– you are 25 or over and have attended a course of advanced further education or have successfully completed its part-time equivalent.

The National Union of Students (NUS) negotiates with the Department of Education and Science about grants and the conditions under which they are awarded. From September 1977, the prescribed maximum amount is to be: £1,145 for London; £1,010 elsewhere; and £785 if living at your parents' home. The actual amount of an award is decided according to a means test on the student's parents. Parents are expected to make up the grant to the prescribed maximum, but cannot be legally forced to do so.

If you fall into one of the following categories, you may be considered **independent**, in which case you will receive a grant in your own right which is not determined by your parents' income:

– you are aged over 25; *or*

– you have worked for three years (including up to six months' registered unemployment, any period claiming sickness, invalidity or maternity benefit and any period spent by married students caring for children); *or*

– there are other special circumstances (e.g. your parents cannot be traced).

If you are granted independent status, but are married, your grant will be means tested on your spouse's income. (If you do not fall into the 'independent' category, your grant will be assessed on your parents' income even if you are married.)

If you are aged over 26, and have worked for three out of the six years before 1 September of the year when your course starts, you may be eligible for a higher **mature student's award**.

Education authorities may also make **discretionary grants** to students who are not on designated courses, or who do not qualify for a compulsory grant on a designated course. It is always worth applying. The *NUS Survey of LEA awards* (latest edition February 1977) details the attitudes of individual LEAs to such awards.

Local authorities may request information in order to assess a student's and the parents' resources.

Disciplinary powers of LEAs

The discretion to award or refuse grants can be used by LEAs as a strong disciplinary weapon. Withdrawal of a grant usually means the end of a student's academic career. But LEAs are obliged to act reasonably, and must first consult the college authorities. The precise form of this consultation is not laid down, and LEAs do not have to accept the advice of the college. In law, both the original initiative and the final decision rests with the discretion of the LEA.

The local authority can only withdraw a mandatory grant in accordance with the regulations. But if the LEA, for instance, discovered that you had a criminal record, they could argue that you had shown yourself by your conduct unfit to hold an award. One local authority has withdrawn a grant in such circumstances, and the NUS is challenging their decision.

If the LEA had not followed a proper procedure in deciding to withdraw or refuse a grant (e.g. by not giving the student proper notice), a complaint could be made to the local government Ombudsman (see p. 516). If the LEA acts unreasonably in withdrawing or refusing a grant, a complaint could be made to the Secretary of State for Education, who has a general duty to ensure that LEAs carry out their duties reasonably (see p. 436).

Rights within college

When a college makes an offer of a place, and the student accepts the offer, the college and student have entered into a **contract**. Although it would be easier if the terms of the contract were all in one document, they are usually found in a number of documents, including the prospectus, application form, college regulations, letters between the college and applicant, and so on. The student does not, however, have any freedom to negotiate about the terms of the contract. The college sets out the terms to the student who has no alternative but to accept them or give up the chance of an academic career.

If a college prospectus gives information about a course which bears no relation to the actual course given, the college would be in breach of its contract and could be sued.

Under the terms of the contract, students have a right to enter and use the various facilities of the college, but they have no legal right to control them and may not always be permitted to invite guests onto the premises. While a group of students may enter the administrative offices of the college to inquire about their grants, if the same students entered the same offices in order to paralyse college administration by an occupation, they would be acting outside the terms of the contract and may be committing a trespass (see p. 207).

College authorities may ask the police to help remove students who have refused to leave the premises when asked. The police may intervene when invited; the circumstances when they can enter premises without being invited are set out in Chapter 1 (see p. 27).

The police can enter and search a student's room in a hall of residence without a warrant if the warden has given permission.

Disciplinary powers of the college authorities

Most colleges have some form of disciplinary code, but in many institutions the Vice-Chancellor, principal or governors have wide discretionary powers. Normally the courts will only act to restore a legal right that has been denied by a college if it is considered that the college acted in bad faith or adopted an inadequate procedure. For instance, the courts may intervene if a student was expelled after a hearing which did not conform to the disciplinary procedure of the college or for an offence not contained in the college's disciplinary code.

There is nothing to prevent a college from meting out 'double discipline' and punishing a student for an offence which has already been tried in a criminal court.

If you are involved in a disciplinary offence, you should always seek advice and, if possible, representation. The National Union of Students will always give advice, and NCCL may be able to help (particularly in a case involving discrimination on grounds of sex or race, or against homosexuals).

Student unions

In almost every institution of higher education running degree-level courses and in most colleges of further education, membership of the students' union is automatic. In most cases, the LEA will pay the union fees. Most of these unions are affiliated to the National Union of Students.

More information

Schools

Judith Stone and Felicity Taylor, *The Parent's Schoolbook*, Penguin (90p) – a detailed run-down of the education system for parents.

G. Taylor and J. Saunders, *The New Law of Education*, Butterworth (£7 – or in your local reference library) – legal framework of the education system, with the texts of all governments plus commentary.

Where to Look Things Up, ACE (£1·20) – a guide to the major sources on all important educational topics.

Advisory Centre for Education (ACE), 32 Trumpington Street, Cambridge (0223-51456).

Campaign against Secret Records on Schoolchildren, 10 Argyle Road, Swanage, Dorset (Swanage 2861).

Confederation for the Advancement of State Education (CASE), 1 Windermere Avenue, Wembley, Middlesex.

Department of Education and Science, Elizabeth House, York Road, London SE1 (01-928 9222).

National Society for Mentally Handicapped Children, Pembridge Hall, 17 Pembridge Square, London W2 (01-229 8941, 01-727 0536).

National Union of School Students, 3 Endsleigh Street, London WC1 (01-387 1277).

Society of Teachers Opposed to Physical Punishment (STOPP), 27 Raleigh Court, Lymer Avenue, Dulwich Wood Park, London SE19.

Further and higher education

Judith Booth, *Grants for Higher Education*, ACE.

Anthony Arblaster, *Academic Freedom*, Penguin (60p).

Campaign for Academic Freedom and Democracy, 186 Kings Cross Road, London WC1 – set up under NCCL's sponsorship.

Department of Education and Science, Further Education Information Service, Elizabeth House, York Road, London SE1 (01-928 9222).

National Institute of Adult Education (England & Wales), 35 Queen Anne Street, London W1 (01-637 4241).

Training Opportunities Scheme (TOPS), 162–8 Regent Street, London W1 (01-214 6000) or local 'skillcentres' or employment offices – training and re-training for people over the age of 19; allowance paid during training.

Workers' Educational Association, Temple House, 9 Berkeley Street, London W1 (01-402 5608) – will provide list of addresses of WEA district secretaries.

22. Housing

This chapter covers:

It deals mainly with the legal position between a tenant and a private landlord. *If you are a council tenant, see pp. 458–9 and 418.*

Housing law is extremely complicated and confusing. It is most important that you seek expert advice with any difficulty. You can get help from a citizens' advice bureau, a local law centre, a solicitor (see p. 494 for how to claim legal aid) or the rent officer.

What kind of tenancy do you have?

According to the law, there are a number of different kinds of private tenancies. It is important to know which kind you have.

If you entered into an agreement with your landlord when you became a tenant, and the original tenancy agreement was for a specified period or ran from week to week or month to month, etc., until you receive a notice to quit or your rent is increased, then you are a **contractual tenant**.

If you are a contractual tenant you may also be **protected** under the Rent Acts, which means that you can apply to have a fair rent fixed and that your landlord cannot evict you except in certain limited circumstances. See p. 445 for full details of which tenants are protected and which are not.

If you were a protected tenant, then you will become a **statutory tenant** if you go on living in the same place at the end of the period for which you were a contractual tenant and you will have the same rights as a protected tenant under the Rent Acts.

You are a **controlled tenant** if you have been in occupation since 7 November 1956 or earlier of *unfurnished* premises which had a rateable value of up to £40 in Greater London or £30 outside London on 7 November 1956. The premises are *not* controlled if you share any part of the living accommodation, e.g. a kitchen, with the landlord. Bathrooms are not counted as part of the living accommodation, so you can still be a controlled tenant even if you share the bathroom with your landlord. Some protected tenants are also controlled tenants. A protected tenant or a statutory tenant who is *not* a controlled tenant may be called a **regulated tenant**.

You are a **Part VI tenant** if your tenancy was granted after 14 August 1974 and the following applies:

- your landlord provides board or attendance (for instance, cleaning the premises) and you pay for this as part of the rent;
  or
- your landlord shares part of the premises such as the kitchen;
  or
- you do not have exclusive use of any part of the premises.

A **licensee** is a person who has the right to remain only as long as the landlord is prepared to allow it (e.g. 'squatters' licensed by the local authority.)

The Rent Acts 1968 and 1974

The Rent Acts 1968 and 1974 were designed to give tenants security, and to regulate the amount of rent the landlord can charge. If your tenancy is covered by the Rent Acts you are a **protected tenant**. It is important to know whether you fall into this category.

PROTECTED TENANTS

In general, all premises which are let as a 'separate dwelling' are covered by the Rent Acts, provided that:

- you occupy the place as your home (it does not matter if the premises are furnished or unfurnished); *and*
- the rateable value is no more than £1,500 in Greater London or £750 elsewhere (property rated higher is regarded as 'luxury accommodation' and is not covered by the Acts).

Premises which you also use for business purposes are not covered by the Rent Acts but may be covered by the Landlord and Tenant Act 1954; you should seek legal advice on this point.

UNPROTECTED TENANTS

You will not be protected by the Rent Acts if:

- you have a tenancy granted on or after 14 August 1974 and the landlord lives in another part of the same building, except where the building is a block of flats (if you are an **unfurnished tenant** and your tenancy started before 14 August 1974, then you will be a protected or statutory tenant even though you have a resident landlord);
- the premises are let at a low rent which is less than two thirds the rateable value of the part of the building you occupy (e.g. you have a long leasehold and pay a small ground rent);
- your landlord provides board or any other attendance;
- you live in a hall of residence or other accommodation provided for students by an educational institution;
- the premises are let for holidays;
- you rent a house let with other land beside the site the house stands on and a normal-size garden;
- you rent a house let as part of an agricultural holding of more than two acres of land, and you also farm the land (seek legal advice to find out if you are protected by agricultural legislation);
- the Crown is the immediate landlord;
- the immediate landlord is a public body, such as a local authority, the commission or development corporation of a

new town, housing corporations and housing trusts (no council tenants are protected);
– you are a priest required to live in a parsonage house within a parish.

Fair rents

Protected tenants

If you are a protected tenant (as set out on p. 445), you can apply to the rent officer to get a fair rent fixed as soon as you actually become a tenant. You cannot apply to the rent officer before you become the tenant.

The landlord must tell you what the previous rent was if the property has been let during the last five years. In most cases, you can't be charged more than this, even if the rent was not included on the local **rent register**.

If the rent has been registered, you can check the amount by inspecting the rent register at your local town hall. (A citizens' advice bureau can help, if necessary.) If the landlord has been charging you more than the registered rent, you can claim it back for up to two years, and this can be deducted from any future rent you pay.

THE RENT OFFICER

You or the landlord can apply, separately or together, to the rent officer to fix a fair rent. You can get the application form from the rent officer at the local town hall, or from a citizens' advice bureau. The rent officer decides the fair rents for private tenants of non-resident landlords. It does not matter whether you are a furnished or unfurnished tenant. The rent officer also sets the fair rent for *unfurnished* tenants of resident landlords who have been there since before 14 August 1974.

A fair rent is decided by taking into account a number of factors, including the age, state of repair, character and locality of the accommodation, but *scarcity of accommodation should not be taken into consideration*. The rent officer will need to inspect the accommodation, and will then ask you and the landlord to discuss the rent with him. Any documents which the rent officer receives will be given to everyone involved. The discussion will be informal, and if you all agree to a reasonable rent and the rent officer is satisfied, that rent will be registered. The registered rent includes all payments to be made to the landlord, except for rates.

THE RENT ASSESSMENT COMMITTEE

If you object to the rent officer's decision, you must put this in writing within twenty-eight days of getting the decision. The matter will then be referred to the rent assessment committee. It may be some time before the committee can meet, and since they may increase the rent you should try to put some money aside each week to cover this. The rent increase cannot be back-dated more than four weeks before you received the notice of increase.

It is helpful to get expert advice from a valuer, land agent or surveyor. You can apply for legal assistance under the green-form scheme (see p. 494) to help meet the costs of getting an expert opinion.

A local law centre should also be able to help you prepare your case. You can either put your case in writing, or go to the committee hearing and give oral evidence. You have no automatic right to call an expert witness, but in practice you are allowed to do so. You can question an expert witness called by the landlord. You should ask for the reasons for the decision in writing, in case you have grounds for appeal. Appeals on a point of law can be made to the High Court, but you will need to get advice from a solicitor about this.

NOTICE TO INCREASE RENT

A notice to increase rent can have the effect of ending your contractual tenancy and creating a statutory tenancy (see p. 444 for what these terms mean). This notice is necessary where an application has gone to the rent officer and the rent has been increased.

There is a system of phasing the increase, and you should check with the rent officer who will explain the way in which this works. The increase cannot be dated earlier than the date the rent was registered, and in any case cannot be back-dated for more than four weeks before you receive the notice.

Controlled tenants

If you are a controlled tenant (see p. 445), your rent cannot be increased except in certain circumstances laid out in the Rent Act 1968 and the Housing Rents and Subsidies Act 1972. Your landlord can apply to the rent officer for a fair rent certificate if your home is improved to reach a specified standard or has already reached that standard. The **specified standard** means that the property:

- has all standard amenities – bath, hand basin, sink, hot-water supply and lavatory of an approved standard; *and*
- is in good repair with regard to its age, character and locality; *and*
- is fit for human habitation, taking into account natural lighting, ventilation, drainage, freedom from damp, internal arrangement, sanitary conveniences, facilities for preparing and cooking food and disposing of waste water.

No improvements can be carried out without your consent, but the landlord can apply to the county court if you withhold consent unreasonably. Any rent increase will be phased over a period of two years.

Part VI tenants

You can apply to the rent tribunal to have your rent reduced. Application forms are available from a citizens' advice bureau or from the local tribunal office.

Tenants usually apply to the rent tribunal after they receive a notice to quit. This is because, when you apply to the rent tribunal to have your rent reduced, you will automatically be given security of tenure (i.e. the right to stay in the property) for six months. But you can apply to have a reasonable rent fixed at any time. You cannot apply for security of tenure by itself: you must make an application for a rent reduction.

The law is complex and your landlord may be represented by a lawyer, so you should try to get advice from the Surveyors' Aid Scheme, Shelter, a local law centre or a solicitor (see p. 496 for who can claim legal aid).

Members of the tribunal will visit your home, often on the morning of the hearing, and you should be there to show them anything relevant (e.g. damp, bad drainage, etc.). At the hearing, you are allowed to call witnesses and produce documentary evidence such as letters, plans, rent books and agreements. You will be questioned by the tribunal and by the landlord or his representative. You or your representative can also question the landlord and his witnesses.

The tribunal will give its decision either at the end of the hearing or by post. You should always ask for the reasons for their decision to be given in writing, in case you have grounds for an appeal to the High Court on a point of law. But you will need legal advice before considering an appeal.

Rent rebates and allowances

Tenants of private landlords can have part of their rent paid back by the local council, depending on income, the size of the family and the level of the rent. (See p. 418 for more information.)

Tenancy agreements, rent books, repairs, etc.

You should ask your landlord to explain any written agreement to you before you sign it. If you do not fully understand it, go to a citizen's advice bureau and ask them to explain it to you.

If your agreement mentions holiday, board or attendance, this probably means that you will not be protected under the Rent Acts (see p. 446). You should also check to see if there is any clause saying that the landlord has been living in the house or flat and will require it back at the end of the tenancy, as this will affect your security (see p. 456).

Part of your agreement with the landlord may be spoken, instead of being written down. You should always ask for the following information, if it isn't written down:

– how much rent you are to pay;
– does the rent include the general and water rates;
– does the rent include electricity, gas and telephone;
– will the landlord be responsible for decoration;
– will the landlord be responsible for repairs such as blocked drains;
– the exact day your tenancy begins;
– is the rent to be paid weekly or monthly;
– is the rent to be paid in advance or in arrears;
– exactly how much of the house or flat you occupy and which parts you may have to share.

Rent book

It is a criminal offence for a landlord to fail to provide you with a rent book if you pay rent weekly. You should keep the rent book and make sure that everything you pay is correctly noted in the book. The rent book should also give the following information:

– the name(s) of the tenants;
– the date the tenancy began;
– the name and address of any agent employed to collect the rent;
– the name and address of the landlord (the agent must in any case give you this information within twenty-one days of when you ask for it);
– the amount of rent payable, and whether it includes rates, electricity, gas, etc.;
– any terms of agreement between yourself and the landlord if you do not have a written agreement.

Make sure the rent book does not include printed terms which you have not agreed with the landlord. If your rent book does not include all the relevant information, report the matter to your local authority. They have the power to prosecute the landlord or the agent.

Deposits, key money, fees

Once you have paid a deposit, it is difficult to get it back if you decide not to take the tenancy, though in law you can get the deposit back if you have not made a definite agreement to take the accommodation.

It is a criminal offence to pay or receive a premium for the privilege of living in certain premises. All key money for the granting, transferring or renewing of a lease or tenancy is illegal. An excessive amount asked for furniture, fittings or fixtures is key money in disguise. You should ask for a list of furniture and fittings with the price clearly set out – the value should be the true market value of each item. If you are asked for key money, you should report it to the local authority, who have the power to bring a prosecution. The maximum penalty is a fine of £100 and the return of the premium.

The landlord may ask you for a deposit as security against non-payment of rent, electricity, gas or phone bills, or damage to furniture or fittings. Get a receipt for any deposit you pay and see that it states clearly under what circumstances the landlord is to pay it back to you. Ask the landlord for an inventory (i.e. a list) of the contents of the premises, which shows clearly the condition of the items. Check the list yourself. Ask the landlord to sign the inventory, but never sign one yourself until you have checked it.

Agents may charge you a fee for finding you accommodation *only if you actually take a tenancy*. Ask the agent for a receipt for any money paid and make sure the receipt is signed by the agent, as agent for the landlord, and that it states clearly for what purpose the money was paid.

Repairs and decoration

Landlords are legally obliged to carry out the following repairs even if you have signed an agreement accepting responsibility for them:

- repair of the structure and exterior of the premises including drains, gutters and external pipes;
- keeping in proper working order the water supply, gas, electricity, sanitation and fuel supply for heating water (Housing Act 1961).

Tenants must:

- take care of the premises and use them properly;
- not alter the structure by knocking down walls, removing partitions or doors, etc.;
- repair damage or breakages done by you, your family or visitors; *and*
- keep the premises wind- and watertight.

If an agreement requires you to be responsible for keeping the premises in a good state of repair, you should insist on the phrase 'fair wear and tear excepted' being included.

If the landlord has undertaken to carry out repairs and decorations in a written agreement but fails to do so, you can take the matter to the county court (Housing Act 1974, s. 125). See p. 245 for how to bring a county court action.

Local authorities have wide-ranging powers to force landlords to carry out repairs and improvements. If you have any complaint, you should contact your local public health inspector at the town hall and ask them to inspect the premises.

Assigning and sub-letting

To **assign** means to transfer or dispose of your interest in the premises, though as the original tenant you will still be liable for the rent if the next tenant fails to pay. You can only assign your interest in premises where you have an agreement for a fixed period of time.

Sub-letting means that you remain the tenant to your land-lord, but allow someone else into the premises who becomes your tenant.

Some agreements forbid assigning or sub-letting, and you should try to add a clause allowing you to assign or sub-let with the consent of the landlord. The courts may allow you to assign or sub-let if the landlord is behaving unreasonably. You should get advice from a citizens' advice bureau, a local law centre or a solicitor.

You will stop being protected under the Rent Acts if you assign or sub-let the whole of the premises you occupy, or if you sub-let at a rent greater than the amount you pay the landlord.

Rates

You should remember that all tenants pay rates, as well as owner-occupiers, and you may be able to get part of the rates back in the form of a rate rebate. Information about rent and rate rebates and allowances is given on p. 418.

The rateable value of your property

Every landlord and owner-occupier has to pay rates to the local council, based on the rateable value of the property. (Tenants pay the rates to the landlord, who then makes the payment to the council.) The rateable value is decided by valuation officers, working for the Inland Revenue.

When you receive a notice from your local valuation officer about the proposed rateable value of your property, you will also be sent the necessary forms for making an objection. The valuation officer will try and negotiate with you, if you object, so that the matter can be settled without a hearing at the local valuation court. There is an enormous backlog of cases, so a hearing could be delayed for up to two years.

If your case does go to a hearing, try to get help from the Surveyors' Aid Scheme or Shelter. Your case must be thoroughly prepared because the law on rating valuation is very complicated. The valuation officer presents his case first. You are allowed to call witnesses, produce relevant documents and question witnesses. If the case is not too difficult, the court will give its decision soon after the hearing. Or they may decide to inspect your property and postpone the decision until a later date.

You should always ask for reasons for the decision in writing in case you want to appeal. You can appeal to the Lands Tribunal within eight days of the original decision. But you will need expert legal advice for this.

Notice to increase rates

The landlord can increase your rent to cover a rate increase by serving a notice of increase in the form laid down by law. The increase cannot be back-dated more than six weeks before you receive the notice.

Eviction

Protected tenants

If you are a protected tenant (see pp. 445–6), the landlord can only evict you legally by getting a **possession order** from a court. It is difficult for a landlord to get a possession order; the court can grant an order in the following circumstances:

- the landlord can provide suitable alternative accommodation reasonably suited to the needs of you and your family, considering its rent, size and distance from your work;
- you are in arrears with the rent or have committed other breaches of the tenancy agreement;
- you have been convicted of using the property for immoral or illegal purposes and have caused a nuisance or annoyance to the neighbours or have damaged the property;
- the condition of the premises or furniture has deteriorated because you have damaged or neglected them;
- you have given notice to quit and the landlord has contracted to sell or re-let the property;

- you have sub-let the whole property without the landlord's consent;
- you have sub-let part of the premises for more than the maximum rent due for that part;
- the accommodation went with a job which you no longer hold and the former employer needs it for another full-time employee;
- the landlord needs the accommodation for himself or his family. This only applies to property purchased by that landlord before 1956 and if the court decides that the landlord and his family would suffer greater hardship than you would if you were evicted;
- the landlord was originally the owner-occupier of the premises and gave written notice, when the tenancy agreement was made, that he might want to re-occupy the premises. The landlord must have lived elsewhere throughout the tenancy, and must need the premises for himself or some member of his family who lived with him when he last lived in the house;
- the landlord acquired the premises in order to live there after retirement and gave notice of this intention at the time the tenancy agreement was made;
- the tenancy was for a period of not more than eight months, and the landlord told you in writing that it was to be used for holiday purposes only.

If you receive a **notice to quit**, make a note of the date when you received it, and seek advice immediately from the rent officer, a citizens' advice bureau or a local law centre. The notice may be ineffective if you are a protected tenant. The notice must be in writing and give a minimum of four weeks' notice, ending on the day you pay rent. Any notice served since 31 March 1976 must be in a statutory form and contain set wording at the bottom to make it valid. Even after a notice to quit has been sent to you, you cannot be forced to leave until the landlord gets a court order.

COURT ORDERS

If your landlord has taken out a summons against you to get possession, and you want to stay, seek help immediately. You can apply to have the hearing **adjourned** (i.e. postponed) if you need time to get proper advice. You should apply for an adjournment at once, as you will have to pay costs if you apply for an adjournment on the day of the hearing. You can get an application form from the offices of the county court.

If you are not represented by a lawyer, you should go to court yourself for the hearing. If the judge does make an order of possession against you, ask for further time in which to find somewhere else to live.

WHAT HAPPENS TO THE FAMILY IF THE TENANT DIES?

If a protected or statutory tenant dies, then the tenancy can be taken over by certain members of the family. If the tenant was a man, then his widow can take over the tenancy if she was living with him at the time of his death. In any other case (e.g. if the tenant was a woman or if there was no widow) then any member of the tenant's family who lived with him or her at the time of death and for the previous six months can take over the tenancy. If there is more than one relative involved, they can either agree between them what is to happen or ask the county court to decide.

The new tenant becomes a statutory tenant even if the tenant who died was a protected tenant.

If the new tenant dies, then the rules can operate again to pass the tenancy to another member of the family, but then the tenancy cannot pass again in this way (Rent Act 1968).

Local authorities and housing associations have their own rules about what happens to families of their tenants.

Part VI tenants

If you are a Part VI tenant (see p. 445), you can apply to the rent tribunal if you are given a notice to quit. But, as explained on p. 449, you must apply for a fair rent to be fixed. You must apply to the tribunal *before* the notice to quit runs out.

The tribunal has the power to extend the period of notice, before you have to leave, to six months. (But they cannot give you this extension if the tenancy was for a fixed period of time, such as six months or one year.) The landlord will be informed of your application, and a date will be set for a hearing. The landlord can object to any extension of time, but if the tribunal agrees to extend the period of notice, you can keep going back to the tribunal for further extensions. The landlord can apply to the tribunal to *reduce* the period of notice if:

– you fail to stick to the terms of your agreement;
– you are guilty of nuisance or annoyance to the next-door neighbours;
– the condition of the premises has deteriorated because you have damaged or neglected it.

The landlord cannot evict you without a court order. But the court will normally grant an order if a valid notice to quit has been served and expired, and if any extension given by the rent tribunal has also expired. But the court can delay the eviction for between twenty-eight days and six weeks, so even if you have no grounds for objecting to the eviction order, you should apply for this extension to give you more time to find somewhere else to live.

Council tenants

Because public bodies are exempt from the Rent Act, council tenants have no legal security. Councils still have to get a court order before you can be evicted, but they do not have to prove the same reasons for evicting you as a private landlord. Councils are allowed to evict tenants 'for the better execution of their housing duties', which means that council tenants can be evicted for having unkempt gardens, disturbing the neighbours and so on. In practice, councils rarely evict tenants for anything except rent arrears, and the courts will not usually make a possession order against a council tenant for anything except rent arrears.

The court will usually give the council a 'suspended possession order'. This means that you will not be evicted, provided that you pay the current rent and part of the arrears each week.

Rents for council tenants are fixed by the local authority. You will probably not be allowed to redecorate the outside of your home, or make any structural alterations, without permission. If you have any problems, you should consult the local tenants' association or a local councillor (contact the local Conservative, Labour or Liberal party, whose address will be in the telephone directory, if you don't know who your councillor is).

Council tenants can get their rent reduced, depending on their income and the size of the family. (See p. 418 for more details.)

Homelessness

The social services department of the local authority has a duty to provide temporary accommodation for the homeless in an emergency, such as a flood. They are also meant to provide accommodation for homeless families, although single people without children are generally left to fend for themselves.

Councils will not rehouse families who are 'voluntarily' homeless (i.e. who leave their previous homes without being evicted), and some councils treat battered women who leave their husbands as 'voluntarily' homeless. For this reason, you must be careful before agreeing to a possession order which includes the words 'by consent'.

Harassment and illegal eviction

It is a criminal offence for anyone to evict a tenant without a court order, or to drive out or try to drive out a tenant by threats, violence or any other means. A landlord can be fined up to £400 or given six months' imprisonment for a first offence. These offences apply to all tenancies of whatever kind. (Rent Act 1965.)

If you think there is an immediate danger to yourself or your family, you should first contact the police. They are reluctant to interfere in what they describe as private disputes, but the landlord can be prosecuted by the police if he has committed another offence against you, such as assault.

It is also an offence for a landlord to cut off your gas or electricity or harass you in any other way to make you leave. If this happens, you should contact the harassment officer or housing officer at your local town hall, who should write to the landlord, explaining the law and warning him that he can be prosecuted. Most local authorities are reluctant to start prosecutions as the procedure is slow, and will not always help you exercise your rights.

In an emergency, you can get legal aid (see p. 499) and apply to the county court for an order (**injunction**) preventing your landlord from taking any action to harm or inconvenience you. This can be done within twenty-four hours. You can also apply for legal aid and take a court action against a landlord who keeps or disposes of any of your belongings, or wrongfully evicts you.

I shall sue you in the County Court for this, wicked landlord!

Squatting

People occupy empty houses because they are homeless or because they live in bad and overcrowded conditions. The desperate shortage of housing in some areas coupled with the existence of many vacant properties has made squatting inevitable. The 1971 census showed that there were 675,000 empty dwellings in England and Wales, mostly awaiting 'redevelopment'. It is estimated that there are about 50,000 squatters in Britain, 30,000 of whom are in London. These are a small percentage of the total number of homeless.

Most squatting is done in houses owned by local authorities and they are sometimes reluctant to throw people out as it draws attention to the inadequacy of their own housing provisions. Some local authorities have negotiated with squatters and licensed their short-life properties to squatting associations on the understanding that the buildings will be vacated when required for rehabilitation or demolition, and that the families involved will not lose their priority on the council housing list. Sometimes these squatters pay a nominal rent to the local authority.

In law an unlicensed squatter is a trespasser, that is, a person who is on another's property without that person's permission. The owner or lawful occupier is always entitled to possession against the squatter provided the eviction procedure laid down by the court is complied with. *A squatter is not a criminal.* Trespass is not generally a criminal offence. Disputes over the occupation of land and buildings are dealt with by civil courts. They are disputes between individuals or bodies such as companies and housing associations or local authorities, not between individuals and the state. But squatters may become involved with the criminal law if they commit offences other than the mere act of trespass. Some further offences are being proposed in the Criminal Law Act (see p. 17).

Starting a squat

Apart from the Criminal Law Act (see p. 17), entering property with intent to squat is not an offence, BUT

– it is a criminal offence under the Criminal Damage Act 1971 to cause even the slightest **damage** to any item of the owner's property without the owner's consent. This includes dismantling 'machinery' (e.g. cooker, heaters or lavatories). Carrying tools which could be used to cause damage is also an offence under this Act.
– Squatters have been threatened with **theft or burglary**

charges. Burglary means entering a property with intent to steal or cause damage, or stealing or causing damage. Theft means taking property belonging to someone else with the intention to permanently deprive the owner of it. It is also an offence to carry tools for use in burglary or theft or specially adapted for such use. For these reasons, care must be taken not to take or damage any of the owner's property.

– Although trespass itself is not a criminal offence, agreeing with someone else to trespass in certain circumstances did involve committing the offence of **conspiracy to trespass**. The Criminal Law Act has abolished this offence (see p. 17).

THE POLICE

If you occupy premises the neighbours may call the police. Tell them that you are not burglars but are squatting and that it is a civil matter between you and the landlord. The only grounds on which the police should involve themselves is to ensure no breach of the peace takes place, if a crime has been committed, or if they assist bailiffs carrying out a lawful eviction. See p. 26 for information about police powers of entry to homes. The police have no right to enter private premises simply in order to make inquiries or because they think there is something wrong.

CONNECTION OF GAS, ELECTRICITY AND WATER

In most houses which have been empty for any time essential services – gas, electricity, water – will have been disconnected. The appropriate statutory authorities are obliged to supply these services to the 'owner or occupier' of premises on request. It should be none of their business whether you own or rent the house or not. But a recent court decision could mean that the electricity boards are not *obliged* to supply but can do so if they wish. However, if an electricity board does agree to supply but then cuts off the supply on grounds other than non-payment of bills, they could probably be sued for breach of contract, and it might be possible to obtain a court order for reconnection.

The gas and electricity boards can ask for deposits before

reconnection and sometimes they demand very high deposits from squatters. If this happens, it may be better to ask for a slot meter instead of paying by quarterly account. An electricity board has no power to charge for reconnection itself unless the electricity was disconnected before because bills were not paid or the house is more than fifty yards from the mains supply. They can disconnect a supply only for non-payment of bills and must give notice that they intend to do so (see p. 224).

It is an offence to steal gas or electricity, that is to use them and not pay for them. It is, therefore, best to arrange immediately for a supply with the appropriate authority and to be prepared to pay for the services used.

Water can usually be connected by turning on the stop tap.

It is important that you do not create a health hazard through insanitary conditions or overcrowding. In general, it is better to settle in quickly and to look after the property to show that you are a serious occupant and not a dosser.

Eviction from a squat

BY FORCE

An owner can evict trespassers using **reasonable force**. Reasonable force is difficult to define and depends on the circumstances. An owner or his agent (like private bailiffs or detectives) who uses more than reasonable force runs the risk of conviction for causing a breach of the peace, or assault or other similar offences. An owner who forces an entry in order to evict squatters may be guilty of **violent entry** (see p. 17), unless the owner is a **displaced residential occupier** (see p. 17).

Most owners now prefer to evict squatters by obtaining a possession order from a court and leaving the eviction to court bailiffs.

THROUGH THE COURTS

Owners can apply for a **possession order** even when they do not know the names of the squatters occupying their property, provided they have taken reasonable steps to discover the names. The order can be granted within seven days, or less in cases of emergency. This procedure can be used in all cases where the occupiers are trespassers even when the persons in occupation originally had the permission of the owner to occupy but the owner has withdrawn that permission. If it is established that the occupiers are trespassers there is no defence against the posession order, unless the owner has committed some technical legal error (e.g. failing to take 'reasonable steps' to discover the names of all the occupiers). It is not a defence that you are homeless and destitute. You can ask for an adjournment of the hearing to prepare your case.

If you have a licence from a local authority to occupy short-life property, you cannot be evicted unless you have been given **reasonable notice**. What is reasonable depends on all the circumstances, but this may be no more than one or two weeks. If you remain after that you can be evicted in the same way as an unlicensed squatter.

When the possession order has been obtained by the owner it takes effect immediately. The owner then has to issue a **writ** (in the High Court) or **warrant** (in the county court) in order to be able to execute the possession order. The eviction order is carried out by the High Court sheriff or the county court bailiff. They may ask the police to assist them. A possession order may be executed against *all* persons found on the premises whether or not they are named.

It is an offence to assault a county court bailiff or High Court official in the execution of his duty. It is also an offence to resist a court official who is executing a possession order if you are a squatter. The Forcible Entry Act 1429, under which squatters could be charged with forcible detainer, has now been repealed. The police could also charge you with more straightforward offences like assault or causing a breach of the peace. It is not part of the police's duty to assist in evictions. If they do they are acting as private citizens. This means they cannot bring charges of assaulting the police in the execution of their duty, or obstructing the police. It can be argued that if police officers or people other than bailiffs try to evict on their own initiative, then the squatter has the right to resist and to prosecute or sue for assault.

More information

Squatting, Trespass and Civil Liberties (NCCL) (50p).

Advisory Service for Squatters, 2 St Pauls Road, London N1 (01-359 8814).

Campaign Against the Criminal Trespass Law, 6 Bowden Street, London SE11 (01-289 3877).

Campaign for the Homeless and Rootless (CHAR), 27 Endell Street, London WC2 (01-240 2691).

Release, 1 Elgin Avenue, London W9 (01-289 1123) – provides advice for squatters.

Shelter, 86 Strand, London WC2 (01-836 2051).

Shelter Housing Aid Centre (SHAC), 189a Old Brompton Road, London SW10 (01-373 7841).

Much of the law on housing has been brought together in the Rent Act 1977 and the Protection from Eviction Act 1977.

23. Medical rights

This chapter covers:

Treatment under the National Health Service (NHS) is usually free, with the following exceptions:

– if you have recently arrived from abroad, you may have to pay (see p. 473);
– dental treatment is usually charged for, but is free for some people (see p. 417);
– you can have your eyes tested free once a year, but spectacle frames (other than the basic NHS frames) and contact lenses will usually be charged for (see p. 417);
– there is a prescription fee of 20p per item, but some people (e.g. children under 16 and pensioners) can obtain all prescriptions free (see p. 417), contraceptives are usually free;
– your GP is allowed to charge you for certain vaccinations and other treatment (see p. 474);
– in some circumstances following a car accident, when you may have to pay medical fees and claim them back from an insurance company or the Motor Insurers' Bureau (see p. 159).

You and your doctor

Choosing a doctor

If you are registered with the NHS, you have the right to be treated by any general practitioner (GP) you choose, provided the doctor is willing to accept you onto the list of patients. If you don't know a GP in your area, you can consult the list of local doctors which is kept by the district family practitioner committee and which you can see at the local library. Or you can ask friends or neighbours to recommend a doctor. If you still have difficulty, contact the family practitioner committee; the address is in the telephone directory.

If you are joining the NHS for the first time or have lost your NHS card, you will have to fill in a form at the doctor's surgery. This will ask for details of where you lived before, previous doctors and (if you have come to this country recently) when you arrived here and where you have come from. You will then be given an NHS number. You should keep your NHS card somewhere safe and take it with you when you first go to see a new doctor.

Changing your doctor

You can change your doctor at any time you like, provided the new doctor is willing to take you onto the list of patients. But a doctor can refuse to accept you, for instance if he or she already has enough patients. A doctor can also refuse to go on treating you, but a doctor who does this should give you reasonable warning. The doctor does not have to give you an explanation of the refusal to go on treating you or your family. If you have difficulty finding another doctor, you should contact the family practitioner committee in your area. As long as you are on a doctor's list, the doctor has to provide you with the medical services you need.

Getting information from your doctor

You may find it difficult to get full information from your doctor about treatment or an operation which is being proposed for you. Doctors are traditionally very secretive and guard their 'clinical freedom' jealously. (For instance, the Health Service Ombudsman is not allowed to investigate matters concerning clinical freedom – i.e. decisions about diagnosis and treatment.) If the doctor does not give you a satisfactory explanation, for instance about the drugs which are being prescribed for you, try to insist on a full answer.

The doctor is meant to answer any questions you have about other possible courses of treatment, the risk of the proposed operation, and so on. If a doctor deliberately misleads you, he or she has effectively obtained your consent to an operation or treatment by deceit. If this happens to you, you could sue the doctor for damages, but you would have to be able to convince the court that, as a reasonable person, you would have refused the operation or treatment involved if you had been given truthful answers to your questions. A doctor would not have to pay you damages if the court was persuaded that you had been deceived in your best interests – for instance, because telling you that you had cancer would seriously damage your mental health.

Will doctors keep what you tell them secret?

As a general rule, doctors must not give away any information they have learned about you while treating you. But there are exceptions. For instance, doctors have to report to the authorities if a patient has a particular infectious disease or veneral disease (VD). A doctor can be ordered by a court to disclose information about a patient. A doctor will not be penalized for reporting a criminal offence.

Your doctor will not give information about you to your solicitor without your consent. If you are taking legal advice about an action for personal injuries, or applying to the Criminal Injuries Compensation Board (see p. 108), you will need to sign a form authorizing the doctor to provide medical information.

Doctors and hospital workers also have to provide a great deal of information about their patients for statistical and research purposes. (For instance, if a woman goes to her doctor for a cervical smear test, the doctor will fill in a form which includes name, address, husband's occupation, number of births, miscarriages and abortions.) This information goes to the regional health authority. When you leave hospital, details about you and the treatment you were given are included in a survey called the 'hospital activities analysis'. In most of these cases, your name and/or your address is included on the form. You should ask the doctor or nurse if you are worried about this happening (although not all hospital doctors realize that information about their patients is collected in this way). If medical information about you is passed on to someone who should not have it, contact NCCL.

The position is even more difficult if the patient is aged under 16. It is in the doctor's discretion whether or not to tell the parents or guardian something which the patient disclosed in confidence. The Department of Health has advised GPs that, if a girl under 16 asks for contraceptive advice and supplies, the GP should respect the girl's wishes if she does not want her parents told. But equally, a doctor who did decide to tell the parents something which a young patient had told the doctor – even if the patient had not been asked for and had not given consent – would probably not be guilty of improper conduct. In the end, however, the doctor's conduct would have to be judged on the basis of the particular circumstances of the case.

Much the same applies to young people aged over 16 but under 18. Normally, their wishes will be respected and parents have no redress if the doctor does not give them information about their children. But if the doctor decides that it is in the patient's best interests to pass on information to the parents, then, depending on the particular circumstances involved, the doctor would probably not be guilty of misconduct.

Dentists

You should ask a dentist to provide you with dental treatment on the NHS. A fee is normally charged to cover part of the costs of dental treatment, depending on what the dentist actually does for you. You can get free dental treatment if:

– you are under 21 (but if you are between 16 and 21 you will be charged for dentures);
– you are expecting a baby or have a baby under twelve months old;

- you are getting supplementary benefit or family income supplement;
- you qualify on 'low-income grounds' for free prescriptions
  and/or free milk and vitamins.

If you have difficulty finding a dentist to accept you, you
should contact the local family practitioner committee, which is
also responsible for dental services.

Going to hospital

Normally, if you need to see a hospital doctor or specialist – e.g.
to have a blood test – you will have to get an appointment
through your GP. You cannot choose which hospital you will be
treated at. But no patient can be denied treatment, and if you go
to hospital at any time you should be seen by a duty doctor
(although you may be referred to the casualty department of
another hospital). This is most likely to happen in an emergency,
or if your GP is not available.

Your own GP will also have to make an appointment for you
to see other NHS specialists, such as an optician or a psychiatrist.

Can you ever be forced to go to hospital?

Normally, no one can be forced to go to the hospital or accept
treatment against their will. But in certain circumstances the
police do have the power to take someone to hospital; this is
explained fully on p. 374 (Mental Health Act 1959). Someone
with an infectious disease can be forced to go to hospital if a
magistrate signs a detention order (Public Health Act 1936).
Finally, someone who has a chronic disease or is aged, infirm or
physically incapacitated and living in insanitary conditions, can
be taken to hospital if this is in his or her own interests or will
prevent injury to someone else's health or serious nuisance to
other people. In this case, either a medical officer of health or a
magistrate has to sign the order (National Assistance Act 1948).

Having your baby at home

Although the trend is for women to go to hospital for childbirth, and there has been a decline in district midwife services, a mother who wants to have her baby at home can insist that it is her right. But it is probably not advisable to insist on giving birth at home if there are likely to be complications and the doctor advises a hospital birth, particularly since it would be very difficult to sue the doctor if something went wrong.

A doctor or midwife present at a birth must notify the local medical officer of health within thirty-six hours (Public Health Act 1936).

Giving your consent to medical treatment

Except for the three situations where you can be forced to go to hospital (see above), you have to give your consent to any medical treatment. A doctor who treats you without your consent could be sued for assault. Giving your consent does not always mean that you sign a form: for instance, holding your arm out for an injection means that you have given your consent. And in an emergency, obviously, a doctor will treat a patient who may be unconscious.

If you are going into hospital for an operation under anaesthetic, the doctor should get your consent in writing. This means that you should first of all be told what the operation involves and why it is needed. If English is not your main language, you should ask for an explanation in the language you understand best, and the hospital should find an interpreter.

You should not sign a consent form before finding out to your satisfaction what the operation involves. This is especially important if the form refers both to the specific operations and to any other treatment which may be found to be necessary.

Operations on children

Someone under the age of 16 cannot consent in law to medical, surgical or dental treatment. The parent or guardian will have to sign the consent form. As with operations on adults, the parent or guardian should only sign the consent form after getting a full explanation of what treatment or operation is proposed for the child. A local authority which has taken over parental rights (see p. 362) can also consent to treatment for a child in their care.

Once a child reaches the age of 16, he or she can consent to treatment. But a parent or guardian *also* has the right to consent to treatment on behalf of a child who is aged 16 but under 18. Even where the 16- or 17-year-old does not consent, the parent may consent on the child's behalf, provided that the treatment is 'for the benefit of the child'. A girl aged under 16 would, for instance, need her parent's consent to an abortion. In theory, the parents could force an abortion on an unwilling girl, although doctors have been known to refuse to operate in such circumstances. A girl who was going to be operated on against her will could be made a ward of court (see p. 365) to stop the operation. A girl aged 16 or 17 could consent herself, and does not need her parent's consent as well.

STERILIZATION OF CHILDREN

A child under 16 can be sterilized if the parents or guardian agree. (A local authority which has taken over parental rights, or which has a child in care, can also agree to the operation on behalf of the natural parents.) Following the case of an 11-year-old handicapped girl in Sheffield, whom doctors proposed to sterilize, it became clear that a number of handicapped girls and boys are sterilized each year. In one case, a hysterectomy was performed on a 12-year-old handicapped girl.

According to the Department of Health, sterilization should only be carried out in exceptional circumstances (e.g. where there is a serious hereditary disease which cannot be detected before birth; where a woman is so mentally handicapped that she could not care for a child; or where a girl's severe physical and mental handicaps would make menstruation extremely difficult to cope with).

It is possible to prevent the sterilization of a child by applying to have the child made a ward of court. This procedure, which can only be used by someone with a close interest in the child (e.g. a social worker, relative or teacher) is described in detail on p. 365.

Can someone coming from abroad get NHS treatment?

If you are 'ordinarily resident' here (see p. 265 for what this means), you are entitled to free NHS treatment. The same applies if you come here with permission to settle (see p. 279) or on a work permit (see p. 275). In addition, the UK has reciprocal arrangements with some countries which allow citizens of those countries to receive free treatment here; and EEC regulations allow a citizen of a Common Market country to receive free medical treatment. Your doctor or the hospital will give you details.

If you come here specifically in order to get medical treatment, you will have to pay for it as a private patient. This can mean that, if you are, for instance, the child of a work-permit holder and you come here after your father or mother arrived here, and you need medical treatment for some illness which you had before arriving, you may be expected to pay for the treatment. In an emergency, you should be treated free. If you have any difficulties, you should contact the **Joint Council for the Welfare of Immigrants** (see p. 310).

Complaints against your doctor or the NHS

This section tells you what to do if you are unhappy about the way your doctor, the hospital or anyone else in the health services has treated you. In really serious cases, you may be able to sue for negligence; this is described on p. 48.

There are a number of official organizations which deal with people's complaints about the health services. The family practitioner committee deals with complaints against GPs, dentists, chemists and opticians working under the NHS. Various professional bodies deal with accusations of professional misconduct against doctors, nurses, midwives, chemists and opticians.

Finally, the Health Service Ombudsman can investigate certain complaints. Each of these is dealt with in turn below.

Family practitioner committee (FPC)

You will find the address of your local FPC in the telephone directory or you can get it from a local citizens' advice bureau. The FPCs are responsible for the vast majority of doctors, dentists, chemists and opticians who provide their services under the NHS and who have contracts with the local FPC.

The FPC will deal, for instance, with complaints that a doctor has failed to visit, has refused to issue a certificate so that you can claim sickness benefit, or has charged for medicine or treatment which should have been free. The FPC can also tell you which things the GP is allowed to charge for (e.g. certain vaccinations).

Now say AAAargh!

If you want to make a complaint to the FPC, you should write to the Administrator, setting out your complaint. The Administrator will then forward it to the chairman of the committee dealing with whichever part of the service you are complaining about. There are separate committees for doctors, dentists, chemists and opticians. Administrators are normally happy to discuss a complaint informally and can advise you whether or not your complaint can be dealt with by the FPC.

You must make your complaint *within eight weeks* of the event you are complaining about. If your complaint is late, the committee will recommend to the Secretary of State whether or not to allow an investigation. If an investigation is refused, you can appeal to the Secretary of State. If there is a good reason for the delay – e.g. if you were seriously ill during the eight weeks – then your complaint will usually be investigated, but if you delay for a long time it may be impossible to investigate your complaint. There would have to be exceptional circumstances to justify an investigation after a year or more from the date of the event you are complaining about.

On the basis of your letter, the chairperson of the committee may decide that the doctor (or whoever you are complaining about) has in fact done their duty, according to the contract with the FPC. In this case, you will be told that you have fourteen days in which to send in a further written statement giving more details of your complaint. If you do not send in a further statement and the chairperson decides that a full hearing is unnecessary, your complaint will go to the committee to consider it.

If the chairperson decides that your letter of complaint does raise a serious question, then it will be sent to the doctor (or whoever you are complaining against) for comment. You will be sent a copy of these comments and you have a right to reply to them. The chairperson will then decide whether the complaint should go to the committee, or whether a full hearing is needed. If the chairperson decides that a hearing is necessary because, for instance, you and the doctor disagree about what happened or if the doctor does not send in any comments, the chairperson will ask the Administrator to arrange a formal hearing.

You have the right to be present at the hearing. Beforehand, you will be sent copies of all the correspondence, statements and any comments you or the doctor have made, which will be used as evidence at the hearing. You can give evidence, bring witnesses along to help you, and question the person you are complaining about or any of their witnesses.

You are not allowed to be represented by a lawyer or paid advocate at the hearing. But you are entitled to have someone with you, to speak for you or to sit beside you and advise you. The FPC will pay travelling costs and subsistence allowance, if necessary.

The committee then draws up a report which goes to the FPC. On the basis of the facts in the report, the FPC decides what conclusions to draw (e.g. that the doctor was at fault) and what action to take (e.g. that the doctor should be cautioned or money withheld from the doctor). Although the committee will also draw conclusions and make recommendations in its report, the FPC is not bound by them.

The report of the committee, together with the FPC's views, is then sent to the Secretary of State. It will usually also be sent to you and the doctor (or whoever you are complaining against). You have a month to appeal against the decision. The doctor may appeal against the decision, and also make representations about the recommendations (e.g. that they are too severe). You have no right to make representations about the recommendations (e.g. that they are not severe enough).

The Secretary of State considers any appeal or representations and decides whether to hold a hearing (which will be dealt with by a small committee with a legal chairperson) or whether the decision can be made on the written documents alone.

Professional medical bodies

Each branch of the medical profession – doctors, dentists, nurses, midwives, opticians and chemists – has its own professional body, dealing with disciplinary matters. If you think that a family doctor has not given you the proper service you are entitled to, you would complain to the family practitioner committee as explained in the last section. But if a doctor had behaved unprofessionally – for instance, by having sexual relations with a patient, or breaching a patient's confidence – the complaint would go to the professional body concerned. Each of the professional bodies is dealt with below.

GENERAL MEDICAL COUNCIL

Anyone can practise medicine on people, but doctors employed under the NHS must be registered with the General Medical Council which tries to make sure that anyone registered with them has a proper standard of education and training. If you make a complaint of professional misconduct about a member of the General Medical Council, it will be considered by the disciplinary committee. This committee may find that your complaint is unfounded; or it may issue a warning to the doctor, place him on probation, suspend him or remove him from the register. The doctor can appeal against suspension or removal from the register to the judicial committee of the Privy Council.

If you want to make a complaint about professional misconduct, you should write to the Registrar, **General Medical Council, 44 Hallam Street, London W1.**

GENERAL DENTAL COUNCIL

If you have a complaint about a dentist, you should write to the Registrar, **General Dental Council, 37 Wimpole Street, London W1.**

GENERAL NURSING COUNCIL

This council was set up under the Nurses Registration Act 1919, and has twenty-two elected members, who are nurses, and twenty appointed members, of whom at least six are nurses. If you have a complaint against a nurse, you should write to the Registrar, **General Nursing Council, 23 Portland Place, London W1.**

The council's solicitor will investigate the complaint, usually by interviewing you, seeing witnesses and taking a statement from the nurse. The solicitor's report is then put before the investigating committee, which also deals with reports from the police about a nurse's criminal convictions.

The investigating committee may decide that your complaint is outside their scope, or that the nurse has behaved unprofessionally and should be reprimanded. Or they may refer the complaint to the disciplinary committee. Your complaint will be presented by the council's solicitor, while the nurse is entitled to be represented by her own lawyer. The disciplinary committee can hear witnesses, and decides whether misconduct has been proved and, if so, what should be done. They can remove a nurse from the professional register.

CENTRAL MIDWIVES BOARD

If you have a complaint against a midwife, you should write to the Registrar, **Central Midwives Board, 39 Harrington Gardens, London, SW7**. Your complaint will be considered by a 'penal cases committee' and may then go to the disciplinary committee. Both you and the midwife are entitled to be represented by a lawyer at any disciplinary hearing. The rules established by the board for disciplinary hearings against midwives are very complicated, and it is probably worth getting legal advice.

GENERAL OPTICAL COUNCIL

Anyone who tests eye-sight or supplies spectacles or other optical aids (e.g. contact lenses) must be registered by the General Optical Council. (This does not apply to registered doctors, who are covered by the General Medical Council.) If you have a complaint about the professional conduct of an optician, you should write to the Registrar, **General Optical Council, 41 Harley Street, London W1**.

The British Optical Association publishes a code of conduct for opticians and any complaint by a member of the public will be investigated by the association and referred, if necessary, to the association's council and the disciplinary committee. This committee can expel, suspend or reprimand a member, or order the optician to pay you compensation. You should write to the Secretary, **British Optical Association, 65 Brook Street, London W1**.

THE PHARMACEUTICAL SOCIETY OF GREAT BRITAIN

If you have a complaint about a chemist, you should write to the Registrar, **Pharmaceutical Society of Great Britain, 17 Bloomsbury Square, London WC1.** The society has a disciplinary committee with the power to remove a member from the register of pharmaceutical chemists on account of criminal convictions or misconduct.

Health Service Ombudsman

The Ombudsman (or Health Service Commissioner) covers regional health authorities, area health authorities and family practitioner committees. (He also covered regional hospital boards, boards of governors, hospital management committees and executive councils which were wound up on 1 April 1974. But he can deal with complaints against these bodies arising from something which happened before April 1974.)

The Ombudsman can deal with your complaint if you suffered hardship or injustice because a health authority failed to provide a proper service (e.g. poor food in a hospital); or if a health authority failed to provide a service which it has a duty to provide; or if there has been bad administration affecting the service (e.g. lack of communication between the staff, or failure to give you full information).

WHAT THE OMBUDSMAN CANNOT DO

The Ombudsman cannot investigate:

1. Any complaint which you have taken to a tribunal or court.
2. Any complaint which you could have taken to a tribunal or court, but chose not to. But if the Ombudsman decides that it was not reasonable for you to go to court, he can still investigate the complaint.
3. The correctness of a doctor's clinical judgement (i.e. the diagnosis or the particular treatment). But if the treatment involved bad administration (e.g. the drugs you were given were not

what the doctor prescribed), you can complain to the Ombudsman.

4. Complaints about doctors, dentists, chemists or opticians who
   provide services under a family practitioner committee. (See
   p. 474 for how to complain to the FPC itself.)

5. Personnel matters, such as staff appointments or dismissals,
   pay, discipline or pensions.

6. Action taken in relation to contractual or commercial transactions.

7. Matters which are the subject of an inquiry set up by the
   Secretary of State to investigate a serious incident or major
   breakdown in the health service.

8. Complaints about special hospitals directly controlled by the
   Department of Health (e.g. Broadmoor, Rampton). These are
   dealt with by the general Ombudsman (Parliamentary Commissioner for Administration) (see p. 514).

HOW TO COMPLAIN TO THE OMBUDSMAN

If you want to complain to the Ombudsman, you must first of all
give the health authority the chance to investigate and reply to
your complaint. If you do not know which authority is responsible for the matter you are complaining about, you should ask
your local hospital or citizens' advice bureau, or contact the area
or regional health authority (address in the telephone directory).
If the authority fails to reply to you, or you are not satisfied with
their explanation, you should then:

1. Write your complaint and send it to the **Health Service
   Commissioner** (i.e. Ombudsman), **Church House, Great
   Smith Street, London SW1.** You should complain within a
   year of the incident you are complaining about, although the
   Ombudsman has the power to extend this time-limit if he
   thinks that would be reasonable.

2. Give your full name and address.

3. Say which authority is responsible for the incident you are
   complaining about, and give the full name and address of the
   place where it happened.

4. Set out what happened as clearly and fully as possible. A local councillor, the citizens' advice bureau or the community health council can help you write the letter.
5. If possible, send the Ombudsman copies of any letters you have written or which you have had from the health authorities about your complaint.

WHAT HAPPENS NEXT

The Ombudsman will decide if your complaint comes within his terms of reference. If he decides that it does not and you still want to follow the complaint up, contact your MP. If the Ombudsman decides that he can take up your complaint, he will write and tell you that an investigation has been started.

The Ombudsman can examine the records of the health authority and interview anyone about your complaint. The Ombudsman's staff will usually visit you or ask you to come and see them; your expenses will be paid and you will be compensated for loss of time. Occasionally, the Ombudsman will decide to have a formal hearing and may decide that you and the health authority should be legally represented. The Ombudsman can also decide to pay your legal costs.

WHAT CAN THE OMBUDSMAN DO?

The Ombudsman will send a report of his investigation to you, the health authority and anyone else with an interest. *He has no power to force the health authority to implement his recommendations.* You can publicize the report, and you should contact the local press and MP to help make sure the report is properly followed up.

Suing a doctor or hospital for negligence

The law requires a doctor to exercise a reasonable degree of care and skill in the care of patients. One judge put it this way: 'A man need not possess the highest expert skill . . . it is sufficient if he exercises the ordinary skill of an ordinary competent man exercising that particular art . . .'

If your doctor fails to exercise reasonable skill in diagnosing what is wrong with you and treating you, and as a result you suffer unnecessary pain or increased suffering or any other damage, you can sue the doctor for negligence.

This applies whether the doctor is working as a general practitioner, or whether he is employed by a hospital. In the case of a hospital doctor, you may also be able to sue the hospital authorities.

NURSES AND OTHER HOSPITAL WORKERS

It is not only the doctor who has a legal duty to look after you properly. Other staff – nurses, anaesthetists and so on – have to exercise reasonable skill and care in their job. If, for instance, you were given the wrong drugs or the wrong gas under anaesthetic, you might be able to sue the individual responsible for negligence. You would also be able to sue the hospital authorities, since they are responsible for their staff. Hospitals are insured against possible claims for damages.

HOW TO FIND OUT IF YOU COULD SUE FOR NEGLIGENCE

If you think a medical worker or hospital has been negligent, you will need to consult a lawyer and get proper advice about whether or not you could bring a successful action. Your complaint would have to be serious: if you are complaining about poor food, you should complain to the hospital authorities and then, if necessary, the Ombudsman (see p. 480). But if you had been given food poisoning, you might well consider suing the hospital for negligence.

WHAT DOES 'SUING FOR NEGLIGENCE' INVOLVE?

A negligence action is likely to be difficult. It could take a long time and be very expensive. But it is now possible for your lawyers to apply to the court to get relevant documents – such as medical records – from the hospital or doctor before you decide whether or not to start an action. These documents can then be examined by medical experts employed by your lawyer, who will be able to advise whether or not you have a strong case. You may be able to get legal aid to cover at least part of the cost (see p. 496).

You must usually start a negligence action within three years of the event you are complaining about, or within three years of when you first knew that you had suffered serious injury or that the injury was caused by the events you are complaining about. The court can let you start an action later than this, but it is difficult to persuade them to give you permission.

Finally, if you do sue a doctor or hospital for negligence, it will be up to you and your lawyer to show the court that there was negligence. This usually involves calling other doctors as expert witnesses. More information about legal actions for damages is in Chapter 11.

More information

Patients' Association, Suffolk House, Banbury Road, Oxford (Oxford 50306).

Your local community health council: address in telephone directory.

24. Death

Registration

The doctor who looked after someone who has died has to deliver a death certificate to the Registrar of Births, Marriages and Deaths, and must also give a notice of the signing of the certificate to the nearest relative. The cause of death on the certificate will be included in the register, unless there is to be an inquest or post-mortem. In this case, the coroner will tell the registrar of the findings. If someone dies in hospital, the death certificate is normally issued by the doctor who regularly looked after the patient.

Inquests
When does an inquest have to be held?

If a coroner is informed that there is a dead body in the area which he covers, then he has to hold an inquest if one of the following three things applies:

- there is reasonable cause to suspect that the person died violently or unnaturally; *or*
- the person died suddenly and the cause of death is not known; *or*
- the person died in prison, or in such a place or circumstances that an inquest is needed.

What is an inquest for?

The purpose of an inquest is to decide who the dead person was; how, when and where she or he died; who (if anybody) should be charged with murder, manslaughter, infanticide or causing death by dangerous driving, or of being an accessory to the crime; and what information should be given to the Registrar concerning the death. If you disagree with the coroner's verdict, you can appeal against it by applying to the **Attorney General, The Law Courts, Strand, London WC1.** (You can ask the clerk of the coroner's court for more information about this.)

The coroner or the coroner's jury can also make recommendations to prevent future deaths in similar circumstances, but they cannot pre-empt the question of civil liability. For instance, if someone died in an industrial accident, the coroner cannot decide that the employer was negligent: that would have to be decided by a court.

The procedure for an inquest

All inquests are held in public, except where national security is involved. Witnesses are summoned to appear, and are usually questioned first by the coroner, and then by anyone (e.g. a relative, or a lawyer representing the family) whom the coroner decides has a proper interest in the matter. The coroner can refuse to allow improper or irrelevant questions, and no witness can be made to answer incriminating questions. Legal aid is not yet available, so a family who wanted to be represented at an inquest would have to pay legal fees themselves. No one except the coroner can insist on any particular witness being called.

Post-mortems

A post-mortem examination involves anything more than a purely external examination of the body. It is only lawful if it is carried out:

– on the instructions or at the request of the coroner; *or*
– under the Human Tissue Act 1961; *or*
– under the Anatomy Act 1832.

We explain what can happen in each of these cases below.

If a coroner orders a post-mortem

The coroner can order a doctor to make a post-mortem before deciding whether or not to hold an inquest. Wherever practicable, the post-mortem should be carried out by a pathologist with suitable qualifications and experience, and with access to laboratory facilities.

If someone has died in hospital, and the coroner wants a post-mortem performed, he should not ask a pathologist working for the hospital, or connected with it, to do the post-mortem if:

– the pathologist does not want to do the examination; *or*
– the conduct of a member of the hospital staff is likely to be called into question as a result of the death; *or*
– a relative of the dead person asks the coroner not to allow an examination by the hospital pathologist.

But if getting another pathologist with suitable qualifications and experience would mean too long a delay, the coroner still has the discretion to ask a hospital pathologist to do the post-mortem.

A hospital can be represented at a post-mortem by a doctor, but it cannot interfere with the actual examination. The post-mortem will take place at the hospital if it has suitable accommodation and the hospital authorities consent, unless the coroner decides it should take place somewhere else. The report of the post-mortem goes only to the coroner, but he has the power to give a copy to anyone who asks for it.

If there is no reason to believe that an inquest will be held or that the coroner will order a post-mortem, an unofficial post-mortem can be done to establish or confirm the cause of death. In this case, the post-mortem has to be done with the authority of the person 'lawfully in possession of the body' (e.g. the hospital but *not* an undertaker) and on the instructions of a registered doctor.

Using parts of a body for medical purposes

If the dead person requested that his or her body should be used for medical purposes, then whoever is lawfully in possession of the body can authorize the doctor or pathologist to remove any part of the body, in accordance with the dead person's request. The request must have been made either verbally, in front of at least two witnesses, during the person's last illness or in writing at any time (Human Tissue Act 1961).

If the dead person did not request that his or her body be used for medical purposes, then the person lawfully in possession of the body first of all has to try and find out if the dead person ever expressed an *objection* to having his or her body used for medical purposes. If the dead person did object, or if the surviving spouse or a surviving relative objects to having the body used in this way, then no part of the body should be removed. If there are no objections, then the body can be used for medical purposes.

In any case, the only person who can remove part of a body is a fully registered medical practitioner who must have satisfied himself by a personal examination that life is extinct.

Anatomical examinations on a dead body

Providing that the following conditions are obeyed, a dead body can be examined for anatomical purposes (Anatomy Act 1832):

- The person who does the examination must be licensed, and the Secretary of State for Health must be notified of the place where the examination is carried out.
- The person in lawful possession of the body (e.g. the hospital, but *not* an undertaker) must request or consent to the examination. There is no obligation for the hospital to ask the dead person's relatives for their consent. But if a relative does object, then the examination must not take place, nor can it take place if the dead person expressed a written objection or during his last illness made a verbal objection before two witnesses.
- The examination cannot take place for forty-eight hours after death, and twenty-four hours after notice of the removal of the body has been given to the inspector of the district.
- Twenty-four hours after the body is removed from the hospital (or wherever it is being kept), the person conducting the examination must send the inspector the death certificate and a form stating the name of the person or authorities from whom the body was taken, when the body was received, the date and place of death, and the sex, name, age and last address of the dead person.

- The body must be removed in a decent shell or coffin and must be decently buried or cremated after dissection, according to the dead person's religion or beliefs.
- A certificate of burial or cremation must be sent to the inspector within twelve months after the day when the body was received for dissection.

After your death

If you want to make sure that your body is used in the way you want after your death, you should make your wishes known in writing, and by telling your nearest relatives, your doctor, and (if you go to hospital) the hospital authorities. This applies whether you want your body used for medical purposes or not.

After a relative's death

You cannot stop the hospital from allowing a relative's body to be used for medical purposes if your relative indicated that he or she was quite happy to have the body used in this way. If your relative did not leave any directions, and you do not want it to be used, you should make your objections known to the doctor who treated your relative, and also to the hospital where your relative died. If neither the dead person, nor you as a surviving relative, makes your objections known, the hospital authority can allow the removal of any part of the body or the use of the body for anatomical dissection.

The *Sunday People* reported in August 1976 that a mortuary attendant claimed to have removed pituitary glands from dead bodies which had had a post-mortem performed, and sold them to hospitals. This would be illegal, since it is only under the laws set out above that someone can dissect a body or remove any part of it.

More information

What To Do if Someone Dies, Consumers' Association (£1·25 including post).

25. Legal services

Most of this book is about your legal rights. Many of these rights can only be achieved with some kind of legal help. This chapter is about who can help you, where you can find them and how you can pay for their services.

Who can help you

Solicitors in private practice

About 30,000 solicitors practise in England and Wales and most of them work in private firms of which there are around 14,000. There is one solicitor to every 1,640 of the population. But their offices are not evenly spread through the country: many are clustered around commercial centres. Solicitors are trained in the law to help people with their legal problems and earn a living by charging clients for their advice or assistance in pursuing cases. Many make a lot of money out of conveyancing (buying and selling houses, buildings and land), probate (wills) and matrimonial disputes (custody, divorce, etc.). Some firms specialize in a particular type of work and many will not be able to help a client with a legal problem outside their specialism. A great deal of their work is done in their own offices but they do represent clients in the lower courts – magistrates' courts and county courts (which handle minor civil matters). With more serious civil and criminal cases, when it is necessary for the client to be represented by a barrister in a higher court or when more complicated legal advice is required, this has to be arranged by a solicitor. Nobody can go straight to a barrister for legal help.

You can find a list of solicitors practising in your area in the yellow pages of the telephone directory, at a citizens' advice bureau or other public information service, or from a court office. Solicitors are not allowed to advertise. Not all do legal aid work and your local citizens' advice bureau may be able to advise you about which solicitors are best suited to help with your particular case. For each area of the country referral lists have been prepared showing the names of all the solicitors in practice in the area and the work they do. These lists are available from citizens' advice bureaux, town halls, public libraries and other advice agencies like housing aid centres.

It is often wise to telephone to arrange an appointment before visiting a solicitor's office. It is possible to change your solicitor if you are not happy with the way he or she is handling your case. You should ask your solicitor to pass on all the papers to the new one. If you owe your solicitor any money, you will have to pay this before your papers will be passed on to a new solicitor.

Law centres

Since 1970 there has been a growth in the number of law centres. In October 1976 there were twenty operating, the majority in London. See p. 507 for their addresses.

They may be funded by local authorities, by the Home Office through the Urban Aid Programme, by charities and by legal aid fees. The solicitors they employ are paid a salary which is not dependent on how well their work pays. They have the same rights as solicitors in private practice and can handle any case right up to the highest court of appeal. Sometimes the help they give is free, sometimes they use the legal aid schemes, but clients are never charged. They do not usually help people who could afford to pay a solicitor in private practice. Most of them only help people who live within the area around their office, in the same London borough for example.

The kind of work they do is very different from many private firms. Most of it is concerned with housing (helping tenants in particular) and they also give legal advice and assistance on employment, welfare benefits, juvenile crime, immigration, family violence, planning, and many other matters. Because of pressure of work, some law centres find it necessary to limit the kind of work they can take on. They are informal friendly places and may employ staff other than solicitors, like social workers and public health inspectors. They often assist organizations within the community with their legal problems, like tenants' associations or immigrant groups.

Legal advice centres

Legal advice centres only give advice. If a case has to go to court, they will refer the client to a solicitor in private practice. Most of them are run by lawyers in private practice who give voluntary help, usually one or two evenings a week. A list of the centres can be obtained from the **Legal Action Group, 28a Highgate Road, London NW5,** for 50p plus s.a.e. They are very useful places to seek initial advice about a problem and they may help you in negotiations with a landlord, for instance, if no legal action is involved. You may find the address of one in your area from a citizens' advice bureau or local information service in the library.

Citizens' advice bureaux and other agencies

There are about 700 citizens' advice bureaux throughout the country mainly in urban areas. They give advice on a wide range of subjects, especially legal aid, welfare benefits and landlord–tenant problems. The quality of their advice varies because they are mainly staffed by laypeople. (However, some employ solicitors – see p. 511.) A large number of citizens' advice bureaux have now instituted rota schemes of local solicitors. These schemes enable clients to meet a solicitor informally and for no charge at the citizens' advice bureau office. The solicitor can give free legal advice but if the case has to be pursued further, it will be referred to the solicitor's private firm. You will find the address of your nearest citizens' advice bureau in the telephone directory.

There are a number of other agencies which provide legal advice and assistance listed on p. 587, like the Child Poverty Action Group, Release, and the National Council for Civil Liberties. Some of these agencies employ solicitors who are usually specialists in the area of law with which the organization is concerned.

If you have a legal problem which may be dealt with by a tribunal (see p. 258) you can get advice and assistance from a solicitor before the hearing but they will probably not represent you before the tribunal unless you pay them. There is no legal aid available for representation before most tribunals. Some organizations help in such cases, for example trade unions advise their members on such things as redundancy, equal pay and unfair dismissal.

Duty solicitor schemes

If you have been charged with a criminal offence and are appearing in a magistrates' court you may get legal help from a duty solicitor. These are solicitors who are on duty at the magistrates' court on a rota basis and offer their services to defendants who are appearing without representation, particularly defendants who have been kept in custody overnight. They will advise about applying for legal aid and bail and whether or not you should plead guilty. If you get legal aid, you don't have to retain the duty solicitor who initially helped you unless you want to.

There were about eighty duty solicitor schemes operating in February 1977 at the following courts:

Altringham, Gtr Manchester	Cardiff
Balham Juvenile, London	Chelmsford
Barrow-in-Furness	Christchurch, Hants
Bedford	Cleethorpes, Humberside
Billericay, Essex	Coventry
Birmingham	Croydon, Gtr London
Blackpool	Dorchester, Dorset
Blandford, Dorset	Dudley, West Midlands
Bolton	Ealing, London
Bournemouth	Eastbourne, Sussex
Bradford	Esher & Walton, Surrey
Bridport, Dorset	Gillingham, Dorset
Brighton, Sussex	Great Yarmouth, Norfolk
Bristol	Grimsby, Humberside
Bury, Lancashire	Guildford, Surrey
Cambridge	Harrow, London

Hastings, Sussex
Hartlepool, Cleveland
Hendon, London
Highbury Corner, Gtr London
Highgate, London
Hove, Sussex
Leeds
Leicester
Liverpool
Luton, Bedfordshire
Manchester
Marylebone, London
Medway, Kent
Newport, Gwent
Norwich
Nottingham City
Nottingham County
Poole, Dorset
Portsmouth
Radstock, Somerset
Richmond, London
Rochdale, Gtr Manchester
Salford, Gtr Manchester
Salisbury

Shaftesbury, Dorset
Sheffield
Sherborne, Dorset
Slough, Berkshire
Solihull
Southampton
South Western London
Strangeways, Manchester
Stratford, Gtr London
Sturminster Newton, Dorset
Sunderland, Tyne & Wear
Sutton, Gtr London
Sutton Coldfield, West
   Midlands
Swindon
Teeside, Cleveland
Tottenham, London
Waltham Forest
Wareham, Dorset
Weymouth & Portland, Dorset
Willesden, London
Wimbledon, London
Wimborne, Dorset
Wolverhampton

McKenzie advisers

If you decide to represent yourself in court you are entitled to have a friend with you to advise and help during the case. He or she is called a McKenzie adviser (see p. 102).

How to pay

If you need legal services for a problem prior to any court proceedings which may be involved and if you don't have much money, you may get free legal advice and assistance from a solicitor. Depending on your income you may have to contribute towards the solicitor's costs. This would arise, for instance.

if you rent a flat and the landlord asks you to sign an agreement and you want to know what the agreement involves. If the solicitor feels that the terms of the agreement should be changed she or he may write and negotiate with the landlord on your behalf.

If you need legal services for a problem which involves some court proceedings and you don't have much money, you may get free legal aid to pay for your case to be prepared and for you to be represented in court by a solicitor or barrister. Depending on your income, you may have to contribute towards the legal costs of the case. This would arise, for instance, if your landlord went to court to get a possession order against you, or if you were charged with an offence by the police.

These schemes are available from most solicitors and they work on the principle that you pay what you can afford towards legal costs and the state pays the rest.

Green-form scheme

Legal advice and assistance (up to the value of £25) is available to anyone over 17 who wants advice or assistance about the law, provided they qualify financially. (Someone acting for a child under 17 can also get help.) You can get this help with claims for welfare benefits, rent and tenancy problems, employment problems, cases of discrimination, housing repairs, etc. There is no application form to fill in. You just walk into a solicitor's office and ask for legal advice. The solicitor completes a form which takes a few minutes. It is green and the scheme has come to be known as the **green-form scheme**. Under this scheme, a solicitor can do any type of work short of actually acting in court. He or she may write letters, take statements, attend meetings, advise in their office, advise in prison, visit you at home, conduct negotiations, draw up agreements, draft wills and handle a number of different types of problem. The solicitor can help you to act yourself by advising you on what to do, or use the scheme to help you to apply for the appropriate type of legal aid (see below).

You can qualify:

– if your disposable capital (which means savings that are not tied up in essential things like clothes, tools for work, or other standard personal household property) is not over £300. You are allowed to deduct from your savings £125 for your first dependant, £80 for your second and £40 each for any others; *and*

– if your disposable income (which means your income after tax, insurance and deductions for your dependants) is not above a certain level or you are receiving supplementary benefits or family income supplement. You pay a contribution towards the solicitor's fees on a sliding scale, according to your income, as follows:

Disposable income in the week before you seek advice	Maximum contribution you pay to the solicitor
under £20	nothing
£20–21	£4·00
£22–23	£7·00
£24–25	£10·00
£26–27	£13·00
£28–29	£16·00
£30–31	£19·00
£32–33	£22·00
£34–35	£24·00

The solicitor assesses your income. To arrive at your **disposable income** from your total weekly income, you deduct tax, NI contributions and the following amounts for dependants:

Spouse					£7·95
Dependant or child under 5					£3·60
Dependant or child aged 5–10					£4·35
,,	,,	,,	,,	11–12	£5·35
,,	,,	,,	,,	13–15	£6·50
,,	,,	,,	,,	16–17	£7·80
,,	,,	,,	,,	18 or over	£10·15

(These figures are accurate from April 1977. The amounts go up twice a year.)

There is a snag. If you get any money back as a result of the advice and assistance provided by a solicitor, you may have to pay the rest of the legal bill from it. But this does not apply if the money you recover is for maintenance or affiliation, social security (National Insurance) benefit, rent rebates or allowances, or if you recover the legal costs from the other side in the dispute. Your solicitor can write to the Law Society, which administers the scheme, for permission not to claim payment out of money you receive if it would cause you hardship.

Civil legal aid

Under the legal aid scheme, if you qualify financially, you can get help from a solicitor with things like divorce, claims for damages for injury at work or in a road accident, or most other matters which may involve a court case. The expense of these cases can be considerable, running into hundreds, or even thousands of pounds: with legal aid, you can get help free or cheaply. It is not available for proceedings before most tribunals (see p. 258). (Criminal cases, e.g. where the police are prosecuting you, are dealt with on p. 500.)

The scheme is administered by the Law Society and you have to convince them that you have a reasonable chance of winning your case, that the case is worth fighting and that you qualify financially. You can get application forms from a solicitor, a citizens' advice bureau or a court office. The forms are very long and complicated and you will probably need help from a solicitor to complete them (see p. 494).

You send the completed forms to the local secretary of the Law Society Aid local office (address in the telephone directory). You will then be interviewed by the Supplementary Benefit Commission who will examine your financial position. You must show them your bank statements, rent book, wage slips, etc. The Supplementary Benefit Commission then tell the Law Society how much they think you can afford to pay. In the meantime, a panel of solicitors at the Law Society will have considered whether your case stands a reasonable chance of succeeding.

They will then write to your solicitor either rejecting your claim for legal aid, or offering you legal aid for nothing or with a contribution. If you are required to pay a contribution you will be told what the maximum will be if the case turns out more expensive than estimated. You have twenty-eight days in which to accept the offer. If you accept, the legal aid certificate goes to the solicitor who can then start work on your case. This whole process takes between six to ten weeks (see p. 499 for emergency cases). Your contribution is payable over a year, but you may have to pay a lump sum at the start of the case depending on the amount of your disposable capital.

You can qualify for civil legal aid:

- if your **disposable capital** (which means savings that are not tied up in essential personal and household property) is not more than £1,400. If you own a house you are allowed to deduct from the market value of the house:
  - £6,000;
  - the amount of any outstanding mortage;
  - 50 per cent of the balance.

  The amount that this leaves over counts towards your disposable capital. If you own the house jointly with someone else it is only your share that is taken into account, unless you own jointly with your husband or wife and are living with them. There are special rules for other circumstances but in all cases the Law Society can decide to ignore that £1,400 limit and in any case of doubt you should apply to them to do so. If the house or any other capital asset is the subject matter of the dispute for which you want legal aid, its value can be ignored but if you win the case you will have to repay the amount spent on legal aid.
- if your **disposable income** is not above a certain level. Disposable income is what is left from your take-home pay, less the amount of rent or mortgage repayment, less allowances for your dependents. The allowances for dependants are the same as for the green-form scheme (see p. 494). The *annual* amounts for the dependants' allowances are as follows:

Spouse					£413·40
Dependant or child under 5					£187·20
Dependant or child aged 5–10					£226·20
,,	,,	,,	,,	11–12	£278·20
,,	,,	,,	,,	13–15	£338·00
,,	,,	,,	,,	16–17	£405·60
,,	,,	,,	,,	18 or over	£527·80

In assessing disposable income and capital the resources of your spouse and any children under 18 will also usually be taken into account if you are living together, unless you want legal aid for a dispute between yourselves.

If your disposable income is less than £665 a year *and* your disposable capital is less than £300, legal aid will be free. If your disposable capital is over £300 you may have to contribute the whole amount above £300 towards the cost of legal aid. If your disposable income is more than £2,085 a year you cannot get legal aid. If it is between £665 and £2,085 you will have to contribute one third of the amount you have over £665.

The table on p. 499 illustrates the levels of income at which people in different family circumstances will be able to claim legal aid.

If you win any damages, you may have to use these to pay towards the legal costs of the case. But this does not apply if the money received is for maintenance or affiliation, transfer of the matrimonial home, or interim payments of damages (where your opponent is prepared to pay some damages but quibbles about the total amount).

If your application for legal aid is refused you can appeal under certain circumstances. You cannot appeal against the amount of your contribution decided by the Supplementary Benefit Commission, but you may be able to get the commission to have another look at the figure, especially if your financial circumstances have changed. Ask your solicitor to consider the matter and, if she or he agrees, to write to the Law Society. If your application is turned down because the Law Society does not think you have a reasonable chance of winning, you can appeal to a more senior panel of solicitors. You may attend their hearing. Quite a high proportion of these appeals are successful. But

	Income from all sources, after deducting income tax, NI contributions and rent	
Applicant	Maximum permitting free legal aid	At or above this point, applicant is ineligible for legal aid
Single person	£769 (£14·78 wkly)	£2,190 (£42·11 wkly)
Married couple, one child aged 4	£1,369 (£26·32 wkly)	£2,790 (£53·65 wkly)
Married couple, two children 4 and 8	£1,595 (£30·67 wkly)	£3,016 (£58 wkly)
Married couple, three children 4, 8 and 13	£1,933 (£37·17 wkly)	£3,354 (£64·50 wkly)
Single parent, two children 4 and 8	£1,182 (£22·73 wkly)	£2,603 (£50·05 wkly)
Married couple no children	£1,182 (£22·73 wkly)	£2,603 (£50·05 wkly)

These examples assume that the Supplementary Benefits Commission (which works out the applicant's financial entitlement) will make an allowance for all the money paid in rent or equivalent.

(The figures are correct as from November 1976, but are usually changed every year and are now higher.)

this does not apply if your application for legal aid was for a hearing in an appeal court.

IN EMERGENCIES

You can obtain legal aid within a few hours with the help of a solicitor. Legal aid may be granted without any financial assessment at the time. If, however, when an assessment is done later you are found to be outside the financial limits for legal aid, you may have to pay the whole of your solicitor's bill. It is advisable to apply for legal aid in this way if it is a real emergency, for instance, if your husband beats you brutally, or if your landlord evicts you.

Criminal legal aid

Criminal proceedings occur if you are charged with an offence. This means that the police or someone else prosecutes you for doing something which is a crime. This could mean anything from murder or assault, to possession of drugs, theft or motoring offences. (Some other bodies like the Inland Revenue or the Post Office can bring criminal proceedings as well as the police.) See Chapter 1 for information about police powers on questioning, arrest, bail, etc. All criminal cases are first heard in magistrates' courts. If the offence is more serious the case will then be heard in the Crown Court before a jury (see p. 77 for a description of the different courts). Criminal legal aid is available to allow you to obtain a lawyer to defend you.

In 1975 90 per cent of applications for criminal legal aid were granted but the majority of defendants in magistrates' courts still appeared without representation.

Court procedure and the rules of evidence are complicated and most people are very confused when they are confronted with legal proceedings against them. Unless your case is very trivial you need a lawyer to defend you. Even if you are not guilty you cannot assume that your innocence will be believed. And if you are found guilty you may need a lawyer to present what are called 'mitigating factors' to the court so that you get a reduced sentence.

Criminal courts are meant to grant legal aid when the defendant cannot afford to pay for his or her own defence and if it is in the interests of justice that they should be defended.

If you qualify financially (see p. 502) you should get legal aid if:

- you might lose your liberty;
- you might lose your livelihood;
- your reputation might be damaged;
- your case involves complex law;
- you cannot follow the proceedings because you cannot speak English;
- you are ill;

- the defence involves tracing and interviewing witnesses, or
  cross-examining expert witnesses appearing for the prosecution;
- your defence involves cross-examination of a child or a witness
  on whom you have allegedly committed an assault.

Today no one is refused legal aid if it is likely that if they are
found guilty of the offence they will be sent to prison. On the
other hand, it is rare to get legal aid for motoring offences unless
you might be disqualified and then be unable to earn a living
because your work depends on your having a driving licence.
The practice of the courts in granting legal aid varies enormously.

Most criminal cases start in one of three ways:

1. You receive a summons from the court after the police have
   laid an information, that is alleged to a magistrate that you
   have committed an offence. Less serious cases start in this way.
   If you want legal help when you receive a summons, you can
   go to a solicitor (or law centre) and ask for legal advice so that
   you can find out what is involved, what the penalties are if you
   plead guilty or are found guilty of the offence, and discuss
   whether or not to plead guilty. If you decide that you would
   like the solicitor to help in court, legal aid is usually necessary.
   The solicitor will have application forms which must be
   completed for you to sign. If you have not seen a solicitor, you
   can get an application form from any magistrates' court.
   When it is completed, it is sent to the court where you have to
   appear. Either the magistrates' clerk or the magistrates themselves will decide whether to grant you legal aid. There may be
   a contribution (see p. 502). Within a day or so the legal aid
   order is sent to your solicitor, or if you do not know of a
   solicitor when you apply for legal aid, to a solicitor whom you
   choose from a list which the court staff give you. You can
   receive this initial advice under the green-form scheme (see
   p. 494) if you are financially eligible.
2. You are charged by the police with an offence. Charges are
   presented in the police station and the police can then grant
   you bail or keep you in custody. If you are granted bail the

chances are that you will have to attend the magistrates' court the following day. Sometimes you would not have to attend court for a week or so but this is rare. This means that you have to get a solicitor quickly if you want advice before you go to the court. If this is not possible you can apply for legal aid when you arrive at the court. You can either obtain the forms from the court office and complete them before your case comes up or you can apply in court to the magistrate.

3. If you are charged by the police and kept in custody you will have no chance of seeing a solicitor before you attend court unless the police allow you to call a solicitor from the police station and the solicitor comes down to talk to you there. Whether the police do this depends on how serious they think the charge is. The more serious the charge the less likely they are to allow you to see a solicitor. What this means is that as soon as you get to the court you must ask the magistrates for legal aid and they will always adjourn the case so that you can get legal representation.

There is no income limit for legal aid in a criminal case. In other words, however wealthy you are you may get legal aid in some circumstances. If your resources do not exceed £50 (or if you are married, the joint resources of you and your spouse do not exceed £80) you cannot be refused legal aid on financial grounds. If your income was not more than £440 in the previous year (or if you are married, the combined income of you and your spouse was not above £720) you cannot be ordered to pay any contribution.

The court itself is responsible for granting criminal legal aid. It will get details of your income from the application form which is quite long and complicated. If your income is above these levels, you may have to pay some part of your costs if the court makes a **contribution order**. There is no means of telling what contribution you may be ordered to pay but it is unlikely that it would be more than £20 before the case is heard. After the case the court can revise the contribution order or make one for the first time, but even then it is unusual for an order to be much above £50. In many cases no contribution order is made at all.

If a contribution order is made which you cannot afford, you or your solicitor can ask the court to refer the matter to the Supplementary Benefit Commission. They will investigate your financial position but the court is not obliged to follow their advice.

If you are acquitted of the offence and you have been ordered to make a contribution towards your legal aid costs, your solicitor or barrister ought to ask the court to say that your contribution should be repaid.

If you think your solicitor's bill is too high, you can question it. You must do this within a month. If the solicitor refuses to reduce the fee, you can ask him or her to get a certificate from the Law Society stating that in their opinion the sum charged is 'fair and reasonable'. If they suggest a lower fee, you will only have to pay that. You can also ask for the bill to be 'taxed'. This means it will be checked by a court official who may reduce it.

Complaints against lawyers

The legal profession in this country is rigidly divided into two branches: barristers and solicitors. There are 3,646 practising barristers in England and Wales and about 30,000 solicitors. Barristers usually act as advocates which means they represent people (mainly in the higher courts). Solicitors provide advice and legal assistance and they often represent clients in the lower courts (see p. 490). The training and conduct of solicitors and barristers is governed by their professional associations: the Law Society for solicitors and the Senate of the Inns of Court and the Bar for barristers.

These two bodies investigate complaints against their members if it is alleged that they have broken any professional rules. *They do not deal with complaints of negligence.* Negligence means that a lawyer has been careless or has not handled your case as cleverly as he or she might have done. The only remedy in such cases is to sue the lawyer for negligence in a civil court. It would be necessary to get legal assistance to pursue such a case. You would need to prove that you had suffered because of the lawyer's negligent action. Nearly all lawyers are insured against

being sued for negligence so they can pay any damages that might be awarded to you.

Solicitors

THE LAW SOCIETY

You may make a complaint to the Law Society about your solicitor if he or she:

– has persistently delayed answering letters;
– has not accounted for money held on your behalf;
– has breached confidentiality by telling someone else about your case;
– has acted for another client whose interests conflict with yours;
– has taken advantage of your age or inexperience;
– has overcharged;
– has acted dishonestly;
– has offended against other professional rules.

To make a complaint write to the **Law Society, 113 Chancery Lane, London WC2**, setting out the reason for the complaint as clearly as possible. Keep a copy of your letter. You must say in your letter that you give the Law Society permission to show the letter to your solicitor for his or her comments. The Law Society will then investigate the complaint and this may involve examining the solicitor's accounts or even restricting his or her right to practice whilst the complaint is being investigated. If the complaint is upheld but is not very serious, the solicitor will merely be informed of this by the Law Society.

Solicitors' disciplinary tribunal

If the complaint is upheld and is more serious the Law Society may bring the solicitor before the solicitors' disciplinary tribunal. The tribunal, which is composed mainly of solicitors, may order a solicitor to pay a fine or stop practising as a solicitor. He or she could be struck off the register for good or for a period of years. The tribunal cannot order a solicitor to pay compensation to the client. It is possible to make a complaint about your solicitor direct to the disciplinary tribunal but you may have to pay all the costs if the application is rejected.

The Law Society cannot:

– give you legal advice directly;
– order your solicitor to hand over any papers if the costs have not been paid;
– compel a solicitor to act for you;
– recommend a solicitor by name;
– tell your solicitor how to work as long as professional rules are being obeyed;
– deal with allegations of negligence;
– collect private debts;
– investigate complaints about judges, magistrates or barristers.

THE LAY OBSERVER

If you make a complaint to the Law Society and are dissatisfied with the way in which they have dealt with it, you can have the matter reviewed by an official called the Lay Observer. This only applies if the matter occurred on or after 1 January 1975. The matter must be referred to the Lay Observer within three months of the notification of the Law Society's decision. Write to the **Lay Observer, Royal Courts of Justice, Strand, London WC2**, setting out the grounds of your complaint. *The Lay Observer is under a statutory duty to consider written complaints about the way in which the Law Society handled a complaint against a solicitor.* He does not consider the complaint itself. He makes a written report to the Law Society who may reconsider the matter. Most of those who wrote to the Lay Observer in the first year of his operation complained that the law was too slow, too expensive and too difficult to understand. He considered 140 complaints in 1975 but in only two did he disagree with the Law Society's decision and the solicitors concerned were told 'that their conduct was deprecated'. The Lay Observer cannot give legal advice, intervene in the proceedings or a decision of a court, express an opinion about a solicitor's charges, or consider the question of legal aid being granted or refused.

Barristers

You can make a complaint to the Senate of the Inns of Court and the Bar about your barrister if he or she:

- has disregarded your instructions;
- has taken instructions from someone other than a solicitor;
- has acted for another client whose interests conflict with yours;
- has touted or advertised for business;
- has breached the professional rules in some other way.

To make a complaint write to the **Secretary of the Senate of the Inns of Court and the Bar, 11 South Square, Grays Inn Road, London, WC1**. Your letter will be referred to a member of the professional conduct committee who considers and investigates the complaint and then presents the matter to the full committee. The committee then decides whether to dismiss the complaint, to admonish the barrister, or to bring the case before the barristers' disciplinary tribunal. If the complaint is upheld by the tribunal, it may order that the barrister be disbarred, suspended for a period, reprimanded or ordered to return or forego fees. A barrister who has been convicted by the tribunal can appeal to a panel of High Court judges.

The Senate of the Inns of Court and the Bar will not deal with complaints concerning administration associated with the case, the way a barrister conducts a case in court, the cost of the case, the length of time the case has taken, or the fact that the client lost the case because of the inefficiency of the barrister.

In the year ending 31 March 1976, 116 complaints against barristers were considered. Of those seventy were rejected and twelve were referred to the disciplinary tribunal. Two barristers were reprimanded and one disbarred.

Law centres

For information about law centres, see p. 490.

In September 1976 the following law centres were in operation:

BALHAM NEIGHBOURHOOD LAW CENTRE
92 Balham High Road,   Mon, Tues, Thurs 10.30–5.30
London SW12   Mon & Wed 7–9
01-673 8602   Sat 10.30–1
                          24-hour emergency service

Only covers the Balham, Bedford and Nightingale wards of Wandsworth, except for emergency illegal evictions and battered wife cases, where the whole of Wandsworth is covered.

BIRMINGHAM: HANDSWORTH LAW CENTRE
102 Homstead Road,
Handsworth
(021-554 7553)

BIRMINGHAM: SALTLEY ACTION CENTRE
2 Alum Rock Road,
Saltley
(021-328 2307)

BIRMINGHAM: SMALL HEATH COMMUNITY LAW CENTRE
477 Coventry Road,   (No opening arrangements or
Birmingham 10   telephone yet.)

BRENT COMMUNITY LAW CENTRE

161 Church Road,
London NW10
01-451 1122

Advice sessions: Tues 5–6.30
Thurs 5.30–8
Other times by appointment

Restricted to residents of Brent.

CAMDEN COMMUNITY LAW CENTRE

146 Kentish Town Road,
London NW1
01-485 6672

Mon & Wed 10–9
Tues & Fri 10–6
Thurs & Sat 10–1
24-hour emergency service

CAMDEN: WEST HAMPSTEAD COMMUNITY LAW CENTRE

6 Midland Parade,
West End Lane,
London NW6
01-328 4501
24-hour emergency service

Tues 6–8 at Housing Aid Centre,
West End Lane
Wed 7–9 at 60 Mill Lane
Thurs 11.30–1 at 61 Kingsgate
Road, NW6
Sat 10–1 at 6 Midland Parade

CARDIFF: ADAMSDOWN COMMUNITY TRUST

103–4 Clifton Street
Adamsdown, Cardiff
0222-498117

Mon–Fri 9–6

COVENTRY: HILLFIELDS INFORMATION AND OPINION CENTRE

31 Primrose Hill
Hillfields
Coventry

(For further details contact
Coventry Legal & Income Rights
Service, 62 Lower Ford Street,
Coventry 0203-23051.)

HACKNEY ADVICE BUREAU AND LAW CENTRE

236–8 Mare Street,
London E8
01-986 8446

Mon–Fri 9.30–5.30
Mon & Thurs open until 8

Clients are seen initially by citizens' advice or consumer advice unit if they call in. Otherwise by appointment.

HILLINGDON COMMUNITY LAW CENTRE
63 Station Road,   Mon–Fri open for making
Hayes,   appointments
Middlesex   9.30–5.30
01-573 4021   Clients seen by appointment
                                    2–5.30

Clients must live or work in Hillingdon.

HOLLOWAY LAW CENTRE
c/o Martin Luther King Centre
Sheringham Road
London N7
(01-607 2524)

ISLINGTON COMMUNITY LAW CENTRE
161 Hornsey Road,   Mon, Wed, Fri 10–6
London N7   Tues 10–1 & 7–8.30
01-607 2461   Thurs 10–6
                                    Sat 11–1
                                    24-hour emergency service

LAMBETH LAW CENTRE
506–8 Brixton Road,   Mon–Fri 9.30–5.30
London SW9   24-hour emergency service
01-733 4245   Appointments preferred

LIVERPOOL: VAUXHALL LAW AND INFORMATION CENTRE
Silvester Street,   Information officers at the centre
Liverpool 5   screen clients before referring
051-207 2004   them to the solicitors at the centre.

MANCHESTER LAW CENTRE
595 Stockport Road,   Mon–Fri 10–6 (except Wed pm)
Longsight,   Mon & Thurs 7–9 also
Manchester 12
061-225 5111

Restricted to residents of City of Manchester, *not* Greater Manchester.

NEWCASTLE-UPON-TYNE: BENWELL COMMUNITY LAW
PROJECT
85 Adelaide Terrace,
Benwell
(0632-31210)

NEWHAM RIGHTS CENTRE
309 Barking Road,   Mon–Fri 9–6 by appointment or
East Ham,   telephone
London E6   *Advice Centres:*
01-471 8226   Tues 6.30–7.30
                           St Francis's Church (basement)
                           Grove Crescent Road, Stratford
                           E15
                           Thurs 6.30–7.30
                           Congregationalist-Methodist
                           Church, Wakefield Street, East
                           Ham E6

No appointments needed for advice centres. Restricted to London Borough of Newham (E6, E7, E12, E13, E15).

NORTH KENSINGTON NEIGHBOURHOOD LAW CENTRE
74 Golborne Road,   Mon, Wed, Thurs 9.30–9.30
London W10   Tues & Fri 9.30–6
01-969 7473   Appointments necessary for
                           evenings
                           24-hour emergency service

PADDINGTON NEIGHBOURHOOD ADVICE BUREAU AND
LAW CENTRE
465 Harrow Road,   *Law Centre:*
London W10   by appointment only, except for
01-969 9425   emergencies
                           Advice Centre:
                           Mon 10–1
                           Tues 10–4 & 6.30–8
                           Wed 1–4 & 6.30–8
                           Thurs 10–1 & 6.30–8
                           Fri 10–4

SOUTHWARK: ADVICE CENTRE IN THE BLUE
190–92 Southwark Park Road,
London SE15

SOUTHWARK: EAST DULWICH CENTRE
Lordship Lane,
London SE22

SOUTH WALES ANTI-POVERTY ACTION COMMITTEE
Bethesda Chapel,
Bethesda Street,
Merthyr Tydfil
0865-6252

TOTTENHAM NEIGHBOURHOOD LAW CENTRE
13 Portland Road,   Mon–Fri 10–6
London N15   Open-door policy for advice.
01-802 0911/2

TOWER HAMLETS NEIGHBOURHOOD LAW CENTRE
341 Commercial Road,   Mon 10–1
London E1   Tues 7–9 by appointment
01-790 6311   Fri 2–6
                           24-hour emergency service

WANDSWORTH: GARRATT LANE LAW CENTRE
170 Garratt Lane,
London SW18
01-870 7389

Solicitors in citizens' advice bureaux

Increasingly, organizations other than law centres are employing
salaried solicitors to advise clients and provide a back-up service
for lay advisors.

BIRMINGHAM CITIZENS' ADVICE BUREAU
Dr Johnson House, Colmore Circus,
Birmingham B4
021-236 0864/5

LEWISHAM
2 Lewisham Way,
London SE14
01-692 0057

NORTH KENSINGTON INFORMATION AND AID CENTRE
140 Ladbroke Grove,
London W10
01-969 2433

NOTTINGHAM
2 St James Terrace
Nottingham
0602-411792

WALTHAM FOREST
167 Hoe Street,
Walthamstow E17
01-520 0939

26. Complaints against government, public authorities and the professions

This chapter deals with complaints against:

– national and local government, p. 513
– public authorities, p. 518
– the professions, p. 523

Complaints against the police are dealt with in Chapter 1 (see p. 64); complaints against the NHS and the medical profession and other medical workers are dealt with on p. 473; complaints against businesses are dealt with on p. 226; and complaints against lawyers are dealt with on p. 503.

National and local government

This section describes the different procedures for making a complaint against national government; local government; and the public authorities which provide energy (e.g. gas and electricity), transport and communications.

In general, if you have a complaint about the way in which one of these bodies has treated you, or the facilities or services it provides, you should firstly complain direct to the body concerned. If you are not sure who exactly to complain to, consult the citizens' advice bureau for your area. It is best, if possible, to complain in writing and you should always keep a copy of your letter and the replies you receive.

If you are not satisfied with the reply you get, then you should use one of the procedures set out below. But many of the procedures are inadequate and bureaucratic. They are not always well advertised, and there are considerable differences in how easy it is to have a complaint investigated, how independent the complaints body is, and how effective the body is in remedying people's grievances.

These complaints procedures are not designed to change the *policy* of the department or authority concerned. Many people make complaints about things which are policy, and are disappointed when the complaint is rejected. In such cases, only a change of policy will make any difference, and that will only be achieved if enough people draw attention to the problem.

Central government

If you have a complaint about any action affecting you taken by a government department, you should first of all complain directly to the department itself. Keep a copy of your letter, and give them a reasonable time (at least a month) to reply.

In some cases you will have a right to appeal to a tribunal, as described on p. 259.

If you are dissatisfied with their reply, but do not have a right to appeal to a tribunal, you should consider making a complaint to the Ombudsman (whose full title is the Parliamentary Commissioner for Administration).

THE OMBUDSMAN

The Ombudsman's job is to investigate whether or not a government department has carried out the law properly. He cannot investigate whether or not the law itself is fair. So any report he makes will only concern the way in which the job has been carried out.

Although most government departments can be investigated by the Ombudsman, there are a number of areas which the Ombudsman cannot deal with. The Ombudsman cannot deal with any of the following matters:

– a complaint which you have made to a tribunal, or which should have been made to a tribunal (e.g. a supplementary benefits complaint which could have been dealt with by a supplementary benefits appeals tribunal);

- a complaint which you have taken to court;
- any complaint relating to local government (see p. 516 for information about the Local Government Ombudsman); the health services (see p. 479 for information about the Health Services Ombudsman); the police, the armed forces or foreign affairs; government contracts; government authorized action taken to investigate crime or protect state security.

In order to complain to the Ombudsman, you must write to an MP who must ask the Ombudsman to investigate your complaint. The MP need not necessarily be your own MP. You should send the MP the following information:

- your full name and address;
- the name of the department you are complaining about;
- a statement giving your consent to an investigation by the Ombudsman;
- the basic facts of your complaint.

You do not need to include every detail of your complaint in the letter to the MP. If the Ombudsman decides to investigate, you should have a chance to go into the details later.

You must make your complaint within *twelve months* of when the action you are complaining about happened.

You can apply for legal assistance under the green-form scheme (see p. 494), to help you prepare your case for the Ombudsman. But in most cases you shouldn't need a lawyer to represent you during the investigation. If you do have to take time off work, or pay any costs (e.g. travelling) in order to be interviewed by the Ombudsman, you should ask the Ombudsman to pay your expenses and compensation for loss of earnings.

The address of the Ombudsman is: **Parliamentary Commissioner for Administration, Church House, Great Smith Street, London SW1 (01-212 7676).** You can get a free leaflet from this address, giving more information about the Ombudsman's powers.

Once the Ombudsman has investigated your complaint, by interviewing you and officials from the department and any other people involved, he will prepare a report. If the Ombudsman decides to uphold your complaint, he can make *recommendations* about what action the department should take. But he has no power to force the department to implement those recommendations. It is important, therefore, to follow up the Ombudsman's report by contacting your MP, writing to the Minister concerned, and asking your local newspaper to publicise the case.

Local government

If you have a complaint about any action affecting you taken by the local authority, you should first of all complain to the local authority department involved (e.g. social services department, housing department). Make your complaint in writing, and keep a copy of your letter. Give them reasonable time (say, one month) in which to reply.

If you are not satisfied with the reply, or you get no reply within a reasonable period, complain to your local councillor. If you don't know who your local councillor is, ask at the local public library, or contact the Conservative, Liberal or Labour party in your area (address in the telephone directory).

Most local authorities do not have their own internal complaints procedures, so the way your complaint will be handled will depend on the way that local authority works. But if you are not satisfied with the result, you can then complain to the Local Government Ombudsman (whose formal title is the Commissioner for Local Administration). There are separate Commissioners for England and Wales, for Scotland and for Northern Ireland. (Addresses on p. 517.)

THE LOCAL GOVERNMENT OMBUDSMAN

The Local Government Ombudsman can investigate all local authorities except parish councils, and also all water authorities and police authorities. The Ombudsman will not investigate the following:

- local authority policy on rates and charges (e.g. charges for home-help services);

– some educational matters, such as the internal conduct of schools, or the quality of teaching.

Like the national Ombudsman, the local Ombudsman can only investigate the *way* in which a matter has been handled, and not the merits of the decision itself.

If you are not sure whether your complaint is something that the Ombudsman can deal with you should make the complaint anyway. It is up to the Ombudsman to decide whether or not he can deal with your complaint, and he generally takes a broad view of his powers.

In order to make a complaint, you must ask your local councillor to refer your written complaint to the Ombudsman. If the councillor refuses to do this, you can then write direct to the Ombudsman.

If the Ombudsman decides that your complaint falls within his powers, he will carry out an investigation. If you need to be represented by a lawyer during the investigation, your costs can be paid, but the Ombudsman prefers to keep investigations as informal as possible. When the investigation is completed, the Ombudsman will then make a report of the findings which will be sent to you. But the Ombudsman has no power to force the local authority to obey his recommendations, so it is important for you to follow up the report by contacting your local councillor and the local press.

The addresses of the Ombudsman are as follows:

– Commission for Local Administration in England, 21 Queen Anne's Gate, London SW1 (01-930 3333).
– Commission for Local Administration in Wales, Derwen House, Court Road, Bridgend, Mid Glamorgan (0656-61325/6).
– Northern Ireland Parliamentary Commissioner for Administration, and Commissioner for Complaints, River House, 48 High Street, Belfast (Belfast 33821).
– Commission for Local Administration in Scotland, 125 Princes Street, Edinburgh (031-226 2823).

You can obtain a free leaflet from each of these bodies, giving more detailed information about how to make a complaint.

Public authorities

Energy

This section deals with the public authorities which supply gas, electricity, water and coal.

If you want to complain about the supply, service or appliances of any of these, you should go direct to the local showroom or office. If the matter is not put right, you should use the formal complaints procedure described below.

GAS

You should write to the local Gas Consumers' Council, which is an independent body. There is a council in each area covered by a gas board, and you can find the address in the telephone directory. The council will refer the complaint to the board to see if the matter can be sorted out. If this does not work, the consumers' council, will itself consider the complaint.

If you are not satisfied with the action of the consumers' council, you should write to the **Secretary of State for Energy, Department of Energy, Thames House S, Millbank, London SW1.**

ELECTRICITY

You should write to the local Electricity Consultative Council, which is an independent body. There is a council in each area covered by an electricity board, and you can find the address in the telephone directory. Different consultative councils have different procedures for handling complaints, but most will try to solve a complaint by informally negotiating with the board at local level. If you are still not satisfied, you should write to the **National Electricity Council, 30 Millbank, London SW1.** If this does not solve the problem, write to the Secretary of State for Energy (address above).

WATER

If you have a complaint concerning the local water authority, you should take it up with the local Ombudsman (see p. 516). The Ombudsman can investigate complaints against water authorities, unless your complaint is about the level of charges for water.

COAL

If you have a complaint about your supply of coal, you should complain first of all to the coal merchant. If this does not work, you should write to the local panel of the Approved Coal Merchants Scheme, which will investigate your complaint. You can get the address from the **Approved Coal Merchants Scheme, 2 Turnpin Lane, London, SE10.**

If this is not satisfactory, write to the **Domestic Coal Consumers' Council, Thames House S, Millbank, London SW1.**

Transport

This section deals with complaints against British Rail and state-controlled freight haulage, water- and air-transport authorities.

RAILWAYS

If you have a complaint about rail services or British Rail shipping services, you should write to the divisional manager for the relevant British Rail area. You will find the address in the telephone directory, or you can get it from the local library or citizens' advice bureau. If your complaint is not dealt with satisfactorily, you should write to the local Transport Users' Consultative Committee which is an independent body. There are eleven of these committees covering Great Britain, and you can get the address from the telephone directory, public library or citizens' advice bureau.

The consultative committee will try to reach a settlement with

British Rail. If they do not succeed, and they decide to uphold your complaint, they can ask the Central Transport Consultative Committee to take the matter up with the Secretary of State for the Environment. He can direct British Rail to carry out the consultative committee's recommendation.

If you want to complain about a proposal to withdraw a particular rail service, you should write direct to the local Transport Users' Consultative Committee, without writing first to British Rail.

PORTS

If you have a complaint about the services in a particular port, you should write to the Port Users' Consultative Committee. You will find the address in the telephone directory covering that area. If the committee cannot deal with your complaint to your satisfaction, you should write to the Transport Users' Consultative Committee for the area (see above).

NATIONAL FREIGHT CORPORATION

If you have a complaint against the National Freight Corporation (which includes British Road Services and National Carriers), you should write to the local Transport Users' Consultative Committee (see above on 'Railways').

WATERWAYS

There is no formal complaints procedure for the British Waterways Board. Other than by taking civil action in the courts (see pp. 246–58 for a description of what this involves), the best way of making a complaint is to write direct to the **British Waterways Board, Melbury House, Melbury Terrace, London NW1.**

If this does not produce a satisfactory result, write to the **Inland Waterways Amenity Advisory Council, 122 Cleveland Street, London W1.**

NATIONAL BUS COMPANY

There is no formal complaints procedure for the National Bus Company or its subsidiary companies, the local bus companies. Apart from taking civil action in the courts (see p. 246), the best way of making a complaint is to write to the managing director of the company involved. If this is not satisfactory, write to the Traffic Commissioners for the area (address in the telephone directory).

LONDON TRANSPORT

Bus and underground services within London are the responsibility of London Transport; Green Line buses come under the National Bus Company (see above). If you have a complaint about London Transport, you should write direct to **London Transport, 55 Broadway, London SW1**.

If this is not satisfactory, write to the **London Transport Passengers' Committee, Room 33, 26 Old Queen Street, London SW1**.

Dear London Transport, you have taken me for a ride...

Communications

This section deals with complaints against the Post Office, the BBC, independent radio and television companies and the press. Except in the case of the Post Office, there are no formal, statutory complaint procedures for any of these bodies.

POST OFFICE

If you have a complaint about the postal service, telephone or other telecommunications service or the Giro, first write direct to the post office or post office department concerned (address in the telephone directory). If this is not satisfactory, write to the **Post Office Users' National Council, Waterloo Bridge House, Waterloo Road, London SE1**. The council has the power to arrange for a full investigation of your complaint.

General complaints about services can also be directed to the local Post Office Advisory Committee, but these committees do not handle individual complaints. The address of these committees can be obtained from the local post office.

BBC

If you have a general complaint about a BBC programme or about programme policy, you should complain direct to the **BBC, Broadcasting House, Portland Place, London W1**.

If you believe that you personally have been unjustly or unfairly treated in a programme, you should write *within thirty days* of when the programme went out, to the **BBC Programme Complaints Commission, 31 Queen Anne's Gate, London SW1**. When you do this, you have to give a written undertaking not to pursue your complaint through the courts. If the Commission decides that your complaint falls within their powers, they will conduct a thorough investigation, and the results will be broadcast and published in the *Listener*.

INDEPENDENT RADIO AND TELEVISION

If you have a complaint about any programme which appears on a commercial radio or television station, you should first of all contact the station concerned. If you are dissatisfied with their answer, you should write to the **Independent Broadcasting Authority, 70 Brompton Road, London SW3.** If their reply is unsatisfactory, you should write again, asking them to refer the complaint to the Complaints Review Board. The board will investigate your complaint in detail and report back to the IBA, which will write to you.

THE PRESS

The easiest way to complain about an article in a newspaper is to write to the editor. If you do not want your letter considered for publication, you should mark it clearly 'not for publication'. If you are not satisfied with the editor's response, you can complain to the **Press Council, 1 Salisbury Square, London EC4.** You must make your complaint within three months. You should send the Press Council:

– a full statement of your complaint;
– copies of any correspondence about the article;
– a copy of the page of the newspaper containing the article.

The Press Council will investigate your complaint, and may ask you to attend a hearing. Neither you nor the newspaper can be legally represented, but the council will pay your expenses. A statement of the council's findings will be sent to you, and will normally be issued to the press. The Press Council has no legal status, but is a voluntary body established by the newspaper industry itself. Experience has shown that it is conservative in its findings.

The professions

Complaints against the medical profession are dealt with in Chapter 23; complaints against lawyers are dealt with in Chapter 25.

There are a number of professional bodies which can deal with complaints against their own members. Each body has its own complex set of rules. The general pattern is that there is an investigation or practice committee, which will investigate a complaint, see whether the matter can be amicably resolved and, if not, decide whether or not to refer the case to a disciplinary committee.

Professional bodies will usually *not* deal with complaints of professional negligence, which can be dealt with by means of a court action (see pp. 482–3 for a description of what this involves). Furthermore, they will not deal with a complaint that you have been over-charged, although they may sometimes negotiate or arbitrate in a dispute over fees.

The disciplinary committees consist of other members of the profession. They do not include lay members, and they usually meet in private. The person you are complaining against has the right to be represented by a lawyer, but you do not. The case will instead be presented by the investigation committee. Disciplinary committees have a number of penalties at their disposal, but usually cannot award compensation to a successful complainant. The most severe penalty is to stop the guilty party from describing or representing him or herself as a member of that particular body. For example, although anyone can call themselves an 'accountant', the Institute of Chartered Accountants can prevent someone describing himself as a 'chartered accountant'. In most cases, the person complained about has a right to appeal against the findings of the disciplinary committee, but neither the investigation committee nor the complainant has a right of appeal.

If you want further information, or wish to make a complaint, you should write to the appropriate address given below.

Actuaries
Secretary, Institute of Actuaries, Staple Inn Hall, High Holborn, London WC1.

Architects
Secretary, Royal Institute of British Architects, 66 Portland Place, London W1.

Certified Accountants
Secretary, Association of Certified Accountants, 22 Bedford Square, London WC1.

Chartered Accountants
Secretary, Institute of Chartered Accountants in England and Wales, PO Box 433, Chartered Accountants' Hall, Moorgate Place, London EC2.

Chartered Insurers
Secretary General, Chartered Insurance Institute, 20 Aldermanbury, London EC2.

Chartered Surveyors
Secretary, Royal Institution of Chartered Surveyors, 29 Lincoln's Inn Fields, London WC2.

Cost and Management Accountants
Secretary, Institute of Cost and Management Accountants, 63 Portland Place, London W1.

Incorporated Architects and Surveyors
Secretary, Incorporated Association of Architects and Surveyors, 29 Belgrave Square, London SW1.

Quantity Surveyors
Secretary, Institute of Quantity Surveyors, 98 Gloucester Place, London W1.

Valuers and Auctioneers
Secretary, Incorporated Society of Valuers and Auctioneers, 3 Cadogan Gate, London SW1.

27. Northern Ireland

This chapter deals with:

In 1972, the Government suspended the Stormont Parliament, which had been responsible for much of the legislation in Northern Ireland since partition, and imposed direct rule from Westminster. Despite direct rule, however, there are a number of crucial differences between the law in Northern Ireland, and the law in England and Wales. The Northern Ireland (Emergency Provisions) Act 1973, which is described in the first part of this chapter, does not apply in the rest of the UK. Many British laws, such as the Race Relations Act, either do not apply in Northern Ireland or have special equivalents. It is impossible to give a comprehensive guide to Northern Ireland law here: an entire book is needed. But this chapter highlights the most important differences.

Emergency powers

The most important legislation affecting Northern Ireland is the Northern Ireland (Emergency Provisions) Act 1973, which replaced the earlier Special Powers Acts of 1922 and 1933. Under the Emergency Provisions Act, the Army and police have special powers to question and arrest people, and to search people and premises.

Questioning

If you are questioned by a member of the security forces (i.e. a soldier on duty or a police officer) *you must answer questions about your identity and movements.* It is an offence to refuse or fail to answer to the best of your knowledge (penalty is £100 fine and/or six months in prison). This applies whether you are questioned at home or in the street.

NCCL's view of the law is that questions about your movements are restricted as follows: if you are at home, you should say how long you have been there; if you are stopped on the street, you need only say where you have come from and where you are going. (You do not have to answer questions about where you were last night or last week.)

You must also tell the security forces *anything you know about recent explosions or any incident endangering life,* or any person killed in an incident or explosion. Make the questioner be as specific as possible. Do not repeat rumours or what you have read in the newspaper. You should answer only what you know from your own personal knowledge to be a fact. When in doubt, say, 'I don't know.'

You do *not* have to do any of the following:

- fill in army 'census' forms. The Army Headquarters in Lisburn has denied authorizing any census and you should contact your local advice centre if you learn that a census is being conducted in your area;
- allow the security forces to photograph you or your family;
- give the security forces the names and ages of your children, except to identify them if they are present;
- give the Army photographs or other information about your family;
- answer general questions about your house or its occupants, like 'What colour is the wallpaper?' etc.
- answer questions about your religion.

Arrest

The Emergency Provisions Act gives the security forces special powers to arrest suspects. In particular:

1. If you are arrested as a suspected terrorist, you may be detained for up to seventy-two hours. You must also submit to being

photographed and having your palm and finger prints taken, even before you are charged. (Section 10.)

2. If you are arrested for any other reason (except under the Prevention of Terrorism Act, see p. 534) you must be charged with a criminal offence and brought before a magistrate within forty-eight hours, or released. The police do *not* have the right to photograph or fingerprint you without your consent before you are charged.

You should ask the security forces under what power they are arresting you. The police must tell you the reasons for the arrest, but a soldier need only identify himself as a member of Her Majesty's forces. The Army can only detain you for four hours: after that, they must either release you or hand you over to the Royal Ulster Constabulary (RUC) or military police for the remainder of the detention period.

QUESTIONING AFTER ARREST

If you are arrested, you must answer questions about:

- your identity (name and address);
- your recent movements, i.e. where you have come from and where you were going when you were arrested;
- recent explosions or other incidents. Ask the questioner to be as specific as possible and unless you know anything as a fact from your own personal knowledge, say, 'I don't know anything about it.' Do not repeat rumours or gossip.

Otherwise, you have the right to remain silent and you are under no legal obligation to answer any questions.

WHAT YOU SHOULD DO IF ARRESTED

If you are arrested, you should:

- try to make sure that someone in your family or a friend contacts your local community leader, a solicitor or your local advice centre as soon as possible;
- ask for a solicitor. If possible, name a specific solicitor and

give the address. Every arrested person has the right to consult a solicitor before making a statement or answering any questions, except on the subjects listed above;

– see a doctor immediately you are released if you have been ill-treated. Even if your injuries seem minor, it is important that a record should be made, both for a possible claim for damages and for your own future protection;
– after your release, contact your local advice centre. It is important for them to have a record of every arrest, to help prevent harassment.

You should *not*:

– sign any document. You do not have to sign any kind of medical certificate before being released;
– believe everything the security forces tell you. Although it is difficult to avoid giving in to promises or harassment, it is better in the long run not to say anything you do not want to say.

Searches

A member of the Army or the RUC can stop and search you for arms, ammunition or explosives in any public place. If you are at home, the person searching you must have reason to suspect that you possess arms or explosives.

The security forces may search your home if:

– the search is authorized by a commissioned officer of the Army or an RUC officer of the rank of chief inspector or above;
– they have reason to suspect that there may be arms or explosives in your house; *or*
– they are searching for a person who they have reason to believe is unlawfully detained and in danger in your house.

In either case you should ask under what authority the search is being conducted.

Under the Emergency Provisions Act, the security forces can only search for people or munitions (arms, explosives, etc.). They have no right to go through private papers, books, etc. without a

I've found one of the Little People!

warrant. If they are looking for a person, they have no right to search places which are too small for someone to hide (e.g. drawers).

If the security forces search your home, you should:

– accompany them during the search. Do not give the Army or police any chance to leave anything behind or take anything without your knowledge;

– insist that any damages done or items taken are listed in writing on a sheet provided by them. You should sign this sheet. If you are not sure that everything has been listed, or you could not be with every soldier all the time, sign the sheet 'with reservations'. If you are not happy with the official list, make your own complete list as soon as possible and contact your local advice centre or a solicitor, who will forward a copy of the list to the authorities. Compensation should be paid for all damage caused by the security forces. (If no damage is done and nothing is taken, you do not have to sign any form.)

– make a record of any conversation or search as soon as possible afterwards, as you may want to use it later in evidence.

The security forces also have the right to *enter your home* if they consider it necessary in the course of their operations. But this does *not* allow them to search the house or question the inhabitants except in the circumstances outlined above.

Detention without trial (internment)

The Secretary of State for Northern Ireland has the power to detain suspected terrorists without trial. This power has not been used since December 1975, but it remains in existence.

Banned organizations

Under the Emergency Provisions Act, there are five proscribed organizations: the Irish Republican Army, the Cumann na mBan (women's section of the IRA), Fianna Eireann (junior section of the IRA), Saor Eire and the Ulster Volunteer Force. (Sinn Fein is no longer a proscribed organization.)

It is an offence to belong to, profess to belong to, solicit or invite financial or other support or make or receive any financial or other contribution for, a proscribed organization. The maximum penalties for any of these activities are: in the magistrates' court, six months' imprisonment and/or a £400 fine; in the Crown Court: five years' imprisonment and/or an unlimited fine.

Troops

The *Manual of Military Law* states:

When called to the aid of the civil power soldiers in no way differ in the eyes of the law from any other citizens; although, by reason of their organization and equipment, there is always a danger that their employment in aid of the civil power may in itself constitute more force than is necessary.

The law is clear that a soldier must come to the assistance of the civil authority where it is necessary for him to do so, but not otherwise. No excessive force or display must be used, and a soldier is guilty of an offence if he uses that excess, even under the direction of the civil authority, unless the circumstances are such that he has no opportunity of ascertaining and judging the facts of the case himself and is therefore compelled to accept the opinion and appraisal of the situation of the civil authority concerned.

There is, however, considerable uncertainty about the extent of the power of the civil authority to summon troops to its aid. The power to call in the Army rested under common law in the Commissioner of the Metropolitan Police, magistrates in the counties, and mayors in the cities – all of whom are JPs. In April 1974, however, the office of JP was taken away from the mayors and the Commissioner of the Metropolitan Police (Administration of Justice Act 1973). Since then, both the Home Office and the Ministry of Defence have stated that the police, rather than the magistrates, are the civil authority who can in practice call on the military for assistance. Furthermore, Roy Jenkins MP, when Home Secretary, announced that the Home Secretary has the power himself to call in the military, although Parliament has passed no law enacting such a power. The Home Secretary did not quote any common law authority for his statement, but was presumably relying on the Crown's residual legal power to direct the disposition and use of the armed forces – a prerogative whose exact limits are far from clear.

In Northern Ireland, of course, the Army is in a different position – although until 1972, the legal basis for its operations was thoroughly doubtful. Under the Government of Ireland Act 1920, the Stormont Parliament had no right to legislate on the armed forces. Nonetheless, it made regulations conferring special powers on the armed forces, unrestrained by the Westminster Government, even though lawyers consistently pointed out that Stormont and the Army in Northern Ireland were acting unlawfully. In February 1972, the divisional court in Northern Ireland ruled that the Army had had no lawful right to arrest John Hume, a Stormont MP and civil rights leader. Faced with the prospect that the courts would rule unlawful much of the Army's activity in Northern Ireland, the Government was forced to produce a Bill – which was rushed through Parliament in seven hours – conferring on Stormont the right to legislate for the power of the armed forces, and legalizing its activities over the previous fifty years.

Use of Firearms

Soldiers serving in Northern Ireland are issued with a copy of a document called the 'Yellow Card'. The Yellow Card sets out the Ministry of Defence's views as to when soldiers are and are not allowed to open fire, and also contains operational instructions for soldiers.

It would be very useful if it were possible to reproduce the Yellow Card in this book. That would make clear to members of the public precisely what powers soldiers have to open fire, could save a lot of misunderstanding and could even help to save lives. It would also enable civilians to tell whether individual soldiers had exceeded their instructions, and if so, then to complain to the local army authorities who could be asked to take action against the soldiers involved.

However, the Yellow Card is a classified document and possession or publication of it could well be a breach of section 2 of the Official Secrets Act 1911 (see p. 327). The 'copyright' of the Yellow Card belongs to the Crown (acting through the Ministry of Defence) and that also means that it is not possible to reproduce the document without permission. The Ministry of Defence has actually refused permission for the Yellow Card to be reproduced in this book, despite the fact that it has often been referred to in the press and elsewhere. The use of the copyright laws in this way is another form of censorship (see Chapter 13).

However, certain principles governing the use of firearms by soldiers serving in Northern Ireland are clear. Whatever action is engaged in by the troops should involve no more than the minimum force necessary. For example, soldiers should fire at particular targets (e.g. particular people) and not fire arbitrarily (although sometimes automatic fire can be used if there is no danger to unarmed people). As a general rule, soldiers should not fire more rounds than are necessary.

Generally a clear warning should be given by soldiers before firing starts unless they or other people are under attack or are about to come under attack. In these exceptional cases a soldier can fire without giving a warning. Even after a warning, a soldier can only fire in particular circumstances, mainly if it is the only way to stop action likely to endanger life or limb, or to arrest somebody who has killed or seriously injured a soldier or someone else.

Despite a wide impression to the contrary, troops at a road block are not entitled to fire at a vehicle that refuses to stop unless the occupants of the vehicle are doing something to endanger life (such as throwing petrol bombs or firing from the car).

Despite the restrictions placed on soldiers, unarmed civilians have been killed on a number of occasions by the Army in Northern Ireland, and the courts have found it difficult to resolve the conflicting needs to ensure effective Army operations against terrorists, and provide judicial supervision of executive and military power in an emergency. The Attorney General for Northern Ireland in 1976 referred to the House of Lords the case of a soldier who shot and killed an unarmed civilian whom, the soldier claimed, he honestly – though wrongly – believed to be an IRA member. The soldier ordered the civilian to halt and when he did not do so he killed him. The trial judge found that the soldier fired because he believed that the man trying to escape *might* be a terrorist. The judge said that mere failure to halt did not justify opening fire, but that the situation in Northern Ireland and the possible presence of armed guerrillas had to be weighed against the death of an innocent man. The soldier's action was, however, clearly outside the scope permitted by the Yellow Card, which refers only to situations where the soldier is certain that someone has a firearm and is about to use it, or is otherwise taking or about to take offensive action – not to someone who has simply refused to halt and appears to be trying to escape.

Prevention of Terrorism Act 1976

The Prevention of Terrorism (Temporary Provisions) Act 1976 applies *throughout the UK*. It is based on the Prevention of Terrorism Act 1974 which was rushed through Parliament after the pub-bombings outrage in Birmingham in November 1974. The Act gives the police the power to arrest and question suspects and detain them for up to seven days; to search people and places; it also allows the Secretary of State to make an exclusion order removing someone from Great Britain or Northern Ireland (or in some cases, from the UK entirely); to ban terrorist organizations.

In Northern Ireland, therefore, the police (but not the Army) have special powers under the Prevention of Terrorism Act in addition to their powers under the Emergency Provisions Act, described in the previous section.

This section deals with the following provisions of the Act:

Arrest and questioning

Under the Prevention of Terrorism Act, a police officer can arrest you without a warrant if he has reason to suspect that:

– you belong to or support any section of the Provisional or Official IRA (see 'Banned organizations', p. 542); *or*
– you are subject to an exclusion order, or you have helped or harboured someone who is subject to an exclusion order; *or*
– you are concerned in the 'commission, preparation or instigation of acts of terrorism', whether or not these are concerned with affairs in Northern Ireland (see p. 539 for what this means); *or*
– you fail to disclose as soon as reasonably practicable information which might help prevent an act of terrorism or lead to the arrest, prosecution or conviction of a terrorist.

The police can detain you initially for up to forty-eight hours. You can then be held for a further five days with the consent of the Home Secretary or Secretary of State for Northern Ireland. During this time *the police do not have to charge you with an offence or take you before a magistrates' court.*

If you are arrested under the Prevention of Terrorism Act, the police have the right to *photograph* and *fingerprint* you, even if you do not consent. They can use 'reasonable force' if you refuse to cooperate.

In Northern Ireland, these powers are separate from the police powers under the Emergency Provisions Act. They can *either* arrest you under that Act as a suspected terrorist and detain you for up to seventy-two hours (see p. 527), *or* they can arrest you under the Prevention of Terrorism Act and hold you for up to seven days.

QUESTIONING AFTER THE ARREST

You have the right to remain silent when the police question you and refuse to answer until you have consulted a solicitor. But it is a criminal offence not to pass on information to the police (or in Northern Ireland, the Army) which you know or believe might be of material assistance to the police in:

– preventing an act of terrorism; *or*
– catching, prosecuting or obtaining a conviction against someone involved in terrorism;

The maximum penalty for failing to give information is a fine of £1,000 and/or six months' imprisonment in the magistrates' court, and an unlimited fine and/or five years' imprisonment in the Crown Court. The police can arrest you without a warrant if they reasonably suspect you of committing this offence. The Attorney General must give his consent before a prosecution can be brought.

At the time of writing this guide, no prosecutions had been brought against people for failing to give information, and it is therefore impossible to say in what circumstances the charge is likely to be brought.

DETENTION AT PORTS OF ENTRY

If you are entering or leaving Great Britain or Northern Ireland, you can be detained at a port or airport by an **examining officer**. The Secretary of State can appoint immigration officers and some customs and excise officers, in addition to police officers, as examining officers with powers of arrest and detention.

Examining officers can:

- arrest without a warrant anyone who appears to them to be concerned with terrorism;
- detain a person for up to seven days for questioning and for the Home Secretary to consider whether or not the person should be excluded;
- detain a person for a further five days *after* questioning is finished, if the Home Secretary consents (making a total maximum of twelve days' detention);
- require a person who is being questioned to produce a passport or other papers establishing nationality and identity, and to produce any other documents which the examining officer considers relevant;
- require someone travelling to or from Northern Ireland to complete an embarkation form;
- search any baggage and retain any article which they consider may be relevant in a court case or in consideration of an exclusion order.

It is an offence not to comply with the examining officer's directions; maximum penalty is a fine of £200 and/or three months' imprisonment.

WHAT TO DO IF YOU ARE ARRESTED UNDER THE PREVENTION OF TERRORISM ACT

If you are arrested under the Prevention of Terrorism Act, the police will almost certainly not allow you to contact family, friends or a lawyer. But you should ask them to tell someone in your family where you are being held. After you are released, you should contact the NCCL, which is monitoring the way the Act is working, or your local advice centre.

Searches

Under the Prevention of Terrorism Act, a police officer may stop you in the street and search you, without a warrant, in order to find out whether you have any documents or other articles on you which would be evidence of possible involvement in terrorism, support for a banned organization (i.e. the IRA at present) or breach of an exclusion order. If any such evidence is found, then the police officer can arrest you (see p. 535 for more on arrests).

If a policeman has a warrant to search any *premises* under the Prevention of Terrorism Act (see below), he can also search any person found on those premises.

SEARCH OF PREMISES

Under the Prevention of Terrorism Act, a senior police officer (superintendent or above) can sign a document authorizing a search if he considers the case is an emergency and immediate action is necessary 'in the interests of the state'. Otherwise, the police can apply to a magistrate for a search warrant in the usual way (see p. 31).

Any police officer, using these powers of search, can seize any documents or other articles which he has reasonable grounds for suspecting are evidence of an offence concerning a banned organization (see p. 542) or an exclusion order (see below). He can also seize anything which he reasonably suspects is evidence which would justify the Home Secretary (or Secretary of State for Northern Ireland) in banning an organization, or making an exclusion order against an individual.

Exclusion orders

In order to understand the way exclusion orders work, it is important to remember that the **United Kingdom** means Great Britain and Northern Ireland; **Great Britain** means England, Scotland and Wales.

Under the Prevention of Terrorism Act, any Secretary of State (usually the Home Secretary or the Secretary of State for Northern Ireland) can make an exclusion order against someone if:

– it appears to him expedient, in order to prevent acts of terrorism intended to influence government policy or public opinion with respect to Northern Ireland affairs; *and*

– he believes that the person is trying or may try to enter Great Britain or Northern Ireland, with a view to being concerned in the commission, preparation or instigation of acts of terrorism.

'Terrorism' is defined as the use of violence for political ends and includes any use of violence for the purpose of putting the public or a section of the public in fear. 'Commission, preparation or instigation' covers any involvement in terrorism – from planning, providing information or equipment, to actually taking part.

THE EFFECT OF AN EXCLUSION ORDER

The exact effect of an exclusion order depends on whether or not you are a citizen of the UK.

If you are a UK citizen

You cannot be excluded or banned from the UK completely. You can be excluded from Great Britain and sent to Northern Ireland unless:

– you are ordinarily resident in Great Britain and have been for the last twenty years (not counting any time in prison in the UK, Channel Isles or Isle of Man); *or*
– you were born in Great Britain and have been ordinarily resident there all your life; *or*
– you have already been excluded from Northern Ireland.

You can be excluded from Northern Ireland and sent to Great Britain unless:

– you are ordinarily resident in Northern Ireland and have been for the last twenty years (not counting time spent in prison); *or*
– you were born in Northern Ireland and have been ordinarily resident there all your life; *or*
– you have already been excluded from Great Britain.

If you want to object to an exclusion order on any of these grounds (see 'Making representations' below), it is up to you to prove your case.

The exclusion order means that you are prohibited from entering or being in either Great Britain or Northern Ireland (depending on which you are excluded from). If you are in Great Britain when an exclusion order banning you from Great Britain is served on you, you will be removed to Northern Ireland; the same applies, in reverse, if you are in Northern Ireland when an order is made banning you from there.

If you are not a UK citizen

You can be served with an exclusion order banning you from entering or being in part of the UK. If you are in the UK when the order is served on you, you will be sent back to the country with which you are most closely connected. It does not matter how long you have lived in the UK.

Once an exclusion order has been made against you, notice of the order must be served upon you, and you can be arrested without a warrant. The exclusion order notice must tell you your rights to make representations against the order.

MAKING REPRESENTATIONS AGAINST AN EXCLUSION ORDER

You have the right to:

- make representations against the exclusion order, provided you do so *within ninety-six hours* of when the notice is served on you; *and*
- request an oral hearing before a government-appointed adviser.

If your representations are not considered frivolous, they will be referred to the adviser and, if you asked for an interview and have not already left the country, you will be given an appointment with the adviser. The Secretary of State will then decide whether or not to cancel the order. You will be kept in custody at the police station until the final decision is made.

If the exclusion order is not cancelled when you make representations, it will last until the Secretary of State decides to cancel it.

If you are served with an exclusion order you have *no right* to:

– know the evidence on which the exclusion order was made or cross-examine witnesses;
– call witnesses to support your case;
– have a public or formal hearing of the representations, or appeal to a court;
– know why the representations were successful or not.

CRIMINAL OFFENCES RELATED TO EXCLUSION ORDERS

It is a criminal offence:
– not to obey an exclusion order once notice has been served;
– to help any person who you know, or ought to know, is subject to an exclusion order to enter the country against the order;
– to harbour a person who is subject to an exclusion order.

The police can arrest you without a warrant if they reasonably suspect you of committing one of these offences. The Attorney General must give his consent before you can be prosecuted. The maximum penalty is a fine of £1,000 and/or six months' imprisonment in the magistrates' court, or an unlimited fine and/or five years' imprisonment in the Crown Court.

WHAT TO DO IF YOU ARE SERVED WITH AN EXCLUSION ORDER

If you are served with an exclusion order in Great Britain, you should contact **NCCL, 186 Kings Cross Road, London WC1 (01-278 4575)** who can arrange for you to see a solicitor. It is also important for NCCL to have details of the case in order to monitor the way the Prevention of Terrorism Act is operating. If you need help outside office hours, contact **Release (01-603 8654)**. If you are in Northern Ireland, contact your local advice centre.

Although you will be kept in custody while your representations are being considered, it is worth making representations against an exclusion order, since a number of these orders have been cancelled as a result of representations. You should also consider appealing to the European Commission on Human Rights (described on p. 577); contact NCCL for advice and help.

Banned organizations

The Home Secretary or the Secretary of State for Northern Ireland has the power to proscribe any organization which appears to him to be concerned in or encouraging terrorism occurring in the United Kingdom and connected with Northern Irish affairs. At the time of writing, only the Irish Republican Army had been banned under the Prevention of Terrorism Act (see p. 531 for organizations which are banned in Northern Ireland but not in the rest of the UK).

It is a criminal offence to:

– belong to a proscribed organization;
– raise or receive money or goods on behalf of a proscribed organization;
– encourage any other form of support for a proscribed organization;
– organize a public or private meeting of more than two people in support of a proscribed organization;
– organize a public or private meeting addressed by a member of a proscribed organization, whether or not he is speaking about Northern Irish affairs.

The maximum penalty for any of these offences is a fine of £1,000 and/or six months' imprisonment in the magistrates' court, or an unlimited fine and/or five years' imprisonment in the Crown Court. The court may also order a convicted person to forfeit any money or goods held for a proscribed organization.

A person cannot be found guilty of membership of a proscribed organization, if all his activities in it took place before it was proscribed (November 1974, in the case of the IRA). The person charged has to prove this.

It is also a criminal offence to display, carry or wear in public anything which arouses a reasonable fear that you are a member or supporter of a proscribed organization, even if you are not. The maximum penalty is a fine of £1,000 and/or six months' imprisonment; the case can only be heard in the magistrates' court.

Other criminal offences

There are a number of other criminal offences relating to terrorism in the UK connected with Northern Irish affairs. It is an offence to:

- ask for a gift or loan which you intend will be used in connection with terrorism;
- receive or accept any money or goods which you intend to be used in connection with terrorism;
- give or lend or make available in any other way any money or goods if you know or suspect they will be used in connection with terrorism.

The maximum penalty is a fine of £1,000 and/or six months' imprisonment in the magistrates' court, or an unlimited fine and/or five years' imprisonment in the Crown Court. The court can also order the convicted person to forfeit any money or property held for use in connection with terrorism.

A person can be arrested without a warrant on suspicion of committing any of the offences listed above.

The Attorney General's consent is necessary before a prosecution can be brought.

Main differences in the law

This section is set out under the chapter headings used for the rest of this book. Under each heading, the major points of difference between the law in England and Wales, and the law in Northern Ireland, are given. For more information, contact one of the organizations listed on p. 584.

The powers of the police

The Emergency Provisions Act, which gives the security forces in Northern Ireland additional powers, is dealt with in the first section of this chapter (see p. 526).

The official procedure for making complaints against the police is similar to that in England and Wales, although there is a separate Police Complaints Board.

Your rights in the criminal courts

Following the Diplock Report in 1972, *jury trial* was suspended for specified terrorist offences. These cases are heard by a single judge.

COMPENSATION FOR CRIMINAL INJURIES

The system of compensation differs significantly in Northern Ireland from the rest of the UK (see p. 109).

Applications for compensation should be made with the assistance of a solicitor and should be sent to the Criminal Injuries Division of the Northern Ireland Office.

Compensation for damage to people is provided under the Criminal Injury (Compensation) Act (Northern Ireland) 1968 and compensation for damage to property is provided under the Criminal Injury to Property (Compensation) Act (Northern Ireland) 1971.

Applications are referred by the Northern Ireland Office to the courts, which decide in principle whether compensation should be paid. For personal injury, compensation is available to the victim or, in the case of death, to the victim's dependants. Compensation for damage to property is only paid if the damage was caused maliciously by an unlawful assembly (see p. 157) or by members of a proscribed organization.

If the court decides that compensation should be awarded, the Secretary of State assesses the amount. The applicant can appeal to the courts against the amount assessed.

The law is likely to be significantly amended during 1977.

Prisoners

Some prisoners convicted before March 1976 of 'political' offences have 'special category' status but this is not available to those convicted after March 1976.

The parole scheme for England and Wales does not apply in Northern Ireland but under the Treatment of Offenders (Northern Ireland) Act 1976 prisoners are entitled of remission under licence of up to 50 per cent of their sentence. A subsequent conviction renders the offender liable to serve the full remainder of the original sentence.

The authorities have a wide discretionary power to grant parole for public holidays and special family occasions.

Public order

Anyone who intends to organize a public procession must give written notice of the proposed time and route to a district inspector, head constable or sergeant of the RUC at least seventy-two hours before the procession is due to start. The RUC may impose conditions on the march, if there are reasonable grounds for suspecting that a breach of the peace or serious public disorder will result. The Secretary of State may make an order allowing one procession to take place, but banning all others in the same area for up to one month; alternatively, he may ban all processions for up to one year.

It is a criminal offence to:

- take part in a public procession, knowing that notice has not been given to the police;
- take part in a public procession knowing that it contravenes an order given by the RUC or the Secretary of State;
- use threatening, abusive or insulting words or behaviour or do anything with intent to provoke a breach of the peace at any public place, meeting or procession;
- break up a public procession;
- wilfully obstruct traffic or hinder any lawful activity by sitting, kneeling or lying down in a public place;
- trespass in a public meeting or interfere with any lawful

activity in a public building (i.e. any building owned, occupied or used by or on behalf of a government department, local or public authority, grant-aided school or further or higher education body).

It is also an offence to act in a disorderly manner in order to disrupt a lawful public meeting. If an officer of the RUC reasonably suspects anyone of committing such an offence, and the chairperson of the meeting asks him to do so, he may ask that person for his name and address. It is an offence to refuse to give this information or to give a false name and address. (Public Order Act (Northern Ireland) 1951, amended by the Public Order (Amendment) Act (Northern Ireland) 1970).

Sex

The Abortion Act 1967 and the Sexual Offences Act 1967 do not apply in Northern Ireland. Any homosexual act, even if it takes place between two consenting men aged over 21 and in private, is illegal.

The age of consent for girls is 17. If a man under 24 is charged with having illegal sexual intercourse with a girl under 17, it is not a defence for him to claim he thought she was 17 or over.

The worker and the law

As from 1 December 1976, the law relating to unfair dismissal, redundancy, equal pay, sex discrimination, etc. is the same as in England and Wales. Complaints under these laws will be heard mainly in industrial tribunals. The Equal Opportunities Commission for Northern Ireland will have the responsibility of overseeing the implementation of the equal pay and sex discrimination laws: **Equal Opportunities Commission, Lindsay House, Callendar Street, Belfast 1.**

The Fair Employment Act 1976 is designed to reduce discrimination on grounds of religion. It sets up the Fair Employment Agency which has a duty to promote manpower integration and will try to achieve the aims of the Act by the use of conciliation.

However, it does have the power to prosecute firms after receiving and investigating a written complaint of discrimination on grounds of religious or political beliefs. Until 1979 the Act will only apply to firms which have more than twenty-five employees.

The address of the Fair Employment Agency is: **Lindsay House, Callendar Street, Belfast 1.**

Race discrimination

The Race Relations Act 1976 does not apply in Northern Ireland. The Prevention of Incitement to Hatred Act (Northern Ireland) 1970 makes it an offence to publish 'threatening, abusive or insulting words with intent to stir up hatred or arouse fear of any section of the Northern Ireland public on the grounds of religious belief, colour, race or ethnic origin, or to use in a public place threatening, abusive or insulting words with such an intent'. It is also an offence to circulate, with intent to cause a breach of the peace, false statements or reports likely to stir up religious or racial hatred or fear.

Marriage and divorce

The Matrimonial Causes Act 1973 does not apply in Northern Ireland. Divorce is still based on the concept of the 'matrimonial offence': adultery, wilful desertion for three years, wilful failure to maintain, incurable insanity, cruelty, sodomy and bestiality.

Welfare and social security benefits

The equivalent to the social security office is the local office of the Ministry of Health and Social Services, known as the social services office. Local advice centres exist to help claimants. The **Association of Local Advice Centres** can be contacted c/o Joe O'Hara, 54 Lisburn Road, Belfast 9.

Legal services

Solicitors in Northern Ireland belong to the **Law Society of Northern Ireland, Chichester Street, Belfast 1.**

The green-form scheme does not apply in Northern Ireland. Thirty minutes of legal advice is available, free or partly free according to your income, from solicitors who participate in a scheme operated by the Law Society. For further information, contact your local citizens' advice bureau or the Law Society of Northern Ireland (Legal Aid Department).

More information

Association for Legal Justice, 25 Divis Street, Belfast.

Belfast Housing Aid Society, 16 Howard Street, Belfast.

Cara/Friend (Northern Ireland Gay Rights Association), 4 University Street, Belfast.

Catholic Marriage Advisory Service, 11 College Street, Belfast.

Citizens' Advice Bureau (NI headquarters), 28 Bedford Street, Belfast.

Coleraine Women's Group, c/o E. Eveson, Social Administration Department, New University of Ulster, Coleraine.

Equal Opportunities Commission, Lindsay House, Callendar Street, Belfast.

Fair Employment Agency, Lindsay House, Callendar Street, Belfast.

Family Planning Association of Northern Ireland, 28 Bedford Square, Belfast.

1974 Committee for Homosexual Law Reform in Northern Ireland, c/o Box 44, Belfast.

Northern Ireland Civil Rights Association, 2 Marquis Street, Belfast.

Northern Ireland Womens' Rights Association, 14 Fitzwilliam Street, Belfast.

Ulster Citizens' Civil Liberties Advice Centre, 25 Devinish Drive, Monkstown Newtownabbey, Co. Antrim.

28. Scotland

The law of Scotland differs considerably from that of England and Wales. It is impossible in one chapter to cover adequately the differences – ideally there should be a separate guide. This chapter highlights some of these differences in important areas of the law, and should not be regarded as comprehensive.

The **Scottish Council for Civil Liberties (SCCL), 214 Clyde Street, Glasgow (041-424 0042)** publishes factsheets on the law, takes up individual cases concerning civil liberty issues, organizes campaigns, and may be able to refer you to appropriate specialist organizations in Scotland.

Many of the terms used in Scottish law will be unfamiliar to English or Welsh people travelling in Scotland, and we therefore give a brief glossary of these terms below.

Advocates–depute	advocate (barrister) appointed to act as prosecutor in the High Court of Justiciary. During the time of the appointment, the advocate can do civil work but not criminal defence work.
Art and part	similar to 'aiding and abetting'.
Cite, citation	summons.
Indictment	document specifying the charge in solemn procedure (see below).
Interim liberation	bail pending the hearing of an appeal in solemn procedure (see below).
Lord Advocate	the Scottish equivalent of the Attorney General.
Means inquiry diet	court hearing to inquire into a person's financial position.
Not proven	one of three verdicts available to a Scottish jury; has the same effect as a 'not guilty' verdict.

Procurator fiscal	public prosecutor; a qualified solicitor or advocate who acts as full-time prosecutor in all the criminal courts except the High Court of Justiciary.
Solemn procedure	the judge sits with a jury; usually applies in more serious cases.
Summary procedure	the judge sits without a jury.
Supervision requirement	requirement that a child undergoes compulsory supervision either at home by a social worker or in a residential establishment.

Main differences in the law

Powers of the police

In Scotland, the police investigate crime under the direction of the procurator fiscal (public prosecutor), who is a legally qualified official, independent of the police. (See p. 557 for more details.)

Where the police have reason to suspect that someone has committed an offence, they must report the circumstances to the procurator-fiscal who will decide what charge, if any, should be made. He will also decide whether to cite (summons) the person to appear, or to apply to the sheriff for **warrant to arrest**. In certain circumstances, the police can act on their own initiative and **arrest without a warrant**. Each of these three procedures is dealt with in turn below.

CITATION

You may be cited to appear before a summary court (see p. 556 for a description of the different courts). The citation may be sent by registered post or recorded delivery or, more commonly, be served personally on you by a police officer or other official who comes to your home or work-place.

The citation can require you to attend at the court on a certain date to answer the charges. In practice, for minor offences and particularly traffic offences, the procurator fiscal may inform you that personal attendance is unnecessary and that you can plead by letter or through a solicitor. If you intend to plead by letter, check that the convictions libelled (listed) in the citation are correct. You may also explain in a letter to the judge any mitigating circumstances.

ARREST WITH A WARRANT

Citation may not be used where a person is to be tried by solemn procedure (see p. 550). In order to obtain a warrant (a court order authorizing your arrest) the procurator-fiscal presents a petition to the sheriff. The sheriff may inquire into the merits of the case, but in practice almost all warrants are granted without any inquiry.

Warrants for arrest are less common in summary procedure, but can be obtained, for instance, where the accused person is not at any address known to the police.

If you are arrested on a warrant, you have the right to see the warrant. But a police officer may make an arrest even if he does not possess the warrant, provided he knows that a warrant has been issued.

ARREST WITHOUT A WARRANT

You can be arrested without a warrant if you are reasonably suspected of committing an offence – whether the offence would be tried by summary or solemn procedure. (Scots law does not make the distinction between arrestable and non-arrestable offences; see p. 37.) In Scotland, a police officer may arrest someone without a warrant if the arrest is necessary in the interests of justice: in particular, he may arrest someone whom he sees committing a crime, or running away from the scene of a crime, or someone who, according to credible information, has committed a crime.

Arrests without a warrant are common for offences such as assault, breach of the peace and theft, where the accused is arrested at the time the offence is committed.

In addition, there are a number of statutes which give the police the power to arrest without a warrant. Under the Prevention of Crime Act 1953, a police officer may arrest a suspect without a warrant if he is not satisfied that he or she has given a true name and address. The Burgh Police (Scotland) Act 1892 and various local laws extend police powers further, particularly in relation to offences of dishonesty. Finally, a number of UK statutes such as the Misuse of Drugs Act 1971 (described in Chapter 6) and the Prevention of Terrorism Act (described on p. 535) also extend police powers of arrest.

P.C. McVitie requests the pleasure of your company at the Police Station at 2 p.m. R.S.V.P.

Under Scots law, an arrest is not clearly defined. It seems that you may not be under arrest, even though you are clearly not free to go about your business. Therefore, if the police ask you to go to the police station, in circumstances where you have little choice but to obey, ask him if he is arresting you. If he says that he is not, and you do not want to go, refuse the 'invitation'. But if the police insist, you would be well advised not to resist. Similarly, if you believe that you are being unlawfully arrested, do not resist, but accompany the police and later use your right to make a formal complaint (see p. 555).

SEARCH OF PEOPLE

The police may search you if:

- you consent to the search;
- you have been arrested (with or without a warrant);
- before an arrest, but only in cases of urgency (e.g. if the police reasonably believe that evidence may be destroyed);
- they obtain a search warrant (such warrants are rare; it is more usual to obtain a warrant to arrest, and then search);
- an Act of Parliament authorizes the search.

The police power to search a person includes: taking fingerprints, photographing, examining the body for surface marks, examining clothing. It does *not* entitle the police to take blood samples or make other physical intrusions, unless you consent or they obtain a warrant.

SEARCH OF PRIVATE PREMISES

The circumstances in which the police can search premises are similar to those for searching an individual. But:

- if the police arrest you without a warrant, they are not entitled to search premises without a warrant, except possibly the place where the arrest is made;
- the procurator fiscal may remove articles to be examined without obtaining the suspect's consent, provided that the consent of the person with custody of the articles is obtained (e.g. a laundry owner in the case of clothing).

POLICE QUESTIONING

The police are entitled to ask anybody questions, but no one is obliged to answer, or even to stay and listen (unless, of course, they are under arrest).

The Judges' Rules which govern questioning in police stations in England and Wales do not apply in Scotland. Instead, the police work under the supervision of the procurator fiscal, and the courts also control police behaviour to some extent by refusing to admit evidence which they consider to have been improperly obtained.

The police are not entitled to question a person who has been arrested. Indeed police questioning of a person under serious suspicion may also be held objectionable by the courts. Answers or statements made in response to police questions after you are arrested, or while you are under serious suspicion even if you have not been arrested, should not be admitted as evidence at your trial. But statements made voluntarily are always admissible.

If you are under serious suspicion or have been arrested, make no statement to the police unless your legal adviser is present.

If you have any complaints about police harassment, make them at the first opportunity to your lawyer or to the court.

YOUR RIGHTS WHILE IN POLICE CUSTODY AFTER ARREST

1. The police may search you.
2. The police should not question you.
3. You should be cautioned and charged with an offence. (The police do not decide the final charge, but must report to the procurator fiscal who makes the final decision. The words of the caution are the same as in England and Wales; see p. 45.)
4. Your property should be listed and packaged in your presence. Do not sign the list if it is inaccurate. Otherwise, sign immediately below the end of the list in such a way as to prevent any additions.
5. You should be given the opportunity of a private interview with your solicitor. The police should inform your solicitor of your request, but you have no right to telephone the solicitor yourself. The morning before you appear in court, a duty solicitor will advise you.
6. If you are to appear in the district court, the police have a discretionary power to grant you bail. You are unlikely to be released if you are charged with an offence against property, if you have no fixed address or you do not have enough cash. You should ask for release anyway. The police should not ask for more than £20; the average is about £10. The police are

often also willing to contact someone else who can provide the money for you. Cheques are only accepted from a solicitor. (For some road-traffic offences and a few other offences, the procurator fiscal can authorize your release with or without bail.)

7. You should be brought before a court on the first day (except Sunday and a few public holidays) after your arrest. So if you are arrested on a Saturday night, you will not appear in court until Monday morning.

8. The police have discretion to allow friends or family to see you, but you have no right to such an interview.

You should inform your solicitor or the court at the first opportunity if any of these rights are infringed, or if the police have used violence or put undue pressure on you.

COMPLAINTS AGAINST THE POLICE

If you believe that a policeman has committed a *criminal offence*, you should complain to the procurator fiscal (address in the telephone directory). The procurator fiscal will ensure that your complaint is investigated, and may direct a police officer to interview you and other witnesses or may carry out the interviews himself. If the procurator fiscal considers that there is sufficient evidence to prosecute, the police officer will be prosecuted in the usual way in the criminal courts. Although the procurator fiscal is an independent element in the Scottish police complaints procedure, it is undermined by the fact that the procurator fiscal may make his decision on the basis of police reports alone.

Whether or not the procurator fiscal decides to prosecute, your complaint will also be investigated by the police on the instructions of the deputy chief constable of the area to find out whether there has been a breach of police disciplinary regulations.

Disciplinary offences

Actions by the police which do not amount to a criminal offence may be a breach of police discipline. A senior police officer, usually from another force, will be appointed to investigate, and will submit a report after interviewing you and considering any other evidence. The report is confidential and you will only be told the result. If the complaint is upheld and considered serious, the police officer will be charged with a disciplinary offence and a hearing will be held, to which you may be called as a witness. You will be told whether the charge is upheld, but you cannot know what penalty is imposed.

Local inquiry

If your complaint is very serious, contact your MP and ask him to write to the Secretary of State for Scotland, asking for a local inquiry. Such inquiries are, however, very rarely held.

Civil action

You may be able to bring an action for damages if you have been assaulted, unlawfully arrested, etc. This is very complicated and you should get legal advice.

Your rights in criminal courts

There is a basic difference between **summary procedure** where a judge sits without a jury and **solemn procedure** where a judge sits with a jury. Not all levels of courts use both procedures.

DISTRICT COURTS

District courts were set up in May 1975 to replace the burgh (police) and Justice of the Peace courts. They deal with a great volume of minor traffic offences and other minor offences. With a few exceptions the maximum sentence in these courts is a £100 fine or sixty days' imprisonment. Justices of the Peace, who preside in district courts, are not legally qualified. Stipendiary magistrates, who are legally qualified, may be appointed to sit in this court with the same powers as a sheriff (see next section).

SHERIFF COURTS

Sheriff courts deal with offences considered by the procurator fiscal or defined in law as serious enough to merit trial before a sheriff. The maximum sentence that a sheriff sitting alone can impose is three months' imprisonment or a fine of £150. If the sheriff sits with a jury, the maximum sentence is two years' imprisonment or an unlimited fine. The case can be sent to the High Court of Justiciary for sentence if the sheriff considers his powers of sentence inadequate.

HIGH COURT OF JUSTICIARY

The High Court is the only court which can try some offences, such as murder and rape. It generally hears the most serious cases. The maximum sentence this court can impose is life imprisonment or an unlimited fine, although the death sentence still applies for treason. The judge always sits with a jury in the High Court.

COURT OF CRIMINAL APPEAL

The Court of Criminal Appeal (not the House of Lords) is the final court of appeal in criminal cases.

PROSECUTION

The majority of prosecutions are carried out by public prosecutors, called **advocates-depute** in the High Court of Justiciary and **procurators fiscal** in the other courts. These public prosecutors are appointed from advocates or solicitors and are independent of the police. *The police in Scotland never prosecute.* A private individual can only prosecute if a personal interest in the case can be shown, and with the consent of the public prosecutor or the court. Designated officials such as customs officers may also prosecute where specific statutory powers exist.

The public prosecutor has very wide discretion in deciding whether to make a charge, what charge to make, what previous convictions to libel and whether to proceed by summary or solemn procedure. This discretion is limited by specific legal provisions and also by directions from the Lord Advocate. The public prosecutor has power to supervise police investigations and in more serious cases will usually take statements from witnesses.

Summary procedure

If you are prosecuted under summary procedure, your case will be heard by a judge without a jury. You will receive a copy of the charge and previous convictions libelled before you appear in court. If you are not called on to plead, the case will be continued (adjourned), usually for seven days. You may be kept in custody, so you must ask for bail (see p. 562).

If you plead guilty, the judge may sentence you immediately or may defer sentence for a few weeks until a medical or social-background report is prepared. Ask for release pending preparation of the report.

If you plead not guilty, a date will be set for trial. Ask for bail. If you are in custody a duty solicitor will be available to represent you (see p. 573). If you have been cited (summonsed) to appear, you may qualify for legal aid (see p. 573).

Solemn procedure

If you are prosecuted under solemn procedure, your first appearance in court will be made in private with the public and press excluded. The duty solicitor will offer you free representation. Generally no plea or declaration is made at this stage, but you may if you wish make a judicial declaration (i.e. a statement made in private before a sheriff, who can ask questions. The procurator-fiscal and your solicitor will also be present).

This is now rare in practice, but may be useful if, for example, you wish to tell the judge about your defence or about some unfairness in the investigation. You may be committed (remanded), usually for one week for further investigation. Since you may be kept in custody, you should ask for bail. *If you remain in custody, the trial must be completed within 110 days,*

*and if this period is exceeded you must be released and can never again
be prosecuted for the offence charged.*

The document containing the charge, called the **indictment**,
will be served on you some time after committal. Not less than
six days after service of the indictment, a pleading diet (a diet
is a court hearing) will be held. At least nine days must elapse
before the trial diet. If you want to plead guilty, tell your
solicitor to inform the prosecutor and the procedure will be
speeded up.

The trial

Scottish and English procedures vary considerably though it is
only possible to note some of the main differences. There are no
opening speeches in Scotland. The **rule of corroboration** applies
which requires that evidence from two independent sources
must be available to prove material facts. Many rules such as the
exclusion of hearsay evidence apply in both Scotland and England, but care must be taken as the Scottish interpretation often
differs.

Juries consist of fifteen people. To be eligible for jury service,
a person must be aged between 21 and 60 and satisfy a minor
property qualification (Jurors (Scotland) Act 1825). In practice the
property qualification is ignored when the jury lists are drawn up.

The jury may choose one of three verdicts: guilty, not guilty or
not proven. A verdict of **not proven** has the same legal effect as
a verdict of not guilty. A simple majority verdict is needed.

SENTENCE

If the prosecutor does not move for sentence, no sentence can be
imposed. Before sentence, the judge may adjourn the case to
obtain medical, social-background or other reports. You may be
kept in custody during this time, so ask to be released on bail.

Absolute discharge

In summary proceedings, an absolute discharge can be given
without proceeding to conviction. This means that no conviction
will be recorded against you.

Admonition

A court may dismiss a convicted person with a reprimand or admonition, if this appears to be a just way of dealing with the case.

Fine

There are restrictions on the maximum fine a court may impose (see p. 556). The court often allows time to pay a fine, or payment by instalments. The powers of a summary court to impose imprisonment in default of payment are restricted. Usually, where a person defaults a **means inquiry diet** will be held (i.e. a hearing to inquire into the person's financial position). The court may allow additional time to pay or may impose imprisonment. Periods of imprisonment for failure to pay a fine are laid down by statute, but the period may be reduced to take account of part payment.

Probation

The principles of probation (see p. 95) are similar in Scotland and England but some differences exist. In summary cases, the order is made without proceeding to conviction.

Imprisonment

If you are sentenced to a term of imprisonment, any time spent in pre-trial custody is not automatically deducted from the period of your sentence, but the court does have discretion to deduct it.

Young offenders cannot be sent to prison, but may be detained in a young offenders institution, a detention centre or a borstal. There are also restrictions on the imprisonment of first offenders aged over 21.

Detention in the precincts of a court

In summary cases, a court may detain a convicted person within the precincts of the court until evening, instead of imposing a prison sentence.

Deferred sentence

A court may defer sentence for a period. At the expiry of the period, the court may impose any sentence including imprisonment which could have been imposed at the time of the conviction. If the court is satisfied as to the good behaviour of the person involved, it will generally admonish or fine the convicted person.

Conditional discharge, binding over and suspended sentence do not apply in Scotland.

APPEALS

The appeals procedure is very complex and you should apply for legal aid and representation. You should also apply for **interim liberation**, i.e. bail pending the hearing of the appeal. If you are released and fail to appear, your appeal may be dismissed.

Review of decisions of summary courts

There are three methods of appeal against decisions of summary courts, to the High Court of Justiciary:

1. Appeal by **stated case**: the grounds on which a stated case may be obtained are varied. The method, which can be used by both the accused and the prosecutor, is frequently used to appeal against alleged procedural irregularities and errors of law.
2. Appeal by **Bill of Suspension**: this is often used where there is some fundamental injustice or defect in the proceedings. Only the accused can use this procedure.
3. Appeal by **Bill of Advocation**: this is appropriate for obtaining a review of the earlier stages of prosecution, but cannot be used to review the merits of a case. Both the accused and the prosecutor can use this procedure, but it is now rare.

Review of decisions of the sheriff and jury and High Court of Justiciary

An appeal against decisions of the sheriff and jury, or of the High Court of Justiciary is made to the Court of Criminal Appeal, which is composed of at least three judges of the High Court. An appeal may always be made on a question of law. In other cases, an appeal may only be made if the trial judge or appeal court consents. Only the accused may appeal to this court, except that the prosecution may be able to appeal against the sheriff's decision by advocation, as in point 3 above.

There is no appeal to the House of Lords in criminal cases.

BAIL

In Scotland, bail takes the form of a cash deposit made by anyone including the accused. Bail amounts are very low and sums of £10 or less are common even for serious offences. However, there is no right to bail and it is often refused because of the person's previous criminal record, no fixed address, likelihood of interference with witnesses or evidence, etc.

Except at the stage of committal for further investigation, an accused person can appeal to the High Court of Justiciary against refusal of bail or the amount of bail set. The accused can also return to the court which set bail for a review of the decision because of a material change of circumstances. The prosecutor can always appeal against a decision to grant bail.

Public order

BREACH OF THE PEACE

The offence of breach of the peace has a far wider application in Scotland than in England, and provides the authorities with a very powerful weapon. Almost any unorthodox behaviour could technically amount to a breach of the peace, and it is left to the discretion of the police and prosecutors to decide whether a particular act is an offence. In the past it has been used to deal with noisy gatherings in private houses, attempted suicides, peeping toms, and a schoolmaster who made indecent suggestions to pupils.

OBSTRUCTION OF THE POLICE

This is only an offence if there is a physical act of obstruction (Police (Scotland) Act 1956). The maximum penalty that can be imposed is a fine of up to £50 and three months' imprisonment on summary conviction. A second conviction within two years of a previous similar offence carries a maximum penalty of nine months' imprisonment.

INSULTING WORDS AND BEHAVIOUR

This is an offence under the Public Order Act 1936 but is normally prosecuted as breach of peace.

MOBBING AND RIOTING

Anyone who knowingly takes part in a violent or menacing group or demonstration may be guilty of the offence of mobbing and rioting. The essence of the offence is intimidation by numbers or by threat of violence.

ART AND PART

Art and part is similar to aiding and abetting, with some differences. For instance, it is not criminal in Scotland to help a person after an offence has been committed, unless the help itself amounts to an offence or indicates that the helper had prior knowledge of and had agreed to the offence.

CONSPIRACY

The development of conspiracy laws has been different in Scotland. In general, less use has been made of conspiracy charges.

MEETINGS AND PROCESSIONS

The Public Order Act 1936 (see Chapter 4) applies to Scotland. Also local legislation gives local authorities considerable powers to restrict access to public parks, the use of loudspeakers and in some cases to regulate or ban processions in the streets. The English law of trespass does not apply in Scotland.

MEETINGS ON PRIVATE PREMISES

Although there is no law of trespass, you do not have the right to hold meetings on other people's property without permission. You would almost certainly be ordered to leave and you would possibly be charged with breach of the peace. If you damage the property you may be charged with malicious mischief.

RIGHTS OF POLICE TO ATTEND MEETINGS ON PRIVATE PREMISES

The right of the police to enter meetings held on private premises has never been established in Scottish law. They would probably have to show that there was an urgent threat to public order to justify such action.

BINDING OVER

There is no 'binding over' procedure in Scotland, though in exceptional circumstances, for example under a local Act in Aberdeen, it may be used as an alternative to a fine or imprisonment.

Sex

HOMOSEXUALITY

The Sexual Offences Act 1967 does not apply in Scotland. All male homosexual activity is illegal under common law. Successive Lord Advocates have, however, directed that homosexual conduct in private between consenting adults over the age of 21 should not be prosecuted. There is nothing to prevent the Lord Advocate from withdrawing this protection, and the Scottish

Minorities Group with the support of SCCL have campaigned for statutory protection.

INCEST

Sexual intercourse between two consenting adults may be an offence if the persons are related by blood or marriage in certain ways, e.g. mother and son or father-in-law and daughter-in-law (Incest Act 1567).

INDECENCY

Indecent exposure may be an offence under the Vagrancy Act 1824 (see p. 180). Other kinds of 'indecent' conduct may be an offence under statute or common law. Breach of the peace (see p. 149) often covers such conduct and may be charged instead of more specific offences.

PROSTITUTION

The Street Offences Act 1959 does not apply in Scotland. The Burgh Police (Scotland) Act 1892 makes it an offence for a prostitute to solicit people in the street for the purposes of prostitution. It is also an offence for anyone habitually or persistently to solicit or loiter for the purposes of soliciting women or children for immoral purposes.

Workers and the law

The law relating to contracts of employment, redundancy, unfair dismissal, race and sex discrimination, etc. is virtually identical in Scotland and is described in Chapters 8 and 10. There is, however, a separate court structure. Scottish industrial tribunals are administered by the **Central Office of Industrial Tribunals, West Nile Street, Glasgow,** which is headed by a President appointed by the Lord President of the Court of Session. Actions such as recovery of wages due may be brought in the sheriff court (see p. 566).

Your rights in the civil courts

SHERIFF COURTS

Sheriff courts can deal with actions of debt or damages without any financial limitation. The procedure is complicated and written pleadings are essential. Trial is normally before a sheriff-substitute sitting without a jury. It is possible to appeal to the Sheriff Principal and/or the Inner House of the Court of Session.

A new procedure for certain cases in sheriff courts came into effect on 1 September 1976. This replaces the old small-debt procedure, and is designed to make it easier for someone to take a case to court without being legally represented. There are new rules and standard forms which apply to a variety of actions, in particular for payment of money, sequestration of rent and recall or variation of a decree for aliment (Summary Cause Rules, Sheriff Court, 1976). It is not possible to describe the procedure in detail here, but it is important to remember that there are time-limits for most stages of the procedure. You should get legal advice as quickly as possible if you want to start an action, or have to defend an action which is being brought against you.

COURT OF SESSION

The Outer House of the Court of Session deals with many cases similar to those dealt with in sheriff courts though they tend to be more complex. But it is the only court which can deal with divorce and some other actions. Trial is usually before a judge alone but some actions, particularly reparation actions, are heard before a judge and jury of twelve people.

The Inner House of the Court of Session usually acts as a court of appeal though some cases can be brought before it in the first instance. Three judges hear appeals but in specially difficult cases, more than three judges may sit.

HOUSE OF LORDS

The House of Lords is the final court of appeal for Scottish civil cases.

Censorship and secrecy

The Obscene Publications Acts 1959 and 1964 do not apply in Scotland. Publishing an obscene work intended to corrupt public morals is a common-law offence and no defence of literary merit is allowed. Prosecutions are usually brought under the Burgh Police (Scotland) Act 1892 or similar local legislation, with the result that local prosecutors use their own initiative to prosecute. Since May 1975, local prosecutors have come under the control of the Lord Advocate and a more centralized control is expected. In the past, the Lord Advocate has been slow to authorize such prosecutions. Private prosecutions are virtually impossible. The maximum penalty is a fine of £10 or sixty days' imprisonment.

Marriage and cohabitation

Scots law is very different from English law. Some of the differences are mentioned here but for further information you should look at *Law of Husband and Wife in Scotland* by E. Clive and J. Wilson, and *Marriage, Divorce and the Family* by D. Nichols.

COHABITATION

Scots law recognizes a form of irregular marriage known as 'cohabitation with habit and repute'. The man and woman must live together and be known as husband and wife and this must continue for a considerable period while both parties are free to marry.

DIVORCE

The Divorce (Scotland) Act 1976 came into effect on 1 January 1977. This means that the ground for divorce is basically the same as in England and Wales (see Chapter 15), that is, that the marriage has irretrievably broken down. The Act lays down five different circumstances which the court must take into account.

Divorce may be granted if:

- husband and wife have not lived together for the two previous years, and both consent to the divorce; *or*
- husband and wife have not lived together for the previous five years.

Adultery by the defender (i.e. the partner who is not bringing the action for divorce), desertion by the defender for a period of two years, and unreasonable behaviour by the defender are also indications that the marriage has irretrievably broken down.

The Act also makes a number of changes in relation to financial provision. In particular, the person who is divorced no longer forfeits the right to periodical allowance and a capital payment. Thus, if a wife who has committed adultery is divorced by her husband, the husband may still be ordered to pay her maintenance and a share of the capital assets. In adultery cases, it is no longer possible to sue the lover as a co-defender to the action.

With regard to custody of children, the Guardianship Act 1973 (see p. 343) applies in Scotland.

Children

The age of criminal responsibility is 8. There are no juvenile courts in Scotland. There is a system of reporters and children's hearings (Social Work (Scotland) Act 1968). The Lord Advocate may also prosecute a child in serious cases in the sheriff court or the High Court.

REPORTERS

Reporters, assisted by deputies and assistants, are appointed by regional district authorities. Reporters usually have legal or social work qualifications.

A child may be referred to a reporter in the following circumstances:

- if a criminal offence has been committed by a child, the police will usually refer the case to the reporter, though in serious cases the procurator-fiscal will be notified;

- if the child is beyond the control of his or her parents;
- if lack of parental care is likely to cause the child unnecessary suffering or seriously impair the child's health or development;
- if the child is falling into bad company, or is exposed to moral danger;
- if the child has been the victim of certain specified offences such as incest or is likely to live with someone who has committed such an offence;
- if the child fails to attend school without reasonable cause.

In most cases, the referral is made by the social work department; in the last case, it is made by the head-teacher.

The reporter, who has a semi-judicial function, may decide on one of the three following things:

- to take no action. The reporter may inform whoever referred the child that no action will be taken, and some reporters also tell the parents and warn them that further misbehaviour may lead to the child being referred to a children's hearing;
- to refer the case to the local authority social work department, if the parents accept voluntary supervision of the child;
- to refer the case to a children's hearing.

CHILDREN'S HEARINGS

A lay tribunal of three people, including at least one man and one woman, is drawn from the children's panel, which should represent a cross-section of the community and is appointed by the Secretary of State on the recommendation of an advisory committee.

If the reporter refers a child to a children's hearing, a copy of the reasons for referral will be sent to the parents with at least seven days' notice of the hearing date.

The hearing is not open to the public. The press may attend, but publication of information is restricted. Usually only the child, his or her parents, a social worker and the reporter or a representative are present. Free legal representation is not available. The chairman will explain the purpose of the hearing and ask whether the parents and child accept the grounds of referral.

If the grounds of referral are disputed, and the child is not discharged, the case goes to the sheriff court to decide whether any ground of referral exists. Legal representation is available under the legal aid scheme (see p. 573). If a child denies committing a particular offence, the matter will be dealt with by the sheriff. If it appears that the child has committed any offence this will amount to grounds for referral, and the case will be returned to the children's hearing.

If the grounds of referral are accepted or are established at the sheriff court, the hearing will discuss the case informally with the people attending and may decide to dismiss the case or impose a **supervision requirement**. A supervision requirement means that the child must undergo compulsory supervision either at home by a social worker or in a named residential establishment. If the parents want to appeal against the decision, they can ask for written reasons from the reporter and appeal to a sheriff within twenty-one days of the hearing.

Both the child and parents have the right to ask for a review of a supervision requirement after three months, or after six months where the same supervision requirement was continued after the first review hearing. The local authority, usually the social work department, has the right to ask for a review at any time. The reporter must in any case arrange for a review after nine months and before the end of a year from the date the requirement was made. There is a right of appeal to the sheriff court against any decision of a children's hearing.

Mental patients

The treatment, care and reception of mental patients in Scotland is governed mainly by the Mental Health (Scotland) Act 1960. The patient or nearest relative can appeal to a sheriff for release if it is decided to continue detention.

The Mental Welfare Commission, which has no English counterpart, is an independent body of seven to nine commissioners appointed by the Secretary of State for Scotland. The commissioners inquire into cases, visit patients and look after their general welfare. The commission can recommend a patient's release, unless the patient is detained under special restrictions, for instance a convicted murderer committed to mental hospital by the court.

Welfare and social security benefits

The same system of social security and supplementary benefits (see Chapter 20) applies in Scotland. Prosecutions for fraud are the responsibility of the procurator fiscal.

An important Scottish difference is that regional social work departments can make small cash payments to people in need, even where there are no children in the household (Social Work (Scotland) Act 1968). In practice, however, Scottish social work departments do not seem to be more generous as a result of their wider powers.

Education

Every education authority must ensure that adequate and efficient provision is made for primary, secondary and further education in its area (Education (Scotland) Act 1962). The Secretary of State and the education authorities must have regard to parents' wishes so far as is compatible with the provision of suitable instruction and training and the avoidance of unreasonable public expenditure.

RELIGIOUS EDUCATION

Every public and grant-aided school is open to pupils of all denominations. Parents may withdraw their child from religious instruction or observance so long as it does not place the child at any disadvantage.

SCHOOL ATTENDANCE

If a child fails to attend school without a good reason, the education authority may serve an attendance order on the parents. Parents may appeal to the sheriff court against the order. If an attendance order is in force, and the child still fails to go to school, parents must satisfy the court that there is a reasonable excuse. For a first offence, the maximum penalty is a fine of £10 and for a second offence a fine of £20 or imprisonment not exceeding one month.

COMPLAINTS

Complaints should be made to the head of the school or the local education authority. The Secretary of State will consider complaints and if satisfied that an education authority, the school managers, or anyone else has failed to discharge a duty he will make an order declaring them to be in breach of their duty. He may also make arrangements for the duty to be fulfilled. Alternatively the Court of Session, on application by the Lord Advocate, may order specific performance of the duty.

Housing

Scots common law is different from English law, but much of the statute law covering leases and rents (see p. 445) is similar. The Rent (Scotland) Act 1971 consolidates some of the legislation, but this is very complicated and you should get advice from a lawyer or local authority rent officer.

Landlords are obliged to keep in repair the structure and exterior of the house and the installations for the supply of water, gas, electricity, sanitation and heating (Housing (Scotland) Act 1966). The local authority can serve notice on the landlord requiring him to carry out repairs.

SQUATTING

If you squat without the consent of the owner, you may be evicted by civil process, and the owner may obtain an interdict forbidding continued occupation. The police can evict squatters under the Trespass (Scotland) Act 1865 which makes it a criminal offence to occupy private property without consent.

Legal services

LEGAL AID

Legal aid in civil proceedings

You can get legal aid for proceedings in sheriff courts, the Court of Session, the House of Lords, the Lands Valuation Appeal Court, the Lands Tribunal for Scotland, the Scottish Land Court and the Restrictive Practices Court. You will not be able to get assistance for representation at tribunals such as social security or industrial tribunals, but you may get help from a voluntary legal aid centre (see below).

You can apply for legal aid through a solicitor to the Legal Aid Committee. They will only grant a certificate if they are satisfied about the merits of your case and that you cannot get help from another body. You will only be eligible for help if your income and capital fall below a certain limit; your solicitor or a citizens' advice bureau will explain this. You may be asked to pay a contribution.

Legal aid in criminal proceedings after an arrest

If you are arrested and brought before a district or sheriff court, you can get free advice and representation from the duty solicitor as of right. If you are arrested, but released on police bail, you should ask to see the duty solicitor though this will not always be allowed.

In summary cases, the free representation continues until the end of the pleading diet. This means that if you plead not guilty, the solicitor applies for bail. If you plead guilty, the solicitor will make a plea for mitigation, even if the case is postponed to allow for a report, such as a social-background report, to be prepared.

In solemn procedure, the free aid continues until you are granted bail or committed for trial.

Legal aid in other criminal proceedings

If you are cited to appear to go for trial you can make an application to the court for legal aid. The forms are available from the court. *In summary cases*, you must satisfy the court that you cannot pay for the defence and that it is in the interests of justice that legal aid be granted. *In solemn procedure*, you need only satisfy the financial test to obtain aid. There is some variation among courts in the way financial tests are applied, but if you qualify you will not be required to contribute to the costs.

Legal aid for appeal in criminal proceedings

If you need legal aid for an appeal, you must apply to the Supreme Court Legal Aid Committee. You will have to satisfy the committee that you are unable to pay, that substantial grounds of appeal exist and that it is reasonable that help be granted.

LEGAL HELP FROM VOLUNTARY ORGANIZATIONS

There are citizens' advice bureaux in most major towns, and you should find their address in the telephone directory. In Edinburgh, Glasgow and Dundee, there are citizens' rights centres and a variety of other voluntary legal centres. Most of these centres will arrange representation for you at tribunals as well as offering other help.

COMPLAINTS AGAINST LAWYERS

If you believe that a lawyer has committed a criminal offence, you should report the matter to the procurator-fiscal.

Otherwise, you should make your complaint against a solicitor in writing to the Secretary of the Law Society, 26 Drumsheugh Gardens, Edinburgh. The complaint will be investigated and if the solicitor cannot give a satisfactory explanation, disciplinary hearings may be held after which the solicitor may be censured, fined, or have his or her practising certificate suspended.

A lay observer has now been appointed, to whom you can write if you are dissatisfied with the way in which your complaint has been investigated. You should write to the Office of the Lay Observer, Melville Street, Edinburgh.

A complaint against an advocate (barrister) should be addressed to the **Dean of the Faculty of Advocates, Parliament House, Edinburgh.**

More information

Scottish Association for the Care and Resettlement of Offenders (SACRO), 1 Strathmore House, East Kilbride, Glasgow.
Scottish Child Poverty Action Group, 11 Castle Street, Edinburgh 2.
Scottish Council for Civil Liberties (SCCL), 214 Clyde Street, Glasgow (041-424 0042).
Scottish Minorities Group, 60 Broughton Street, Edinburgh 1 (031-556 3637).

29. European Convention on Human Rights

The European Convention for the Protection of Human Rights and Fundamental Freedoms was signed by the fifteen member states of the Council of Europe on 4 November 1950. It came into force on 3 September 1953. By the Convention, nations have agreed to submit to international control all their actions which concern basic human rights. The Convention provides legal protection for these rights.

The UK has ratified the Convention, together with four of the five 'protocols' (i.e. additions). It has not ratified the fourth protocol, which deals in part with citizenship and immigration. The main parts of the Convention and protocols which set out the rights and freedoms guaranteed by the Convention are given on pp. 580–86.

States who are members of the Council of Europe can make complaints against other governments under the Convention. The following countries are members of the Council: Austria, Belgium, Cyprus, Denmark, France, Greece, Holland (Netherlands), W. Germany, Iceland, Ireland (Eire), Italy, Luxemburg, Malta, Norway, Sweden, Switzerland, Turkey, UK. Individuals – whatever their nationality – also have the right to make a complaint about the UK Government (and against other governments who recognize the right of individual petition).

Complaints are dealt with first by the European Commission of Human Rights, and may go later to either the Court of Human Rights or the Committee of Ministers at the Council of Europe. The Commission and Court each consist of one person from each country who is a member of the Council. The Committee of Ministers is a political body, consisting of government representatives from each country. These bodies are not part of the Common Market.

The Convention allows governments to derogate from (i.e. depart from) the standards it sets 'in time of war or other public emergency threatening the life of the nation'. The UK has given notice of such derogation in relation to Northern Ireland (to permit internment, and other emergency measures which would otherwise be in breach of the Convention). The government can never derogate from certain articles of the Convention – such as the article guaranteeing freedom from torture.

How to use the Convention

If you believe that any of your rights under the Convention has been violated, you can write direct to the **Secretary of the Commission of Human Rights, Council of Europe, Strasbourg, France**. Any individual, group of people, or non-government organization can apply directly to the Commission. But it is better to get legal advice, from a solicitor or from an organization like NCCL, so that your application can be presented as effectively as possible. Your application should include:

– name, age, address and occupation;
– name, address and occupation of your representative (e.g. your lawyer);
– the name of the government against whom you are complaining (e.g. the UK Government);
– as far as possible the object of the application and the articles of the Convention which you think may have been broken;
– a statement of the facts of your case, and the reasons you think these amount to a denial of your rights under the Convention;
– any relevant documents and, in particular, any judgment or other official document connected with your application;
– evidence that you have 'exhausted your domestic remedies' (as explained below).

The Commission then has to decide whether your application is **admissible** (i.e. falls within their terms of reference). The application will be referred to one of the Commission's members – the *rapporteur* – who can ask for further information from you or the Government, before reporting on the case to the Commission. The Commission can then decide to ask for further information, or to invite the Government to make observations on whether or not the application should be admitted. You will be sent a copy of the Government's observations, and can in turn make observations yourself. The Commission can hold an oral hearing at this stage, and can give you legal aid to cover your costs.

The following things are taken into account in deciding whether or not to admit an application:

- you have brought your case within six months of the date when the appeal court, or whatever body you finally appealed to, took its decision;
- the application is anonymous (anonymous applications are automatically inadmissible);
- it covers a situation which has already been dealt with by the Commission or some other international process;
- the application is incompatible with the Convention, or 'manifestly ill-founded' or an abuse of the right of petition. Under these broad conditions, the Commission rejects the majority of applications;
- domestic remedies have been exhausted. It is vital to show in your application that you have done everything possible by way of appeal to a court of law or tribunal. 'Domestic remedies' do *not* include discretionary or political remedies, such as a complaint to the Ombudsman, so you can take a case to the Comission even if you have not involved the Ombudsman.

How the Commission reaches a decision

If the Commission decides that your application is admissible, it will then examine the substance of your case. You and the government will usually be asked to present written observations on the merits of the case, and the Commission will usually hold a hearing at Strasbourg. The Commission then reaches a provisional opinion on the merits of the case – which is not published – and tries to reach a friendly settlement (i.e. a negotiated agreement) between the opposing parties.

If a friendly settlement is agreed, the Commission prepares a report with a brief statement of the facts and the solution reached, and sends it to the government, the Committee of Ministers, and the Secretary General of the Council of Europe, who publishes it. Previous decisions of the Commission are available free of charge from the **Secretary General, Council of Europe, Strasbourg, France**. If there is no friendly settlement, the Commission draws up a report and states whether there has been a breach of the Convention. The report can include dissenting views from individual members of the Commission. During the three months after the report is published, the case can be referred to the Court of Human Rights by the Commission itself or any government involved (or whose citizen is involved) in the case. *The individual applicant does not have the right to refer the case to the Court.* The Court's decision is binding. If the case is not referred to the Court, it is left to the Committee of Ministers to decide (on a vote of at least two thirds of its members) whether there has been a violation of the Convention. If it decides that the convention has been breached, the Committee may also decide what measures the government concerned should take.

It is very rare for cases to be referred to the Court. In the only individual case against the UK Government which has been referred to the Court, the Court decided that the limitation on prisoners' correspondence with their lawyers, contained in the Prison Rules, was in breach of Article 8 of the Convention. Although the applicant is not directly involved in the case when it gets to the Court, it is normal practice for the Commission, when presenting its case to the Court, to invite the applicant's representatives to help the Commission with this job.

The effect of the Convention

Between 1955 and 1973, 6,402 individual complaints were made. 121 were declared admissible, forty-two of these against the UK. The largest group of complaints against the UK concerned the treatment of East African Asians, under the immigration laws. The procedure for handling complaints under the Convention is extremely cumbersome, and it can take years for a decision to be finally reached. Despite these delays, and the limited nature of many of the rights guaranteed by the Convention, it represents a useful measure for further protecting civil liberties in this country.

The rights and freedoms protected by the Convention are set out in Articles 2 to 14, and Protocols 1 and 4. These articles and protocols are reproduced below. (The remaining articles and protocols concern the procedure for enforcing the Convention, and are not included.)

Rights and freedoms protected by the Convention

ARTICLE 2

1. Everyone's right to life shall be protected by law. No one shall be deprived of his life intentionally save in the execution of a sentence of a court following his conviction of a crime for which this penalty is provided by law.

2. Deprivation of life shall not be regarded as inflicted in contravention of this Article when it results from the use of force which is no more than absolutely necessary –
   a. in defence of any person from unlawful violence;
   b. in order to effect a lawful arrest or to prevent the escape of a person lawfully detained;
   c. in action lawfully taken for the purpose of quelling a riot or insurrection.

ARTICLE 3

No one shall be subjected to torture or to inhuman or degrading treatment or punishment.

ARTICLE 4

1. No one shall be held in slavery or servitude.
2. No one shall be required to perform forced or compulsory labour.
3. For the purpose of this Article the term "forced or compulsory labour" shall not include –

a. any work required to be done in the ordinary course of detention imposed according to the provisions of Article 5 of this Convention or during conditional release from such detention;

b. any service of a military character or , in case of conscientious objectors in countries where they are recognised, service exacted instead of compulsory military service;

c. any service exacted in case of an emergency or calamity threatening the life or well-being of the community;

d. any work or service which forms part of normal civic obligations.

ARTICLE 5

1. Everyone has the right to liberty and security of person.
No one shall be deprived of his liberty save in the following cases and in accordance with a procedure prescribed by law:

a. the lawful detention of a person after conviction by a competent court;

b. the lawful arrest or detention of a person for non-compliance with the lawful order of a court or in order to secure the fulfilment of any obligation prescribed by law;

c. the lawful arrest or detention of a person effected for the purpose of bringing him before the competent legal authority on reasonable suspicion of having committed an offence or when it is reasonably considered necessary to prevent his committing an offence or fleeing after having done so;

d. the detention of a minor by lawful order for the purpose of educational supervision or his lawful detention for the purpose of bringing him before the competent legal authority;

e. the lawful detention of persons for the prevention of the spreading of infectious diseases, of persons of unsound mind, alcoholics or drug addicts or vagrants;

f. the lawful arrest or detention of a person to prevent his effecting an unauthorised entry into the country or of a person against whom action is being taken with a view to deportation or extradition.

2. Everyone who is arrested shall be informed promptly, in a language which he understands, of the reasons for his arrest and of any charge against him.

3. Everyone arrested or detained in accordance with the provisions of paragraph 1.c of this Article shall be brought promptly before a judge or other officer authorised by law to exercise judicial power and shall be entitled to trial within a reasonable time or to release pending trial. Release may be conditioned by guarantees to appear for trial.

4. Everyone who is deprived of his liberty by arrest or detention shall be entitled to take proceedings by which the lawfulness of his detention shall be decided speedily by a court and his release ordered if the detention is not lawful.

5. Everyone who has been the victim of arrest or detention in contravention of the provisions of this Article shall have an enforceable right to compensation.

ARTICLE 6

1. In the determination of his civil rights and obligations or of any criminal charge against him, everyone is entitled to a fair and public hearing within a reasonable time by an independent and impartial tribunal established by law. Judgment shall be pronounced publicly but the press and public may be excluded from all or part of the trial in the interests of morals, public order or national security in a democratic society, where the interests of juveniles or the protection of the private life of the parties so require, or to the extent strictly necessary in the opinion of the court in special circumstances where publicity would prejudice the interests of justice.

2. Everyone charged with a criminal offence shall be presumed innocent until proved guilty according to law.

3. Everyone charged with a criminal offence has the following minimum rights:
   a. to be informed promptly, in a language which he understands and in detail, of the nature and cause of the accusation against him;
   b. to have adequate time and facilities for the preparation of his defence;
   c. to defend himself in person or through legal assistance of his own choosing or, if he has not sufficient means to pay for legal assistance, to be given it free when the interests of justice so require;
   d. to examine or have examined witnesses against him and to obtain the attendance and examination of witnesses on his

behalf under the same conditions as witnesses against him;

e. to have the free assistance of an interpreter if he cannot understand or speak the language used in court.

ARTICLE 7

1. No one shall be held guilty of any criminal offence on account of any act or omission which did not constitute a criminal offence under national or international law at the time when it was committed. Nor shall a heavier penalty be imposed than the one that was applicable at the time the criminal offence was committed.

2. This Article shall not prejudice the trial and punishment of any person for any act or omission which, at the time when it was committed, was criminal according to the general principles of law recognised by civilised nations.

ARTICLE 8

1. Everyone has the right to respect for his private and family life, his home and his correspondence.

2. There shall be no interference by a public authority with the exercise of this right except such as is in accordance with the law and is necessary in a democratic society in the interests of national security, public safety or the economic well-being of the country, for the prevention of disorder or crime, for the protection of health or morals, or for the protection of the rights and freedoms of others.

ARTICLE 9

1. Everyone has the right to freedom of thought, conscience and religion; this right includes freedom to change his religion or belief, and freedom, either alone or in community with others and in public or private, to manifest his religion or belief, in worship, teaching, practice and observance.

2. Freedom to manifest one's religion or beliefs shall be subject only to such limitations as are prescribed by law and are necessary in a democratic society in the interests of public safety, for the protection of public order, health or morals, or for the protection of the rights and freedoms of others.

ARTICLE 10

1. Everyone has the right to freedom of expression. This right shall include freedom to hold opinions and to receive and impart information and ideas without interference by public authority and regardless of frontiers. This Article shall not prevent States from requiring the licensing of broadcasting, television or cinema enterprises.

2. The exercise of these freedoms, since it carries with it duties and responsibilities, may be subject to such formalities, conditions, restrictions or penalties as are prescribed by law and are necessary in a democratic society, in the interests of national security, territorial integrity or public safety, for the prevention of disorder or crime, for the protection of health or morals, for the protection of the reputation or rights of others, for preventing the disclosure of information received in confidence, or for maintaining the authority and impartiality of the judiciary.

ARTICLE 11

1. Everyone has the right to freedom of peaceful assembly and to freedom of association with others, including the right to form and to join trade unions for the protection of his interests.

2. No restrictions shall be placed on the exercise of these rights other than such as are prescribed by law and are necessary in a democratic society in the interests of national security or public safety, for the prevention of disorder or crime, for the protection of health or morals or for the protection of the rights and freedoms of others. This Article shall not prevent the imposition of lawful restrictions on the exercise of these rights by members of the armed forces, of the police or of the administration of the State.

ARTICLE 12

Men and women of marriageable age have the right to marry and to found a family, according to the national laws governing the exercise of this right.

ARTICLE 13

Everyone whose rights and freedoms as set forth in this Convention are violated shall have an effective remedy before a national authority notwithstanding that the violation has been committed by persons acting in an official capacity.

ARTICLE 14

The enjoyment of the rights and freedoms set forth in this Convention shall be secured without discrimination on any ground such as sex, race, colour, language, religion, political or other opinion, national or social origin, association with a national minority, property, birth or other status.

First Protocol to the Convention

ARTICLE 1

Every natural or legal person is entitled to the peaceful enjoyment of his possessions. No one shall be deprived of his possessions except in the public interest, and subject to the conditions provided for by law and by the general principles of international law.

The preceding provisions shall not, however, in any way impair the right of a State to enforce such laws as it deems necessary to control the use of property in accordance with the general interest or to secure the payment of taxes or other contributions or penalties.

ARTICLE 2

No person shall be denied the right to education. In the exercise of any functions which it assumes in relation to education and to teaching, the State shall respect the right of parents to ensure such education and teaching in conformity with their own religious and philosophical convictions.

ARTICLE 3

The High Contracting Parties undertake to hold free elections at reasonable intervals by secret ballot, under conditions which will ensure the free expression of the opinion of the people in the choice of the legislature.

Fourth Protocol to the Convention*

ARTICLE 1

No one shall be deprived of his liberty merely on the ground of inability to fulfil a contractual obligation.

ARTICLE 2

1. Everyone lawfully within the territory of a State shall, within that territory, have the right to liberty of movement and freedom to choose his residence.

2. Everyone shall be free to leave any country, including his own.

3. No restrictions shall be placed on the exercise of these rights other than such as are in accordance with law and are necessary in a democratic society in the interests of national security or public safety, for the maintenance of *ordre public*, for the prevention of crime, for the protection of health or morals, or for the protection of the rights and freedoms of others.

4. The rights set forth in paragraph 1 may also be subject, in particular areas, to restrictions imposed in accordance with law and justified by the public interest in a democratic society.

ARTICLE 3

1. No one shall be expelled, by means either of an individual or of a collective measure, from the territory of the State of which he is a national.

2. No one shall be deprived of the right to enter the territory of the State of which he is a national.

ARTICLE 4

Collective expulsion of aliens is prohibited.

*This Protocol has not been ratified by the UK.

Appendix A. Organizations which give help and advice

Adoption Resource Exchange, 39 Brixton Road, London SW9 (01-582 9802).

Advisory Centre for Education (ACE), 32 Trumpington Street, Cambridge (0223-51456).

Advisory Service for Squatters, 2 St Paul's Road, London N1 (01-359 8814).

Age Concern, Bernard Sunley House, 60 Pitcairn Road, Mitcham, Surrey (01-640 5431).

Albany Trust (Homosexuality), 16–20 Strutton Ground, London SW1 (01-222 0701).

Alcoholics Anonymous, 11 Redcliffe Gardens, London SW10 (01-325 9669).

Amnesty International, 10 Southampton Street, London WC2 (01-836 7788).

Apex Trust (Prisoners' employment), 9 Poland Street, London W1 (01-734 4658/9).

Association of British Adoption Agencies, 4 Southampton Row, London WC1 (01-242 8951).

Association for the Prevention of Addiction, 9 James Street, London WC2 (01-836 1373).

Automobile Association, Fanum House, Stanmore, Middlesex (01-954 7373/7355).

Belfast Housing Aid Society, 16 Howard Street, Belfast B1.

British Pregnancy Advisory Service, Guildhall Buildings, Navigation Street, Birmingham 2.

Brook Advisory Centre, 233 Tottenham Court Road, London W1 (01-580 2991, 01-323 1522).

Campaign for Homosexual Equality (London office), 22 Great Windmill Street, London W1 (01-437 7363). (National office) P.O. Box 427, 33 King Street, Manchester (061-228 1985).

Catholic Housing Aid Society, 189a Old Brompton Road, London SW5 (01-373 4961).

Catholic Marriage Advisory Service (London), 15 Lansdowne Road, W11 (01-727 0141). (Northern Ireland) 11 College Street, Belfast.

Charity Commission, 14 Ryder Street, London SW1 (01-214 6000).

Child Poverty Action Group (CPAG), 1 Macklin Street, London WC2 (01-242 3225).

Citizens' Advice Bureaux, National Citizen's Advice Bureaux Council, 26 Bedford Square, London WC1 (01-636 4066).

Citizens' Rights Office, 1 Macklin Street, London WC2 (01-405 5942).

Claimants' Union, The Albany, Creek Road, London SE8 (01-692 1047).

Commission for Racial Equality, Elliot House, 10–12 Allington Street, London SW1 (01-828 7022).

Commissions for Local Government (local government Ombudsmen), see p. 517.

Confederation for the Advancement of State Education (CASE), General Secretary: Mrs B. Bullivant, 81 Rustings Road, Sheffield 11 (0742-662467).

Consumer Aid Centre, 200 Kilburn High Road, London NW6 (01-328 4743).

Consumers' Association, 14 Buckingham Street, London WC2 (01-839 1222).

Cruse National Widows' Association, 126 Sheen Road, Richmond, Surrey (01-940 4818).

Defence of Literature and the Arts Society, 18 Brewer Street, London W1 (01-734 3786/6900).

Down and Connor Family Welfare Society, 43 Falls Road, Belfast 12.

Equal Opportunities Commission, Overseas House, Quay Street, Manchester (061-833 9244).

Family Planning Association, 27 Mortimer Street, London w1 (01-636 7866).

Family Planning Association of Northern Ireland, 28 Bedford Street, Belfast.

Family Rights Group, 35 Wellington Street, London wc2.

Gay Switchboard, 5 Caledonian Road, London n1 (01-837 7324).

Gingerbread, 9 Poland Street, London w1 (01-734 9014) – for one-parent families.

Gypsy Council and National Gypsy Education Council, 18 Poynz Road, Battersea, London sw11 (01-228 2884).

Howard League for Penal Reform, 125 Kennington Park Road, London se11 (01-735 3773).

Independent Personnel: Martin Luther King Foundation, 154 Balham High Road, London sw12 (01-675 0941).

JAIL (Justice Against Identification Laws), 271 Upper Street, London n1 (01-359 8034).

Joint Council for the Welfare of Immigrants (JCWI), 44 Theobalds Road, London wc1 (01-405 5527).

Justice (British Section of the International Commission of Jurists), 2 Clements Inn, Strand, London wc2 (01-405 6018).

Law Centres – see p. 507.

Law Society, 113 Chancery Lane, London wc2 (01-242 1222).

Law Society of Northern Ireland, Chichester Street, Belfast 1.

Law Society of Scotland, 26–7 Drumsheugh Gardens, Edinburgh 3.

Mental After-Care Association, 110 Jermyn Street, London sw1 (01-839 5953); 78 Barrowgate Road, London w4 (01-995 9702).

Motor Insurers' Bureau, Aldermary House, Queen Street, London EC4 (01-248 4477).

National Association for the Care and Resettlement of Offenders (NACRO), 125 Kennington Park Road, London SE11 (01-582 7172).

National Association for Mental Health (MIND), 22 Harley Street, London WC1 (01-637 0741).

National Council for Civil Liberties, (NCCL), 186 Kings Cross Road, London WC1 (01-278 4575).

National Council for One-Parent Families, 255 Kentish Town Road, London NW5 (01-267 1361).

National Marriage Guidance Council, 3 Gower Street, London WC1 (01-935 2838).

National Society for the Prevention of Cruelty to Children (NSPCC), 1 Riding Street, London W1 (01-580 8812).

National Union of Students/National Union of School Students, 3 Endsleigh Street, London WC1 (01-387 1277).

National Women's Aid Federation, 51 Chalcot Road, London NW1 (01-586 5192).

Northern Ireland Civil Rights Association, 2 Marquis Street, Belfast.

Patients' Association, Suffolk House, Banbury Road, Oxford (0865-50306).

Ombudsman (Parliamentary Commissioner and Health Service Commissioner's Office) Church House, Great Smith Street, London SW1 (01-212 7676).

Police Federation, 15–17 Langley Road, Surbiton, Surrey (01-399 2224).

Pregnancy Advisory Service (British), 58 Petty France, London SW1 (01-222 0985).

Pre-School Playgroups Association, Alford House, Aveline Street, London SE11 (01-582 8871).

Preservation of the Rights of Prisoners (PROP), 339a Finchley Road, London NW3 (01-435 1215).

Radical Alternatives to Prison (RAP), Eastbourne House, Bullard's Place, London E2 (01-981 0041).

Release, 1 Elgin Avenue, London W9 (01-289 1123; 01-603 8654 emergency).

Royal Automobile Club, 89 Pall Mall, London SW1 (01-930 2345).

Schools Council, 160 Great Portland Street, London W1 (01-580 0352).

Scottish Association for the Care and Resettlement of Offenders (SACRO), 1 Strathmore House, East Kilbride, Glasgow.

Scottish Child Poverty Action Group, 11 Castle Street, Edinburgh 2.

Scottish Council for Civil Liberties, 314 Clyde Street, Glasgow C1 (041-424 0042).

Shelter Housing Aid Centre (SHAC), 189a Old Brompton Road, London SW10 (01-373 7841).

Shelter, 86 Strand, London WC2 (01-836 2051).

Society of Teachers Opposed to Physical Punishment (STOPP), Secretary: 27 Raleigh Court, Lymer Avenue, Dulwich Wood, London SE19.

Trades' Union Congress (TUC), Congress House, 23–8 Great Russell Street, London WC1 (01-636 4030).

United Kingdom Immigrants' Advisory Service (UKIAS), 7th Floor, Brettenham House, Savoy Street, London WC2 (01-240 5176).

Ulster Pregnancy Advisory Service, 198 Stranmillis Road, Belfast 8.

A Woman's Place, 42 Earlham Street, London WC2 (01-836 6081).

Appendix B. Public order and related offences

Offence	Authority	Penalty
ASSAULT		
Common	Offences Against Person Act 1861, s. 42	*Summary:* 2 months or £50*
Aggravated, on woman or child	ditto, s. 43	*Summary:* 6 months or £500
Occasioning actual bodily harm	ditto, s. 47	5 years
On police officer in execution of his duty	Police Act 1964, s. 51(1)	*Summary:* 6 months and/or £100*
With intent to prevent apprehension	Offences Against Person Act 1861, s. 38	2 years
Wounding or inflicting grievous bodily harm with or without weapon	ditto, s. 18	5 years
Ditto, with intent	ditto, s. 18	life
BEHAVIOUR		
Threatening or abusive words or writing	Metropolitan Police Act 1839, s. 54(13) Public Order Act 1936, s. 5 amended *re* penalties by Public Order Act 1963, s. 1	£20 *Summary:* 3 months and/or £100*

* indicates throughout this section that the offence or penalty has been amended by the Criminal Law Act (see pp. 17–20).

Offence	Authority	Penalty
Threatening or abusive words or writing in public where racial hatred likely to be stirred up	Race Relations Act 1976, s. 70	*Summary:* 6 months and/or £400* *Indictment:* 2 years and/or unlimited fine
Public nuisance, i.e. act or omission endangering life, health, property, morals or comfort of the public	common law	imprisonment for life and/or unlimited fine
Being a suspected person loitering with intent to commit a felony	Vagrancy Act 1824, s. 4	*Summary:* 3 months or £100
Violent or threatening	Local Government Act 1933, s. 249	£20
	Town Police Clauses Act 1849, s. 29	£10
	Metropolitan Police Act 1839, s. 58	£10
Blasphemy	common law	imprisonment for life and/or unlimited fine
Conspiracy* (see p. 17)	common law	imprisonment and/or unlimited fine

MEETINGS

Offence	Authority	Penalty
Infringement of police regulations governing route, parking, etc.	Metropolitan Police Acts 1839, ss. 52 and 54	£20
Infringement of police directions *re* route, etc. in anticipation of serious public disorder	Public Order Act 1936, s. 3	*Summary:* 3 months or £50*

Offence	Authority	Penalty
Infringement of Dept of Environment regulations *re* parks and gardens	Park Regulations Acts 1872 and 1926; Trafalgar Square Act 1944 and Regulations 1952; London Government Act 1963, s. 58	£20 £5
Unlawful assembly (i.e. an assembly of 3 or more persons) a) for purposes forbidden by law or b) with intent to carry out any common purpose, lawful or unlawful, such as to endanger the public peace or put firm and courageous persons in that neighbourhood in fear	common law	life imprisonment and/or unlimited fine
Rout (i.e. an unlawful assembly on the move)	common law	imprisonment for life and/or unlimited fine
Riot (i.e. a tumultuous disturbance of the peace by 3 or more people who assemble together of their own authority with an intent mutually to assist each other against anyone who shall oppose them in the execution of some enterprise of a private nature and afterwards actually execute the enterprise in a violent and turbulent manner to the terror of the people)	common law	life imprisonment and/or unlimited fine

Offence	*Authority*	*Penalty*
Affray (i.e. fighting by two or more people to the terror of HM's subjects)	common law	imprisonment for life and/or unlimited fine
Endeavouring to break up a public meeting or inciting others to do so	Public Meeting Act 1908, s. 1 (as amended)	*Summary:* 3 months and/or £100*
Wearing uniforms in connection with political objectives	Public Order Act 1936, s. 1	*Summary:* 3 months and/or £500
Management or control of a quasi-military organization	Public Order Act 1936, s. 2	*Summary:* 6 months and/or £100*

OBSTRUCTION

Of police in execution of their duty	Police Act 1964, s. 51(3)	*Summary:* 1 month and/or £20*
Of customs officers	Customs and Excise Act 1952, s. 10	*Summary:* 3 months and/or £100* *Indictment:* 2 years and/or £500*
Of highway without lawful authority or excuse	Town Police Clauses Act 1847, s. 28	£20
	Metropolitan Police Act 1839, s. 54(4)	£20
	Highways Act 1959, s. 121	£50
Of public footpath or thoroughfare in disobedience to police regulations (London)	Metropolitan Police Act 1839, s. 54	£20

Offence	Authority	Penalty
Breach of orders regulating crowds and preventing obstruction during processions, rejoicing or illuminations or when streets are thronged or liable to be obstructed	Town Police Clauses Act 1847, s. 21	£20

OFFICIAL SECRETS

Spying	Official Secrets Act 1911, s. 1	14 years and/or unlimited fine
Wrongful communication of information	ditto, s. 2	2 years and/or unlimited fine

PROPERTY (DAMAGE)

Attempting to cause explosions or making or keeping explosives with intent to endanger life or property	Explosive Substances Act 1883, s. 3	20 years
Destroying or damaging property belonging to another	Criminal Damage Act 1971, s. 1(1)	*Summary:* 6 months and/or £400* *Indictment:* 10 years and/or unlimited fine
Destroying or damaging any property and endangering the life of another	ditto, s. 1(2)	life imprisonment and/or unlimited fine

Offence	Authority	Penalty
Arson	ditto, s. 1(1–3)	*Summary:* 6 months and/or £400* *Indictment:* life imprisonment and/or unlimited fine
Threats to commit offences under s. 1	ditto, s. 2	*Summary:* 6 months and/or £400
Cutting or injuring electricity wires with intent to cut off the supply	Electric Lighting Act 1882, s. 22	5 years and/or unlimited fine

PROPERTY (ENTERING)

Excessive picketing (i.e. using violence or intimidating by watching or besetting the residence or workplace of another in order to compel that other to do or abstain from doing something he has a legal right to do)	Conspiracy and Protection of Property Act 1875, s. 7	3 months or £20

PROSCRIBED ORGANIZATIONS†

Membership of	Prevention of Terrorism Act 1976, s. 1(1)	*Summary:* 6 months and/or £400* *Indictment:* 5 years and/or unlimited fine

†At January 1977 the only proscribed organization was the IRA.

Offence	Authority	Penalty
Raising or receiving money or goods on behalf of	ditto	ditto
Encouraging any other form of support for	ditto	ditto
Organizing public or private meeting of more than 2 people in support of	ditto	ditto
Organizing public or private meeting addressed by member of	ditto	ditto
Displaying, carrying, wearing in public anything which arouses reasonable fear that you are a member or supporter of	ditto, s. 2(1)	6 months and/or £400*
Asking for gift or loan intended for use in connection with terrorism	ditto, s. 10(1)	*Summary:* 6 months and/or £400* *Indictment:* 5 years and/or unlimited fine
Receiving or accepting any money or goods to be used in connection with terrorism	ditto	ditto
Giving or lending or otherwise making available money or goods, knowing or suspecting they will be used in connection with terrorism	ditto, s. 10(2)	ditto

Offence	*Authority*	*Penalty*
SEDITION		
i.e. exciting discontent or dissatisfaction between sections of the public	common law	imprisonment and/or unlimited fine
WEAPONS		
Going armed to terrify the Queen's subjects	common law	imprisonment and/or unlimited fine
Possessing offensive weapons (i.e. any article adapted for causing injury or intended by the possessor for offensive use)	Prevention of Crime Act 1953, s. 1 (amended *re* penalty by Criminal Justice Act 1967)	*Summary:* 3 months and/or £200* *Indictment:* 2 years and/or unlimited fine and forfeiture of weapon
Having an offensive weapon while at a public meeting or on a public procession	Public Order Act 1936, s. 4	*Summary:* 3 months and/or £50*
Possessing firearms with intent to endanger life	Firearms Act 1968, s. 16 (amended *re* penalties by Criminal Justice Act 1972)	life and/or unlimited fine
Use of firearm, or imitation, to resist arrest	Firearms Act 1968, s. 17	life and or unlimited fine
Possession of firearm with intent to commit serious offence	Firearms Act 1968, s. 18	14 years and/or unlimited fine

Offence	Authority	Penalty
Carrying firearms in a public place	Firearms Act 1968, s. 19	*Summary:* 6 months and/or £400* *Indictment:* 5 years and/or unlimited fine
Trespassing with a firearm on land	Firearms Act 1968, s. 20(2)	*Summary:* 3 months and/or £20
ditto, in a building	ditto, s. 20(1)	*Summary:* 6 months and/or £500* *Indictment:* 5 years and/or unlimited fine
Causing explosions likely to endanger life or proprety	Explosive Substances Act 1883, s. 2	life imprisonment and/or unlimited fine
Throwing fireworks into street	Explosives Act 1875 (amended *re* penalty by Explosives (Age of Purchase) Act 1976)	£200
Possessing explosives under suspicious circumstances	Explosive Substances Act 1883, s. 4	14 years
Possession of airguns, shotguns and similar weapons *if under 14*	Airguns and Shotguns Act 1962	3 months or £20
Possessing anything to be used to commit an offence under the Criminal Damage Act	Criminal Damage Act 1971, s. 3	*Summary:* 6 months and/or £400 *Indictment:* 10 years

Appendix C. Index of Acts of Parliament

Note: *A more comprehensive list of statutes affecting public order is contained in Appendix B.*

Index

The NCCL protects Civil Liberties in the United Kingdom

NCCL is an independent voluntary organization which protects individual civil liberties, and the rights of political, religious, racial and other minorities in the UK.

Founded in 1934, NCCL is financed solely by membership and affiliation fees, and by donations. It is a pressure group, campaigning on issues such as the right to a fair trial; the right to privacy; immigration and race relations; police powers; women's rights; freedom of expression and association. NCCL provides legal advice, takes up cases of individual injustice, makes representations to government and authorities, presses for legal reform through the Parliamentary Civil Liberties Group and publishes a wide range of pamphlets and reports on individual rights. Although based in London, NCCL has fifteen local groups.

NCCL works in close cooperation with the Cobden Trust, a registered charity which undertakes research and education on civil liberties. NCCL and the Cobden Trust publish factsheets on police powers, which have been translated into Hindi, Bengali, Urdu, Gujarati and Punjabi. They also organize training courses for people representing complainants at industrial tribunals.

You can get more information about NCCL and the Cobden Trust, together with a full publications list, from 186 Kings Cross Road, London WC1.

If you value liberty, join NCCL

Membership rates:

> Individuals £5·00 (£4·50 by bankers' order)
> Couples £6·50 (£6·00 by bankers' order)
> Students,* claimants, OAPs £3·00
> * Please say which college and when your course ends.

> Add 50p to these rates if you also wish to join the Campaign for Academic Freedom and Democracy (CAFD).

( ) I wish to join NCCL and have completed the bankers' order/ enclose £ · in payment of my first year's subscription. (NCCL Giro No. 584 0104.)
( ) I enclose £ · as a gift.
( ) I wish my organization to be affiliated. Please send me the list of affiliation fees based on membership.
( ) I wish to make a covenanted donation to the Cobden Trust. Please send me a form.
I would like more information about
( ) Scottish Council for Civil Liberties
( ) Campaign for Academic Freedom and Democracy
( ) NCCL Rights for Women Unit
( ) Cobden Trust

NAME_____

ADDRESS_____

_____

_____

PLEASE USE CAPITAL LETTERS

Bankers Order

Please pay to the account of the National Council for Civil Liberties, William & Glyns Bank, 25 Millbank, London SW1P 4RB (Account No. 71186914)

the sum of (in words)_____

_____(amount in figures) £

on the date   197   and every year on the
_____
same day until otherwise notified.

Name and address of your bank
_____

_____

_____

Your name and address
_____

_____

_____

*Signature*_____

Please send this form to NCCL, 186 Kings Cross Road, London WC1 and we will send it on to your bank.

More About Penguins and Pelicans

Civil Liberties in Britain
Barry Cox

Britain is one of the freest countries in the world; but the
rights which many of us take for granted are not protected
by charter and their maintenance needs constant vigilance;
The 1930s were a particularly dangerous time when
governments attempted to regain powers which they had
had during the First World War. But the 1970s may be an
even more dangerous decade. As more people become aware of
their rights and are prepared to assert them, there will be
attempts to restrict them.

Civil Liberties in Britain is a history of the civil rights
movement, of how the basic rights – of association, assembly,
expression and movement – have been threatened and fought
over for the past fifty years; and a survey of the areas in which
personal freedoms are open to abuse – the courts, the police,
legislation, industry and the armed services.

Barry Cox concludes that while there have been some
changes for the better since 1934, when the National Council
for Civil Liberties was founded, we have no reason for
complacency.